Britain After Empire

Britain After Empire
Constructing a Post-War
Political-Cultural Project

P. W. Preston
Professor of Political Sociology, University of Birmingham, UK

palgrave
macmillan

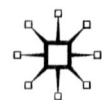

© P. W. Preston 2014

All rights reserved. No reproduction, copy or transmission of this publication may be made without written permission.

No portion of this publication may be reproduced, copied or transmitted save with written permission or in accordance with the provisions of the Copyright, Designs and Patents Act 1988, or under the terms of any licence permitting limited copying issued by the Copyright Licensing Agency, Saffron House, 6–10 Kirby Street, London EC1N 8TS.

Any person who does any unauthorized act in relation to this publication may be liable to criminal prosecution and civil claims for damages.

The author has asserted his right to be identified as the author of this work in accordance with the Copyright, Designs and Patents Act 1988.

First published 2014 by
PALGRAVE MACMILLAN

Palgrave Macmillan in the UK is an imprint of Macmillan Publishers Limited, registered in England, company number 785998, of Houndmills, Basingstoke, Hampshire RG21 6XS.

Palgrave Macmillan in the US is a division of St Martin's Press LLC, 175 Fifth Avenue, New York, NY 10010.

Palgrave Macmillan is the global academic imprint of the above companies and has companies and representatives throughout the world.

Palgrave® and Macmillan® are registered trademarks in the United States, the United Kingdom, Europe and other countries.

ISBN 978–1–137–02382–7

This book is printed on paper suitable for recycling and made from fully managed and sustained forest sources. Logging, pulping and manufacturing processes are expected to conform to the environmental regulations of the country of origin.

A catalogue record for this book is available from the British Library.

A catalog record for this book is available from the Library of Congress.

Contents

Preface   vi

Acknowledgements   viii

1 After the Empire: Establishment Designs, High Arts and Popular Culture in Britain   1

2 Foundation Myths: The War, Wartime and 'Continuing Britain'   19

3 Grand Designs: Patrician Reformers, Subaltern Demands and the Ideal of Welfare   40

4 Making Enemies: The Cold War   62

5 Voices of Complaint, Voices of Assertion   82

6 Patrician Retreat: Quickening Change in the 1950s and Early 1960s   97

7 Affluence Attained, Affluence Doubted   112

8 Corporate World, Media and Politics   138

9 Amongst the Bullshit Industries   157

10 Familiar Utopias: New Technologies and the Internet   177

11 Continuing Britain: Contemporary Political Culture Unpacked   196

Notes   218

Bibliography (Readings/Viewings)   257

Index   267

Preface

This text tracks the intermingled intellectual/moral responses of elites and masses to the collapse of the British state-empire system in the years immediately following the end of the Second World War. It asks how the elite sought to fashion a new project/identity for itself, how its ideas were disseminated and how ordinary people responded. The elements of these political-cultural processes are sought in elite designs (policies, plans, declarations and the like), high arts (novels, theatre, fine arts, art-house film and so on) and popular culture (radio, film, television, newspapers and magazines and lately the burgeoning realm of digital media). Establishing this project entailed a creative mixture of denial and confection. The former dismissed the hitherto peripheral territories of empire as of little enduring relevance, parts of an empire accumulated in a fit of absent-mindedness, and given away in due time in a peaceful consensual fashion, whilst the latter reworked the collective memory of the now shrunken core territories, claiming that Britain was a long-established nation-state, now legatee of empire, recent victor in a virtuous war, favoured ally of America and something of a model for other countries-in-general. This political-cultural product of these interlinked manoeuvres can be tagged 'continuing Britain'. Against this comfortable, deluded tale, the present text presents a rather more sceptical view: that the British polity comprises an entrenched, enlightened oligarchic elite, in thrall to the USA via finance, defence and ideological nostalgia, ordering a demobilized acquiescent mass content with welfare-buttressed debt-fuelled consumerism. The frame of the polity is resilient, the passing detail fluid, and the possibilities of internally generated reform seemingly slight, but not altogether absent. With this in mind, unpacking the accumulated logic of the post-war political-culture might help uncover novel intellectual spaces, which might, in turn, help drive change.

* * * * *

A companion volume will turn to the counterpart to this story of the creation of continuing Britain and look at the 'Empire after Empire' and track the ways in which the dissolution of the state-empire system provided opportunities for aspiring local replacement elites to seize power, construct states, fashion nations and thereafter, one way or another, pursue economic and social development. Together, therefore, these texts assert that the starting point for any discussion of the political history of Britain in the twentieth century – and of its present-day unfolding political culture – is a recognition of the ineluctable centrality of the collapse of the state-empire system; an experience, it might be noted, replicated in several other European countries, and whose consequences, taken together, run down to the present in the form of the European Union.

Acknowledgements

This text is one of a sequence dealing with the political culture of my home-patch, Britain, but its origins, like those of its companion volumes, lie elsewhere; in travel, in the experience of other cultures and in the curious experience of looking at my own country from the outside, with to some extent outsider's eyes. The first moves in these enquiries were made whilst I was living and working in Bielefeld, later on further materials were added in Tokyo, Hong Kong and most recently Bangkok. And, as scholarship is a collective endeavour, I should like to offer my thanks to friends, colleagues and students scattered around these and other places in Europe and East Asia.

1
After the Empire: Establishment Designs, High Arts and Popular Culture in Britain

In the late summer of 1939 the British elite ruled a state-empire system[1] that embraced territories and peoples spanning the globe, an empire upon which 'the sun never set', within which an identity was available to all – 'British' – and where, amongst that elite, various problems notwithstanding, the future health of 'the Empire' was taken for granted. Yet six years later, in the summer of 1945, it was clear that the system could no longer be sustained; the metropolitan core elite could command neither the economic resources, nor the military capability, nor the politico-intellectual convictions that were necessary to sustain their state-empire and within a few years it was dissolved. In the hitherto peripheral territories a number of new states were formed – in Southeast Asia, South Asia, the Middle East, Africa and the Caribbean – and their place within the wider evolving industrial-capitalist system ordered under the rubric of state formation, nation-building and economic advance, or, in brief, development, where the precise pursuit of this goal was inflected by sometimes violent disputes, both local and international, as to the most effective course of action. All this is reasonably familiar: the empire dissolved, some parts did well, others, not so well. The other part of the tale, events in the hitherto core, are not so well known. It is here that a species of putative common sense reigns: the empire lost, the core continued. It is a poor story, for in the hitherto core areas, that is, in this case, the British Isles, the elite had perforce to rethink their own location within a radically changed environment; one that had seen the dissolution of a state-empire system centred on their hitherto core territory, the subordination of that territory to the requirements of newly established global powers and the mobilization of their domestic population around claims for economic, social and political reform. Cast in terms of extant elite interests and self-understandings, the episode was a catastrophe – a loss of empire.

This text tracks the intermingled intellectual/moral responses of elites to that loss of the state-empire and the identities attached thereto in the years following the end of the Second World War. It looks at how the elite reimagined their place in the world, the ways in which they fashioned this new project; the various components, the means whereby it was put into practice and the ways in which these policies and ideas found expression when deployed amongst the wider population. The elements of this still unfolding process will be sought in elite designs (policies, plans, declarations and the like), high arts (novels, theatre, fine arts, art-house film and so on) and popular culture (radio, film, television, newspapers and magazines and lately the burgeoning realm of digital media).

Overall, the text will argue that the elite's creative response to the loss of state-empire entailed both denial, as the peripheral territories were reimagined as of relatively little consequence, and confection, such that the hitherto core areas were imaginatively reworked as a long extant nation-state, 'continuing Britain'. This process saw the construction of a distinctive politico-cultural project: one that was biased towards finance, overly committed to the military-industrial complex, subordinate to the United States and resentful of its inevitably ordinary place within the organizations made in mainland Europe. In these demanding circumstances the elite reconceptualized Britain, presenting it as the legatee of empire, the victor in a virtuous war, number one ally of America and something of a model for other countries-in-general. Having detailed these elite-sponsored tales, this text, in an engaged fashion,[2] will go on to argue that an appreciation of the scale of the catastrophe which overcame the British elite, and the unsustainable nature of their response, are necessary conditions of a better grasp of the realities of the circumstances of the contemporary polity and its possibilities for the future.

State, nation and public sphere

The text is grounded in European social theory.[3] In the realms of politics, modernity, the complex of social practices informed by core commitments to reason, science and intellectual/material progress,[4] can be unpacked around the interrelated ideas of states, nations and public spheres. Understood in these terms, the shift to the modern world of science-based industrial capitalism was organized institutionally through the parallel construction of liberal markets and bureaucratic-rational states. The two are complimentary: thus liberal markets require order, and states set the rules within which liberal markets function, and liberal markets are productive, and so generate the wealth necessary to fund the machineries of these states.[5] The construction of bureaucratic-rational states was legitimated amongst the masses of populations in terms of ideas of nation.[6] States laid claim to territorial sovereignty and exclusive control of resident populations, and the apparatus of control (armies, police, bureaucrats and so on) was legitimated in terms of an idea of common identity amongst the population, an idea of nation.[7] This intellectual/moral apparatus fostered obedience and loyalty and was promulgated through numerous mechanisms embracing official ideologies and bureaucratic routines, routine social practices and the pervasive diverse realms of culture/media. Thereafter, all these mechanisms worked to aid the construction of an idea of nation. But these same mechanisms were also available to carry other ideas. The crucial social institution took shape in the novel spaces and instruments of emergent urban life, coffee shops, theatre, newspapers, pamphlets and so on, all the paraphernalia which allowed individuals to constitute and belong to a novel collective sphere – the public sphere.[8] This was an arena within which all contributors were in principle equal and which in total functioned to generate a reflexive, critical appreciation of the nature and direction of the political community in question; a nascent form of democracy.

Jurgen Habermas[9] makes use of the historical sociology of the development of the public sphere in England, coupled to philosophical reflections on the nature of human language, in order to argue that the development of the modern world produced a distinctive sphere of social life, what he called the public sphere. First, the institutional vehicles for this sphere of life were clubs, societies, coffee houses and other places where people could gather informally and talk freely about the world that they inhabited (information, opinion, gossip, argument and maybe plans for more explicit commentary – pamphlets, novels or journalism). Second, the social function of the public sphere serves the organized political community by providing a sphere of critical commentary separate from those institutional forms created or dominated by the elite. Third, such commentary will be very diverse, but it will be governed by the intrinsic logics of human communication – that is, the inherent tendency towards rational consensus. Habermas argues that collective, free debate tends towards the production of rational consensus and is the essence of a democratic polity. Thus fourth, Habermas links the fundamental character of human communication and the public sphere, and the goal of democracy.[10] It is here that we find the line of reflection (for politicians, policy-makers and commentators) which links state, nation and public sphere: the last noted is crucial to the constitution of the former pair and it also carries the promise of democracy. Subsequent commentators have pursued a series of debates: the nature of the state, the nature of national identities, the promise and performance of the public sphere and the related subordinate question of the responsibility of intellectuals/scholars to engage with these processes so as to foster progress.

Overall, the complex process of the shift to the modern world sees the social construction of states, nations and the realm of the public sphere. The links are intimate: the public sphere offers the promise of progress towards democracy and political agents, policy-makers and commentators have made it an arena of contestation, a battleground for ideas and agenda-setting.

Texts, text-analogues and readings

The rise of the modern world, and along with it the construction of states, nations and the public sphere, forms the general frame within which subsequent social theorists have operated, and to which reflexively they have turned their attention. Unpacking some of its elements generates a broad idea of politics (matters of power and its legitimation) and a distinctive role for collective systematic reflection (arguments in the public sphere). The arguments placed in the public sphere can take many forms, deploying materials from the arts, humanities, social sciences, policy and politics. These interventions can be summed as 'texts' and they can be analysed as 'texts' or 'text-analogues'.

Human language considered

The background to the main tradition of work in this area – that is, the interpretation of arguments deployed in the public sphere in order to make sense of our forms of life – lies in interpretive/critical philosophy.[11] These materials are rooted in continental philosophy. The key claim is that the social production of meaning is fundamental to humankind. Or, put another way, what is special about humans is that they operate within socially created webs of meaning and these meanings inform social practices, or, informally, we act in the world in the light of the ideas that we have about our world.[12] Or, again, after Hans-Georg Gadamer,[13] all human knowing is carried in language.

At first meeting these are unexpected claims, yet, contrary to our routine experience of the world where talk seems to be transient and inconsequent, or 'just words', it is through language that we constitute and act in our worlds. In the twentieth century, reflections on the nature of language have taken three forms: first, hermeneutics, the characterization of language as embedded in history, thus humankind dwells within meanings/practices carried in traditions; second, linguistics/semiotics, the characterization of language as a formal system for making signs, thus humankind dwells within formal systems of rules; and third, ordinary language philosophy, the characterization of language as a socially constituted body of rules serving practical purposes, thus humankind dwells within forms of life carried by language games.[14]

These reflections coincide in the claim that human beings inhabit language-carried webs of meaning. Such meanings inform or find expression in our routine social practices. Stocks of meanings/practices are carried in tradition. Specific actions initiated by individuals draw upon the common social stock of meanings. Yet the stock of meanings is not fixed; new ideas inform new social practices; new social practices produce new ideas whilst other ideas/practices fall into disuse.

Texts and text-analogues

The links between the intellectual traditions noted above which are concerned with elucidating the nature of language and the realms of the public sphere can be found in three technical terms: text, text-analogue and reading; these let us analyse the social world as suffused with meanings; any cultural construction or any social practice.

As noted, three streams of work underpin the idea of the text. First is hermeneutics, originally concerned with the detailed exegesis of biblical texts. Here the focus of attention is on syntax, semantics and provenance of versions of the bible – the aim is to discover the accurate version in order to uncover its true meanings – so as to access the word of God. The philosopher Wilhelm Dilthey[15] moves the idea of the exegesis of texts into the wider social world, in his case, history, so meanings are embedded in history. This work is subsequently further developed in the philosophical hermeneutics of Gadamer.[16] Second, associated with Ferdinand de Saussure,[17] linguistics/semiotics, where the focus of attention is the analysis of language as a formal system of arbitrary signs. Meanings are carried in formal sets of rules. The idea of signs allows many cultural constructions to be analysed. Third, ordinary language philosophy, which is concerned with analysing language as a rule-governed practical activity. Here the aim is to show how language has meaning in use; associated with Ludwig Wittgenstein and moved into the social sciences by Peter Winch.[18]

Hermeneutics begins with the analysis of biblical texts, but the strategy can be used much more widely as these reflections on language enable the shift from analysing texts to analysing text-analogues – 'cultural texts' – the social world can be read as comprising meanings, and discrete meanings can be picked out and analysed as if they were texts – cultural products carrying meaning (arguments deployed) can be analysed as if they were texts. Thus enquiry moves from text: which carries meanings; is constructed; has an audience in view; and is context bound; to text-analogue: which carries meanings; is constructed; is a limited specific exercise in sense-making; has an audience in view; is context bound and can be identified and analysed in self-conscious commentary. In sum, texts carry meanings. And the idea can be applied to any specific cultural artefact: books, films, pamphlets, statues, public rituals, or the layout of entire cities. Human social practices are inscribed with meaning, and these can be read, as texts or text-analogues.

Of course, texts can be just that – publications – words strung together to interpret the world in favour of this or that course of action. Numerous examples can be cited, all devoted, one way or another, to deploying arguments in the public sphere. Thus Milton Friedman has made arguments on behalf of the liberal market bourgeoisie in pursuit of an ideal free market in his scholarship and political writing; organizations such as the British Medical Association or the Confederation of British Industry making arguments on behalf of memberships in pursuit of sectional concerns in policy advocacy and public relations activities. Individuals such as Jeremy Clarkson who uses television and journalism in order to make arguments intended to entertain and make a splash. And in the arts, Gunter Grass has made extensive interventions in public discussion around the theme of German history, society and politics in the wake of the 1930s collapse into National Socialism and its subsequent reconstruction within the frame of the West. These issues have been pursued in a sequence of novels: the *Tin Drum*, which chronicles the fall of pre-war Danzig and the start of the Second World War; *My Century*, which reviews the politics of the continent; and *Crabwise*, which opens up the issue of German suffering in the Second World War.[19] And, in a similar way, J.G. Ballard might be taken as an analogous figure writing in English. In the latter years of his life he produced a sequence of novels focused on contemporary life[20] whilst publishing three texts that detailed his own.[21] The novel sequence offers a critique of contemporary urban/suburban life where the familiar is reworked after the style of science fiction writing the distanced/distorted rendering of the familiar carries the moral commentary, pointing to the comfortable amoral character of modern life.

Art-house films can be read as texts. The director is invested with the same concerns and intentions as a creative author and so the result can be analysed in an analogous fashion. By way of examples, Lars von Trier, a Danish director, has made films examining European history in the wake of the end of the Second World War detailing the moral confusions of the period, and in *Europa* he examines the lives of people living in the ruined continent;[22] Ridley Scot, an English director, has made mainstream films and whilst some of these are straightforward Hollywood entertainments, one film was distinctly art-house in tone/style, thus *Blade Runner* was set in a near future of large corporations and crowded urban areas, part dystopia and part film noir;[23] or Peter Greenaway, another English director, has made a series of art-house films, which are characterized by their formal stylized reflections built around apparently straightforward themes: English manners in *The Draughtsman's Contract* or the business of dying in *Zed and Two Noughts* or contrariwise the psychological dynamics of childhood, youth and adulthood in *The Pillow Book*.[24]

Any cultural artefact can be treated as a text-analogue and it can then be read so as to reveal its social meaning. Thus 'reading the city', where meaning is embedded in building design (architecture/space) or in urban layouts (space)[25] and where the city-as-a-whole can be read as spectacle via the role of flaneur.[26] Or 'reading popular culture' such as television reality shows, Wooten Basset memorial parades or flying the flag of St George around national team football matches where the game is taken to exemplify both individual and national character. Or, again, 'reading printed images' in order to decipher the ideas carried in photojournalism or cartoons. And then, the wide territory of 'reading political activities', for example, in order to unpack the mix of claims in ministerial statements, or to grasp the nature of Royal Family work in declaring things open or giving honours or holding parades,[27] or to uncover the claims to legitimacy in rituals such as Prime Minister's Questions (PMQs), the state opening of parliament or elections.[28] And, one more example, 'reading the City of London' through the creation of an anthropology of traders-as-tribe,[29] or the deconstructing bonus recipients' declarations ('because we're worth it'), or unpacking the rhetoric of press reports on the city-organized business of gambling, skimming, tax avoidance and sundry other 'financial service activities', all cast in terms of 'the market'.

8 Britain After Empire

Texts are ways of making sense; their construction embraces a subtle dynamic involving context, theorist and audience. In this process, the text-maker will always have a particular audience in view; texts are addressed to specific audiences. Such audiences can be understood in simple terms to be either passive or active: first, in the former case the meanings on offer are simply accepted (repetition, reassurance, familiarity, habit and the like); then, second, in the latter case the meanings are offered but quite how they will be received depends on the reactions of the audience – messages are encoded and then they must be decoded – where these cannot be predicted in advance.

Texts, text-analogues and readings

This provides an intellectual base for three ideas: texts, text-analogues and readings. These enable the analysis of the production of cultural meanings; in particular in the sphere of the political life of the community, the various ways in which arguments are made and deployed via the media in the public sphere. Such 'arguments' can take many forms: flags, parades and anthems (official arguments); statues in the park (official arguments); urban forms (exemplifying ideas of architects, planners and local political agents); popular songs or pulp fiction or television soaps (commercial popular art); art-house movies, novels, museums and theatres (high art); journalism, commentary and public statements by political actors (public realm of political life); formal statements made in parliament, or by parties or state agencies (formal public realm).

So, returning to the original concerns, there are two strategic issues: the promise of the public sphere – which can address meanings to various audiences in pursuit of a rational citizenship within the community; the performance – the public sphere can be directed towards the optimistic goal but it can also be used to distract or mislead or misdirect publics. And, here, the debates about promise/performance go round and around: amongst the left, in terms of the extent of intentional deceit on the part of the powerful, and amongst the right, in terms of the interlinked notions of the role of education and the levels of achievement of the masses.

Locations and forms of argument deployed

Very many agents are able to deploy arguments and the audiences addressed are equally diverse and so the public sphere is a rich environment: such arguments may be understood broadly (any way of placing argument into the public sphere (from state or corporate world through to architecture, film, arts, print, broadcast and so on)); or understood narrowly (that is, the familiar products of the realms of print and broadcast journalism and so on). But the field is neither random nor chaotic: first, common themes emerge, most generally (given a concern for politics) the nature of power, its efficiency (or otherwise) and its legitimacy (or otherwise);[30] and second, particular agents have particular institutional bases (state, corporate world and public sphere)[31] which shape their arguments; and third, relatedly, particular media have their own intrinsic logic (thus, an artist with paint, a writer with words, a musician with their instrument, an architect with bricks and mortar or a bureaucrat with rules and regulations[32]).

Locations, agents, fields and logics

The range of arguments deployed in the public sphere is vast: from enticing brand names on a cereal packet celebrating an energetic modern lifestyle, through to spare government consultation documents reviewing policy options, or general work from commentators tracking events in the world of one sort or another. But the field of argument is not random or chaotic: particular agents have particular institutional bases. Agents don't float free of the social world upon which they comment, they will all have a definite location or context and they work within the confines of this context; agents have particular intellectual resources or skillsets available – they can do some things, they cannot do all things, so they contribute in definite ways; and these arguments are not directed randomly at the world-in-general, rather they are precisely targeted – that is, their messages however they are made have audiences-in-view.

(i) Locations and agents: State, commerce and social world

The modern world is both highly productive and highly regulated, or disciplined in Foucault's sense, and the same is true of the public sphere. There are many agents involved in making and deploying arguments in the public sphere: the state, the corporate world and the diverse spheres of ordinary life. And, of course, each runs to its own institutional or organizational agendas.

First, the state addresses its population in diverse ways: schematically, order/control, the baseline of the state's activities in regard to its population, plus, relatedly, legitimacy, the enabling function of popular acquiescence. With regard to the former, the state has extensive interests in surveillance and control, and this can be advertised (cameras in Muslim areas of Birmingham, or photographs in the press of GCHQ in Cheltenham, or pictures of warships in the newspapers, or signs in airports, written in bombastic type, saying 'UK border'[33]) or explicitly and demonstratively permitted (thus the 2012 proposals to allow the security bureaucracy to read all internet-carried materials).[34] The state gathers information and releases survey materials as part of routine state planning (census, Social Trends, Ordnance Survey). The state has extensive interests in welfare (hence forms, regulations and ID documents). And, with the latter, the state has extensive interests in its own legitimacy (thus flags, parades and anthems, sacred sites, and official ideology or the national past) as it promulgates its various projects, from the mundane through to grand designs, enshrining them in policy documents, regulations and law.

Second, the commercial world devotes huge resources to the production of texts for a variety of audiences: the routine materials of commerce (headed notepaper/stationary, company logos and, in Japan, a company philosophy or 'vision statement' and company song), the routine materials of reporting to shareholders/state authorities (glossy brochures, formal accounts) and the material used to address customers (logos, brand identities plus print and broadcast advertising campaign materials). One aspect of a 'consumer society' is the pervasive nature of the messages deployed by corporate agents.[35]

Third, individuals and groups create their own texts which are deployed both in ordinary life and the public sphere: gossiping, complaining, graffiti on walls, 'writing to my MP', writing to the 'local paper', joining clubs, societies or even a political party. The realms of ordinary life are rich in activity; these form a dense cross-cutting network, rich in the production of meanings.

(ii) Available fields: High arts, popular/commercial arts and folk arts
;Contemporary debate revolves around the idea of texts. A written text is easy to identify, words written on a page and carrying meaning, thereafter an argument by analogy opens up the idea of a text-analogue: any cultural product (painting, film, artefacts, rituals or urban form) which carries meanings can be designated a text and analysed for its meanings. This general area of work involves the social science and humanities; in recent years pursued as 'cultural studies';[36] and these enquiries draw on economics, sociology, politics and the resources of the humanities in order to analyse the meanings carried in texts/text-analogues.

Cast in these terms we can distinguish high arts, commercial arts and popular arts. First, the high arts of painting, music and literature: such work can be analysed in terms of its context (what is the environment within which it is made?), the thoughts of its creators (what do the artists involved have in mind?) and the audiences to whom it is addressed (which reading public and what expectations of responses?) (for example, Canaletto's London-as-Venice, for the rich public;[37] Georg Groz's bourgeoisie as fools, for the radical left public;[38] Graham Greene's innocently corrupt American CIA agent, for a general English reading public). Second, the commercial sphere of film, television, radio, newspapers, fashion and popular music: such work can be analysed in terms of its context (the market environment in which organizations must operate and in which they must place their product), the thoughts of its manufacturers (what concerns motivate them) and the audiences to whom it is addressed (which market segment, what price schedules and what expectations of rewards; for example, Hollywood trash for cable television, BBC middle-brow classic serials for their popular channels, Malcolm McClaren inventing punk for self-understood rebels and Vivienne Westwood selling the clothes variant to the middle classes). Third, the sphere of popular taste, opinion and memory: thus the local-level consumption of such high arts as might be proffered ('classic FM'); thus the local-level consumption of proffered commercial products ('it's the Sun what won it'); thus the local-level maintenance of the intellectual/moral resources of the local community (for example, pubs, football, rugby, angling, hunting, shooting, village or town fairs and festivals, and regional cuisines). Such local resources will include class-inflected activities, such as middle-class 'regattas' versus working-class 'bingo', and they might also include self-conscious activities, thus folk music or folk-dancing. Such patterns of taste will be accompanied by ways of deploying argument: recycling commercial materials (thus 'celebrities'); recycling commonplace attitudes (satirized in *The Royle Family*); and recycling commonplace memory (the empire, the depression years, the war).

(iii) Logics: Producers and consumers

Any medium will have its own intrinsic logic, what can and cannot be done with the medium in question: for example, writing or (quite different) building. Thus writing, along with music and film, are routinely described in terms of their particular genre – high-brow, art-house, commercial, popular and so on – and each revolves around a distinct way of addressing an audience. And architecture, urban plans, memorials and so on also have their own intrinsic logics: what can and cannot be done with the medium in question. These cultural objects can be unpacked in terms of their creators' intentions or their public function; the ideas embodied in buildings or city layouts; the functions of memorial spaces; or the ideas/responses the constructor had it in mind to try to invoke in their audience.

The producer of the text will always have an audience in mind, which can be addressed and can react in a variety of ways. The range of possible recipients is just as diverse as the social world itself. Audience responses can be unpacked in a variety of ways: audiences can be conceived as essentially passive (reading obvious clues, passing the time and being entertained) or essentially active (responding creatively to the producers clues/ambiguities, so maybe being entertained, maybe learning).

All this points to a trio of ideas – locations, agents and audiences. It is their interactions that shape the argument deployed in the public sphere. Much more could be said but for the present purposes it is enough to note the multiplicity of agents making and deploying arguments and it is enough to note the density of meanings through which members of society routinely move. It might also be added that one argument typical of intellectuals suggests that there is something to be said for being aware of these agents and the meanings they promulgate; that self-awareness is a desirable goal and it is the personal aspect of the wider promise of democracy carried in the media.

After the empire: Establishment designs, high arts and popular culture in Britain

Turning to the post-Second World War period in Britain, the elite's response involved denial and confection, with the former, dismissing the collapse of empire in terms of the loss of non-essential peripheral territories, whilst the latter centred on the elaborate political project of 'continuing Britain'. These linked strategies carried the elite's response to the collapse of the state-empire system within which they had been embedded. The loss of empire was a political-cultural catastrophe. The response can be tracked in government designs, high arts and popular culture; it is the intermingling of these claims, their clashes, their conflicts and their squabbles, which together constitutes the ever-shifting public sphere. It is here that elite and mass contrive a contested compromise in respect of the nature of the polity and its appropriate route into the future.

* * * * *

The historical trajectory of the state can be grasped in simple schematic terms of four phases, which together reach an inflection point in the years immediately following the Second World War: first, the shift to the modern world, which begins, entirely by accident, in Northwest Europe and secures an early advance in Britain; and then second, the process of intensification and expansion, which characterized the long nineteenth century, which saw the intensive internal development of an industrial-capitalist political economy along with the creation of a vast peripheral sphere spread around the planet. It was in the third phase, which saw the construction and consolidation of a number of European-centred state-empire systems – Danish, Dutch, Belgian, Italian, Spanish, Portuguese, German, Czarist and French[39] – that the system now remembered as 'the British Empire' was assembled. However, notwithstanding the scale[40] and drama of empire, the system did not long survive; in the fourth phase, a series of revolts in peripheral territories placed increasing pressure on the system, which subsequently imploded as conflict broke out in the core territories of the system, interstate warfare in Europe and also in rather different form in East Asia.[41] The result was a general crisis: the political-economic pattern of the global system along with its associated state-empire political form broke down – extensive economic, social and political distress characterized the first half of the twentieth century.

The collapse encompassed the state-empire system. The elite dealt with the loss of state-empire by utilizing a mixture of denial and confection: the scale and nature of the general crisis was simply disregarded and the loss of peripheral empire territories represented as of little weight; whilst the core territory was quickly reimagined as a long-established, self-contained, so to say, nation-state – that is, 'continuing Britain'. The confection is built up of a number of layers. There is a 'deep history' in the stylized remembrance of the self-contained past – it is the elite's summary of the past, an abstract-general stylized recollection, presented as unproblematic, essential and timeless.[42] There is a more immediate base layer found in the ideas circling around 'the war' and 'wartime'; the moment when a long-established nation-state stood alone (and so on). Together, these ideas constitute the foundation myth of contemporary Britain, and subsequent years have added further elements as passing events have been read into the overall story: together these materials shape the contemporary public sphere of the polity.

The public sphere is an arena of debate with many contributors, many conflicts, many novelties and many reiterated themes: in all, fluid, popular and democratic. These various contributors create 'arguments deployed'. Many of these are routinely presented in a non-discursive fashion: ideas can be embedded in routines and simply taken for granted; ideas can be embedded in concrete and walked past or through in everyday life (buildings, statues, memorials and so on); and ordinary social routines are infused with meanings (and as state-ordered liberal markets produce unequal societies, the social world is not 'flat' (and that this might be supposed shows how hegemonic ideas infuse the social world, they work 'behind our backs')). But many of these ideas can be presented more or less self-consciously, in discursive forms: talk, writing, images, songs and so on. Together these disparate contributions constitute an unfolding tradition: a set of ideas about the polity; the set is not fixed (ideas wax and wane in influence); the set is not definitive (ideas are introduced into discourse and they can fall away); the set is not agreed (there are many ongoing arguments about which ideas could/should be utilized, and many of these arguments are never resolved); and the ideas are both constitutive (establishing the polity in discourse) and a resource (providing a means to the critique of established ideas/practices and a means to grasp unfolding change impacting established ideas/practices of the polity).

Substantive enquiry in this text will look at post-Second World War Britain; tracking the shifting nature of discourse within the public sphere; the project of 'continuing Britain' will be sought in establishment designs, high arts and popular culture. The text will uncover the layers of meanings that underpin contemporary debates. This process of excavation will be ordered around a trio of ideas: events, ideas and residues. These posit a process whereby incidents within the general flow of life are read by participants in terms of the idea of 'events' (not just something or other happening, but something of significance (famously, former Prime Minister Harold Macmillan, when asked what had been the most difficult thing to deal with as Prime Minister, replied: 'events, dear boy, events')), which are grasped in terms of definite 'ideas', new formulations serving to grasp and underscore the significance of those episodes in question, and which, thereafter, in greater or lesser measure, leave a permanent 'residue' within the political culture, they become a part of tradition, of collective memory or the national past.

Overall, this is a reflexive process; these ideas are used, amended and passed on as the polity reads and reacts to change. In this process, ideas will be debated, themes reiterated and territories now familiar sketched out.

Layers of meanings

The resources now available to those operating in the public sphere can be grasped in terms of a series of layers: the deep history invokes stylized elements of the record of the polity, the immediate base layer is laid down by the events of the Second World War, subsequent layers include welfare and the Cold War, and thereafter further events lay down more layers of ideas. The contemporary pattern is a contingent, comprising the deep history, core themes put in place after the war,[43] along with an agglomeration of additions. The materials adduced sketch out a number of post-war phases, very roughly tracking the decades.

First, in the 1940s/1950s, the crucial episode of the collapse of the state-empire system was grasped in terms of the idea of 'continuing Britain' and the reimagined nation-state's history was grasped in terms of a set of claims centred on the ideas of parliamentary sovereignty, the rule of law and the constitutional monarchy[44] with, thereafter, the polity animated by the culture of liberal individualism, and all these elite ideas find related expression amongst subaltern classes. Thereafter, and in the foreground, there were a series of claims built around the experience of war, and to these were added further notions reflecting the more transient preoccupations of the post-war period. These include the rhetoric of wartime, themes of heroic victory, nostalgia for empire and remembered war, and these are the crucial base of elite and popular thinking; then rhetoric of welfare with fairness, equality, cradle-to-grave care, planning and rights, recalling and expressing a political compromise between elite and mass in the years following the war, now available as an elaborate rhetoric of welfarism; plus the demands of the new great powers in respect of their nominal allies and suffusing the politics of Europe, the rhetoric of the Cold War with its Manichean politics, institutionalization of military exterminism (weapons of mass destruction) and legions of domestic enemies – in particular, spies. Then towards the end of this opening phase, within an environment of full employment, was the appearance of a dissenting counter-rhetoric, the rhetoric of complaint associated with angry young men, youth rebellion, rebellion in the arts, the end of deference and the discovery of the working classes.

Second, in the 1960s/1970s, the immediate post-war era came to an end as a number of factors came together: generational change, economic prosperity and social differentiation coupled to the weakening grip upon people's imaginations of inherited class-cultural hierarchies. The upshot was a period of inchoate (and oversold) social change. It was a matter of changing generations. The post-war baby boomers began to move into positions of influence (but not power). They constituted a novel social category; as a result of the welfare state, they were socially secure, enjoyed good health and were relatively well educated.

In addition, this generation were used to a domestic economy of full employment. In this, of course, their experience was sharply different from that of their parent's generation, where the 1930s was disfigured by depression and war. And then, from the early 1950s onwards, the post-war long boom underpinned an early consumerism. Thereafter, third, there were the social and political benefits of a longish period of domestic peace (not so in the peripheral territories of the fading state-empire where wars of colonial withdrawal were fought, blamed on others and conveniently forgotten).[45] And all these combined to encourage the younger generation to speak out, and in the 1960s these changes reached an early apogee – a mix of youthfulness, experimentation in the arts, changes in social mores and the whole ensemble wrapped in a range of absurd claims carried in the media – thus the nadir of 'swinging London'.[46] Later, the wave of creative change subsided, declining slowly into the 1970s with their economic and political problems.

Then, third, in the 1980s/1990s, the nature of political discourse changed quite sharply: the fag end of the 1960s saw accelerating relative industrial decline, social instability (strikes, riots involving recently arrived migrant groups) and a rapidly fraying post-war consensus (social democracy was no longer fashionable intellectually, politically or socially – that is, those groups which had carried the project either shifted to internecine indulgence or withdrew their commitment altogether).[47] The political right seized their chance. A diagnosis of present ills was available (had been since the latter years of the Second World War) and it was cast in terms of the rhetoric of the liberal marketplace: individual action, individual responsibility, the denigration of the state and the critique of welfarism. In the 1980s, in the domestic guise of the New Right, this became the rhetoric of corporate advance: the market, liberalization, deregulation, the enemy within and without (Cold War II), violence, class victory/defeat and corporate media. And this was complemented by the rhetoric of corporate success: corporate world, corporate power, corporate media, business efficiency, bottom line, media aggression, populism and a pervasive commercialism.

And now, fourth, in the early decades of the new century, the population of the country has been presented with the rhetoric of digital revolution. Based on novel technologies and burgeoning consumer industries, grand claims have been made for the nature of the present. In one respect, read positively, these claims amount to another technologically based utopia (the idealistic promise of e-government, e-democracy and e-citizens), whilst, inevitably, read negatively, they signal another technologically based dystopia (the burgeoning spheres of state e-surveillance along with corporate world promulgated e-consumption).

Ideas are laid down over time in common culture. Received culture informs contemporary thought and action, and it is passed on, modified by responses to events, as an available resource. In each of these schematic phases, events generate ideas, which leave their mark: claims to welfare, claims to individual self-expression, claims to business action, claims to utopian futures nascent in the machineries of the internet. These layers of meaning both underpin contemporary debates within the public sphere – they are an available repertoire of concepts – and allow novel events to be grasped and taken up in debate. The set is diverse (many strands of ideas), carried in a variety of media (texts and text-analogues) and contingent;[48] there is no essence to the culture of the polity, rather, there is only the currently available living stock of ideas, those currently informing those practices, which in total constitute the polity.

Britain, going forwards

Cast in these terms, the contemporary British polity comprises an entrenched (but not closed) enlightened elite, a soft oligarchy,[49] adjusting to the loss of empire, in thrall to the United States (via finance, defence and ideological nostalgia), ordering a demobilized acquiescent mass content with welfare-buttressed consumerism. The elite have read their shifting circumstances in the light of the demands of their own continuation in power and the available resources of the political-culture that they have long commanded. A national past is available which celebrates the longevity of the polity whilst giving pride of place to a stylized memory of the Second World War. In reality, the war years marked a politico-cultural catastrophe, but they are now cast in terms of a founding myth that presents 'continuing Britain' as legatee of empire, victor in a virtuous war, number-one ally of America and a model for other countries-in-general; thereafter, this core set of claims has been supplemented by later ideas: the notion of welfare, habits of popular complaint or protest, and recently the widespread enthusiasm for debt-fuelled consumerism.

Domestically, the structural framework of the polity is resilient, the passing detail fluid and the possibilities of internally generated reform seemingly slight. However, the demands of the wider world have to be met and so whilst the overall pattern might well remain the same, the detail, the precise character of the unfolding elite-sponsored political-cultural project, might be more open to question. As the 2008/10 financial crisis[50] has shown, events are unpredictable, so the future is not closed and alternative scenarios can be envisaged;[51] and in the event that they are rationally developed, they will be so on the basis of the critical apprehension of resources available to the elite and the mass, the available resources of inherited tradition, the sets of ideas that currently inform the British polity.

2
Foundation Myths: The War, Wartime and 'Continuing Britain'

The Second World War marked the beginning of the end of the state-empire system of the British Empire – the dissolution of a set of territories accumulated over several centuries took only a couple of decades – and the British elite and wider population of the hitherto central territory, the British Isles, were confronted with the task of making sense of events and making sense of the place in the world of their newly constituted, territorially limited nation-state polity – this process involved both denial, thus the empire was downgraded as never essential, and confection, thus the newly restricted territory was reimagined as the unproblematic continuation of a long-established polity. Much of the work of the elite was pragmatic – inevitably – first, the attempt to secure so far as they could continuing economic access to their lost overseas sphere – then the parallel task of the reconstruction of state, society and economy within their newly delimited domestic territorial sphere – and finally some of their work was cultural, that is, the construction of novel narratives able to mobilize and order their local population – it is here that the occasion of the ideas of 'the war' and 'wartime' can be found – together they came to provide a new foundation myth for the polity as the unfolding mixture of elite denial and confection gave rise to the idea of a 'continuing Britain'.

The Second World War radically undermined the economic, military and intellectual/cultural (or 'soft')[1] power of the British state-empire elite and they were obliged to adjust to the demands of the political-cultural project of the newly powerful American elite. The project pursued by the American elite was defined in terms shaped by the experience of the Great Depression and the wars following and the elite made an argument which urged that prosperity was the key to ensuring that there would be no further catastrophic wars and the keys to that future were to be found in the machineries and practices of a liberal trading sphere. The means to that goal was a mix of institutions, that is, the United Nations and the Bretton Woods organizations, and power, that is, the economic, military and soft power of the United States. The situation of the British elite and the polity they controlled was one of subordination within the newly delimited American sphere. The British elite were obliged to accept this circumstance; there was no alternative. The country was broke, its population determined upon the goals of welfare rather than overseas possessions, and in any case there was little appetite to make any pragmatic or moral argument for empire. It had had its day.

The British elite were left with direct control (subject to the demands of the newly powerful American elite) of the hitherto core areas[2] of the state-empire system and the political-economy, society and culture (including politics) of this unit had to be reworked (or, the reworking imposed by circumstances had to be grasped, a matter of reading and reacting to enfolding change) and they were reconstituted in their current form; that is, as a nation-state.[3] In geographical terms, it was a radically shrunken sphere. In 1945 the British elite may have represented themselves as a great power, victorious in a recent war, but the shock of the loss of empire ran deep and the elite were obliged to accommodate this loss as best they could, formulate a plan for the future and thereafter, so far as they could, explain the new situation to their population. What they came up with, as they were subordinated within the American sphere, was, in brief, a tale of the 'continuing British' as victorious in a morally righteous war – this was the element of active remembering and what was equally actively forgotten was the business of the now defunct state-empire – it endured in heritage-mode, a tale of adventures, victories and general exotica. Thus was history shorn away and subordination decently veiled – the price tag, as Tony Judt[4] might have put it, was buying into the systematic deceit. There were a number of elements to their evolving macro-strategy: first, dealing with the political economy of the disintegrating state-empire system; second, looking to the social consequences of events; and third, offering an explanation/interpretation which rendered these upheavals intelligible.[5]

In regard to the political-economic profile of the now disintegrating state-empire system the British elite sought to protect their long-established interests. First, the elite sought to defeat or delay any changes within the hitherto peripheral territories; in brief, British business interests were to be protected so far as possible. This was a rational response, one that gave rise to patterns of relationships that came to be tagged, in the literature of critical development theorists, neo-colonial: thus, for example, support for conservative social groups in Malaya/Singapore and Brunei; thus, for example, the otherwise curious decision to actively reoccupy Hong Kong and thereafter to maintain their grip up until 1997; thus, for example, British meddling in the Middle East in order to protect oil interests – Iran 1953 or Egypt 1956; plus other, minor, examples, in sub-Saharan Africa, for example, Kenya or Rhodesia and so on. Then, second, the elite sought to reinvigorate the domestic business scene – celebrations of new technology (some of it derived from wartime production, for example, aircraft), assumptions of the continuing advance of established industries (consumer goods, for example, cars or consumer durables), indicative central planning, tri-partite conversations in regard to industry and so on. In the event, arguably[6] something of a disappointment to those involved, as a literature on 'decline' quickly took shape. And third, the elite sought new formal alliances: the Bretton Woods machinery was imposed, but the relationship with mainland Europe was open to negotiation and (notoriously) the British elite refused to become involved in the machineries of a nascent union of European states, thus, the 1951 European Coal and Steel Community (ECSC) and the 1957 European Economic Community (EEC), preferring instead to build an alternative in 1960, European Free Trade Association (EFTA).[7]

In regard to the social consequences of the disintegration of the state-empire system, the elite response had to accommodate/address a number of consequences/problems, both external and internal, as populations either reordered themselves in line with new structures of power, or where this was not possible, saw sections of the population physically relocated. Externally, in the new territorial settlement, the hitherto inclusive British sphere, no matter how bifurcated by ethnicity and class and religion (and so on), was subject to radical deconstruction and social ties were reworked. First, in the 'dominions', kith and kin in former peripheral territories became separated from what had been the motherland, as Australia,[8] New Zealand and Canada[9] had perforce to look to their own economic and political interests. Second, within newly created states, minority groups, which had hitherto lived successfully within the state-empire system, found their situations in question (thus, ethnic minority groups in newly formed states in Southeast Asia or religious communities in South Asia or settler minorities in East Africa and Southern African states). Third, occasionally groups were left behind as the tide of empire ebbed, and all had to adjust to new circumstances, and such adjustments could be problematic (settler rebellions in Africa, minority group expulsions in Africa and India, minority group repression in Burma, or cultural-dissolution, as with Peranakan or Eurasian groups in Singapore, or more recently, the Falkland Islanders living with neighbours unreconciled to their status). And, internally, within the now metropolitan core territory, there was significant population movement: hitherto overseas dwellers, expatriates or refugees or migrants, relocated to the territory of the core; and others travelled the other way, emigrating to former white dominions, as career opportunities in what had been the empire were foreclosed. Attention turned to the newly constituted domestic sphere. And some of this took time: thus the slow reduction in colonial holdings and the related slow reduction in overseas military deployments (thus for a long while the BBC radio broadcast *Two Way Family Favourites* and in the 1960s empire nostalgics marked the final 'withdrawal from east of Suez').

And all these changes had to be rendered intelligible and managed; the elite had to read and react and formulate a project. Here, arguably, as attention turns to matters of elite self-understandings and the tales told to the masses, the continuing problems begin. So, in regard to the politico-cultural consequences of the disintegration of the state-empire system: the first element of elite public reaction was a sustained denial of reality, both recent past and present (history of state-empire system actively forgotten, subordination to America veiled), coupled with the stylization of 'the war' and 'wartime' and the claim to 'victory in a virtuous war'; plus, the second element was the public confection of a new self-image predicated on a largely delusional claim to a deep historical continuity – the 'continuing British' – a long-established, distinctive nation-state.

There are two caveats to this judgement: first, flagged by the world 'public', it is sometimes difficult to believe that the elite did not realize what was going on, in other words the public face may have been cover for a much more self-conscious decision to accommodate themselves to the demands and opportunities of subordinate status within the American sphere, opportunities which have been pursued (hence the machineries of contemporary subordination in defence, finance and nostalgia); and second, whilst this judgement made in hindsight might seem harsh, in defence of the elite, accommodating a politico-cultural catastrophe of this scale might well have taxed the imagination of any elite, thus both the French and the Dutch governments fought wars in futile attempts to sustain overseas empires, the Belgian government sought to retain its African colony before precipitately leaving; and the Portuguese regime did hang-on to territories until almost the end of the twentieth century when domestic revolution occasioned their release. Nonetheless, for the British elite, the core elements of this mix of denial and confection came to revolve around the Second World War. British involvement was embraced in a stylized memory, which became a foundation myth: 'victory in a virtuous war', recalled, familiarly, in the idea of 'the war' and 'war-time', which, in turn, informed the new elite led political-cultural project of 'continuing Britain'.

State-empire dissolution and the tasks of the hitherto core, 1945–56

The focus of this text is on ways of thinking and a simple trio of ideas – events, impacts and residues – offers a schema with which to grasp the ways in which agents have responded to enfolding change and thereafter the ways in which some (but not all) materials have become sedimented in the political-culture of the polity, available, thereafter, as taken-for-granted ideas/assumptions, elements carried within cultural tradition.

There are two aspects to the response of the elite to the collapse of the British state-empire system: denial and confection, together the elite ordered creation of a stylized collective memory; this process sketched out a route to the future and once it was up and running it endured, as alternatives were foreclosed. In the new dispensation minimum change was acknowledged, the scale of the catastrophe that had overcome the elite and their project obscured and a spurious essential continuity affirmed.

The starting point for this response, the given of circumstances, was the experience of war.[10] The elite, concerned to sustain their state-empire,[11] had prepared for war in the late 1930s:[12] an already powerful military was upgraded with new weaponry; a worldwide empire supported the metropolitan core; and the key ally, France, also had a powerful military. In the event the British were forced from the mainland but the state-empire endured for two years, until the Japanese attacks in 1941/2 forced the British out of East Asia[13] and brought the USA into the war. It was this circumstance, along with Soviet allies, which ensured that the British would be part of a general military victory in Europe and in the East. The war was presented to the population, both domestic and empire, as a 'people's war'; that is, embracing many participants and serving their concerns.[14] But this characterization did not endure,[15] and at the end of the war period the episode was subject to various interpretive reworkings – the mainstream version of events has been tagged the 'allied scheme of history'[16] – but for the British elite and population, now shorn of their empire, the war in time became a new foundation myth, a period when the essential character of the long-enduring British was made manifest.

The 'people's empire' and the 'people's war'

The dissolution of empire placed heavy demands on the metropolitan political elite as a new political-cultural project had to be fashioned. The base line for these new endeavours was given, that is, there was an available, indeed, inevitable, starting point in the notion of a 'people's war', the legitimating theorem confected by the elite and widely disseminated and embraced amongst the wider subaltern population. Such overarching theorems can be self-consciously created and revised but the costs are high with the entire business of deploying new argument and extirpating the old.[17]

Wendy Webster[18] has looked in detail at the various themes current within elite sponsored popular thinking over wartime years and into the early 1950s. During the wartime period events were constructed as a 'people's empire' along with a 'people's war'.[19] These themes were heavily promoted, linking Britain, the empire and the war. However, the aspect of empire faded, the nineteenth-century-style colonial empire was reimagined first as a 'people's empire' then as 'Commonwealth' and now in the early years of the twenty-first century as 'heritage'. Thus the loss of empire was never directly acknowledged (some affirming 'the minimal impact thesis'[20]). What was left was wartime; and here 'people's war' gave way to 'the war', with the focus now firmly on the contribution of the core, in particular in the earlier years when 'Britain stood alone',[21] and with this period read as evidence of deep seated traits in the polity, harking back, that is, precisely to the days of empire. So in the terms used in this text – denial and confection – it is in these years that the crucial moves are made; the loss of empire is carefully disregarded as a 'continuing Britain' is confected.

Webster looks at the cultural impact of the loss of empire and whilst her discussion does not deal directly with the high politics or the business of remembering and forgetting flagged by Tony Judt and others,[22] she does identify three 'cultural' narratives:[23] first, 'people's empire', affirming the linkage of domestic welfare with peripheral development, a theme whose apogee was found in 1953 with the Coronation, the conquest of Everest and the idea of a 'New Elizabethan Age'; second, 'England under siege', noting the impact of colonial wars and inward migration; and third, 'national greatness', as exemplified in the Second

World War where the role of empire was progressively elided in favour of the role of the metropolitan core.

First, the 'people's war' and the 'people's empire' stood for inclusion: class divisions amongst the core population were disregarded and conflicts associated with independence movements and race divisions within the empire were similarly set aside. London was presented as the central place of a globally dispersed family. There was a corresponding concern for the home front: J.B. Priestly celebrated 'little England' and this was echoed by George Orwell's inward-looking celebration of England.[24] And the relationship with the United States was carefully managed: the empire was presented as cooperative; and Britain was represented as crucial to the dispersed network of the 'English-speaking people's'.[25] Then, after the Second World War, there was a notion of a 'people's victory', and a parade in June 1946 celebrated the diversity of participants, but this image was quickly changed as the notion of a 'hero's victory' emerged, which let the war take over the cultural territory formerly occupied by the empire.[26] But these changes were not straightforward and for a while the empire remained in view, now as the Commonwealth, celebrated in the coronation of Queen Elizabeth II and the conquest at the same moment of the world's highest mountain, Everest;[27] domestically, there was a flush of optimism, the 'New Elizabethan Age'.

Second, the loss of empire could not be wholly disregarded.[28] The Commonwealth was advanced as a successor and embraced the old territories of empire, revolving around Britain and its revivified monarchy. But the idea was difficult to sustain, with two problems, in particular. First, the sequence of colonial wars, where there were three phases of colonial 'implosion' (1947–8 in South Asia, 1956–7 in the Middle East and 1961–5 in Africa),[29] which required any image of a 'people's empire' to disregard rebellions, violence and war. And second, the problems associated with the arrival of inward migration from the empire; in particular the business of 'colour bars' and race prejudice, which cut directly against an idea of an inclusive Commonwealth. Englishness came to be seen to be in some sense embattled, both settlers in the residual empire territories and people in the metropolitan core, and the upshot was that the Commonwealth dwindled in significance in public discourse. Moving from quasi-empire, to source of threat, to a marginal issue, with immigration controls passed and membership of the EEC in prospect.[30]

Third, as the empire faded, in practice and imagination, memories were reworked and focused on the core territory. The Second World War became a victory of the people of the metropolitan core; other contributions were acknowledged, but as adjuncts to the efforts of the core. But Webster notes that by the late 1950s and early 1960s public discourse was beginning to shift. The angry young men of the theatre attacked what they saw as the moribund attitudes of the elite. The satire boom of the early 1960s followed along this line. But both were ambiguous critiques: attacking the elite for their attitudes, whilst measuring them and the present against the lost past; they offered no alternative, remaining essentially conservative critiques.[31]

And so, overall, in summary form, there were a number of reworked or novel discourses: the wartime military victory came to involve less empire, fewer allies and more core British heroes as the war became the key idea, increasingly a new foundation myth; the idea of an orderly withdrawal from empire was embraced, with the Commonwealth as a species of somewhat ambiguous consolation; ideas of domestic welfare and colonial development were embraced; and the notion of the 'English-speaking people's' was advanced[32] whereby the elite sought to build a link with the now powerful USA. Thus the response to the disintegration of the political-cultural project of state-empire involved two elements: denial, the loss was set aside as of relatively little concern; and confection, the metropolitan core was reimagined as a continuation of a long-established nation-state.

Denial: Addressing the loss of empire

So, first, denial: in the case of the British elite, denial centred upon the catastrophe of the Second World War with its 55 million dead, which was recast as war and wartime, together underpinning an heroic victory in a morally virtuous war.

The Second World War unfolded on an unprecedented scale. Military campaigns engulfed Europe and East Asia, colonial territories in South Asia, Africa and Latin America were drawn in as suppliers and the United States quickly became a military/industrial super-power. The Soviet Union, having suffered catastrophic losses, emerged as a second super-power. In all this upheaval the state-empire systems of the Europeans – including the British – were simply undermined. Militarily untenable, economically unaffordable and politically no longer tolerable, their dissolution in the years after 1945 was rapid, although it was, it might be noted, accompanied by a series of wars of colonial withdrawal and these were more than usually futile exercises (and given events in the hitherto core territories of Europe, more than usually indefensible). Seen in this context, British elite denial involved much active forgetting: first, the collapse of the state-empire system, which was reimagined via the construction of the Commonwealth; then second the subordination to the USA, which was reimagined in terms of a putative relationship mirroring Greece/Rome, or grasped in terms of an overarching construction, the 'English-speaking peoples', or – now notoriously – cast in terms of the 'special relationship'; and finally, third, the relationship with mainland Europe, where polities were in similar situations, was represented as a side issue, and ordered in terms of a deluded and patronizing contrast between a continuing great power and the variously defeated.

(i) Commonwealth

The dissolution of the territories of the state-empire system impacted both hitherto peripheral areas and hitherto core areas. The shrunken territorial unit that comprised the core was reordered as the country now called 'the United Kingdom' or 'the UK'[33] or 'Britain'. The hitherto peripheral territories were recast in a number of ways: first, the slow process of separation that had characterized the political experience of the 'dominions' was accelerated sharply – the experience of the Pacific War had moved Australia towards the American sphere, Canada slowly and seemingly somewhat reluctantly floated free,[34] as did New Zealand and in a different way South Africa; second, other territories were remade as nation-states – initially territories in South and Southeast Asia, later sub-Saharan Africa and the Caribbean; and third, the extensive spheres of informal empire also contracted.[35]

The core elite sought to retain access for economic reasons (trade and investment), social reasons (kith and kin), politico-cultural reasons (elite self-image) and political reasons (status claims within the international system). The mix generated the Commonwealth. The construct went through a number of phases: at first the metropolitan core plus the newly independent former empire territories formed the Commonwealth, where this was taken as a 'continuation-of-empire', reaching an apogee in the 1953 Coronation; but later, with inward migration and the emergence of the political sphere of the EEC, elite interest in and popular support for the Commonwealth began to fade and the organization dwindled in the public consciousness.[36] Overall, the Commonwealth was presented to the population of the hitherto core area as part continuation-of-empire and part apotheosis of the colonial relationship.[37] But it was a confused message and embraced a number of different strands. First, the social aspect of retreat – this could include the obligations owed to various groups within former peripheral territories, in particular, those who were 'kith and kin', in other words, sometime colonial officials and most awkward of all, settlers, and it could include repatriation of colonial officials and local groups likely to be treated as collaborators by incoming nationalists, and it could also include sustaining odd military links such as Gurkhas. Second, the nature of the political relationship with replacement elites, during the process of withdrawal and thereafter – this could include questions about the role of the Queen (head of the Commonwealth and for some former dominions, the head of state) and it could include what has by now become a commonplace, the status shift from 'independence fighter' to 'statesman'[38]). And third, it could include economic issues – control of oil in the Middle East, control of money reserves in Brunei, control of banking centres in Hong Kong, control of income-generating resources in Malaya, and so on. And these social, political and economic issues took no fixed form, varying from place to place. They entered political debate in no fixed form, again varying from place to place and they left no uniform homogeneous legacy for present-day thinking. The dissolution of empire and its transition into the Commonwealth produced a confusion of strands of thinking – ideas that run down to the present day – some associated with the East, some the Middle East, others with sub-Saharan Africa.

In the East, there were elite political and wider public debates about the state-empires. The colonial territories in the East had constituted the jewel in the crown of empire: economic (trade and investment – producing money, jobs and products); social (the social networks of empire saw people moving from place to place (first, migrant workers from the core to the periphery as civil servants, soldiers, managers and assorted hangers-on), second, migrant workers from peripheral territory to peripheral territory, and third, some migrants moving from periphery to core, becoming in the 1950s and early 1960s a source of tension in the former metropolitan core)); and political, control of large populations made the core elite politically powerful within the extant global system. All these linkages provoked vigorous domestic debate about questions of responsibilities, the pragmatics of continuing interests and the demands of quickly shifting circumstances. Yet by 1945 some elements were already lost (concessions in China); some elements were in the process of loss (India,[39] Burma); whilst in other places the colonial power managed to hang on for a while (Malaya,[40] Singapore, Brunei); and in one area the British colonial regime was sustained albeit in a very curious fashion until 1997 (Hong Kong). The collective memory of the British probably records these events today (in the early twenty-first century) in a schematic fashion (if at all): the East was exotic (Somerset

Maugham); the loss of empire involved terrible suffering (Japan); and post-war withdrawal was smooth, except when interrupted by the violence of the local inhabitants (Partition, the Emergency). And today, at a guess, for most people, 'the East' is a tagline on a tourist brochure, with one major exception, the continuing links with South Asia, specifically, the links of settled migrant groups with their countries of origin and associated patterns of continued inward migration and here the idea of the Commonwealth shades into the reading noted by Webster,[41] the link is a problem.

Then in the Middle East there were elite political and wider public debates about the state-empire's role. Here the British had an accumulation of informal empire and mandate territories. After 1945, amongst these, some were quickly lost (Palestine, 1948) some remained (Arabian peninsular) and in some influence was regained (Iran, 1953) whilst in others it was lost (Egypt, 1956).

The informal empire territories related both to oil interests around the Arabian Gulf (these had become crucial territories after the Royal Navy switched from coal to oil-fired propulsion systems and the territories in which these resources were located were drawn into the informal empire of the British) and to the Canal Zone in Egypt, nominally an independent country, again part of the informal empire. After 1945 as the empire began to dissolve away these territories were matters of great concern. The British along with the Americans overthrew the government of Iran in 1953 in order to control oil interests. The British (and Americans) controlled most of the Gulf sultanates for many years after the end of the Second World War, same reason, oil. The British (plus France and Israel) invaded Egypt in 1956 in order to control the Suez Canal. And, the mandate territories covered areas formerly controlled by the Ottoman Empire. After its dissolution following the Great War the French gained territory in the northern Arab lands (now Lebanon and Syria) whilst the British gained territory in the southern Arab lands (now Jordan, Iraq and Israel).

Debates in respect of the former involved: questions of oil supplies, Cold War competition with the Soviet Union and the defence of routes to the Far East. The opening pair are a continuing concern, less for the British than their allies the Americans. The latter ran on until the 1960s when Harold Wilson's government announced the military/diplomatic withdrawal from 'East of Suez'. But it was debates about the latter group, the sometime mandate territories that attained most prominence, in particular the issue of Palestine. The British had signed up to the Zionist ideal of a homeland for the Jews in Palestine, their religiously validated historical homeland, and the catastrophe that had befallen European Jewry during the Second World War provided a final impetus – moral and practical – to the establishment of a Jewish state. But, as was the case elsewhere, the process of carving out a territory from the realms of a disintegrating empire was not straightforward and the incoming Zionists fought guerrilla wars against the British, wars of ethnic cleansing against local Palestinians and outright interstate wars against their neighbours. Thus the establishment of Israel was neither straightforward nor agreed and the local legacies continue to be an urgent matter and the issue remains a live one within British politics.[42]

And, finally, in respect of sub-Saharan Africa there were elite political and wider public debates about the state-empire; prior to 1956, there had been an expectation of slow change-in-general, mixing expectations of some economic development plus local political advance along with a concern for kith and kin settler colonies,[43] but following Harold Macmillan's 'winds of change' speech, the colonies in sub-Saharan Africa were vacated, not easily (rebellions, settler problems).

Harold Macmillan came to power after the debacle of the invasion of Suez and the policy of his government was to withdraw from what was left of the empire as quickly as possible. Macmillan granted the claims of aspirant replacement elites and handovers were quickly organized. The British left West Africa in a relatively short period of time, local economies were strong and crucially there were few white settlers. But the situation was different in East Africa. The British became involved in a small-scale brutal war of colonial retreat in Kenya. The local population was divided along ethnic lines, leading to interethnic conflicts, and there was a large influential white settler group. Withdrawal was accompanied by violence. In other parts of East Africa withdrawal was smoother. The British withdrawal from Southern Africa was more problematical as South Africa and Southern Rhodesia established states built on ethnic separation and white rule – in South Africa it was announced as the policy of separate development – in Southern Rhodesia the situation obtaining in colonial days was run on into the independence period.

Debates about sub-Saharan Africa have had a markedly different character to those relating to the Middle East or Far East. The continuing domestic discourse about Africa is cast in terms of that continents' need for continuing development assistance so claims to knowledge, expertise and ethic have informed British dealings with former colonial territories at both the state level and the non-governmental organization (NGO) level.

And, finally, as an addendum, in respect of all these territories there were the rituals of imperial retreat-cum-continuity. Retreat was evident in the 1953 Coronation, which signalled the New Elizabethan Age plus hand-over ceremonies plus claims to success (colonial rule ends as a job well done). And there were rituals of continuity with Commonwealth Summits or Commonwealth Games plus the cultural linkages, all strategies of popularization. And, in all this, here there was a particular role for the monarchy, which was popular outside Britain, sustained inside.[44]

(ii) English-speaking peoples

In the chaotic aftermath of the Second World War, as the British state-empire system dissolved, elements within the hitherto core area sought new routes to the future. One key issue was their evolving relationship with the emergent power of the USA, at one time a set of English colonies planted in North America, more recently an industrial and military competitor and now clearly the dominant power in the North Atlantic region. As the new situation slowly unfolded itself in elite and mass thinking, a number of strands of response followed: there were elite debates around the status of the USA and the position of the British; popular responses, a mix of war time experiences plus post-war models; and general debates centred on the ideal 'the American dream' of opportunity/consumption. One particular signal of the new situation was to be found in the elite's new rituals of obeisance: the visits of circumstance diminished politicians to the new quasi-imperial centre of Washington.

First, the matter of elite responses to new status of the USA – the record reveals a mix of conflict and cooperation with the terms of trade running strongly in favour of the Americans, a point finally acknowledged in the 1950s. There was conflict about the architecture of the post-war economic settlement (Bretton Woods) and negotiations were conducted by Harry White and Maynard Keynes, in the main the views of the former held sway.[45] The abrupt ending of lend-lease in August 1945 was an early assertion of American priority in the post-war world. There was early cooperation in the anti-Soviet Cold War and the Atlee government did not seek to moderate American policy, Ernest Bevin, foreign secretary, was an enthusiast[46] but there was also residual self-assertion, evident in the decision to go for nuclear weapons, evident also in the failed invasion of Egypt in 1956 and evident a little later as Macmillan deploys idea of Greece and Rome – obliquely acknowledging the situation.[47]

Second, there were popular responses – some resentful memory as the war years had seen millions of American service personnel based in Britain and there had been some friction (a popular complaint was that the Americans were 'over here, over paid and over sexed'), some awkward memory (American army racism where blacks were discriminated against and this rankled with host population), some appreciation (as American personnel and material were evidently indispensible to the war effort) and post-war a new positive opinion forms around popular culture (jazz, pop-music, cinema, comics) and a little later popular consumerism – coke, hamburgers, jukeboxes and so on.

Third, in this period the USA becomes a model, what now would be tagged 'soft power' as economic, military and political power finds related supplementary expression in the realms of culture: in the high arts (for example, in painting) or the intellectual sphere (humanities and social sciences) or popular (images of opportunity/consumption). It is the period of the high tide of the 'American dream' – it is a model centred on the possibility of individual advancement and attainment, increasingly available to American citizens as the economy powered ahead, but still more of an aspiration for the British where affluence belonged to the later 1950s and early 1960s.

And finally, the rituals – patterns of structural power had changed and the response of the British elite had numerous strands (economic, military and diplomatic) but two over-arching themes came to the fore. One of them was a pitch to a novel imagined community – embracing the inhabitants of the hitherto metropolitan core, the members of its dominions and the USA – together wrapped up as 'the English speaking peoples'. The other involved offering a particular reading of the events of the war years, prioritizing the role of the USA and the British, now in terms of the idea of 'the special relationship' and these were cemented in practice via rituals: elite politicians 'visit Washington', elite politicians 'meet the new president', receive gifts ('defence cooperation' – Polaris/Trident), deploy the ritual use of forms-of-words (in particular, uttering or writing in the press the words 'the special relationship').

(iii) The Continent

The metropolitan core of the British state-empire – the European core of the global empire – emerged from the military conflict significantly less damaged than its mainland neighbours. The polities of the Continent had endured catastrophic military campaigns and sustained enormous casualties and material damage. In this context, the British elite could represent themselves not merely as victors in a virtuous war, a global power, but also as the beneficiaries of a relatively undamaged, high-tech and successful economy along with its mobilized, community-minded patriotic citizenry. Some of these claims were correct – the relative economic power, some false, the claims to global power, but in retrospect it is easy to see elite and popular hubris. Being on the winning side in the war was celebrated, whilst all that was lost, that is, a state-empire, was forgotten. This short period – the late 1940s and early 1950s – sees an attitude put in place, one of difference from mainland neighbours, an attitude that runs down to the present, evidenced, notoriously, in Britain's 'semidetached'[48] relationship with the European Union.

First, military – demobilization saw the bulk of the armed forces brought back from various active war zones but British armed forces remained in Germany (and did so until well into the twenty-first century[49]). The occupation involved four powers, later the NATO/Warsaw Pact. The British elite took note of their experience of membership of militarily victorious alliances and comparisons were made (the victorious 'Big Three' versus the variously defeated/occupied). The emergence of the military alliance with the USA became a key part of the self-understanding of the British elite – the claim to the status of number-one ally in Europe.

Second, welfare – the war years had facilitated the embrace by sections of the elite of a programme of social reform. In the event the postwar period saw extensive domestic reform. It was elite sponsored. It was supplemented by extensive political mobilization (Army Education Corps, the Left Book Club and so on). The programme was widely supported. The period also provides material for a Labour Party 'national party past'[50] – that is, the period is recalled as the party achieving an approximation of 'socialism' in Britain.

Third, economic austerity/recovery – the domestic economy had been oriented to the state-empire sphere, not to the mainland. The recovery in Britain was slower than the mainland, producing some surprise and the slow beginnings of a puzzled resentment that finds expression as complaint ('we won the war, so why are we poor?') or analysis ('declinist' work).[51]

Then, rituals are deployed – there are popular symbolic events such as the 1951 Festival of Britain; the 1953 Coronation and the idea of the 'New Elizabethan Age' and there are elite symbolic events such as refusing to join the EEC and instead forming EFTA. There are also cultural inventions (elite/mass) such as the idea of 'the Continent'[52] or general characterizations and stereotypes of national groups.[53]

Confection: Imagining 'continuing Britain'

Then, supplementing denial, the second element is confection. The state project was cast in terms of a continuation of an independent quasi-great power status – economic, social and politico-cultural – a kind of 'continuing Britain'. The newly confected self-image comprised both domestic elements (in the myth of war and wartime underpinning the notion of victory in a virtuous war, the progressive, technologically advanced New Elizabethan Age, plus the welfare state) and international elements (in the bridge between the United States and Europe, the core of the Commonwealth, a model polity, available for emulation by everyone-in-general).

(i) War and wartime

The idea of 'the war' and 'wartime' – the episode is read into collective memory in a specific way – the scale of the disaster could not be hidden – it was recalled selectively.[54] The notion of 'the war' permits events to be recalled in stylized form: first, the 'deliverance at Dunkirk' – a military defeat is reframed as a quasi-religious victory; second, the invention of the Battle of Britain – the military events are framed as the victory of an heroic group – plus, as events are subsequently told and retold, the felicitous availability of novel science-based technologies – with certain military aircraft thereafter aestheticized as beautiful; third, the Battle of El Alamein – the military events are framed not merely as a local victory but as a 'turning point';[55] fourth, the invasion of Normandy, 'D-day' – military events are famed not merely as victory but as the start of the 'liberation of Europe' – neglecting thereby the role of the Red Army;[56] and fifth, VE day – the camps – later Nuremburg – virtuous victory confirmed.[57]

This stylized history can be criticized on empirical grounds – where memory gets the story wrong – Norman Davies's lists, thus, for example, that El Alamein was a small-scale battle compared with those in Eastern Europe and Russia or W.I Hitchcock, who writes about the invasion of Western Europe, and notes the high costs of liberation.[58] The stylized history can be addressed directly, thus, again Davies, writes of the 'allied scheme of history' – an elaborate tale, which more or less systematically skews the history so as to produce a moral victory for the allies with guilt/responsibility reserved exclusively for National Socialist Germany. But the notion of 'wartime' permits the social experience to be recalled in stylized form: community – pulling-together – shared sacrifice; joining up – the forces; freedom from normal constraints – upheaval – change – novelty; a period when action made a difference.[59]

(ii) Standing alone, muddling through

David Edgerton argues that in the late 1930s, Britain was rich and powerful: the science and technology base of the economy was very strong;

war planning oriented to the use of technology was good; and the country's links with the empire and global system were strong. These strengths meant that the elite could contemplate war with confidence – it is true that opinion ahead of the conflict was mixed (with various combinations of appeasement and rearmament advocated)[60] but the country was strong.

The early setbacks were read at the time as a matter of poor equipment/planning and this theme has fed into later post-war discussion, but the setbacks were not occasioned by poor equipment/planning – these failures had other occasions (not specified by Edgerton). The early setbacks in the European theatre – that is, defeats in Norway, France and North Africa – were read into the public sphere and later history in terms of the idea of 'being alone' but this was nonsense as the empire continued its support as did contacts with the rest of the global system[61] – in terms of war production these were not major problems. The setbacks in East Asia were major problems – both at the time (thus, for example, the loss of Malaya's rubber) and later as the empire began to unravel and dominions turned for defence links towards the USA. Thereafter, from early 1942, with the USA and the Soviet Union involved in the war, the British could be confident of their participation in an eventual military victory.

Edgerton takes this record and unpacks the detail whilst challenging some familiar readings of the war experience: post-war theories of 'decline', which posit a lack of concern for national economic development are rejected[62] – the country emerged from the war years with a strong science-based industrial system; post-war anxieties about the welfare state, which is opposed to robust industrial development are rejected as the role of welfare spending was minor until the 1950s; also note the role of experts of all types, adding that the idea that they were not important is odd as the country did have a major science base; and finally, the loss of empire is acknowledged, along with a post-war turning inwards to a militaristic nationalism which ignored both loss of empire and the contribution to military success of empire and allies.

After 1945, Edgerton argues,[63] the elite and masses became more nationalistic and militaristic – the history of recent events was written with the metropolitan population to the fore and the empire, the allies and the global system (which the allies could access) all pushed into the background. A skewed version of the war was produced: all the tales of Britain 'standing alone' and overcoming early problems with arms and supplies through native ingenuity. But this vision is wrong, for the country was rich and powerful and it never stood alone.[64] The war left Britain the most powerful Western European country – economically, scientifically and politically – it was nationalistic and militaristic. But all this was conducted as a species of low politics; there was no Friedrich List-type figure able to interpret the new situation. However, the country had been eclipsed by the very rapid growth of the USA, now the dominant partner amongst the Western allies, and it had either lost or was in the process of losing, stage by stage, its empire. On this last noted, Jeremy Paxman[65] argues that the empire continues to have a residual effect on the population – the refusal to explicitly debate the loss is symptomatic of a pervasive nostalgia for an irrecoverable now stylized past.

(iii) 'Continuing Britain'

The elite response to the catastrophe of the collapse of their long-pursued political-cultural project of state-empire involved denial and confection – the former served to veil loss, the later to offer a route a future intimately linked to that which had been lost. It is a subtle construct. The state-empire system is lost, its loss veiled and a species of continuity is affirmed. Thus, in this creation, the post-war country is more than the residuum of the state-empire system, it is certainly not an historically new unity, rather it is the always existing continuing core, thus there was 'Britain' then there was 'the British Empire' and now once again there is 'Britain' and the process encapsulates an essential continuity – a 'continuing Britain'. It is a nationalist reading.

In this perspective post-war Britain is: first, still a great power within the global system; second, an exemplary polity, evidenced in victory in a virtuous war; third, recovering earlier greatness in the New Elizabethan Age; fourth, disposing of empire in the imaginative creation of a Commonwealth; and fifth, a long-established successful polity offering a model to others.

Running down to the present: Legacies and repetitions

It would be a mistake to see these materials, the ideas of 'the war', 'wartime' and 'continuing Britain', together reworking the catastrophe of the Second World War as a new foundation myth, as in any way fixed or static. They are ways of understanding the political world and like any other set of ideas needs must be actively created and recreated in order for them to pass down the generations, moreover, as they pass down through time, they are subject to the vagaries of collective memory (active misremembering/forgetting), and to the unanticipated demands of events – things crop up, the stock of ideas is deployed and in being so used is replenished and amended – so tradition unfolds not as mere mechanical repetition but as a living set of ideas.

The contemporary political culture of the United Kingdom, most especially those institutions whose members would be inclined to represent themselves as British, evidences an ambiguous relationship to war fighting: part formal revulsion, a learned[66] response legitimated by public remembrance (the response is thus officially sanctioned) and part uneasy affirmation, a response legitimated by elements within collective memory (the stylized histories of empire, with their heroic figures, Nelson, Wolf and so on, their deaths represented in art as pietas, and the stylized memory of the Second World War with the deaths and privations played down in favour of foregrounding episodes of heroism).

On war fighting there are numerous post-Second World War examples to cite: the retreat from empire (fighting successfully 'guerrillas, bandits and terrorists') which has bequeathed to the British Army a (false[67]) sense of itself as particularly skilled at counterinsurgency operations (COIN); post-empire Cold War interventions of an ill-advised or disastrous type (indirect, Iran 1952, or direct, Korea 1950–3); post-empire wars (ill-advised, Suez; more intelligibly, the Falklands); and more recently, wars of choice, 'liberal interventionism', both successful (Sierra Leone), sadly unavoidable (former Yugoslavia) and calamitous (Iraq, Afghanistan). The records of these wars are read into collective memory in terms of the frame of meanings set by the episode of the Second World War.

The contemporary political culture of Britain evidences a prospective and positive understanding of wartime: public opinion is quick to rally to the support of the armed forces (in whatever war they happen to be deployed) – in popular media a distinction is drawn between the particular war in question and the role of the individual soldiers in that war – the latter are celebrated, the former often downplayed – dissent in the public sphere is quickly downplayed, all members of the polity are invited to support 'our troops', or 'our boys' once the military fighting has begun – explicit public rejection is rare. And, in nostalgic mode, on rare public festival days, the elite enjoins the populace to organize 'street parties' – echoing the celebration of the end of wartime.

The contemporary political culture of Britain evidences a stylized reverence for 'the war': a period of sacrifice, community and collective endeavour, a period in which, for individuals, 'action made a difference'. This attitude is seen in annual official remembrance ceremonies and associated charity collections – it is seen in the creation of museums dedicated to the experience and artefacts – it is seen in public ceremonies which have no direct connection with the Second World War – thus the 2011 Royal Wedding had a fly-past of vintage warplanes – it is seen in the sphere of popular culture – television shows such as Tony Robinson's *Time Team* excavating war sites – or Richard Homes's *War Walks* – or in Dr Who ending up in wartime London (again) – or in the voluminous collections of war-related materials in local bookshops.

Thus does 'the war' and 'wartime' run down into the present day, offering resources with which to read and react to contemporary events; be they wars, or sporting events or weddings.

Reforging the nation: The war, wartime and continuing Britain

Measured in terms of the rhythm of life of an individual, the state-empire system collapsed quite slowly. Events were experienced as part of the general political/social background noise for those born just after the war, the baby-boom generation.[68] The empire was more or less intact in late 1945 as territories occupied by Japan were in part recovered (but not those in China save for Hong Kong); thereafter holdings in South and Southeast Asia broke away relatively slowly, those in other parts of the world even more slowly, with the process running on into the early 1960s as it proved difficult to dissolve satisfactorily colonial holdings in Southern Africa.

Metropolitan elite accommodation to new circumstances was measured and a quasi-global role was available: overt Cold War conflicts (for example, the 1950–3 Korean War); wars of colonial retreat (for example, the 1948–58 Malayan Emergency); plus assorted covert adventures in the Middle East (for example, the 1953 overthrow of Mossaddegh's government in Iran). The rhetoric of great power status continued to be deployed, but the focus drifts; it moves away from actual state empire (it had to, as the territories were shrinking and clearly set to shrink further) and towards a nationalist-style reading of the history and character of the core territory of the state-empire system. The key was the recent episode of conflict. This was reimagined. The worldwide collapse of the state-empire system was ignored, the loss was met with denial and the episode recentred upon the war years which were presented as a battle between 'free peoples' and 'tyrannies' and read this way, Britain won through, being victorious in a virtuous war; thus the construct of 'the war' and the invocation of a certain style of solidarity, 'wartime'. These were the cores of a new national foundation myth. A limited territory restricted to the geographical British Isles became the home of a tighter group of people and the wider territories were now reimagined, no longer lost parts of a lost system, but overseas possessions that had always been separate and were now separated, a much less dramatic pattern of change, indeed, these changes could be read as the natural realization of the duties of empire. The mass of the population were invited to buy into into the new story: a new Queen was enthroned, a new Elizabethan Age was celebrated in the press, the Commonwealth was formed, and a new political settlement began to take shape: 'continuing Britain'.

3
Grand Designs: Patrician Reformers, Subaltern Demands and the Ideal of Welfare

The violent manner of the dissolution of the state-empire system created a space within which novel political arguments could be made – in the peripheral areas of the system these demands were lodged by aspirant replacement elites and centred upon political independence and thereafter concerned the business of state-making, nation-building and the pursuit of development – in the core areas, where old structures and ideas had been radically disturbed, there were similar calls from patrician reformers and subaltern groups for change and one set of demands centred upon novel claims in respect of welfare – the assertion of the responsibility of the state to attend to the basic needs of all its citizens and the parallel claim to a human right to such welfare provision. In the former metropolitan core territory, the notion of welfare became one of the defining ideas of the post-war polity – an aspect of the contested compromise between classes that could not easily be challenged, much less significantly changed.

The welfare state can be understood in several ways: first, most obviously, as a current set of state-ordered administrative structures which together act to provide welfare benefits for the population in the fields of health, housing, schooling and general welfare (familiar debate then revolves around the technical detail of provisions, asking whether it is effective, efficient or whatever); or, second, more broadly, as the product of a reform programme, itself lodged in history, the creation of the wartime generation of social/political reformers (debate then revolves around the identity of the reformers and their objectives, and maybe party political allegiances); and then, third, and more broadly still, the welfare state can be read comparatively, as one state form amongst others, thus, competitive liberal states, developmental states, party-state systems and so on.[1]

Grand Designs: Reformers, Demands, Welfare   41

The debates ordered around such characterizations are familiar, and they are concerned, one way or another, with how the system works and with what associated schedules of intended and unintended consequences, but the discussion here has a different focus, not the institutional apparatus, however conceived, or compared, but the experiences of the elites and citizens of Britain, in particular, the nature of the political-cultural ideas both embedded within the institutional apparatus and thereafter more widely disseminated through the social world. In their early versions, as the system was put in place, such ideas would express elite designs and popular wishes, but thereafter, such ideas would be modified as the system bedded down, became accepted and perhaps also taken for granted. So, down the years, there was modification and routinization, and today, the idea of welfare can be unpacked in a variety ways: as a familiar, regular administrative task that demands attention from the permanent government; as an issue/institution which exercises the corporate world and its celebrants in the political world; as an occasionally urgent issue confronting politicians; and amongst the population at large as a taken-for-granted characteristic of modern social life.

So the discussion here is concerned with the political-cultural experience of the elites and masses of Britain, the contexts within which they dwelled, the expectations held and the plans that were made. In which case, the wartime generation, with its elite patrician reformers and a receptive mobilized population, did construct the apparatus of a now well-established (although always contested)[2] welfare-state system, whose apparatus includes not merely the organizations but also the ideas in respect of welfare, which now (again always contested) pervade the political culture.[3]

Episode: The project of the welfare state

The political programme of reform was an elite project. The push for reform was an aspect of the business of mobilizing an empire population for the war effort and plans were made for both the metropolitan core and peripheral areas: thus Beveridge, dealing with the core, published his report in 1942, just as a little earlier elite attention had turned to the colonial sphere.[4] In both core and periphery, reform-minded agents took their chance and advanced claims to reform: in the former, it found expression in the spread of reforms now tagged 'the welfare state', whilst, in the latter, it was realized in the fashion of 'independence' as a wide collection of 'new nation-states' made their appearance on a rapidly reconfiguring global political scene.

In Britain, the work of domestic reform was not all top down and nor was it a matter of suddenly realized conviction, because circumstances demanded an elite response as mass incompetence had not contributed to a second major war in 20 years whereas that of the elite certainly had. There was a broad swell of reformist opinion throughout the population. It was fuelled by various reform-minded groups – the political left were active – and as the state mobilized the population for war, domestic reformers[5] took the chance to advance calls for what were then regarded as sweeping reforms. Paul Addison[6] suggests that one key group was the Army Education Service, offering reasons for fighting and reasons for post-war reform, and reaching, by virtue of their official role, a large number of people. In brief, overall, there was a widespread view that a return to the pre-war status quo ante with its inequalities and elaborate status hierarchies was not an option and all this amounted to an irresistible – if not uncontested – demand lodged by assorted reformers on behalf of the ordinary people of the country.

Post-war domestic reconstruction[7]

In retrospect the programme of domestic reform can be seen to have rested upon a number of crucial assumptions in respect of the key agents, how goals could be realized and not least the ambitious scope of what could be done. It was ambitious. Yet the context for the project, the 1940s, was a gloomy period.

David Kynaston[8] offers a neat characterization:

> Britain in 1945. No supermarkets, no motorways, no teabags, no sliced bread, no frozen food, no flavoured crisps, no larger, no microwaves, no dishwashers, no Formica, no vinyl, no CDs, no computers, no mobiles, no duvets, no Pill, no trainers, no hoodies, no Starbucks. Four Indian restaurants. Shops on every corner, pubs on every corner, cinemas in every high street, red telephone boxes, Lyons Corner Houses, trams, trolley-buses, steam trains. Woodbines, Craven 'A', Senior Service, smoke, smog, Vapex inhalant. No launderettes, no automatic washing machines, wash day every Monday... Abortion illegal, homosexual relationships illegal, suicide illegal, capital punishment legal. White faces everywhere. Back-to-backs, narrow cobbled streets, Victorian terraces, no high-rises. Arterial roads, suburban semis, the march of the pylons... Heavy coins, heavy shoes, heavy suitcases, heavy tweed coats, heavy leather footballs, no unbearable lightness of being. Meat rationed,

butter rationed, lard rationed, margarine rationed, sugar rationed, tea rationed, cheese rationed, jam rationed, eggs rationed, sweets rationed, soap rationed, clothes rationed. Make do and mend.

The elite sought to move forwards. The welfare state was an elite project, it was an elite construction and it was made in a top-down fashion. The key players included patrician reformers,[9] interwar intellectuals (generally repelled by the costs of great depression and variously inspired by the example of the Soviet Union with its planned economy and society, and apparently successful record),[10] and assorted domestic groups and lobbyists (local-level groups arguing for this or that reform or for the concerns of this or that commercial or professional group).[11]

The programme rested upon the work of an active state. It was the key to the project. It was not assembled in any grass-roots up-wards or spontaneous manner. It was designed using the whole panoply of state power: committees, experts, plans and thereafter dissemination to the wider population, which in turn was mobilized, partly on the basis of various sector-specific negative experiences (Northern industrial towns – Jarrow March), partly on the basis of argument (thus Left Book Club or J.B. Priestley's books and broadcasts) and partly on the basis of the various experiences of the Second World War (industrial planning,[12] logistics and the work of the education departments in the armed forces).[13]

The programme was oriented towards reorganizing economic/social practices. The novelty was the turn to a national orientation and the simultaneous embrace of a reform programme. The British state-empire system had been expansive. The keys to its growth had been trade and the military, and social and political matters, welfare or reform (democratization) had come a distant second to matters economic. This had been true of both core and peripheral populations. But as the state empire dissolved away (with the state defending as best it could its holdings), the attention of the elite now turned inwards towards the population of the metropolitan domestic territory. The resultant state/government policy agenda looks quite different: famously, J.M. Keynes[14] – attacking unemployment through the active development of the economy (in ambition, both domestic and international); famously, William Beveridge – attacking the question of social security for the domestic population, with matters cast in terms of the state addressing the five problems of 'want, disease, ignorance, squalor and idleness', which militated against the attainment of a healthy productive life; and, somewhat delayed, famously, Harold Macmillan – announcing a 'wind of change' as the loss of empire was acknowledged.

The programme embraced plans for the future that were expansive and optimistic. Critics who cautioned in favour of modest 'piecemeal social engineering'[15] were disregarded. The mix of elite figures, an active state and an agenda focused on broad reform produced a grand design for the future: Keynesianism informed the goal of a mixed economy within a regulated international economy (hence Bretton Woods), ideas associated with modernism informed the goals of urban reconstruction and development, and the ideas associated with Beveridge informed the goals of welfare; or, in total, the goal of a mixed economy underpinning a modern welfare state.

Arguments deployed

The arguments made in favour of the project of the welfare state were not restricted to the texts produced by experts or politicians or policy specialists or commentators more broadly. Crucially, many of the relevant claims on people's attention, which moved them to action, included what are characterized here as 'arguments deployed', that is, arguments embodied in actions or institutions or memories; that is to say, whilst the creation of the welfare state was organized by elites – it was top down – argument in favour of the project was embedded in a range of social activities and so elite ideas resonated with subaltern desires and this fuelled the project, which thereafter found expression in multiple forms through local government initiatives, social movement work and the wide and deep spread of popular opinion and routine action. The arguments deployed in texts and in practice in the making of the welfare state included the following: the activities and statements of the state; political commentary amongst intellectuals and variously engaged reform groups amongst the population; plus the memory of interwar depression and its associated hardships; and, as war years turned into post-war, the collective memory of sacrifice, that is, the dead, injured and those who had otherwise experienced loss.

The institutional resources of the state provided the key mechanisms: committees, experts, consultations and finally formally presented plans. The state created the plans and drove the programme, which thereafter were promulgated amongst the population. The state began the overall process when it established war aims, where these rehearsed the declarative positions adopted in the 1941 Atlantic Charter. These statements of war aims were thought necessary by the elite to legitimate the prosecution of the war to a population that had a clear memory of the recent Great War, which it viewed negatively, a matter not merely of inhuman suffering and waste but also of elite incompetence and responsibility.

Thereafter the state published a series of plans, which offered creative responses to the unfolding collapse of the state-empire system. And this, it might be noted, was evident quite early on as the sweeping gains of the Japanese in 1941-2 and the related promises made to elite Indian politicians meant that the premier empire territories in the East were lost.[16] Hence, looking to the periphery, the Colonial Development Act 1941, passed in the early years of the war, hence, with attention turned to the domestic core territories, the rest of the planning work which fed into the creation of the welfare state, where the 1942 Beveridge Report, the Butler Education Act 1944 and the Town Planning Act 1949 all embraced the ethic of planned social reform.

Some social elements bought into the project as a result of political sympathies aroused in writings published by critics: famously, in popular engaged publishing the work of the Left Book Club, or on radio J.B. Priestley or in print journalism George Orwell. All argued, one way or another, for broad social change; George Orwell cast the business in terms of the country being a family with the wrong members in charge.

Some social groups were receptive to the plans for welfare on the basis of their direct experience; economic distress or political activism, or both. Economically, northern industrial towns had suffered badly during the depression years, and widespread distress found expression, famously in the Jarrow March. But this was the respectable response, less respectable and much less acceptable to established power holders was the deepening of grass-roots radicalism, evident, for example, in domestic Communist Party activity or in the contributions organized by various grass-roots organizations in support of the beleaguered Republican government in Spain.

The experience of the war years also fed into the pressures for change. As noted, during the wartime period, there was the long-running work of the Army Education Corps.[17] Such activity was supplemented by memories of war – 'sacrifice' – collective memory noted the costs which the war had imposed on the general population and their moral weight asserted in support of claims for reform. And there was vigorous domestic print journalism – the wartime themes of collective mobilization were available to be carried over into post-war reconstruction. And during the war years and after there were many local films,[18] and these saw the recreation of wartime and promises for the future taken as lodged therein.

The war related dissolution of the state-empire system centred on Britain obliged the elite to respond, and whilst much of this was a matter of the immediate exigencies of war fighting, a significant amount of attention was turned to the nature of the post-war world. Plans were drawn up. These dealt with both periphery and core: in regard to the former, in general, acquiescence in withdrawal; and in regard to the latter, amongst other things, the construction of the welfare state.

Grand designs I: The mixed economy

The interwar period saw depression throughout the heartlands of the industrial-capitalist system – in the USA, in Japan and in Europe – and there was a well-advertised contrast drawn by various commentators between the situation of these countries and the circumstances of the Soviet Union, where a planned economy was securing rapid development. The interwar period also saw numerous armed conflicts. There were civil breakdowns, civil wars and interstate wars, which, in due course, were subsumed in a worldwide series of interlinked wars, now variously remembered – for citizens of United States, the Second World War[19] – and, in all, symptomatic of the general crisis of the state-empire system.

Political analysts in the metropolitan core countries offered a number of diagnoses along with associated remedies. In schematic terms these were, first, party-state communist regimes, which argued in terms of a terminal crisis of capitalism necessitating a move towards centrally planned socialist systems; second, mainland European fascist parties, which argued in terms of a cultural collapse occasioned by assorted dissenting groups, necessitating a state-led purge of such groups in pursuit of a state ordered around the ideal of leader/family; third, European and American conservative-minded liberal democracies, which argued in terms of economic policy errors and sought to protect domestic economies, which thereafter were subject to strict financial discipline in the expectation of a spontaneous, market-led recovery; and fourth, a more ambitious programme to reorder the industrial-capitalist economies around the managerial role of the state.

J.M. Keynes,[20] along with others,[21] participated in these debates during the 1930s and 1940s. Rejecting the ideological inclinations of the liberal free market theorists and policy-makers who argued for cutting government expenditure in order to free up the spontaneous energy of the liberal marketplace, Keynes argued instead that in the context of an economic slowdown, cutting government expenditure made no sense, but underpinning the private economy via government expenditure did. In brief, he made the case for liberal-democratic state intervention in the liberal market in order to correct short-term marketplace failures and to build self-consciously for a more inclusive economy and society.

Contrary to the position of market liberals, it certainly was the proper business of the state to correct short-term market failures and to reorder economy and society so as to secure an equitable long-term development trajectory. In Britain this intellectual and political stance came to be tagged 'Keynesianism' and it unpacked within the domestic arena in a range of policy positions, which were oriented towards 'the mixed economy'. In mainland Europe, there were analogues to this package, thus in France, 'indicative planning', or in Germany, the idea of 'the social market', or in Sweden, a variant of 'welfare social democracy'. The overall line of advance was clear: following the problems of the interwar years, and the catastrophe of the war itself, politicians, policy-makers and commentators agreed that states had to engage with the business of building decent lives for the majority of their citizens.[22] This position – intellectual and political – was also echoed in the USA with the programme of the New Deal – and moreover, as the war years dragged on, American policy-makers drew wider lessons, thus it was foolish to work to defeat National Socialism and Japanese fascism if the war was followed by the renewed establishment of nationalistic beggar-my-neighbour economic policies – the conclusion was clear and in practice tremendously ambitious – in addition to domestic action to manage the economy there would have to be an enduring high-level agreement on tariffs and trade – in the event, the material of the Bretton Woods system, the economic counterpart to the political arena of the United Nations.[23]

In Britain, in the early parts of the post-war period, this set of ideas informed domestic policy, and as the now familiar apparatus of the welfare state was put in place (health, education, welfare and so on), the economy was reordered around the precepts of Keynes, or, at least, the state was given a central role. The post-war government nationalized large areas of economic activity. This was not so difficult as the war period had seen a command economy in operation; that is, the ideas of state control were familiar, so putting them into practice required no great leaps of the imagination. These newly acquired economic operations were managed as large-scale integrated state enterprises with top-down management, which in turn reported to Whitehall.[24] And these nationalized industries embraced the 'commanding heights' of the economy: in transport, British Railways; in mines, the National Coal Board; and in steel, the Iron and Steel Corporation. These were paralleled in the general field of welfare with the establishment of the National Health Service (NHS), the new tripartite secondary-school system, and so on. In all this there was no hint of grass-roots democracy – the route to the future was to be organized by technical specialists – acceptable to management and unions – at its best corporatist planning but at its worst a spread of sclerotic state-subsidized special interest groups. Thereafter the extensive private sector was encouraged to plan for the future and in the late 1940s and 1950s it was successful. In total, then, 'a mixed economy', combining a thriving state sector and an equally successful private sector, with the state embracing oversight of both in the cause of national reconstruction and development.

Grand designs II: The modern urban environment

Cities are central to contemporary human social life.[25] In 1945, Britain, like other European countries, held a large stock of war-damaged and war-dilapidated stock. In addition the post-war authorities inherited a large stock of housing left over from early phases of industrialization; in urban areas, concentrated as slums, in rural areas,[26] a dispersed and sometimes picturesque collection of substandard housing.[27] Post-war recovery entailed amongst other things rebuilding extensive parts of cities as well as constructing entirely new settlements. It was a vast undertaking. It was also lodged within the general rhetoric of welfare. However, the process of rebuilding inherited established ideas, albeit quite diverse. The inherited debate revolved around two responses to the rise of industrial society in the nineteenth century: optimists, who celebrated progress, and pessimists, of one sort or another, who looked instead to ameliorate the worst aspects of the new form of life. This tension ran through all later discussions of urban forms and urban regeneration, and into post-war debates, indeed, the experience of post-war reconstruction exercises in turn have resonances that run down to the present day.

(i) Debating urban forms

That city forms should be debated is unsurprising for they are central to our form of life and their development is not (and never has been) socially neutral. City forms embody political power relations ('the rich man in his castle, the poor man at his gate' and so on), city forms embody economic power relations (speculative built squares or terraces in, say, London or Bath) and, when self-consciously planned construction or reconstruction is undertaken, then city forms embody ideologies (as with, say, Bournville).

In the modern period, debates about city forms have been running since the nineteenth century. Modernity and forms of urban life are interlinked. The ideas of political elites can be inscribed in architecture and urban forms. In the modern world, such ideas are, if not commonplace, then widely acknowledged, which means that city-building is a more or less self-conscious activity. Those who construct individual buildings or groups of buildings or whole towns and cities do so with elaborate sets of ideas in mind – ideas summed under the tag 'urbanism' – and these might include ideas about the nature of humankind; ideas about the nature of the contemporary social world; ideas about routes to the future; and at the same time, running through all these debates, ideas about the power of urban form to shape human lives.

These ideas have a modern root in the headlong rush during the nineteenth century into an industrial-capitalist system that had been accompanied by large-scale rural-urban migration. It meant that towns grew rapidly in an unplanned fashion and the upshot was a poor quality of life for many of the inhabitants. The situation provoked a variety of responses as a broad conservative hostility towards industrialization was mirrored by a similarly broad progressive hostility to capitalism. More specifically, there was aesthetic hostility towards the ugliness of rapidly made industrial-capitalist cities; moral hostility towards the loss of those rules associated with small-scale agricultural communities; social hostility towards the material squalor of rapidly made industrial-capitalist cities; and so on. One complex strand of response focused on the material aspect of these industrial-capitalist cities: the layout of districts; the layout of roads, railways and canals; the characteristics of urban utilities, such as water and waste; the characteristics of housing provision (layouts, building standards, occupancy rates, room sizes); and the provision of local amenities (shops, open space, schools and so on). The work of architects and planners embraced the concerns of critics and celebrants of urban industrial-capitalism and sought to provide solutions – it produces a distinctive discourse – part utopian reformism and part mundane practicality. And in this context the growth of urban areas during the nineteenth century was very rapid indeed. Architects, urban planners, social reformers, artists, writers, theorists and politicians had to respond. Within Britain, two broad reactions were available: the first tending to the optimistic, thus the changes were read as a benefit to humankind, in particular, the provision of new technologies and material goods, all of which fostered prosperity in the widest sense, which should be embraced; and the second tending to the pessimistic, where the sum of the changes was read as a threat to humankind, that is, the novel form of life was taken to have clear

50 Britain After Empire

deleterious consequences for human well-being, and these had to be managed. Each generation of architects or planners or politicians have had their own take on these questions and so the responses are varied; here, in turn, are three examples: first, the celebration of the possibilities of modernity which are found in modern architecture and design; second, the ideal of rural craft life invoked in an amended form as a creative defensive response to the demands of industrial society; and third, a range of explicit reactions against modernism in design, where contemporary examples are available, both explicit (post-modernist jokes) and kitsch (nostalgic retro-designs).

(ii) Modern architecture and design

At the outset a clutch of overlapping concepts can be noted: first, the modern (the ideas/practice characteristic of today); second, modernity (the cultural character of the modern world); and third, modernism (an art/design movement celebrating the modern).[28] The ideas enter the language in the late nineteenth century and they provide the widest framework for ideas turned more directly towards the business of design, including architecture and city planning. Around the turn of the twentieth century a number of design traditions took shape and they had in common the fact that they sought to respond positively to the rise of industrial society: in France, the celebration of the possibilities of technology found in art deco; in Vienna, the analogous work of the Wiener Werkstatte; in Britain, such design ethics found expression in some art deco building and public design;[29] and a little later, influenced variously by these experiments, the Bauhaus.

The key aspects of modern architecture and design can be summarized. The first was future optimism: ideas were utopian, that is, architects and designers looked to an ideal future; technology was embraced, thus designers were anxious to make use of the latest technological innovations; work was unsympathetic to past forms, that materials or ideas were historically well known, or old, was not in itself a recommendation, rather the reverse; and relatedly, work was unsympathetic to sentiment, it should be clean and uncluttered by facile sentiment. Then, second was an aspiration towards democracy: it was acknowledged that there was elite provision, thus elites provided resources (designs, finance, leadership) and yet theorists saw the modern movement itself as democratic (as opposed to established elites) and oriented towards a democratic polity. And, third, it was international in practice: in Europe, modern architecture often took public forms, for example, workers' housing (albeit with a mixed record); whereas in the USA, modern architecture often took private forms, for example, office buildings (again with a mixed record).

In all this the Bauhaus remains the quintessential school of modernist design. An adventurous school in Germany during 1919–33, its members designed buildings, furniture, household goods and everyday utilitarian objects – their ideal was to create mass-produced high quality design for modern living for the masses. One figure from this school – Mies van der Rohe – relocated to Chicago in the late 1930s and his slogan, 'less is more', encouraged the design of buildings of austere aesthetic simplicity. These ideas found substantive expression in modern skyscrapers, a design strategy that in subsequent years has gone round the planet. And it is also a design strategy that caught the attention of corporate accountants; less, they realized, might also mean cheaper, a response that has not helped the contemporary urban form. Modern architecture became a key to contemporary design and in Britain during the period of post-war reconstruction, a number of lines of action were undertaken: slum clearance, new estates, new towns and new lines of communication, thus motorways.

So first, there were extensive programmes of slum clearance involving areas of housing inherited from the nineteenth century, often in poor condition and mostly located in urban industrial areas and thus recently subject to war damage (the East End, towns in the Midlands (symbolically, Coventry), Liverpool, Glasgow, southern sea ports – and, rather differently, a range of small market towns, victims of the 'Baedeker raids'). Such programmes involved clearing whole areas and rebuilding. The new build was informed by modernist ideas and utilized tower blocks, large estates, system building. Related to the programmes of slum clearance were the new suburbs with large-scale public housing estates built on the outskirts of these towns throughout Britain. All these forms of building were well received; they were popular, desirable and sought after. Then, second, there were programmes of building new towns. This strategy was not new, for such enterprises had been seen in the nineteenth century. Reform-minded industrialists had built model settlements, for example, at Saltaire in Yorkshire and Port Sunlight in Cheshire. And in the early twentieth century Ebenezer Howard had presented this strategy as a formal ideology/programme, thereby inaugurating the garden city movement.[30] In the post-war period new town-building was energetically pursued in Milton Keynes, Redditch,

Telford and so on. These towns were planned to be ready-made communities in which housing, service facilities and employment were all provided. A final element of this drive to rebuild was found in the creation of a motorway network,[31] which, at the time, was viewed as symptomatic of a bright modern future.

And the ethic of modern design, now routinely criticized, runs down into the present, as do the debates amongst urban designers about the nature of the modern world.

(iii) Rural craft life reimagined

Optimistic responses to the shift to industrial forms of life found expression in varieties of modern design, for example, in architecture and industrial design, but an alternative response was on offer, however, it was not a simple reaction, nor an unrestricted celebration, rather, the tone was ameliorative and accommodative. In one form, as noted, in the actions of late nineteenth-century patrician social reformers, thus, the creation of small-scale utopian manufacturing settlements, for example, Bournville Village in the Midlands, and in another, in line with an explicit manifesto, for example, the Garden City movement.

Bourneville Village[32] was developed in the late nineteenth century by the Cadbury family as a planned community: houses, parks, places of worship, leisure facilities and the factory around which everything revolved. The area is laid out in a neat and tidy fashion around a central area of parkland, with the factory sitting adjacent to the park alongside a canal and railways. The design ethic for the houses is taken from the Arts and Crafts movement of the late nineteenth century. Here the key figure was William Morris, whose approach to design and manufacturing affirmed an ethic of resistance to the social and personal moral coarsening associated with industrial production, coupled to an affirmation of the superiority of craft styles of working, which were taken to be authentically expressive of human skills and creativity.

Bourneville Village was one of a number of similar projects, which were simultaneously backward looking, in their invocation of an idealized rural past, and also forward looking, as they sought a prospective accommodation with the demands of industrial life. Ebenezer Howard, who established the Garden City movement, pursued these general ideas on a larger canvass. In 1902 he published *Garden Cities of Tomorrow* and founded Letchworth in 1904 and Welwyn Garden City in 1919. The ideology written into the urban form sought to combine the best of rural life with the possibilities of urban industrial living, and the design introduced open spaces into the town design and zoning so as to separate out various users. The early experiments were well received, and the idea has taken root and is rehearsed within Britain with varying degrees of success, and copied overseas.[33]

(iv) Explicit reactions: Heritage

Early in the post-war period there was an unexpected statement made in favour of the grand designs – and by implication, pattern of life – of English great houses. Their decaying condition became a concern for the National Trust and this established organization reoriented its work away from recreational land for the masses, towards the preservation of the architecture of these houses. It was an early proponent of what has subsequently been tagged as 'heritage', an often pejorative term suggesting that the buildings and social practices so reconstructed and remembered are done so in an essentially inauthentic fashion, providing a simulacrum of forms of life and serving ambiguous functions with pretty buildings, nice gardens and at the same time a recollection akin to propaganda of particular forms of life.[34] The National Trust, it might be noted, is in the early years of the twenty-first century, the most popular voluntary organization in the country, owning many houses and gardens.

Over many years, Prince Charles has taken an interest in architecture and urban design; he has made his opinions known, and on occasion opposed directly plans for modern buildings.[35] Poundbury is a planned small town championed by Prince Charles and designed by the architect Leon Krier – the design is a self-conscious reaction against modern architecture which is read as anti-human – the design invokes an ideal of small-town England. In Poundbury the design ethic involves small-scale building, mixed housing, traditional-looking designs and mixed zoning – it is an architectural pastiche – inauthentic, pretty and reportedly very popular.

(v) Running into the present

As noted, all these debates run on down into the present. So recently, the epoch of neo-liberal debt-fuelled excess found architectural expression in so-called post-modernist designs – pastiche, playfulness, surface style and so on.[36] And during the early years of the twenty-first century the then Labour government funded a number of signature buildings as keys to urban regeneration programmes and, whilst the styles varied, many were post-modernist, and commentators have been critical of these experiments.[37]

However, running against that fashion, the deeper inclinations of modernism have continued; thus, by way of an example, they have found sustained expression in the work of Norman Foster,[38] which involves high-tech design, using high-tech materials and the latest building techniques. The ethic is clear: the modern world should be embraced and modern design in the guise of architecture can create spaces within which people can flourish. Foster's work includes, amongst others, the Wills Faber building, the HSBC building, the Sainsbury Centre for Visual Arts, Nimes Mediatheque, the Reichstag, Pont Millau, Beijing Airport and St. Mary Axe.[39]

Ideas are embedded in urban form, and through the post-war years there have been a number of broad movements in urban design: the optimistic reconstruction of the 1950s and 1960s, the neo-liberal consumerism of the 1990s and the state-sponsored regeneration projects of the recent decade. Governments have changed, ideological opinions have changed and there have been various fads and fashions in respect of the more superficial elements of urban development, yet running through all these has been a consistent return to modernism and optimism in respect of the future.

Viewed in retrospect the nature of record of 'future-embodied-in-urban-forms' is mixed: (general) success of New Towns; (general) failure of new high-rise housing; general overselling technology (thus, motorways were sold as 'futuristic'). Patrick Wright has pursued these issues and Owen Hatherley has returned to the promise of the post-war period and the failures of recent government exercises in 'signature' building.

Grand designs III: Social development

If the mixed economy was intended to power the rehabilitation of the country and if urban reconstruction was to be its material expression, then the popular social core of the project was to be found in social reforms – the familiar territories of health, schooling and insurance. The overall package, the grand design, would enable individuals to prosper, to reach their potential and to live productive lives.

The NHS was a product of Nye Bevan's reforms. The post-war Labour government built on available reform proposals in order to construct a national health system that promised treatment on the basis of need, was available to all citizens and was funded through general taxation – the new system upgraded the level of health of the population in general – thereafter, the detail and unintended consequences could be recorded.

A new system of schools flowed from Rab Butler's reforms. The Education Act 1944 established a tripartite system of secondary education – grammar, technical and modern – the new system promised education for all funded by general taxation. The reform upgraded the level of education of the population – thereafter the detail and unintended consequences could be spelled out.

The welfare system was inspired by William Beveridge's report and the system promised a social insurance system, which would embrace the entirety of the population. It was to be funded partly by individual contributions and partly by employer contributions, and where these were not possible by state contributions. The system raised the level of material well-being of the population in general, and thereafter there have been many detail discussions of the consequences – intended and unintended.

Broader themes in the public sphere revisited

The project of the welfare state set the terms of post-war reconstruction. It also set the terms for political analysis. Some 50 years down the track it is possible to pick out some of the assumptions that the patrician and subaltern reformers were making; some of these were challenged at the time by proto-neo-liberals but other ideas continue to run down unexamined into the present.

The core of the project embraced progressive ideals. It was optimistic, future-oriented and routinely celebratory of technical expertise. First, the future optimism[40] – the post-war period was culturally optimistic that after the depredations of war, the establishment of a planned science-based economy would enable the creation of a welfare state which in turn would raise levels of living which in turn would give impetus to the system so that a beneficial circuit of economic growth, welfare and social advance would be established. Second, the celebration of technology and expertise – the keys to this welfare utopia and the ideal model to which reforms looked was to be found in the natural sciences as it was thought that pure research informing technological advance would fuel economic growth and the deployment of similar expertise would fuel the processes of social reform, and so reforms to education were one crucial aspect, with all this creating a virtuous circle of expertise, investment and reward. And third, the central role of planning[41] – the ideal in mind allocated a key role to planning and to planners as the social and administrative sciences were to be the analogue to the natural sciences so that experts could plan on behalf of the community. All these intellectual/moral commitments found expression in the grand design of the welfare state. Thereafter, the optimism was reflected and amplified through the mass media – film, radio and print – one tag was deployed after the coronation of the new queen – the New Elizabethan Age.

The idea of the welfare state

The creation of the welfare state significantly reworked not merely the systems of social welfare provision within the United Kingdom but also the general tenor of political life – it impacted the broad political culture, political debate and party self-images – the creation of the welfare state was a kind of political emancipation for the working classes – for the first time, their needs were acknowledged directly.

The welfare state has created downstream cultural impacts. Thus, picking up from the above, the tug between proponents of welfare provision (on behalf of the working classes and middle classes) and the opponents of welfare provision (specifically, the better-off middle and upper classes objecting to provisions for the working classes, veiled in terms of combating scrounging or dependency). More broadly, the welfare state has acted to secure emancipation of the working classes and middle classes and there is a culture of entitlement, maybe not citizenship, but nonetheless tending towards inclusion. However, there are critical voices here: recall Alasdair MacIntyre[42] on emotivist culture or Zygmunt Bauman[43] on postmodernism, celebrating consumers and then identifying 'failed consumers', that is, the poor.

One aspect of the downstream impacts, related to entitlement, is the seemingly open-ended expansion of the welfare system. To some extent this was predictable, for as a system is set up it becomes available for use, and as theory does not translate directly into practice, the uses to which the system is put will vary from those for which it was designed: this might include unanticipated uses (requests for welfare that were never anticipated);[44] gaming (using system for purposes never intended);[45] fraud (manipulating the system); and rising expectations (demands made as a result of the system being in place – thus welfarism). The negative consequence of this open-endedness is that it both saps the confidence of the taxpayers who fund it and opens up a line for otherwise hostile critics.[46] That said, the welfare state was a product of its time and Judt, Addison and Collini pick up aspects of the overall tale, looking at contexts, agents and the complacency of British intellectuals.

Tony Judt[47] details the construction of the Cold War and in parallel the creation of the welfare state. As regards the former, the meeting at

Yalta settled the post-war spheres of influence and whilst these events are subsequently re-remembered by the Americans as 'betrayal', it was a done deal. The meeting at Yalta did not settle the issue of Germany. The Western allies decided against a unified demilitarized state (they took the view that it gave too much geostrategically to the Soviets) and split the country by establishing the Federal Republic. It was one move in the construction of Cold War blocs. So the Iron Curtain was re-established. As in 1917, the Soviets were to be resisted.[48] The bloc system had many aspects. First, the European soft left came to the fore in public politics in an acknowledgement of the working class via a concern for social welfare, whilst, as events unfolded, a sharp intellectual divide was created between communists (plus fellow travellers) and anti-communists. At the same time, the political right wing was eclipsed in mainstream public politics as pre-war politics had seen the right linked to fascism so they, the right, were discredited. However, they were able to re-enter the political sphere as the Cold War bloc system was put into place (for example, Japan, with 'reverse course', or in Germany where anti-Nazi purges were discontinued, or in France where the wartime period was left uninvestigated, or in Britain where pre-war elite sympathies for fascism were quietly forgotten). Second, bloc-think was promulgated, that is, extensive propaganda funded by the two bloc leaders and their subordinate states. Then, third, the British turned away from involvement in mainland politics, invitations to participate in the early moves towards the European Union were rebuffed and the country turned to domestic concerns centred on the welfare state. And, fourth, on a broader historical scale, German-speaking Central Europe, which had been established over centuries and was a long-time source of cultural creativity, was destroyed by war, expulsions and bloc imposition.

As regards the latter point, welfare, Judt notes that the late 1940s were a period of reconstruction from war – the 1950s saw wider economic recovery – this ran on into the 1960s – the period saw economic growth and social democratic policy initiatives, in Britain, the welfare state. Many aspects: post-war long boom, European integration and European economic structural changes as agriculture shrinks and industry expands; the role of planning advances (disputed – available in varieties); the state invests in urban redevelopment; demographics change as the baby boom creates a young age profile (future optimism); and there are the beginnings of consumer society.[49]

At the time, the period was celebrated by the centre left, affirmed by the centre right and slowly disowned by both hard left (for not going far enough as class inequalities continued) and hard right (for giving too much ground to the masses). It was an always-contested project. Paul Addison[50] details the construction of an elite project for social reform, provoked by circumstances, that is, the evident failure of pre-war politics, and the ways in which the masses were co-opted or mobilized for the project.[51] Thus, first, pre-war conservatism evidenced a slate of traits: fiscal conservatism, empire, interwar growth (light industry, suburbs, suburban railways and sprawl) and the policy of appeasement.[52] The second, the wartime coalition: war mobilization, command economy, debt and loss of empire, and drive for welfare state (planning versus market; iron curtain debate recycled); patrician top-down reform (Beveridge Report 1942), supported by popular research (Mass Observation, Gallup Poll, Ministry of Information, supported by popular mobilization (Beveridge Report, BBC, newspapers, photo-journalism, Army Education)). And then, third, mobilizing for reform: John Grierson and the documentary film movement; Tom Harrison and Mass Observation; Allen Lane with Penguin Books; Edward Hulton and *Picture Post*; plus commentators (George Orwell, J.B. Priestly); the Army Education Bureau; and an energetic influential left-wing press (*Daily Herald*, *Daily Mirror*).

Looking at the early post-war period, Stefan Collini,[53] asking what happened to local intellectuals, begins by noting the pre-war position of intellectuals (high modernism, disenchantment from contemporary Britain) and then notes the impact of the Second World War. Intellectuals had been absorbed into the business of war with arguments in favour of the allied cause and plans for the post-war era; all the business of mobilization dealt with by Addison. Collini speaks of the 'long 1950s', a period of satisfaction at the outcome of the war, confidence in British exceptionalism and a Whig view of history as progressive. Intellectuals rallied to the unfolding status quo (unlike, say, France, where intellectuals had to address the business of Vichy, or Germany, where intellectuals had to address the catastrophe of National Socialism). Collini unpacks all this via a critique of two pieces of analysis offered by Noel Annan and Edward Shills, who both offered variants of the line that intellectuals in Britain were absorbed into the ruling circles. Collini thinks both pieces overstate their case but, by way of a comment, it seems there is some sort of case to be made about the complacency of intellectuals in Britain during the long 1950s.

All this feeds into the post-war era creation of the welfare state. It was a self-conscious programme and was debated amongst reformers, ordinary people and intellectuals: critics, in retrospect, identify a certain general intellectual complacency.

Running down to the present: Legacies and repetitions

The welfare state was constructed at a particular time, by a particular group of agents, in the expectation of an equally particular series of results – the creation of a stable, prosperous, healthy industrial capitalism in the domestic sphere of the former state empire of the British. It was a contested compromise, one that held for around 20 years. It remains influential. It has institutional form, intellectual adherents and popular support. Yet this post-war domestic settlement has been subject to numerous pressures. Thus, *internally*, it has generated its own unsupportable demands in respect of welfare as demands for welfare provisions have become both pervasive (many demands made by many groups in respect of many matters) and financially unsupportable because these demands are not merely large (a matter of scale) but open-ended in respect of future growth. The familiar example is health where the mix of an ageing population, ever-advancing medical technology and the given preference of people for a long, healthy life means that health costs could rise in an open-ended fashion – they have to be capped, either by explicit rationing of access or by privatization and rationing by price). Also internally, it has generated its own critics: some perhaps principled (objecting to the potentially moral costs for individuals of state provision, that is, undermining individual self-reliance); some perhaps ideological (objecting to the impact on economic behaviour of welfare systems); and some perhaps opportunistic (the cynical objecting to paying for a welfare system).[54] And, finally, externally, the domestic settlement has been placed under pressure by changes in the wider global system. Two might be noted: first, changes in the peripheral areas of the former state-empire where shifting patterns of international trade have not benefited the hitherto core territory; and second, the recent internationalization of the global economy has reinforced the weight (if not cogency) of domestic neo-liberal argument.

The Keynesian informed active state debated

In the wake of the war years, advocates of collective action ordered by the state affirmed the intellectual/policy role of planning (state as mechanism) and sought the social welfare goal of state-directed reform; key figures included J.M. Keynes and Karl Mannheim, along with reform-minded political actors such as Harold Macmillan, Quentin Hogg and Dennis Healey.

Yet, there was opposition to the role of the state plus counteraffirmations of liberty plus patrician-class anxiety; key figures included

Friedrich von Hayek and Karl Popper (the late version);[55] plus a Cold War theme, which was present in some elite British circles and present in some American circles.[56] So although the ethos of planning for social welfare ran until the 1970s when circumstances changed long-term opponents became more influential. The year 1979 was a breakthrough in Britain for the New Right. This was a distinctive variant of the right as philosophical liberty was transmuted into free market economics (patrician anxiety is rewarded in ironic form with middle-class provincial aspiration). As the programme unrolled, some traditional patrician spheres were remade (City of London, certainly, the universities, somewhat, the Palace, somewhat (search for popularity plus rise of charismatic royals) and the armed forces, a little (rescued from John Nott's cuts by the Argentine invasion of the Falklands/Malvinas)), and the machineries of the state are in part dismantled (financial deregulation, privatization of state holdings) and in part deployed to discipline a recalcitrant working class in pursuit of the governing party's goals.

Thus the Keynesian-informed notion of the mixed economy came to grief during the 1970s through a coincidence of otherwise disparate factors: overweening trade-union arrogance, feeble government policy-making and dull managements combined to shift economy, society and polity into something of a dead-end. The optimism of the post-war period evaporated. A period of confusion ensued and it was at this point that the long-held opposition of liberal market theorists and conservatives (an odd alliance in retrospect, united only in their opposition to the interventionist active state) gained traction. In Britain they were initially known as the New Right, later as their ideas became mainstream they were tagged more simply as neo-liberals. The preference for liberal markets was key to their ideology and policy-making, and it was hugely influential, these ideas ran until the economic debacle of 2008–12, when a long building bubble of debt issuance by the banks, which had fuelled an equally long building asset price bubble which in turn had fed a consumer binge, finally burst and private-sector debt was then repositioned as public debt as the state bailed out the banks. At this point neo-liberals – nothing if not energetic in defence of their ideology and wealth – attempted to rework the crisis as one of sovereign, that is, state, debt. However, as 2013 opened there were few signs domestically of economic recovery, indeed, commentators in the broadsheet press spoke about the possibilities of a 'triple-dip recession', and the government's policy stance, built around the drive to reduce state debt so as to create space for private sector activity, looked ever more implausible. At this point, commentators began to speak about the need for Keynesian-style interventionist spending.

Legacies, repetitions and the idea of welfare today
Crucial legacies: these include overall sympathy from the population for the idea of the welfare state; strong support from population for health services; strong support from medical professionals for health services; variable support from population and professionals for education services; variable support from population and professionals for housing provision; and restricted support from population and professionals for welfare transfer payments. But the system is contested – thus private schooling, private health, private insurance, and private housing.

Repetitions: the idea of welfare is deeply embedded and claims can be voiced to an ever-expanding list of rights. The idea of welfare has become embedded within common thinking. It now extends into many areas as it is a taken-for-granted idea. Alasdair MacIntyre[57] speaks of an emotivist culture, which erroneously asserts putative individual rights/entitlements against a nominally competent state bureaucracy. The cost of these interlinked errors, for MacIntyre, is the loss of a sense of active, morally responsible community. Robert Hughes identifies a corollary:[58] failures in welfare systems are met with complaint, not merely about specific failures but as a general style of treating the system. A rather different point is made by Zygmunt Bauman,[59] who notes that in a rich post-modernist society, where order is secured by consumer seduction, failed consumers – the poor – are subject to the bureaucratic discipline of welfare rolls.

The idea of welfare today is under pressure: both practical, with issues of costs, organization and results; and ideological, with, down the years,[60] the calls from market liberals for cutbacks in the face of the demands of the putative logic of economics or more recently the allegedly unavoidable requirements of an equally unavoidable globalization. But these pressures have been resisted[61] and today the ideal of welfare is embedded in institutions, in the strategizing of elites, in the expectations of the masses and in the common sense of the political culture. Welfare is taken for granted.

4
Making Enemies: The Cold War

In hindsight the Cold War was an elaborate confection, a set of institutionally carried Manichean comparisons, which served to legitimate the military division of Europe into two camps. The Cold War comprised a set of mutually directed institutionally carried actions and claims which assisted the control exercised by respective lead nations over their territories; such activities/claims involved diplomacy, economy, politics, the military and culture. Thus, in respect of culture, the division of Europe into blocs was accompanied by an elaborate system of bloc-think, the creation of two sets of mutual characterizations and two sets of domestic discipline: overt, with politicians, soldiers and policemen, and covert, with propaganda, official deceit and the apparatus of low-level subversion and spying, with the one celebrating liberal democracy, the other state socialism. In the West, and thus in Britain, some elements of these activities became familiar parts of the public sphere, sometimes serious, thus, say, reactions to the construction of the Berlin Wall, and at others less so, thus the vogue for spy novels and later films, but, in all, the Cold War entered popular consciousness as variously expressed Manichean division. Now, decades later, it is clear that it has left its legacies: sometimes with significant political import, thus the habit of state-security machines, now turned to new putative enemies, presently, Islam; at others, merely as cliché, thus the reflex criticism of Russia, or, more popularly, the continuing recourse to certain cultural themes expressed in film and novels of spying: deceit coupled to moral and class betrayal.

The Cold War in Europe can be given two dates: conventionally, from 1946 (Churchill's Iron Curtain speech) through to 1989 (the opening of the Berlin Wall and the collapse of state-socialist regimes in Eastern Europe); or in more scholarly terms, from 1917 (the Russian Revolution) through to either 1989 or the present day (where the former is an obvious date, whilst the latter points to continuing anti-Russian sentiment amongst sections of European and American elites).

In conventional terms the Cold War marked a sharp division of Europe into two nominally competing blocs, where the competition was military, economic, social, political and cultural. The term 'nominally' points to both the continuing nature of European life (whether or not it was slotted into one or other bloc system) and to the overarching role of bloc leaders, that is, the Cold War might have taken place mainly in Europe, at least early on, but it was not made in Europe, the creators were the respective bloc leaders. In the familiar Western version of the Cold War, commentators typically present the Soviet Union as the aggressor with the Western powers having perforce to react. But, in the main, this is propaganda.[1] The Cold War has its origins in European and American elite reactions to communism, which can be dated to 1917,[2] and these involved active participation in Russia's civil war, ran on through the interwar years[3] and after a necessary interval during the Second World War resumed shortly after the fighting ceased, and here a key action was the Western powers' precipitous move in dividing Germany,[4] and so thereafter relations quickly deteriorated. Raymond Aron[5] argues that the Cold War served to legitimate division and discipline bloc members, and draw them into the projects of respective bloc leaders. Thus, the Cold War was largely a construct, a political confection: in the West, it served to order/legitimate the American drive to create a liberal trading sphere; and in the East, perforce, it served to order/legitimate the Russian-centred drive for state socialism.

Episode: Dividing Europe and the process of the construction of an enemy

George Orwell's novel *Nineteen Eighty-Four* posits a global political system with three major blocs which are perpetually at war in some combination or other – the alliances change and as they do so their respective populations (or at least the one we learn about in the novel, the citizens of Airstrip One, part of Oceania) are re-educated, files are amended, history is rewritten and a new public truth is established. The Western Cold War bloc-think version of Orwell's discussion has it that he was referring to the Soviet bloc or to the style of working of state socialist systems, but this is an error; the target was both more specific, that is, England in the late 1940s, and more general, that is, the political habits of elite manipulation and subaltern obedience.

Conservative groups in the United States and Europe were hostile towards the political left; whether it took the guise of the Soviet Union or small-scale local party groups. The 1920s and 1930s saw political conflicts in Europe, the United States and elsewhere, aspects of the general crisis of state-empire systems and thee broad streams of argument found expression: communism, fascism and liberalism. The latter was the sickly child of these debates as conservative elites were only partially supportive, often having greater sympathy with fascism. Patrick Wright[6] notes the political tensions of the early twentieth century with destructive war in Europe, the 1917 Russian Revolution, followed later by economic depression, and in this context, the revolution and its claims for socialism were met with the unreserved hostility from European and American elites: intervention in the Russian civil war, hostility towards trades unions, populist nationalism – and the slide towards fascism and war.

The ready expression of these antipathies was suspended – more or less – for the duration of the Second World War as the Soviet Union was reimagined as an heroic powerful ally, but in 1945 there was a reservoir of available elite-level hostility ready for deployment,[7] and elite-level hostilities resumed fairly quickly after the military campaigns came to an end. The immediate post-war years saw a number of meetings, discussions and arguments – they were turned to the issue of the occupation of Germany and the future shape of Europe – and these elite-level exchanges and negotiations slowly ran into the sand. In time these relationships broke down. The key players were the United States[8] and the Soviet Union; with Britain and France, secondary; others less important, and bloc-thinking was put in place: in the West, elites cast their hostility in terms of liberal markets versus state socialism, whilst in the East the pattern was reversed.

Construction of a package: 'Cold war'

The division of Europe into two blocs was not foreordained, nor was it inevitable, it was, rather, the result of contingent political stances and the contingent interactions of those who affirmed these ideas. It precipitated a 40-odd-year division of the Continent. If there was a single prime mover, then, the Cold War was willed into being by political actors in the United States.[9]

(i) Elite- or state-level actions oriented towards the architecture of the system

These included creating the basic institutional architecture of the bloc system and this involved a number of aspects: military, economic and political.

Initially the division of Europe was made in accordance with wartime agreements made by the three main allies in respect of managing the military campaign against German fascism and its assorted allies; spheres of influence were agreed and lines were drawn on maps indicating where the allied armies should halt their advances. Such agreements were necessary and, notwithstanding subsequent Western bloc-think criticisms of Yalta, they were clear because they had to be, given the numbers of armies involved, the vast numbers of refugees and other displaced persons, and the generally chaotic nature of the economy, society and polity in 1945 Europe. However, whilst relations between the four allied powers (with France having a zone within the American/British areas) began easily enough, later, as domestic American politics began to push their government's policy towards an anti-Soviet stance, the exchanges became progressively more awkward. Elite-level politics and international diplomacy were important arenas of debate and action, but events on the ground drove these exchanges: the radically disturbed populations of these territories had to be reordered; that is, states, borders, economies, polities and crucially people.[10]

In this context a crucial episode was the currency reform of 1948, which was inaugurated by the Western authorities and precipitated the economic division of Germany and thus the Continent. The reforms are associated with Ludwig Erhard – introducing the D-mark on 20 June 1948 – but Carolyn Eisenberg[11] argues that these reforms were made by the Western powers and were part of a long-running United States determination to divide the country and absorb West Germany into the US-centred liberal-market sphere. Thus in the months immediately following the defeat of fascism in Germany, the allied powers had positive exchanges, but thereafter, driven by American policy and supplemented by a number of high-profile episodes, relations became progressively more awkward. In April 1949 the Western allies established NATO. In May 1949 the Federal Republic of Germany came into existence. In October 1949, this was followed by the inauguration of the Democratic Republic of Germany, and later in May 1955 the Warsaw Pact was established. These episodes meant that by late 1949 the political division of Europe had been accomplished.

(ii) Symbolic events to facilitate the creation of the bloc system

Such state-level activity fell within the purview of relevant elites, however, the division of Europe into blocs could not be accomplished without popular involvement (at a minimum, acquiescence) and it is here that official propaganda, journalism and happenstance found their role.

There were a number of these symbolic episodes; some designed, others adventitious; some linked directly to Britain, others merely embracing the territory as part of the US-centred West. They can be logged as a series of dates.

March 1946, Fulton, Missouri, the Iron Curtain Speech: some nine months after the end of the war,[12] Winston Churchill was a guest at a local college and made a speech warning of the rising threat from the Soviet Union. Patrick Wright,[13] who details the history of the deployment of the metaphor, notes that whilst this particular effort is remembered as one of the starting points of the Cold War, Churchill's main concern was to argue for financial help to Britain. Nonetheless, the phrase was picked up and widely reported, and the metaphor became one way in which American and European anti-communist elites could prospectively characterize the situation in Europe. It was a way of making the sense that their liberal trading project needed; plus, more parochially, in Churchill's case, he was a long-standing anti-communist.

March 1947, the Truman Doctrine Speech: the statement was made at a meeting of the wartime allies in Moscow where the central issue was Germany, but for the Americans the wider problem was ordering Europe. The speech had little impact on the Soviets but did galvanize opinion in Washington.[14] The standard story here is that Washington was divided between adherents of the project summed as the New Deal, which was part and parcel of the wider project oriented to the creation of a free-trade area, the better, in the eyes of its proponents, to inhibit any return to depression, nationalism and war, and conservative realists, those concerned with narrow national interests. The former group took the view that it was possible to work with the Soviet Union; the latter group viewed that country as a domestic threat (encouraging the US left) and an international competitor/enemy. During the war years, the New Dealers held sway, but with the death of Roosevelt, the end of the war and the unfolding of the Truman presidency, the conservative realists came to have more influence and over the period of the late 1940s effectively displaced their opponents in government policy-making circles. The Truman Doctrine Speech was thus a key moment in the overall change in policy, a founding document of the Cold War.

July 1947, the publication of the long telegram: to the extent that the emergent doctrine had an intellectual basis as opposed to being rooted in American conservative nationalism, it was provided by George Kennan's telegram sent in February 1946 from Moscow to the State Department and printed in *Foreign Affairs* in July 1947. The piece was very influential and it diagnosed an essentially irrational, suspicious and expansionary polity against which it advocated a policy of containment. Influential at the time; later treated as a foundation document of the Cold War. It was a fate that did not, it seems, please its author, who felt that he had been misunderstood in that in place of patient resistance to Soviet aspirations, his text had been taken to justify worldwide resistance to all and any sign of left-wing activity.[15] Many subsequent critics of United States foreign policy, particularly in the period of the disintegration of state-empire systems which saw nationalist leaders coming to power, have argued that the US Cold War mentality led them to confuse nationalism with the political left. And whilst attacks on the latter were unreasonable, if predictable, confusing them with the former was a gross error and contributed to numerous disasters as the United States supported dictators around the globe provided they declared themselves to be anti-communist.

June 1948, the Berlin airlift: the agreements made at Yalta specified that the capital of Germany, Berlin, would be occupied jointly by the allied powers and this was done however the city lay within the wider Soviet occupation zone and it slowly became a point of contention. In June 1948 the Soviet authorities withdrew permission for road and rail links from the western zones into Berlin and the response of the Americans, British and French was to mount an air-supply operation, which could only be interdicted by the Soviets in actions tantamount to war. So the city was supplied by air and the episode was a public relations gift to the burgeoning Western anti-Soviet camp, demonstrating both the unreasonable nature of the Soviets and the doughty resolve of the Americans and their stalwart European allies.

Summer 1951, the Cambridge spies:[16] in the 1930s, physicists in Europe worked on atomic research. This was the basis for building atomic weapons. After the start of the Second World War the Americans mounted a very large research/production facility in Western United States and it was successful, and in August 1945 two weapons were used against Japanese cities, killing around 200,000 civilians.[17] The United States thus became the sole power to possess this extremely destructive weapon. The Soviet Union sought to master the same technologies using a mix of domestic research, captured German scientists and spying, as their nominal allies were not about to share this technology with other states. An A-bomb was tested in August 1945 and an H-bomb in August 1953. The reaction of the Americans was one of dismay as Soviet success had come much earlier than anticipated and spies were blamed and they turned up at regular intervals. Some of them were scientist spies[18] who had had some contact with the Los Alamos project, some were civil servants in the United States government and many were sent to gaol, some being quasi-ritually executed.[19] But, for the British, one group of spies were of particular and enduring interest, the Cambridge spies. The particular attraction for commentators – newspapers, novelists, film-makers and the like – is to be found in their class position as they were all members of the upper classes, so they were not merely traitors to their countries, but traitors to their class, and perhaps symptoms of a wider problem of elite-level sympathy for the left. The theme of class betrayal has resonated down the decades. Mrs Thatcher famously asked of politicians with whom she had to deal whether or not they were 'one of us', flagging a social/cultural as well as political divide, and these divisions remain, maybe with the class boundaries somewhat redrawn.[20]

August 1961, the Berlin Wall:[21] the Cold War was up and running by 1949/50. In Europe, NATO had been formed; in East Asia the Korean War had begun. Two blocs had coalesced. In Europe, Berlin retained its anomalous status, nominally under four-power control but in practice divided into two sections, West and East. The dividing line had an ambiguous status as it was an interzonal rather than international border and the Americans allowed anyone entering the western sector from East Berlin to exit to West Germany, and by 1961 this had begun to harm the East German economy. In August 1961 the East German authorities constructed a fortified border wall, thereby turning the interzonal border into a species of international border. However, the sight of a wall being built along with people rushing to cross into West Berlin enabled the Western authorities to use the episode as another public relations gift in their propaganda war against the Soviet bloc. It helped fix in place the perception of the Soviet Union and Eastern Europe as one giant prison filled with people trying to escape.

In sum, from 1946 to 1961, Manichean division: the public sphere was suffused with what David Caute tagged 'the Great Fear'.[22] In the USA the domestic process of rebranding the Soviet Union continued apace and a polity which had been an heroic ally in the fight against fascism was represented as a totalitarian nightmare, not merely a disaster for its own people but also a threat – military and politically – to the domestic heartlands of America. Popular anxieties were encouraged around issues such as nuclear bombs, atom spies, communist activists and liberal fellow travellers. The list of internal enemies was very flexible, potentially embracing all those who failed to be explicitly anti-communist. The list of external enemies was similarly flexible, potentially embracing any polity whose domestic political make-up or government policy mix found disfavour with Washington. Many have noted that enemies can be useful to polities – domestic and international – and for the US elite and their European allies, anti-communism met these needs. The habit persists. For the USA, the new external enemy is the world of Islam. This has been echoed somewhat feebly in Britain (and other parts of Europe), first, with government participating in the war on terrorism, and second, with their ill-considered involvement in the USA's wars in Iraq and Afghanistan.

(iii) Cultural policy serving bloc-think

The propaganda war was a significant territory as it sought to foster a set of ideas built around the core Manichean claim to irreconcilable difference, the essence of bloc-think. However, the sharp contrast of this characterization with the earlier celebration of the heroism of the Soviet Union during the war years, coupled with its manifest irrationality, not to mention the rewriting of history against which Orwell had warned, meant that this style of thinking had to be inculcated (state-level actions plus episodes read as symbolic of the elite's conflict) and sustained, that is, routinely remade. The new elite-sponsored reading had to be sold and made to stick, and here a cultural policy was put in place. There were a number of aspects to these policies: covert anti-communist funding, popular hysteria and – as Orwell noted – the (further) development of the elite-controlled machineries of persuasion.

There was covert funding to cultural organizations.[23] The American state financed propaganda by funding leading magazines – here, *Encounter* – nominally independent, they ran materials favourable to the West. Such magazines and their lines of argument were supported by a diverse group of people, now tagged as 'Cold War liberals';[24] they took the money and made arguments against the Soviet Union and the left in general, claiming to be concerned with setting the record straight they were in fact highly partisan and so, in retrospect, their arguments have to be reworked in order to extract the enduringly valuable material and discard the transient propaganda.

The mass media were a channel of communication that recycled government briefings, official and unofficial. The print media routinely ran anti-Soviet stories, helping to sustain the elite narrative of Manichean danger.[25] And the broadcast media also ran stories supporting the overall narrative (and for many years the security apparatus of the state secretly vetted BBC journalists).[26] One theme in this work involved presenting the Soviet sphere as one gigantic prison:[27] a place of captivity, a place from which people wished to escape to the West because there they could find freedom. It is a familiar rhetoric. In highbrow terms, it was built around the notion of totalitarianism. In lowbrow terms it was built upon available memories of captivity in the recent global wars (prisoners of war, concentration camps and so on) plus the use of instructive examples as individual 'escapees' were given media treatment.[28] The idea of captivity gets a further twist in the context of the Korean War when some returned American prisoners showed signs of maltreatment, tagged brain washing.

In all this, new media technologies were a useful aid. Thomas Doherty[29] looks at the intermingling of the growth in numbers of television audiences, the ways in which television images thread their way through the rise of consumer society and how Senator McCarthy used television to add his contribution to wider networks of red-baiting. A number of issues are discussed: blacklisting, for studios a quiet life, for the politicians effective red-baiting; self-censorship, as Cold War anxieties intrude, again, a route to a quiet life; controversial personalities, picked up and puffed up, their fate thereafter was media contingent (thus, Lucille Ball was accused of being a fellow-traveller[30]); and the circus-like nature of the House Un-American Activities Committee (HUAC) hearings, broadcast to a wide audience and thus influential. The episode was later regretted, with the media indicating some unease at their role.[31]

And, in the realm of popular culture, the Cold War reanimated an established literary genre, the spy story. There were many spy stories,[32] and these found expression in both popular novels and films, some of the work was simply entertainment – thus Ian Fleming or Len Deighton – whilst other work had more claim to literary status – John Le Carré – and some more recent, that is twenty-first century film treatments are similarly concerned to recover the cultural atmosphere of the time[33] and – with an eye on current conflicts – to note the self-deceiving justifications offered by participants.[34]

And, as an addendum, states now routinely promulgate this sort of systematic misinformation – commentators root the techniques in the work of the psychologist Edward Bernays who moved this sort of study from the consulting room to the PR office. The substance varies depending on the enemy of the day and much of these materials are deployed domestically, where one political party attacks another or a corporate group runs a lobbying campaign to secure its sectional interest. Thus, in Britain, notoriously, the nuclear industry, oversold down many decades, or, more recently, the security industry, which has been vigorous in making domestic sales in recent years. And these security materials are also deployed in the international arena, as in the case of the Cold War, and as in that case they are part of a play book; part of which is oriented towards undermining targeted foreign governments; and part of which is oriented towards appropriately disciplining domestic populations. In respect of the latter element, recent notable exercises might include justifying the attacks on Afghanistan (home to Al Qaida terrorists) or the invasion of Iraq (weapons of mass destruction (WMD) in 45 minutes) or the overthrow of the government of Libya (bombing to stop a massacre) and so on. A report in early July 2012 pointed to the country of Mali as a new prospective base for Al Qaida terrorism, given that displaced Taureg peoples had gathered there following the overthrow of the government in Libya – in response, one contributor to the attached comment string remarked: 'God almighty, when will this scaremongering stop.'[35]

Themes in the public sphere

For the British elite there was much to be fearful about – the disintegration of the state-empire had created many urgent problems, not all of them concerned elite money and status – and these anxieties were variously addressed (or denied) with the resultant patterns of apprehension energetically distributed around the wider population. These problems included: involvement in the general Cold War (rhetorical claims were made and promulgated via official statements, law, the media and so on); involvement in Cold War low-level conflicts (where the British participated in the Berlin air lift and covertly in funding anti-government groups in Eastern European countries); involvement in civil war (where the British supplied aid to the right wing government during the civil war in Greece (a role later taken over by the USA)); involvement in civil/international war (the British government followed the Americans into the civil war in Korea, represented to the British domestic audience as 'resistance to international communism'); plus various involvements in assorted conflicts in the hitherto peripheral territories of the now disintegrating system of European state-empires. All these issues/anxieties found general expression in the public sphere – the overarching theme was one of loss, where this included: loss of security (danger), loss of status (empire) and loss of trust (people).

Loss of security: The costs of Manichean division
Elite-sponsored Cold War bloc-think represented Europe in various ways: geographical, military and socio-politically. These distinctions found wide expression in official statements, in media commentary, in novels, film and so on.

So first, the continent was divided politico-geographically into blocs, good/bad, with a clear dividing line between the two blocs – the Iron Curtain – which blocked exchanges between the hitherto unified continent; second, militarily the continent was divided into defensive/aggressive powers, where the militaries of the former were cast in terms of a notion of defences, whilst those of the latter were designated as the aggressive forces of an expansionist enemy (all this included both anxieties about the intentions of the Red Army and the recently invented nuclear weapons where anxieties about nuclear weapons were particularly acute). Then, third, economically it was divided into prosperous/poor, with the situation of the former explained in terms of the energizing institution of the liberal marketplace, whilst the situation of the latter was explained in terms of the deadening effect of state-socialist planning; fourth, socially it was divided into individualistic and collectivistic social forms, with the former enabling the individual pursuit of life, liberty and happiness, whereas the latter demanded obedient regimentation; fifth, politically it was divided into free and unfree, with the distinction extensively elaborated both in political philosophical terms (democracy/totalitarianism) and in popular form, thus the West was free, the East was a species of prison with its populations captive; and finally, sixth, culturally it was divided in terms of authenticity/inauthenticity – in the case of the former, the arts were shaped by the individual pursuit of aesthetic excellence and authenticity, in the latter the demands of the state, the pursuit of socialism, required obedience and thereby damaged the arts.

These nominal divisions were cast in Manichean terms; the 'other side' was always dangerous. In hindsight, this apparatus of division seems absurd, with the claims made about the lives of ordinary people particularly overdrawn and foolish, but at the time, once the game of Manichean comparison had been set in motion, it could flood the public sphere and envelope most aspects of people's lives.

Loss of status: The costs of the dissolution of state empire

A number of themes run through the work of John Le Carré; three are of particular note: loss, betrayal and deceit. The first theme is that of loss. The fictional characters whose work he records in his novels are emblematic of the post-Second World War situation of the elite: the state empire has gone, are subordinate to the Americans and they move within a claustrophobic world of banal routine and betrayal. The second theme is betrayal. The traitors are in league with the newly specified enemy, the Soviets, a seemingly straightforward instance of betrayal, yet in psychological terms it seems that Le Carré is diagnosing an episode of displacement – the key figures in the circus suffer betrayal by members of their own class, professional and personal. A subtheme relates to the Americans, those nominal allies who in practice did ensure that domestic elite error (getting involved in war as they did) resulted in the loss of state-empire, clearly matters that cannot be addressed directly. And the final theme noted here is that of deceit. In the novels people lie, organizations lie and the state lies.[36] All these are run together in the novel *A Small Town in Germany*, where officials in the local British embassy work assiduously to block the release of damaging information about a highly placed war criminal in the service of the West.

These are themes that find wider resonances in popular thinking. There is veiled anger at the results of the war ('we won, but others are reaping the benefits'), an ambiguous admiration for the United States (over paid and loud but also offering an unstuffy optimistic view of the future) and a little later a further twist to these responses would be added when the *Empire Windrush* disembarked its passengers signalling a change in the make-up of the local British population and the start of an intermittently acrimonious debate about 'race'.

These themes run down into the present day: residual elite hostility towards Russia;[37] residual elite nostalgia for an imagined pre-war past (great houses, class hierarchies and empire[38] – in sum, 'heritage');[39] confused semi-anxieties about race;[40] and a popular pleasure in the ambiguous entertainments revolving around spies (if not George Smiley, then James Bond).[41,42]

Loss of trust: Writers and dishonesty/betrayal as constant risk in politics/life

In the European tradition with its commitment to the public sphere one distinctive way of making arguments can be captured in the notion of the political writer. Political writing is concerned to respond to the demands of the present: to identify problems, to make diagnoses and to offer solutions. It is an engaged form of writing. It can be based on: intellectual commitments (ethical or ideological ideas); personal experience (politicians, émigrés, activists); or professional interest (journalism, commentary or scholarship). Each would unpack slightly differently – but all are species of action.

In the late 1940s and 1950s there were a number of examples of writers placing arguments in the public sphere: George Orwell, Gunther Grass and as noted John Le Carré. These examples can be unpacked in terms of the trio 'context, agent and audience': the 'context' details the environment within which the writer is working; the 'agent' calls attention to the particular experiences or ideas or foibles of the writer in question; and the 'audience' calls attention to the groups of people whom the writer has in mind when preparing material. The way these elements play together shapes the 'argument deployed in the public sphere'.

Eric Blair invented George Orwell.[43] Orwell's background was a 1930s public schoolboy, colonial policeman and thereafter a traveller in London, Paris and Spain. In Spain he fought for the Republic, but his politics were not straightforward, sometimes anarchist, sometimes socialist, sometimes patriot and finally a perhaps unintended[44] Cold War writer. The last encompassed his goal to be a 'political writer' and this included early novels (*Keep the Aspidistra Flying*); social reportage (*Down and Out in Paris and London*, *The Road to Wigan Pier*); two key texts written during the war years (*Animal Farm* and *Nineteen Eighty-Four*); and much journalism. Orwell's work was distinctive – the persona he constructed was that of a plain-speaking, sensible, no-nonsense man dealing directly with experience but social and political commentary do not work that way as engaged writing is a subtle construction. Orwell's stance was politically conventional/conservative (for all the claims to socialism) and anti-intellectual (that is, his emphatic criticism of abstract writing marked not merely a refusal to engage in critical reflection but also served to encourage a similar refusal in his readers) and, it might be recalled, his writing was also very influential, in particular as a critic of the Soviet Union's style of socialism.

Now Orwell is treated as something of a British national treasure. Stefan Collini[45] considers his work, which was hostile to the political left, in particular, communism, and virulently hostile towards those he tagged as intellectuals. Orwell invents the plain man, speaking directly about how things are. The work fitted readily into the construction of the Cold War, as anti-communism was made the self-evidently correct stance of the plain man, for only posturing intellectuals could think otherwise. One commentator tagged Orwell as a man 'raw down one side and numb down the other'.[46]

Another figure, treated now as something of a national treasure, is Gunter Grass whose early work shares an analogous context, that is, the immediate post-war years, this time in Germany. Grass has made extensive interventions in public discussion around the theme of German history, society and politics in the wake of the 1930s collapse into National Socialism and its subsequent reconstruction within the fame of the 'West'. These issues have been pursued in novels. The sequence of books begins with the *Tin Drum* (1959), which chronicles the fall of pre-war Danzig and the start of the Second World War, and continues with a series of further texts. At the turn of the millennium *My Century* (1999) reviewed the broad pattern of the politics of the Continent. The early work was cast in expressionist terms, tracking the behaviour of adult conflicts through the morally ambiguous eyes of his fictional child protagonist, Oscar. The local dynamics of the slide into fascism are unpacked and displayed, as are the final consequences in military defeat, foreign occupation and the reallocation of the city, now renamed, to the new Polish state.

In *Crabwise* (2002) Grass opens up the issue of German suffering in the Second World War. The losses suffered are addressed in a text which is part novel, part recollection and part political commentary, and which revolves around the loss and memorialization in right-wing websites of the *Wilhelm Gustloff*, a pre-war National Socialist cruise ship named after a murdered Swiss National Socialist and sunk by a Soviet submarine in the Baltic in the closing weeks of the war. Grass acknowledges the losses of the German people in a striking image of thousands of drowned children, their lifebelts working to make them float upside down, and makes the point that if the centre-left don't speak of it the right wing will.

Where the work of Orwell and the younger Grass were shaped by the experience of war, John Le Carré's work inhabits a different double milieu: that of post-war Britain, relatively poor and shorn of its global empire; and that of post-war Europe during the Cold War, poor and divided. Le Carré's early career involved the Foreign Office and spying. He left the Foreign Office after his first few novels were successful and made the territory of realistic spy novels his own.[47] The early work was realistic in style in contrast to then available thrillers, and in *The Spy Who Came in From the Cold* (1963)[48] and *A Small Town in Germany* (1960) he detailed the dishonesty and violence of the British state as individuals were subordinated to the political demands of the moment. Later, in a rather different register, Le Carré's key invention was George Smiley and the world of the circus – with its rituals and nomenclature.

There have been various reactions to all this work. A number of points can be made. First, the domestic literary establishment has dismissed Le Carré as a genre writer, not of any great interest. He falls into a category also inhabited by Somerset Maugham or Graham Greene or Ernest Hemingway, writers who engage with the contemporary social/political world. However, this material constitutes a distinctive mode of social theoretical engagement, dismissal is foolish. Then, second, some pick up on the issue of the Cambridge Spies (issue of class and betrayal) and focus on this – picking out the obvious parallels between the denizens of the circus and the presumed worlds of upper-class spies – again the theme of class/betrayal. And, in similar fashion, some pick up on the issue of scientist spies (committed to a cause versus dishonourable and dangerous) and speculate as to 'why they did it' or where a motive is established whether or not they were correct to 'act as they did', and it is noticeable in Le Carré's fiction that the state or corporate world or their representatives are often corrupt, implying a justification for the role of 'traitor', one who acts from conviction. And third, some recall the atmosphere of the Cold War (Eric Hobsbawm[49] or Sheila Fitzpatrick[50] or in different vein Peter Wright)[51] and make it clear that the period was peculiar and had its own routines and that it is now over (or it is for most people). Overall, politics does run through his work, sometimes elucidatory, at others critical, but his politics are difficult to pin down. The early work is focused on the Cold War – spies – betrayal, loss and alienation, and it seems hermeneutic in spirit, that is, it unpacks a particular social/historical milieu, but the later work is more critical and attacks the corporate world in poor countries and the indifference of rich countries to the damage they cause.

In retrospect, looking at all this work, it seems that the years immediately following the Second World War with its loss of state empire, domination by the USA plus a confected fear of the Soviet Union represent an area of anxiety for the British elite and masses, an important period, whose events and legacies have not yet been fully acknowledged or assimilated.[52]

Wider issues: The Cold War in retrospect

The Cold War runs into the present in a number of ways – noticed and unnoticed – but here these legacies can be considered under two simple headings, the substantive impacts and the ongoing debates amongst commentators.

The Cold War considered substantively

The general crisis destroyed the European centred state-empire systems and it also destroyed the extant systems of Japan and the USA. The post-war global political pattern is cast in terms of nation-states plus the overarching frame of the United Nations coupled to 'the international community'. The interregnum was chaotic. The state empires did not dissolve in a neat and tidy fashion, successor states were not obviously delineated – elites had to take and secure power – and it was during the interregnum that the Cold War was inaugurated and thereafter within a few short years a global bloc system was in place. The Cold War came to involve many countries, but, at least initially, it was focused on Europe and East Asia.[53] In the European theatre, the key protagonists were, on the one hand, the USA plus its Western European allies, and, on the other hand, the Soviet Union plus assorted Eastern European allies, together with the communist bloc or Soviet bloc or the East. In the East Asian theatre, on the one hand, the USA plus local allies in Japan, South Korea, Taiwan along with others in Southeast Asia, and on the other hand the People's Republic of China (PRC), plus its allies in North Korea, Vietnam, Laos and Cambodia.

The nature of division was distinctive: first, political-economic competition – state-socialist planning versus liberal-democratic market; second, military-diplomatic competition – search for military advantage plus related search for allies amongst the post-Second World War non-aligned nations where this included support for favoured local elites, arms transfers, money transfers, proxy wars, covert operations and regime changes; and third, cultural competition – competing claims to status of advanced culture thereby laying claim to the future, in politics, liberal democracy versus communism, in the social realm, individualism versus collectivism, in social science, modernization theory versus state socialist Marxism, and in the arts/humanities work funded by competing states in the arts, journalism, film and popular culture, celebrating individual achievement or responsibility towards the collective good.

The episode was of long duration. A matter of memories: for the West, conventionally, the Cold War began with post-Second World War Soviet intransigence and expansionism; for the Soviet Union, Western hostility was evident from 1917 onwards (as Western powers supported White Russians during the civil war). The Cold War in Europe ended in autumn 1989 with the nature of the ending and immediate consequences debated (we won, end of history, gangster capitalism and so on), whilst the Cold War in East Asia seemingly endures (North Korea/South Korea) (Republic of China/PRC) (USA/PRC). The whole episode has been read in terms of the idea of 'Cold War'; a discourse elaborated across a range of conceptual binary oppositions and deployed via key institutions, in total, producing bloc-think.

The construction of the Cold War

Against the standard arguments to the effect that the Cold War was inevitable given Soviet expansionist designs, it can be analysed in terms of the process of constructing the political, institutional and popular machineries of division. The Cold War was a manufactured product.

(i) The elite-sponsored social construction of an enemy

It is clear – some 50 years after the period in question – that the Cold War was an elaborate elite-level confection where the interests and prejudices of a narrow group of people in government, the military, industry and the media (in power, resources/status, profit and story-telling) found expression in a sustained project of contrived hostility towards its designated enemy. The project had its headquarters in Washington but it found enthusiastic supporters in Europe. Thus, as examples, for Germany, the turn towards the West was part of the process of recovering from the criminal fascist regime. Or for Italy, the alliance with the USA helped cement the institutional power of the alliance between the Catholic Church, business and the mafia, which found expression as the Christian Democratic Party. And for the British, the alliance with the USA served as a partial consolation for loss of empire. It can be read as an early demonstration of the power of the state to secure widespread obedience within target populations and there were early critics: some diagnosed 'repressive tolerance'[54] whilst others spoke of the creation of a 'mass society'.[55]

(ii) The elite's reach within a population

The episode raised the issue of the extent of the possible reach of an elite within a target population, the extent to which 'discipline' can be secured. If the majority of citizens in the West could be persuaded that they were at risk from the Soviet Union, then what other equally implausible claims might powerful elites promulgate? In respect of Britain, one obvious answer would invoke the state's lying ahead of the invasion of Iraq (and such examples could be multiplied) but the deeper questions revolve around the state's habits of manipulation and the role of novel technologies in facilitating such behaviour.

(iii) The role of the arts in puncturing such constructions

Cold War bloc-think was not without its critics. Standard political parties were not effective and the formation of communist parties and the like in Western Europe was quickly embraced by Cold War elites as evidence of the claims to danger which they had been making, likewise the efforts of trades unionists. However, one source of criticism was more successful, the arts. Thus, in literature, the critique of war made by Joseph Heller in *Catch 22* or the critiques of the end-time of colonial days made by Anthony Burgess in *The Long Day Wanes*; in film, standard histories of the Great War were satirized in *Oh What a Lovely War*; the logic of the Cold War was lampooned in *Dr Strangelove*; the military were ridiculed in *Fail Safe* and later, United States involvement in Vietnam was criticized as a doomed colonial adventure in *Apocalypse Now* – and these works stood out amongst a broader output of banal nonsense[56] or outright dross.[57]

Considered in commentary

The Cold War was refracted back into commentary amongst intellectuals and other commentators in Europe and America. There was no agreement at the time and there is none now, although, as time passes, what were highly contested contemporary debates turn into matters considered in more scholarly terms by historians. Even so, there are clear differences in interpretations. One line of debate divides, as might be expected, conservatives and socialists (or members of 'the left') whilst another divides members of the left into two groups, those sympathetic to communist states and those hostile to these states and to those who argued on their behalf (a debate reanimated in respect of the Soviet Union around 1989/91 and ongoing in respect of China).

Gabriel Kolko[58] tracks the process of the construction of the Cold War system amongst American policy makers: first, a concern for interwar depression fed a preoccupation with fixing global economy around a liberal trade model, all of which fed into the construction of United Nations and Bretton Woods system; second, a concern with opposing communism, seen as a threat to the liberal model; third, a recourse to domestic US red-baiting in the context of local elections; fourth, Roosevelt never let red-baiting run, but Truman did; and fifth, then there were wars in Korea and elsewhere in disintegrating territories of former colonial empires plus tensions in Europe over the post-war settlement plus the awkward task of the demobilization of Western European socialists and communists. In this way, the bloc system emerges.

Taking a different tack, Tony Judt[59] tackles the Cold War offering in particular a critical take on the role of the Soviet Union in Eastern Europe. Distinguishing between 'Western democracies and Soviet totalitarianism'[60] he tracks the re-energizing of the long-running Cold War in the years after the end of the fighting, noting the confused objectives of the key players, the USA and the Soviet Union, the British elite's reluctance to associate themselves with Europe, preferring the subordinate's role to the USA, and the French elite's difficulties in accommodating their decline, achieved, Judt notes,[61] in three years, through accepting a European strategy for the future. So, over this period, the USA and the Soviet Union became key players in Europe. The tone is critical of the Soviet Union but Judt does note[62] that pre-war Eastern Europe was not democratic and that what did unfold, that is, division, was most likely inevitable, and certainly any return to status quo ante (quasi-fascist regimes plus millions of ethnic Germans) was wholly impossible. The process of dividing the Continent and setting up the bloc system was accompanied by the manufacture of bloc-think – communism versus anti-communism, mirror projects in the two blocs – and intellectuals figured in the process as did state money, direct or covert. The situation of intellectuals is unpacked further in Judt's later work and here, in conversation, he recalls the difficult circumstances of the time, offers a defence of the CIA (full of 'smart young people')[63] and notes that one had to choose '[between] two large imperial groupings: but it was only possible and, indeed, desirable to live under one of them'[64] – defiant, yes, unpersuasive, certainly. Overall, it was an unhappy period.

In contrast to these commentators, preoccupied with politics, Patrick Wright[65] analyses the cultural aspect of the construction of the Cold War around the metaphor of an Iron Curtain. The metaphor comes from the theatre. The iron curtain was a firebreak between stage and auditorium and shifted into the political realm the Iron Curtain becomes a sharp division between differing or opposing political cultures and the institutional vehicles of division are likely to encompass military, diplomatic, trade and ideological arenas. The metaphor of Iron Curtain is firmly fixed to post-Second World War period. Starting with Churchill's March 1946 speech at Fulton Missouri, which inaugurated the popularly understood split of 'West' and 'East'. But the political Iron Curtain has an earlier history, anticipated in the First World War (Britain/France versus Germany with all the propaganda aimed by both sides at the other, making a clear division) but most clearly deployed in Western European elite reaction to the Russian Revolution where the anti-communist hostility was immediate and profound and sustained. Wright details the involvement of the British political elite: instant hostility; expressed militarily with involvement in civil war; expressed domestically with anti-left propaganda; and expressed in colonies where anti-colonial movements were often tagged as communist. Wright comments that where Hobsbawm speaks of the short twentieth century it could as easily be tagged the long Cold War (1917–89).[66]

Running down to the present: Legacies and repetitions

In British public politics the episode of wartime still counts: official events are still attended by fly-pasts of vintage aeroplanes, with the Spitfire now a mix of heritage and cliché, military museums proliferate, wartime posters are recycled as fashion, large numbers of history books are published. And the system of the welfare state counts: constructed around the same time, deeply popular and now taken for granted. War and welfare are key building blocks in the edifice of 'continuing Britain'. What then of the Cold War? As the elite's apparatus of fear was deployed for around 40 years, it would be surprising if it had not left residues and some of these are obvious, as with a bloated military budget or claims about 'punching above our weight' or recollections of the Cambridge spies, and some are popular, hence James Bond. But some residues are a little more subtly articulated: first, it is easy for the elite to invoke wartime – as with the Falklands or Afghanistan or Iraq or Libya or Mali or the threats directed at Syria and Iran; second, it is easy for the elite to invoke the perils of the enemy within – as with trade unionists, as with Muslims post-9/11 – as with environmentalist activists and other dissenters; third, it is easy for the elite to shift into Cold War-style criticism of perceived enemies – thus of Russia in respect of actions in Georgia or actions in support of Syria or of Iran in respect of its alleged nuclear weapons programme and so on; fourth, it is easy to invoke the alliance with the USA, the special relationship – thus after 9/11 the subsequent bombings in London are referred to as 7/7 (the bombings are thus used as an opportunity to claim a kind of similarity/solidarity with the USA); and, fifth, it is easy for the elite to sneer at the influence of the political left and other dissenting strands of opinion, overall much exaggerated in the context of the British soft oligarchy. Thus does the Cold War run down into the present day – a hangover from the past, a political bad habit, but for the elite, a useful reservoir of already inculcated ideas amongst the masses comprising available fearfulness and available stalwartness, both useful ways of misdirecting and disciplining the population.[67]

5
Voices of Complaint, Voices of Assertion

Contemporary public discourse can be unpacked in a number of ways by identifying the claims of state authorities, those of the corporate world or the wide range of arguments found within the public sphere. In this last noted arena, the 1950s saw novel claims made. In this decade recovery from the depredations of the war years, plus the construction of the welfare state, plus, in particular, the impact of the 'long boom', provided an environment within which newly confident social groups could make their voices hear. Moreover, amongst the clamour were various lines of assertion, denial and complaint. The aspirations of the urban working classes were vigorously asserted, variously mocked and sometimes simply denied by more conservative figures. Today, such assertion and complaint are familiar aspects of the common culture of the United Kingdom – these forms of engagement can be addressed to various audiences – state officials, politicians, and organizations within the corporate world, plus members of other social classes and to life in general.

The recovery from the damage of the years of warfare was well under way by the early 1950s and thereafter the 1950s evidenced a modest prosperity with full employment, steady economic growth, the machineries of the welfare state in place and a young population. In political life, Harold Macmillan's late 1950s electoral slogan caught the flavour of the period when, addressing the population, he advised them that 'you've never had it so good'. The tone was that of the patrician elite addressing the somewhat unwashed masses but the claims were in general terms accurate. Yet the style was by now outmoded as the masses were increasingly inclined to answer back and this response was caught by a number of young artists, in particular, authors, whose work opened up new areas of debate within the public sphere; a somewhat disparate group of them came to be called 'the angry young men'.

What they had in common was a rejection of received hierarchies, or perhaps a disappointment with their record,[1] and as a related theme an assertion of the claims to public attention of the lives of the working classes. Thus, their work could be read as a species of cultural rebellion and viewed as symptomatic of wider changes in society. Nevertheless, not all members of society welcomed these changes and there was a reaction amongst more conservative-minded authors and political commentators. The former group, the angry young men, exemplified an attitude, which sociologists and political scientists would come to identify as a decline in deference, whereas the later group were more inclined to affirm the hitherto existing status quo, either mocking the newly assertive groups or simply denying their claims.

The episode caught a new aspect of longer-established class conflict. Where subaltern classes had responded to elite claims to social superiority with deference, or the defensive assertion of the value of inward-looking working-class community (the social base of oppositional politics),[2] now there was a novel element of cultural assertion, no longer inward looking, signalling a growing self-confidence. Older forms of accommodation and conflict centred on unions, labour organizations and the Labour Party, which continued to be oriented towards bread and butter issues, whilst newer forms of assertion drifted towards the cultural and intellectual spheres, concerned with new patterns of life and more ambitious claims to the necessity of sweeping reforms.[3]

An episode of social rebellion: Context, trigger and argument

Social rebellion requires particular contexts and it is not obvious what they might be for action cannot be read off shifting social circumstances: it cannot be read off class position (as with cruder versions of Marxism); it cannot simply be read off relative poverty (modernization theory); it cannot be read off relative collective powerlessness (theories of totalitarianism); and it cannot be read off official neglect (theories of rightful resistance). Social rebellion also requires particular triggers and again these cannot be directly specified (for the straw that breaks the camel's back looks just like all the others, those already loaded onto its back). Agents can advance arguments for some sort of change, but forms of argument are multiple so rebellion is likely opportunistic, however, one perhaps common theme is that of disjuncture. Rebellion does require some sort of disjuncture between an agent group's perception of the social world and that of the majority of the people within that particular social world. The disjuncture (whether economic, social, cultural or political) opens up the possibility of rebellion, crucially some sort of denial of the legitimacy of the occasion of the disjunction in question: that economic inequality is unreasonable, that social discrimination is unreasonable, that cultural prejudice is unreasonable or that political disenfranchisement is unreasonable. A contingent event will trigger a demand for change and thereafter individual or group dissatisfaction will need to be articulated and ramped up, criticisms will be made and alternatives sketched out and only then can we speak of some sort of social rebellion.

The 1950s in outline

Britain in the wake of the wartime period was poor and worn out[4] and it was against this background that the advances of the 1950s were set. The 1940s and 1950s marked a period of both recovery from the economic impact of the Second World War, evident in war damage and the disruptive impacts of a command economy, and advance, as attention and resources were turned to civilian purposes. Arguably, a somewhat overly placid period,[5] yet the early 1950s were read as successful, with prosperity not merely returning but advancing as novel consumer goods became available. So for the great mass of the population, the 1950s marked the start of a long period of prosperity for many in the working classes, thus, for example, for those rehoused from pre-war slums the prosperity was unprecedented. The domestic scene was stable, modestly prosperous and maybe intellectually complacent.[6] The elite's creative response to the collapse of the state empire in which they had played a key role was in place – denial plus confection – and for the moment, most of the illusions were in place.

The episode of the war had a profound impact upon the economic system, which had sustained the British state-empire system. There were financial losses (from creditor to debtor); there were also market losses (access to mainland Europe blocked, access to East Asia blocked, ready access to Latin America curbed and access to all other areas disturbed); and there were domestic production upheavals (shift from orientation towards consumer marketplace to war materials plus impact of bombing activity plus impact of neglect of maintenance). But, against this should be counted the beneficial impact of planning/management in the production and the funding of scientific research (aircraft, electronics, computing and so on).[7] The economy of 1945 was different from that of pre-war and these differences continued to widen through the 1940s and 1950s such that by the early 1950s the outlines of a modest prosperity for ordinary people were taking shape. In time, significant social change was associated with full employment and the welfare state.

The experience of the war years – in general terms, shared danger/deprivation/loss – plus the extensive propaganda urging collective effort and in time reward, that is, post-war change, fed into the changed circumstances of the by now dissolving state-empire polity by raising demands on the part of the domestic subaltern classes, the majority of the population. As the 1940s turned into the 1950s full employment plus the welfare state plus the first signs of modest prosperity fed, in turn, into expectations of secure social change – that is, an appreciation that the reform achievements of the post-war years would stick, they would not be undone in pursuit of some sort of elite-sponsored return to the status quo ante. This confidence fed into the public sphere where it found various expressions – the state-sponsored popular and successful Festival of Britain of 1951; and a little later new movements in the arts. However, whilst the domestic scene was one of building success, in the background, enfolding all the pleasures of ordinary life lay the disruptive effects of the end of the state empire generated as shifting structural relationships generated novel and acute demands for the elite to manage: peripheral territories were dissolving and new states were taking shape; the war-ruined countries of mainland Europe were making a start on translating ideals of union into practice; and in addition other problems loomed.

In regard to the hitherto peripheral territories of empire, there had been planning for post-war decolonization, expectations were of an ordered process of transition, but post-war reality was different as the dissolution of the state-empire system proved to be a difficult exercise, often running out of the elite's control. There were multiple problems. There were conflicts with the USA (over the shape of the liberal market trading sphere); there were conflicts with aspirant nationalists leaders in many peripheral parts of the state-empire system; there were multiple wars of colonial withdrawal (now glossed over in collective memory); and there was one great last colonial adventure, the invasion of Suez. The Anglo-French-Israeli invasion of Egypt was a fiasco, domestic and diplomatic: the domestic public became engaged in debate and there was strong anti-war opinion; and diplomatically, US threats stopped the adventure and troops were withdrawn.[8] In Britain the domestic spillover was significant for not only was there was significant popular opposition, but at the elite level there was a dual recognition of the ineluctable logic of the end of empire and the power of the USA; so once again, established ideas and hierarchies were undermined.

A number of issues related to the period might be noted: early consumerism; the beginning of the end of deference;[9] the discovery of the working class; and a profound unclarity about the national past in the wake of the largely unacknowledged collapse of the state-empire.

Themes in the public sphere

The 1950s are often characterized as rather vapid with commentators reporting that nothing much happened, that events lacked any great consequence. This is an error. In this period post-war reconstruction continued apace and a modest general prosperity developed. In the late 1950s general election, Harold Macmillan, as noted, advised the masses that their circumstances were now better than ever – a languid patrician claim, which was in significant measure true – there were jobs, houses and welfare.[10] Nonetheless, the period was low key[11] and whilst some commentators saw steadily advancing prosperity, others saw complacency. Nevertheless, in broad contrast, others noticed the rise of new social groups, in particular, the emergence within the working classes of non-deferential groups, those turned not to trade-union activism or local community stability but instead to the possibilities of new consumer life. The social sentiment of this emergent groups was grasped in the words of the protagonist of a novel, the working-class figure of Arthur Seaton who advises the audience – readers and later cinema goers – 'what I want is a good time, all the rest is propaganda'.[12]

Protest and hope for the future: The arts in theatre and literature
The late 1950s and early 1960s saw new work in literature and theatre. The material was characterized by its disdain for received forms, that is, the established themes/styles exemplified by Terrence Rattigan[13] or Noel Coward, and instead writers either presented satirical views of such established themes/styles or moved into new areas by attending to new social groups, where, in particular, they attended to the working classes. There was breakthrough work in theatre and novels, materials recycled a little later in film. These artists had a number of ideas in common: first, rejections of claims to the legitimacy of established social hierarchies; second, attacks on the alleged complacency or failures of old elites; and finally, the presentation of sympathetic treatments of working-class life.

Frank Kermode[14] notes that the 'angry young men' were a disparate collection of people whose characterization as a group was a matter of journalistic labelling, but the tag stuck and it served to help get them noticed. One aspect of their reaction was to be found in the period – one element was that the experience of war – army and hierarchy – seemed to be carried over into peacetime – that, plus contemporary politics gave the angry young men plenty to be angry about – Kermonde sums it up:[15]

> No doubt there did exist what Osborne called a 'climate of fatigue', not yet dispelled even when the war was long over and rationing had at last ended. Gloom about the Bomb, Suez and Hungary displaced memories of the war. Some of the angry young men were old enough to have seen military service and experienced the hierarchical snobberies and enforced deference, which were a painful extension of rigours still normal in civilian life at the time. They could now see these conditions for what they were and, having imagined that they had left them behind in the Army, did not like finding that they remained in force, if slightly weakened. Their resentment was expressed in various ways, and so were their hopes of improvement.

A clutch of works made their appearance in the late 1950s. The most noted of these was John Osborne's play *Look Back in Anger*, which was first performed in 1956.[16] It dealt with the ordinary lives of a group of disappointed young people: the piece was a critique of contemporary society, its social mores and class system. The style of the play and the themes it dealt with were new: the action was set in a poor apartment, the characters were equally poor in dress and material possessions, the characters interacted in an uneasy and unhappy fashion and they voiced critical opinions on the contemporary state of society. The play was successful and via the remarks of a critic, it produced the label 'angry young men', thereafter affixed to other critical pieces.

The discovery of the working classes

If *Look Back in Anger* had introduced into the realms of the arts the theme of the working classes, a flood of similar material quickly followed, all of which, one way or another, looked at the changing circumstances of the working classes and, further, asserted that they should be taken at face value, that is, accorded appropriate respect.

In 1957, John Braine[17] published *Room at the Top* – the novel was an immediate success and, like the play, it was a surprising departure from established material. The novel dealt with social aspiration and class mobility: it dealt with the energy required in the business of 'getting on'; it dealt with the costs and consequences of cross-class marriage, that is, 'marrying above/beneath yourself'; and it dealt with sex, the desire, the difficulties, the contemporary social mores, the consequences of breaching the publicly espoused rules. A later 1962 volume was entitled *Life at the Top*. In 1958 Allan Sillitoe published *Saturday Night and Sunday Morning*.[18] Shelagh Delaney's play *A Taste of Honey* was performed in that same year.[19] The former dealt with the implications of the changing material circumstances of the working classes – in particular, the impact of full employment, the secure context of the welfare state and the experience of early consumerism in the guise of an available modest disposable income, spare cash in other worlds. The novel revolves around the life of Arthur Seaton, a working-class man from the North with a regular factory job and thus a regular income. Seaton is young, male, sexually active, selfish and socially irresponsible. He exemplifies the confidence of the post-war working classes and he exemplifies also a theme of the vigour of working-class male sexuality, but his rebellion is undirected, he merely suits himself, as the new circumstances of working-class life permit. And the latter looked at the coming of age experiences of young working-class women; thus similar themes – newly available money along with changing social mores. More work of this kind followed: in 1959 Keith Waterhouse published *Billy Liar*, a novel about a dreaming working-class boy, and in 1960 Stan Barstow published *A Kind of Loving*, again dealing with the lives of young people within the working classes.[20] Later Nell Dunn offered *Up the Junction*.[21] And a few years later, many of these plays and novels were reworked as films.

Thereafter this theme of working-class life runs down to the present day where it finds various expressions; thus, for example: in Granada Television's 1960 *Coronation Street*;[22] in Ken Loach's BBC 1966 play *Cathy Come Home*;[23] in Terrence Davies' 1988 film *Distant Voices, Still Lives*;[24] in Caroline Aherne's BBC 1998 sit-com *The Royle Family*.[25]

All these materials offer a mix of lines of commentary about the lives of the working classes in Britain, including concern, critique, amusement and assertion. They have it in common that these forms of life are acknowledged, that is, given respect and read as politically significant. Their voices are given a hearing. This is one product of the social and political reform processes associated with the upheaval of the Second World War, as the 'working classes' had not figured before in this fashion in public discourse. In the nineteenth century these groups had made their own inward-looking organizations,[26] they had had reports written about them[27] and patrician reformers had offered ameliorative help.[28] Wider political aspirations had been blocked or only grudgingly accommodated but after the Second World War in the period of the long boom, building in the 1950s, the working classes moved into the mainstream of public discourse,[29] in politics, in the arts and in scholarship.[30]

Reaction and nostalgia: Arts and popular organizations

The 1950s and early 1960s also saw new variants on long-established themes. Familiar elite themes and styles were reaffirmed in pursuit of a species of continuity with pre-war days. In the realms of culture, an affirmation of the worth of elite tastes.[31] In popular culture, there was a range of middlebrow entertainments.[32] In politics, it was a concern expressed in the project – 'continuing Britain' – the claim to the long-established nature of the polity. But others responded differently and one group of artists were content to acknowledge the novelty of the welfare state and thereafter to make it a target of satire or complaint or resentment, key figures included Kingsley Amis, Phillip Larkin and Evelyn Waugh and their work inspired others – writers, artists, organizations and television.

Kingsley Amis[33] and Phillip Larkin[34] pursued a life-long exchange of ideas in respect of their judgements of the world in which they found themselves: occasionally funny, mostly not, their work adopted the form of a long drawn-out complaint about their world.[35] The latter with some eloquence, the former, more overtly reactionary, with, early on, wit, later merely ill manners. Others elected to acknowledge the present via nostalgic denial. One artist in particular, Evelyn Waugh offered an affirmation of an idealized past in the social and cultural world of 'great houses'. The 1945 novel *Brideshead Revisited* offers a lyrical evocation of a world of elite wealth and privilege, a world the author thought was fading.[36] In addition, the nostalgic theme of inevitable, regrettable loss was found in organizations: thus the National Trust[37] or the Council for the Preservation of Rural England.

It is a theme that runs down into the present day: it is found in the numerous BBC television classic serials celebrating the social manners of the English middle and upper classes;[38] it is found in the seemingly equally numerous variants on the theme of life in great houses; it is found in stories of life in fictionalized public schools; it is available in the popular media preoccupation with the Royal Family; it is found in organizations such as the Countryside Alliance; and in politics, it is found in the distinctly downmarket anti-European hostility of right-wing members of the Conservative Party.[39]

Wider issues raised I: Theorizing social change, the responses of artists and intellectuals

A number of issues could be addressed; they revolve around the issue of social change and its often-unanticipated costs. First, amongst the post-war generation that benefited from expansion of university places, there was a concern for class mobility. Hence, the stories of working-class boys going to Oxford. In the arts, this was a long-running concern for Dennis Potter with his sequence of plays *Pennies from Heaven*, *The Singing Detective* and *Lipstick on Your Collar*.[40] Then second, amongst the post-war generation that benefited from the expansion of university places there was a concern for success. Hence, Alan Bennett's *The History Boys*[41] or Frederic Raphael's *The Glittering Prizes*.[42] And third, relatedly, amongst this generation, successful, there was a concern for the working classes that they had left behind; guilt, unease, fears of an unintended betrayal defended in terms of the perhaps somewhat tenuous claims of the benefits of the culture of the university world. In addition, all these themes found academic expression in the work of Richard Hoggart, whose work, later, in conjunction with Stuart Hall, was to establish the discipline of cultural studies.[43]

Wider issues raised II: Critiques of ruling elites

These themes also found expression in the work of figures on the left writing about the Labour movement, as with for example Anthony Crosland's 1956 *The Future of Socialism*. And others were to work this revisionist seam, notably, Ralph Milliband,[44] looking to rouse the Labour Party so that it might at least attempt to translate into practice its often declared radicalism in the optimistic expectation that the ruling order could be replaced, that sweeping change in British society could be secured via the parliamentary road.

These themes also found early opponents – in Friedrich von Hayek and in Karl Popper and in a range of other conservatives – and so far from the Labour Party embracing a more radical programme, such work as it did, running down the consensus line of Keynes, was of little real note. By the 1970s, the post-war reforming impulse was spent, routine set in and complacency came to mark the attitudes of those involved. In time the whole package was decisively repudiated (intellectually and in practical terms) by the 1980s emergence of neo-liberalism – but what goes around comes around and this debate has post-2008 been reanimated.[45]

Wider issues raised III: The claims to attention of subaltern classes

The claims to attention of the subaltern classes have endured but so has class conflict. The Labour Party is no longer associated with an ideology – 'socialism' – but with 'welfarism' coupled to whatever accommodations are necessary to secure a parliamentary majority. The populist right are dismissive, speaking of 'chavs'. The mainstream right do attend to these matters, treating them as an issue related to the welfare budget. Scholarly and policy advocacy work on the situation of the working classes does continue[46] – but it has dwindled – no longer novel, no longer central to public political discourse – merely an aspect of a wider debate about the scope, purpose and financing of the welfare state. The contrast with the artists of the 1950s is stark. Today, at the start of the twenty-first century, no one would look to the working classes for inspiration or a clue as to the nature of the future.

The 1950s in retrospect

From the perspective of the second decade of the twenty-first century, the 1950s are remote and so imagination has to reach a long way back, but it is possible to track the changes and to note the continuing legacies.

In historical perspective, the decades of the 1940s and 1950s were a disaster for the ruling elites of Britain as a state-empire system with overseas holdings accumulated over centuries dissolved away in a few short years. This was not what the elite had had in mind at the start of the war but as events took their economic toll and the power of the USA rose the continuance of the state-empire system looked ever more implausible. A number of key moments could be cited: the 1942 fall of Singapore signalled the loss of empire territories in the East; the 1944/5 results of the debates with the Americans about the shape of the Bretton Woods machinery signalled the new definitive pre-eminence of the USA; and for all those with continuing ideas of state-empire status the definitive moment came in 1956 with the debacle at Suez as an Anglo-French army in secret cahoots with Israel invaded Egypt to the fury of the government of the USA which promptly threatened the British and French with an insupportable withdrawal of extant financial backing and oil supplies.

Compensating for the dissolution of the state empire proved difficult. The response of the elite was in essence one of denial coupled to confection: thus the response involved a mixture of active forgetting (the loss of the overseas territories of empire were ignored) coupled to invention (an essential continuing polity was discovered). The process of active forgetting entailed the claim that the overseas territories of empire were never that significant and in any case were destined to be relinquished just as soon as they were ready for independence. This strategy of denial was facilitated by the celebration of the Commonwealth, the English-speaking peoples and the special relationship with the USA. Thus the empire continued by proxy. The process of invention was turned to the domestic sphere, the hitherto core territory of the state empire was reimagined as a long-established bounded nation-state with roots going back to Tudor times and thence more romantically to the distant days of King Arthur and the peoples who built Stonehenge. It is a confected nationalist tale, a variant reactive nationalism, but the reaction was not directed at a present 'other' but to the territories' own recent experience of loss.

The role of the masses in all this was negligible. They acquiesced in these claims. No alternative political cultural project was advanced by any major party, not the Labour Party and not the Liberals. Other groups were marginal (thus, for example, the CPGB or Committee of 100) and the population not unreasonably turned to enjoy the modest fruits of post-war economic advance within the framework of the newly created welfare state and were content with a modest prosperity, social security and full employment.

It was within this environment that new critical voices were heard. The angry young men were one such group and they left an enduring mark on the culture. They contrived a particular style of anti-establishment dissent, which was angry, resentful and present-oriented (recall Frank Parkin, it was a species of aspiration)[47] and along with this they celebrated, in contrast to the tired ruling elite,[48] a particular vision of the working class as vigorous and energetic; practical evidence of the possibilities of the future.

Some lines of commentary

Tony Judt,[49] looking at the process of loss of overseas empire territories, remarks that the business was unanticipated by metropolitan elites, resented by locally based settlers and others[50] and accomplished in a relatively few years. Nevertheless, the process was confused and often violent. For the British elite the definitive end of empire (rather than) was the 1956 Suez debacle. It had an impact on the elite as they cleaved to the USA, even as empire survived in the guise of a pervasive long sustained nostalgia. It also had impacts on society. The early 1950s had been optimistic, sometimes tagged the 'New Elizabethan age', but after 1956, public discourse changed. It became more critical of received ideas/structures and more realistic/pessimistic. It also acknowledged a wider social mix, in particular taking note of the working class. All this opened the way for the arts with the angry young men. These novelists and playwrights were in the main concerned with domestic matters – dealing with social change, acknowledging new class configurations.

However, at the same time, more broadly the issue of Europe was opened up and the British elite was opposed, thereby missing a boat, which they had to reluctantly scramble upon some years later.

The later 1950s saw continuing economic advance. There were changes on the mainland with the shift from agriculture to the cities and industry. There were significant movements of population.[51] There were new science-based light industries and the outlines of a consumer society taking shape.[52] The same happened along a different line of advance in Britain. The late 1950s and early 1960s saw the take-up of many consumer durables that are now taken for granted: white goods, radios, televisions, cars and the like. There were definite implications for political life as radio and television brought national politics into the domestic sphere more directly than the earlier medium of newspapers and magazines. Moreover, over time, as the prosperity deepened, the baby-boom generations came of age; their inclinations and ideas later feeding the cultural upheavals tagged 'the sixties'.

Turning to the more restricted world of self-conscious intellectuals in Britain, Stefan Collini[53] notes that the tag was never clearly defined and it was never easily embraced. It retained all the whilst the flavour of elitism, dilettantism and practical disutility. Some self-described intellectuals defended the situation, taking the view that such people should be an elite remote from ordinary mass social life whilst others[54] worried and later sought to remedy the situation, giving rise to the New Left, which looked to mainland intellectual models. But in the late 1950s, intellectuals constituted an inward-looking group, self-consciously turning away from mainland work (thus continental philosophy and intellectuals were disparaged).[55]

There is a standard report on their intellectual/social trajectory.[56] Thus the early decades of the twentieth century saw modernist experimentation with the well-connected Bloomsbury group; the interwar years saw ideological splits (in particular, communism and fascism) and mainstream intellectuals drifted rightward, occasionally actively, more often acquiescent ('romantic moderns') and sometimes disengaged (Isherwood's 'I am a camera'). The less significant left rallied to communism or the Spanish republic or to programmes of social reform. The war years saw mainstream and left coming together, minus fellow travelling right, to support war aims built around liberal democracy and social welfare. This alliance ran on into the 1950s: complacent, self-congratulatory and inward/backward looking.

There are further aspects of these diagnoses of this situation and Collini[57] considers a series of familiar ideas are advanced – first, that the model of a polity containing model intellectuals was France – second, that judged against this standard intellectuals in Britain were acquiescent in the status quo, that is, they were somehow second rate, hence their post-war complacency. Collini thinks the tale is more complex but offers no alternative macro-view. He notes[58] that a diagnosis of the trajectory/status of the mainstream was offered by the New Left in terms of the shift to the modern world of the polity in which a long-established elite contrived an accommodation with the demands of modernity, that is, there was no revolutionary break. This left a nimble-footed elite in charge and they co-opted critics, as they appeared, hence the situation in Britain of no real intellectuals. The New Left therefore took it as part of its task to remedy the problem and attempted to do so by importing ideas and models from the mainland.

A further layer to these debates, both those in the 1950s and those amongst subsequent commentators, is constituted by the Cold War. The division of Europe into two blocs produced bloc-think, in both blocs. One aspect of this in the West was a divide between mainstream social democrats and various strands of radical critique associated one way or another with political groups looking to the work of Marx and the various lines of practice of communist parties. The divide could be bitter: cast in terms of a continuum, if Moscow-oriented communist parties lay at one end, then, at the other, lay the adherents/promulgators of Cold War liberalism, at times indistinguishable from conservative reactionaries.[59]

Running down to the present: Legacies, repetitions and developments

The inheritance from the 1950s is not straightforward and the strands have to be disentangled. In general, the lines of complaint inaugurated around this time continued: the poets, novelists and film-makers who advanced the case of the working classes continued go do just that with more books, more plays and more films. So all these arguments in respect of the intrinsic value of the life of the working classes and the moral and political correctness of their self-assertion (and relatedly the work done on their behalf by artists) continued in a variety of contexts: in the workplace amongst trade unionists (assertiveness); in government (through the election of Labour Party governments); in political theorizing (Anthony Crosland, Tony Crossman); in welfare (for example, education (the 1945 act, the later shift to comprehensives, later expansion of universities (Robbins))); and in the media (an old audience whose new forms of life and aspirations were duly noted). However, there is a divide somewhere in the 1970s, when what was a programme of reform took on new aspects, in particular, claims to entitlement and the habit of routine complaint. Nevertheless, there was no simple line of decline. There are also newer forms of social complaint – in the 1960s young people joined in the action – young people remain a social group from which social complaint issues – stylized in rock music; ritualized in recreational drug use; spontaneous in shopping riots;[60] and organized as in anti-racist organizations. Nonetheless, the tone had changed – there is a difference between self-consciously urging the concerns of a newly emancipated class and running with an habituated strategy of demanding more and better welfare for the already emancipated. Increasingly, it seemed, those who called for welfare payments were operating within an intellectual and moral envelope that bore little resemblance to the thinking of the creators of the welfare state.[61]

Against this report on the slow decline of the progressive line, should be placed the reactionary work of a small but well-regarded group of artists and their various outriders in the sphere of popular culture. In the 1950s Kingsley Amis published *Lucky Jim* – it was a well-regarded satire on university life around that time, an attack on a sometime complacent group, but later Amis's politics drifted steadily rightwards and the wit became submerged in a more curmudgeonly social complaint. However, as if to remind that the production of art is never straightforward, Amis offered one variant of the social milieu of such opinion in his novel *The Old Devils*,[62] a tale detailing the amiably nihilistic pastimes of a group of old men, which won the Booker Prize. And in this same vein, a similar characterization could perhaps be made of Amis's friend the poet Philip Larkin, except that commentators do offer the view that some of his somewhat bleak, washed-out, occasionally funny work, will stand the test of time.[63]

This style of social complaint is now available in other forms. Sometimes the complaints are cast as comedy, as with the BBC television series involving Capt. Mainwaring or Basil Fawlty or Victor Meldrew. Some less-than-funny characterizations have been made: Essex girls and chavs.[64] But social complaint crops up in other places: welfare complainants, as noted; lobby groups, thus industry lobbyists complaining about 'red-tape'; pressure groups, thus assorted NIMBYs on assorted planning issues; and the right-wing populist press, thus the *Daily Mail* or Murdoch-world raging against the dying of the light occasioned by welfarism.

* * * * *

In brief, the 1950s saw the welfare state reforms which flowed from the experience of depression and war fixed in place – the state embraced schedules of responsibilities for the basic needs of its population – these responsibilities were read into top-down expert-staffed bureaucratic structures[65] – they have become part of the mental furniture of contemporary inhabitants of Britain. Yet, the result has been subject to criticism, from left and right. On the left, complaints are made that the welfare provisions are not enough, that society reveals continuing areas of shocking neglect (discrimination, disadvantage and disability) and that consequently the state should spend more to alleviate the distress thus identified. On the right, complaints are made that the welfare system is running out of control. It is argued that the numbers of its users continues to expand as ever-newer claims on the state are contrived and that its budget consequently continues along an unsustainable line of increase. The system works to draw people in (the welfare industry) and undermines whatever self-regard they might have once had (they become welfare dependents, inhabiting a dependency culture); and that consequently the state should radically downsize its involvement in these activities. Such a process could be aided by drawing in social organizations, whilst, at the same time contracting out services to the better-equipped private sector. These debates are now part of the general stock of argument lines (plus stereotypes and prejudices and urban myths) that constitute contemporary political culture – if political culture is a contested compromise, the contestation is permanent – but for the moment, in the late 1950s, the optimism in respect of new class groupings came to the fore – the patrician establishment was subject to further criticism.

6
Patrician Retreat: Quickening Change in the 1950s and Early 1960s

The late 1950s saw accelerating economic and social change as the post-war long boom continued and the period of political agreement continued, tagged as 'the post-war consensus'. At the same time the media narrowly understood underwent changes, newspapers reached and passed a peak in terms of sales and then along came television. It spread rapidly. The BBC had broadcast before the Second World War to a tiny audience and it resumed in 1946 (initially to a similarly limited audience) but during the 1950s the infrastructure was upgraded, domestic electrical appliances became more widely available and in consequence the potential audience grew. In 1955 the BBC were joined by ITV and a now familiar duopoly was established and television audiences grew rapidly during the late 1950s. These developments signalled subtle changes in the public sphere as the duopoly of television meant that there was a more or less coherent national audience, yet more diverse voices were made available to it. The patrician elite were in retreat and where the 'angry young men' had attacked the elite for their failures and simultaneously opened the way for an acknowledgement of elements of a newly confident working class, the critics of the later 1950s and early 1960s were more direct and they were aided by serious missteps amongst the elite via a number of scandals. These events/changes took political culture to the threshold of the 'sixties' but for the moment the patrician elite gave ground, at first slowly, thereafter the retreat was headlong.

The late 1950s and early 1960s have been given an assortment of labels: thus, economists characterized the period from the late 1940s through to the early 1960s as the long boom, that is, there was continuous economic growth in output with high levels of employment;[1] sociologists cast discussions in terms of the logic of industrial society, convergence and the end of ideology;[2] and political theorists spoke of an era of orthodox consensus[3] where there were few real disputes between political parties or their supporting organizations. As an exercise in broad description, this was not unreasonable. It was true of Britain; it was also true of the countries that were to form the founding members of the European Union as all were sustained by the demands – successfully met – of post-war reconstruction.

The period was economically successful and commentators spoke of the long boom, a period of sustained rising prosperity. The underlying reasons for this prosperity were characterized in various ways: first, economic growth was built on the experience of war-period state planning and investment in arms-related industry; second, recovery was aided by pent-up demand and demobilized army personnel provided a ready supply of skilled labour; third, US Cold War policy had mixed impacts but there was an influential aid programme; and fourth, post-war political change was built on the back of a widespread determination not to return to the status quo ante, now seen to have decisively failed (ushering in the war years). Social change flowed from these factors: economic growth empowered new social groups, political change created space for their voices to be articulated and new technology was available to speed the broad public appreciation of these changes. Sociologists were disposed to cast these matters in terms taken from the USA.[4] The notion of a fundamental logic of industrialism was embraced. It was another ostensibly non-political politics: function would determine the route to the future, not ideology; the division between capitalism and socialism would be overcome in functionally occasioned convergence; all would become materially prosperous; and as there would be little to argue about, there would be an end to ideology. The period found its major theorist in the American scholar Talcott Parsons and his work offered an elaborate theoretical characterization of modern society, later widely repudiated.

A familiar way of grasping the political dynamic of the era was to speak of the orthodox post-war consensus where this pointed to a putative broad agreement amongst elite-level political players in the permanent government, parliament, parties and key groups within the broad ambit of a corporatist approach to political life in respect of the direction that the country should be taking. The characterization has been challenged. Some have pointed to continuing conflict between social classes, others to disputes within the elite (whether or not to dissolve the remnants of empire, joining or otherwise the European Union). It is better to see the period as a contested compromise and a number of factors can be cited: the long period of warfare had required high levels of production that in turn necessitated elite/subaltern cooperation, which found expression in a mobilized population staffing a command economy; post-war such functionally occasioned cooperation modulated into a species of corporatism centred on tripartite economic planning; and elite-level patrician reformers had taken the opportunity to push for welfare changes. The corporatist welfare state had implemented welfare and employment policies and once in place they were popular, plus the overall economic environment was benign so neither elite nor mass were inclined to press the other but neither elite nor mass were inclined to rest content with the present arrangements; hence contested compromise, a species of balance between contending groups.

All these changes were further aided by changes in the realm of the media narrowly understood. As old practices were revivified (as with newspapers), new technologies making new audiences emerged, in particular, television. Television in particular made a novel contribution to the public sphere. In the late 1950s television took the form of a monopoly public broadcasting system up until the early 1950s when a commercially funded channel began broadcasting, both were free-to-air systems offering an organization-specified mix of programming; the audience had a choice, watch, turn over or switch off. A joke quickly went the rounds: all the goggle box asked of the viewer was their time. The broadcasting duopoly ensured something approaching a single national audience,[5] not something that had existed in such intimate quasi-domestic fashion prior to television, except perhaps through radio,[6] as newspapers served discrete audiences and cinema in the main served purposes of entertainment.[7] The duopoly also allowed some new voices to be heard[8] and agendas other than those of the elite began to infiltrate television output. One aspect of these slow shifts in institutional make-up and cultural output was the emergence of a more direct way of addressing the patrician elite in general and its political figures in particular. Where the 'angry young men' had attacked the elite for their failures, whilst opening the way for the voices of elements of the working classes, the critics of the later 1950s and early 1960s were more direct – they were aided by scandals – and attacks on political figures could be addressed to a wide popular audience. Thus, taken in the round, as the war years fell slowly into the past, economic, social and political change gathered pace and in the modestly prosperous late 1950s and early 1960s new social groups with new aspirations offered a novel media a ready and receptive audience.

Episode: Quickening change in the late 1950s and early 1960s

The business of recovery from the depredations of wartime was well advanced by the late 1950s with rebuilding, the creation of new towns, broad economic advance and growing stocks of consumer goods. Over the decade, change both accumulated and quickened.

Change recalled

After the destruction and losses of 1940s warfare, plus the shortages and problems of the subsequent period of initial reconstruction, the 1950s saw the development of a modest domestic prosperity. It was signalled by the end of rationing, the easy achievement of full employment and the dawning of what in due course would become today's familiar consumer society. The contrast with pre-war days was clear. Where there had been a long drawn-out depression, which had disproportionately impacted areas with older industries, leading to widespread social distress, the post-war years saw a broadening of the light and high-tech industry-based prosperity which had characterized parts of the southeast from the early 1930s onwards.[9] The roots of this change have been widely discussed: the production-oriented system of state planning put in place during the war (in order to ensure the supply of war materials); the creation of at least the outlines of a national consensus in respect of the future, evidenced in the creation of the welfare state; plus the evident need to reconstruct war damage; and finally the determination of the elites of the USA to order a reconstruction of the global economy in the form of a liberal trading sphere. All this pointed in the direction of economic recovery and for the domestic population an unfamiliar general prosperity. And as the rising material prosperity ran through the population, it had a wide social impact.

(i) Reduction of top-down cultural uniformity

As the 1950s unfolded, established evaluative hierarchies were weakened as the pre-war patterns of class identities and class relationships slowly changed. The London-based patrician elite no longer established models of cultural taste for the community at large with agreed variants for middle- and lower-class groups. The style of 'received pronunciation' stopped being the standard of English to which all deferred and slowly became instead just one more accent, and today received pronunciation sounds strange to most ears, ears now attuned to a multiplicity of regional accents and migrant accents (and indeed novel patois). The claims of literary London to privilege in respect of general canons of taste in literature weakened as the concerns and opinions of other social groups found acceptance. Analogous claims in respect of music were undermined. As imported American rock 'n' roll and jazz (in particular) became popular, the claims of the elite in respect of classical music seemed strained and whilst the BBC's third programme served up classical music, other stations offered a wider fare, notably, Radio Luxemburg (and later the pirate stations); plus, as noted, there were also independent voices in theatre and publishing. All in all, the cultural mix was shaken up as novel materials were made available to novel audiences.

(ii) Increased visibility of subaltern classes

This took various forms,[10] sometimes passive, at others active: a celebration of the extant working-class community could be made (and in the 1950s sociologists made many community studies); a determination to better oneself could be made, a matter of getting on; and ambition could be openly averred and where in pre-war days this was a matter of finding a respectable job this continued but now in an era of rising economic wealth it could take the form of proto-consumer expressiveness as some acquired the disposable income necessary for such displays, and this we may hazard was Arthur Seaton's position.[11] Thereafter, there was more overt dissent from received forms of life in politics; some embracing the modest ameliorist welfarism of mainstream subaltern parties, others turning to the marginal groups of socialists, communists, anarchists and the like.

(iii) Media change noted

In the 1950s broadcast media changed. There were changes in public service broadcasting: BBC radio was established in 1922; BBC television began in 1936, was discontinued during the war years and re-established in1946; and commercial television (ITV) was introduced in 1955. Overall, there was a tightly controlled expansion of provision. The state controlled the broadcast media in one crucial respect, issuing licences to operate. It applied to radio and television and later cable/satellite. In regard to broadcast television a second channel was permitted in the middle 1950s and it was funded by advertising but it was also required to operate in some measure like the established public service broadcaster, that is, to serve a general audience and to 'maintain standards' (thereby damaging any chances of running domestic British television on the basis of cheap imported content from the USA). The duopoly created a national audience but there were signs of greater diversity as new voices were heard.

In the 1950s the market for print media, in particular, newspapers, peaked as all reached their widest circulation in the early years of the decade, thereafter, there was a general decline. But for magazines the market began to expand as more disposable income created new audiences, thus, for example, life-style magazines proliferated. At the same time, photojournalism began to decline, except for either specialist products, for example, National Geographic, or niche work, for example, war photography.

Themes in the public sphere

These changes ran through the social world of post-war 1950s Britain – much of the change was embraced – the extent to which it was remarked varied, issue by issue, group by group. One or two of these can be picked out – some were remarked upon at the time, others look more obvious in retrospect.

Future optimism and new technology

The optimism was widespread, certainly amongst the rising middle classes[12] and working classes, the beneficiaries of the new welfare state. In contrast the elite had to accommodate the loss of empire and the rise of the USA and manage the issue of Europe and the product of this work was the notion of 'continuing Britain' where the future was embraced albeit on the basis of a highly stylized version of the past. The general optimism – elite and mass – was dented somewhat by the self-selected debacle of Suez but at the time it was judged an aberration (thus later commentators pointed to the illness of Prime Minister Anthony Eden, adding that it was an illness occasioned by medical incompetence) and the country continued without finding the need for any very great reflection.

Optimism in respect of the future was grounded, in one respect, in a widespread recognition of the relatively novel role of new science-based technologies. The war economy had been underpinned by natural scientific advance across a range of disciplines: stereotypically, the war was a forcing house for new technologies but more prosaically, the war was a forcing house for war machines. In fact the British economy had long been an effective producer of military materials.[13] Broadly, these favoured the training and employment of natural scientists and thus there was some spillover into wider science-based industrial production – later this would be tagged 'spin-off'. The early 1950s saw a celebration of the possibilities of science-based production – commentators spoke of the New Elizabethan Age – there was a broad optimism in respect of the contribution to general welfare that could be made by new technologies.

Critical and subaltern voices

As the 1950s unfolded, there were numerous voices offering commentary and criticism in the public sphere. Amongst them, the so-called angry young men offered not merely criticism of the patrician elite but linked their remarks to what they saw as shifting social relationships, in particular they picked out the nascent cultural importance of the post-war working classes. Their work was thus novel. As they attacked the patrician elite, diagnosing ineptitude and complacency,[14] they helped to make a cultural space for elements of newly confident working classes. These arguments for the working classes did not go unanswered but such reactionary work was for the moment of secondary importance. Thereafter, as the late 1950s turned into the early years of the 1960s, further lines of criticism were opened up as television embraced the comedy work of a group of politically savvy Cambridge graduates. The group that had made its preliminary name in Edinburgh in a show called *Beyond the Fringe* and they were to provide the earliest recruits for what became the satire boom. One show stands for a wealth of activity, *That Was the Week That Was*, or *TW3*; running on Saturday evening in 1962–3 it offered a mixture of sketches, songs and interviews held together by a front man. A British version of 1930s Berlin cabaret, it had an immediate impact, gathering a large audience, plaudits from critics and hostile attacks from those members of the establishment whom it targeted.

It is true that media attacks on political or elite figures was hardly new (thus, famously, James Gilray) but now these attacks had both a mass audience via television and a critical edge that had not hitherto in the post-war period been given voice. It was effective. The public sphere was enriched. Such attacks have changed down the decades and broadcast work has softened, collapsing in many respects into simple and simplistic mockery, whilst newspaper work has become much more severe, in some respects, feral, with politicians seen as fair game and pursued over days and weeks not just in respect of significant issues or errors but over material most would regard as either private matters or simply trivia.[15]

Scandals

The patrician elite did not help their own cause, as a number of episodes became public news. And whilst in the past such episodes would have attracted only restricted interest, now such stories could be made available to a mass audience with television and newspapers reinforcing each other in terms of impact within the public sphere, creating and sustaining a scandal.[16] The media came to enjoy these scandals and down the years they multiplied focusing on a politician or a criminal or indeed anyone who could be made into a story. Some of these targets collaborated, that is, they employed publicity agents and so scandal morphed into celebrity and celebrities could manufacture endless scandal for the media. In the meantime, in the late 1950s and early 1960s there were a number of genuine public scandals; episodes where reputations were destroyed, politics destabilized and new lines of social development opened.

(i) Lady Chatterley's Lover

From 20 October to 2 November 1960 the trial took place of Penguin Books for allegedly publishing an obscene book. The book was D.H. Lawrence's *Lady Chatterley's Lover*: the prosecution called attention to the novel's treatment of sex, its treatment of adultery and its use of unacceptable language, that is, certain words. The defence was one of 'literary merit', which was available as a result of the then reforming Obscene Publications Act 1959. The prosecution made great play with reading salacious extracts from the book – at one point the leading prosecuting lawyer asked the jury if this was a book they would 'allow their wife or servant to read'. The defence team deployed a line-up of figures from the arts and academe all of whom were happy to support the claim that the book was a work of art, even if, one with blemishes here and there. The trial was a *cause celebre* for liberal reformers who read the event in terms of the forces of obfuscatory reaction confronting those concerned with the open discussion of themes central to any and all human life, in this case, sexual relations. It ended with victory for the publishers. The book then sold millions of copies. As a result of the trial, censorship, thereafter, was more or less abandoned in respect of the arts.[17] This area of reform was to be followed by further social liberalization in respect of sexual preferences, abortion law and the judicial use of the death penalty.

(ii) The night of the long knives

Prime Minister Harold Macmillan's 13 July 1962 'night of the long knives' caused a brief political scandal. The prime minister's government was losing popularity and his response – a familiar one in elite-level politics – was to reorganize his cabinet. What was scandalous was the extent of his reordering; that is during the episode he sacked seven members of his cabinet plus a number of junior ministers. Critics inside the party – as well as those outside it – spoke of Macmillan's lack of loyalty to his friends (in particular his ex-chancellor Selwyn Lloyd) and his open opportunism. The prime minister was heavily criticized and the actions were tagged by one critic as 'sacrificing friends to save oneself'. The actions added not merely to a sense of party political loss of direction – something familiar to all parties of government – but to a somewhat wider issue of an elite being out of touch; that is, Macmillan's culling of his cabinet was read in such a way as to assimilate it to the building mood of disenchantment with received authority.

(iii) The Profumo affair

There were two aspects to this particular scandal – first, the detail of the activities of senior figures in government and second the way in which matters were treated in the legal and public spheres. In the case of this last noted, the story was meat and drink to a now distinctly non-deferential press and also in the case of the last mentioned element, in retrospect it is clear that the judiciary joined in what had become a witch-hunt in respect of one relatively minor player. And in regard to the first mentioned element, the behaviour of senior political figures, the transgressions were – by the standards of the day and today's, minor – if kept private – and the crucial error of the key player was misleading parliament in a fashion which allowed him to be characterized as a liar. Put directly, in retrospect, all the puerile prejudices of elite, public and press were on display as sex, class, prostitutes, politicians and spies were run together.[18]

On 5 June 1963 John Profumo[19] resigned as war minister. The context was a scandal involving elite figures, underworld characters, a defence attaché from the Soviet embassy and MI5. The central element of the scandal revolved around the war minister and the defence attaché sharing the sexual favours of a Soho dancer. All the elements of later media scandals were in place: members of the social elite plus senior politicians plus Soviet spies plus sexual goings-on.[20] The press paid great attention to these events and reported them in great detail; much of the information was made available at the trial for Stephen Ward – a medical practitioner – who was accused (in retrospect, falsely) of supplying prostitutes to the rich and famous. Ward committed suicide, adding, thereby, tragedy to the public farce of the trial and assorted press and public witch-hunts.[21]

* * * * *

As with Macmillan's night of the long knives, the scandal was read as further evidence of the decrepitude of the incumbent government and its elite members; the scandal was followed a little whilst later – 25 September 1963 – by the resignation on health grounds of the prime minister, Harold Macmillan. His chosen successor was Lord Home – a choice greeted with glee by opponents of the Conservative Party, but in the event, Lord Home only narrowly lost the 1964 election to Harold Wilson.

The experience of rolling scandals[22] which engulfed the final period of the government of Prime Minister Macmillan turned out to have a lasting legacy, not just their contribution to the collapse of one particular government and its replacement by the opposition party, but the subtle change in the approach to politics on behalf of the media. For during the scandals the media had become involved in an active and aggressive fashion, they had shifted from observers or reporters or commentators to being players and their collective taste for this particular role was to expand over subsequent decades, reaching an invasive apogee with the 2012 scandals surrounding the newspaper publisher News International, matters which occasioned calls for reform, strongly resisted by the industry.[23]

Wider issues: The changing machinery of the public sphere

The public sphere works within available social spaces such as coffee houses, public houses, meeting halls, voluntary organizations, casual social gatherings and so on. In this context, the mass media are one further social space and the nature of this space is directly impacted by the development of technology for new technologies imply new ways of constituting and using a public sphere; schematically, from the telegraph to radio to television to the internet.[24]

The implications of changing technologies became evident in the 1950s as there were new ways to serve existing audiences plus novel technologies could call forth new audiences: television entered directly into people's homes, the audience was a 'family audience', thereafter segmented through the day for children, family and adults. At the same time there were the beginnings of a slow fall-off in general daily and evening newspaper circulations, but with a countertrend in magazine publishing where niche marketing meant that the sector flourished. There was also a slow fall-off in cinema attendances, mitigated by revamps, multiscreens and blockbusters. All this placed television in a powerful position.

Nature and role of public service broadcasting

Public service broadcasting in Britain is firmly associated with the BBC.[25] This organization began in 1922 and its ethos was of providing information, education and entertainment so the organization had a clear idea of its own social role, contributing to national progress. The earliest television broadcasts were in 1929.[26] The BBC began as a private company but from 1927 it was organized as a Crown Corporation, owned by the state, its relations with government being at 'arms length'. Today, it is a dominant force in the public culture of the country: news, arts and popular entertainments. The pattern is sharply contrasted with the USA where public service broadcasting is marginal in a field dominated by commercial concerns where the key to commercial media is the provision of entertainment, thereby making available an audience to paying advertisers.

In Britain the earliest reaction of the cultural establishment to the prospect of commercial television was negative[27] – the intrusion of commercial motives and resultant products and consequent impact upon audiences was read as a general dumbing-down of both broadcasters and viewers in the service of consumerism – making sales of otherwise unneeded products.[28] Yet some institutions can resist these pressures. Stefan Collini[29] picks up the particular case of the BBC's Third Programme (now Radio 3), an elite cultural channel which has survived numerous attacks (precisely for being elitist and relatedly for having a small audience) and records that whilst its character has changed down the generations as other media have evolved (in particular the arrival of television and later a commercial classical music channel) it has offered a platform for intellectuals which has stuck with culture-in-general and backed away from any overt political allegiances.

The arrival of competitors raised the issue of the precise role of public service broadcasting. A role had been sketched out which identified the general public good and insisted on – either explicitly or implicitly – high standards being upheld in the public broadcasting system. In the light of this ideal, when licences were given to commercial firms several areas were picked out, such as the production of news programmes, the production of high-quality programming, and new entrants were required to match established quality standards.

Predictably, commercial broadcasters both acknowledged these restrictions and chafed at their consequences (principally, higher costs and consequently lower profits) and in time a counterargument was formulated. It pointed to a purportedly elitist ethos of the public broadcasting service, to the allegedly overexpensive character of the service and to the seemingly compulsory funding by viewers of public broadcasting service. In later years these lobbyist-style arguments were supplemented by more overtly ideological neo-liberal arguments to the effect that the public broadcasting service should be regarded as a part of the apparatus of the state and that this fact alone was good and sufficient grounds for calling ideally for its abolition or failing that its severe restriction, as the marketplace would surely automatically take its place in serving audiences.

The anti-public service broadcasting arguments were popular amongst commercial industry lobbyists, neo-liberal ideologues and those members of the general public who were well disposed to right-wing populist rhetoric. A symbolic high point of anti-public service broadcasting argument might retrospectively be identified in the 2009 MacTaggart Lecture given by James Murdoch to the audience at the Edinburgh TV Festival – a little later the News International in Britain was in crisis, revealed to have newspaper operations, which, it seemed,[30] were routinely engaged in criminal activity,[31] a scandal that ran on into 2012. At the same time, opinion polls showed strong enduring support for public service broadcasting; an operation, it was noted, in various reports, which commanded not only a measure of global respect for its quality/reliability but also a significant market for its products.

Nature and role of commercial broadcasting

There were early success in the 1950s and 1960s, giving us ITV and ITN, but operators were working within specified constraints, in particular, working within a cultural envelope, which was dominated by public service broadcasting. In this regard, many commentators have called attention to the circumstances in which media products are created and disseminated.[32] Thus print and broadcast media involve complex exchanges between proprietors, regulators, advertisers, journalists, print unions and finally the audiences to whom the product is sold. This final product – the newspaper or magazine or broadcast show – is shaped by these assorted pressures.

One early commercial broadcaster characterized the operation as 'a licence to print money'[33] and broadcasting operations were successful and they have remained successful. And, from the perspective of today, as their scale grew and their operations developed with new forms of production and distribution, so did their overall importance within the economy – in employment, in turnover and in profits – today, the media realm is dominated by very large integrated transnational companies, News International, Bertelsmann, Disney and so on.

From the perspective of the present day, in the second decade of the new century, a distinct trajectory can be identified: first, continuing success – the constraints loosened – the impact of the cultural envelope also loosened – commercial pressures, that is, revenues/costs, pointed commercial broadcasting downmarket – cheaper products, larger popular audiences; then, second, further success – constraint and cultural model are abandoned – commercial broadcasting goes downmarket; until, finally, third, the arrival of digital distribution mechanisms dissolved the commercial broadcasters entirely into a multichannel popular marketplace where broadcast overlapped with internet sites and with videogames and film tie-ins and commercial entertainment and advertising and so on.[34]

The 1950s media and the public sphere

This period saw the beginnings of a retreat on the part of the British patrician cultural elite as new media called forth new audiences and any simple claim to the superior status of say, opera or theatre or serious novels, could no longer be made with any confidence that they would be accepted without challenge. The distinction between elitist/serious and popular was called into question. But it was only the cultural elite that withdrew and so patrician retreat did not entail democratization, rather, over time, the expansion of the gross commercialization of international media conglomerates. Subsequently, as neo-liberalism took hold, an aggressively corporate ethos emerged whilst the deeper elite, the core oligarchy, remained firmly in place.

So this period saw the first steps in the establishment of a powerful corporate sphere in media and the sphere is now well established. It is difficult to envisage significant change – regulation in respect of cross holdings will continue to be an issue – the quality of output will continue to be an issue (dumbing down – celebrity – 24 hour rolling news and so on) – all tending in the direction of trivializing the public sphere (notwithstanding lines of defence pointing to the role of popular entertainment in drawing people into the public sphere). The involvement of such powerful groups in political life will continue to be problematical/debated. Against this – the role of public service broadcasting has survived – in some respects it has prospered – it is innovative – it is creative – it is popular – (hence, it might be supposed, the continual attacks made on the BBC by the political right wing and some sections of the corporate world).

Running down to the present: Legacies and repetitions

Some 40-odd years on from the events noted here, it is difficult to identify continuing cultural residues – the late 1950s have the cultural feel of an interregnum, neither post-war welfare state making nor 1960s rebellion; there is modest prosperity conjoined to a modest politics; the claims of the working classes become less emphatic, whilst scandals undermine public trust in the hitherto patrician elite.

The voices of subaltern classes continue to be heard but perhaps not much remarked upon. On the one hand, the practical claims on public political attention of the working classes are much weaker as the working-class communities of the immediate post-war are much changed (lack of employment, welfare, redevelopment and inward migration) and the trade-union movement post-Thatcher is much weakened and if there was a working-class ethos of community it would have little resonance in a public sphere dominated by the rhetoric of neoliberalism. Whilst on the other, in the arts, the point that they existed and were worth taking note of had been made, repetition did not add anything to this particular message, nonetheless, the claims on general public attention of the working classes continue, however by virtue of being acknowledged and subsequently picked out they have become something of a cliché.

The politics of the period were marked by high-level scandal – a cause celebre was found in the prosecution of Penguin Books in respect of D.H. Lawrence's novel – a drawn-out unhappy scandal was played out around the figure of John Profumo and a political scandal surrounded the decision of Prime Minister Harold Macmillan to sack a large part of his cabinet, including close friends. These events, coupled with the television programme *TW3*, produced a shift in public perceptions of the elite, deference faded, consumption beckoned, rebellion would soon be celebrated (more in theory than in any local practice). The public sphere changed in character – print media had been joined by broadcast media whilst potential audiences had grown on the back of post-war prosperity – so the general tenor of discussion became a little more sceptical of received wisdom, a little bit more prepared to challenge authority. This habit of thought has continued and in some respects it has deepened as, in places, later events have worked to underscore the disinclination towards frankness, which characterizes the elite. At the present time, the early twenty-first century, there is widespread scepticism in respect of the honesty of both media and political figures; both are distrusted and both professions routinely emerge in surveys as the least respected of trades. However, against these trends, there is strong support for public service broadcasting. It is seen as part and parcel of the post-war settlement. The BBC is seen as a great national institution. And, more recently, public service broadcasting has been seen as something of a bulwark against corporate world media, which is seen as profit driven and perhaps unreliable.

7
Affluence Attained, Affluence Doubted

The proto-rebellions of the 1950s, the pronouncements of the angry young men, the discovery of the working classes, were followed by a wider set of challenges to received authority, in Europe, in the United States and in Britain. Now the often inchoate intention was not simply to assert the interests of this or that group but to make a criticism of the post-war settlement in general and to canvass alternatives. Arguably, the impact of the upheavals of the period was greatest in the sphere of the arts and in some areas of social mores. Overall, a period of social/cultural reform but with little political-economic structural change, indeed, the optimistic reform line of the period had its counterpart in all those activities which paved the way for the rise of the neo-liberals who were to command the following decades. Nonetheless, the reforms in the arts and society endured and have been further unpacked down the years. The period is now recalled as 'the sixties'.

The period labelled the 1960s ran from the early years of that decade into the start of the one following and the label points to an interlinked set of events which have in common that they marked a political-cultural break with preceding decades. Some aspects of the package were more important than others. Some were briefly prominent in the mass media. Some seemed important to participants at the time but not now. It is a more than usually contested period; that said, the core aspects can be picked out: reaction against violence, rejection of the states supporting such violence and the presentation of alternative ideas, some sensible, others distinctly utopian.

So first, in the USA, the brutal chaos of the Vietnam, which was made available to a mass television audience and which garnered widespread condemnation. Then second, in the USA, the Civil Rights Movement, which was made available to a wide mass television audience, and which also garnered widespread support. And, third, in the West in general, the widespread rebellion of young people against established authorities, which took differing forms in different places, so there were calls for reforms in university governance and there were calls for an 'alternative society' and there were novel forms of social interaction, in particular, in the area of grass-roots created popular music.[1] Then, fourth, in Britain, there were significant legal reforms which tended in the direction of greater social tolerance including reforms to law dealing with abortion, homosexuality and censorship in the arts/publishing. Next, fifth, in West Germany, the generation tagged the "68-ers' made an intellectual/political rebellion against the subdued political culture of the country and reopened in particular the issue of the years of national socialism. Then, sixth, in France, university students in Paris joining in all these debates and protesting in particular the political culture of the France of Charles de Gaulle provoked a widespread public rebellion, which for a moment looked like it could be a revolution but which thereafter faded away, with the episode tagged 'the events of '68' so that it came to be symbolic of the period. And finally, seventh, in Czechoslovakia, the equivalent intellectual/social movement for change, the Prague Spring, was snuffed out by a Warsaw Pact intervention, provoking amongst other things the demise of Western European communist parties/movements.

The residues of the period are clear: the social liberalization has stuck (abortion law reform, the widespread acceptance of gays and the end of arts/publication censorship); anti-racism law is widespread (the casually deployed prejudice and discrimination of the early post-war years has softened); and reforms in Eastern Europe have now taken place (the post-Cold War 'return to Europe' achieved). But other things have faded: there is no utopian alternative society; there have been no rational reforms to recreational drug prohibitions; and there have been no democratic reforms in Britain. And some things continue just the same, thus, presently, no sign of an end to US military/colonial adventurism or to the pale copy peddled by the British elite.[2]

Episodes: The long boom and the baby boomers

The successes of the early 1950s were consolidated through that decade and ran on into the 1960s and it was a complex social phenomenon: it involved economic success, welfare provision, further media development (television, lightweight cameras, sound-recording equipment and new digital printing technologies) plus the arrival in early adulthood of the members of the post-war baby boom. People were secure and optimistic. But they were no longer acquiescent; they sought 'better societies'; and events in the decade were to provide the trigger for a widespread surge of social protest against established authorities. One trigger was provided by the American Civil Rights Movement, another was provided by the extensively televised warfare in Southeast Asia and yet a third by the demands of young people for democratic change.

All this, the affluence and the conflicts, produced a disposition to protest which slowly changed into a widespread cultural upheaval, no longer specific complaints, rather a broad refusal of received ideas. It was part generational (young people were in the van), part cultural (creativity in arts and politics), part crass-commercial (jumping on the bandwagon) and part mainstream-political (genuine social liberal calls for specific reforms to be enacted via parliament). And disentangling the elements, that is, dividing transient nonsense from enduring change is not simple and so debate will run on.

Economic success – the long boom

The post-war period saw a sustained period of economic growth, which ran from the late 1940s through until the early 1970s, hence the tag 'the long boom'. It was understood and ordered in a quite particular fashion by elite figures who had gone through the experience of depression and war. The depression of the 1930s made an impression upon that generation of politicians and social scientists for there had been widespread domestic distress, concentrated more especially in heavy industries, and there had also been international tensions, with civil wars in Spain and China, disputes between the USA and Japan over China plus events in Europe following the collapse of the Weimar Republic. Prior to the start of the Second World War there was some recourse to an activist role for the state but it was marginal because domestically, many governments responded to failing economies with programmes of retrenchment or austerity, whilst internationally, collective action was all but impossible, neither Europe nor the USA could act effectively.

It was not until the demands of warfare were placed upon the polity that the state was able to undertake the task of organizing the economy and society and it was not until wartime military alliances were formed that broader discussions about international cooperation became effective.[3] In the realms of economics, the demands of war production (in respect of output and the related functional demands of organization (thus, for example, war bonds or direction of labour or reserved occupations and so on)) brought the state unequivocally into the centre of economic and social life. The wartime allies organized planned war economies. The British ran a command economy. These experiences fed into the post-war world: they created the political will for state-planning; they created widespread citizen support for such action, that is, it was seen as legitimate; they created the mechanisms needed to drive such planning, thus the institutions and bodies of social scientific theory, paradigmatically, J.M. Keynes and Keynesianism.

In this fashion, these intellectual and organizational resources were available in the post-war period and moreover not only were the intellectual, political, institutional and social requirements in place, there was also a ready made set of problems to be addressed, that is, the reconstruction of Europe. Britain was comparatively well placed: relatively undamaged, relatively economically strong and relatively scientifically well resourced; however, the immediate post-war years were difficult with the awkward task of demobilization, the costs of the occupation forces in Germany, agreements with the Americans about post-war financial structures and specific loans, issues relating to domestic programmes of economic and social reform, and assorted problems relating to the end of empire in Asia.[4]

Nonetheless, overall the post-war period saw a sustained spell of economic growth, low unemployment, rising prosperity and class mobility. From the late 1940s through until the early 1970s, the British economy, like that of Europe and the USA, advanced rapidly: economic growth was strong and sustained, unemployment was low, the country witnessed not merely material reconstruction (new roads, buildings and the like) but also significant social change – rising prosperity and class mobility.

The strong economy provided an environment within which the welfare state could function successfully: health, housing and welfare benefits. Plus education, which was the key to class mobility in the period of the long boom, for where Arthur Seaton had earlier sought to have a good time, leaving all the rest as propaganda, his successors wanted much more, they wanted social advance, and for many these aspirations were realized. However, as ever, desires did not translate directly into practice and whilst the children of the wartime generation were better educated, better fed, better housed and had the chance of better jobs than their parents, they also came to expect all these benefits. As they had grown up in this environment, they took it all for granted and further demands for change were made and new arenas of social conflict emerged, these were rooted in prosperity, not poverty.

Social change

From the 1940s through to the early 1970s there were rising standards of living. The post-war growth of the economy was sustained over a long period of time and it raised the standards of living of all social classes. It had a particular impact upon the situation of the working and middle classes for they enjoyed both rising prosperity and security, in part a matter of a prosperous economy, in part a consequence of the establishment of the welfare state (with a range of state-led help in respect of health, old age, sickness, housing and so on and all universally available and much of it without the means tests that had made pre-war welfare funds thoroughly offputting). Economic growth was continuous from the late 1940s to the early 1970s; it became a routine expectation amongst elite and masses.

During this period there was a subtle change in social mores; social scientists characterized it as the end of deference and a number of elements can be recalled, as the proto-rebellion of the angry young men was more firmly fixed in place and broadened in its reach. A novel social group coalesced: youth. Nonetheless, the old long-established social hierarchies did not disappear for they were not based simply on long-secured claims to superior/inferior social status, but rooted in economic and political power. That said, the more routine markers of social status divisions were softened as common cultural codes were challenged in lifestyle, personal dress, speech and so on: social tastes changed and the pattern of life of the upper classes and their servants ceased to be a model against which other groups located themselves; personal dress codes changed as commercial culture and affluence created new patterns of dress and now old upper class derived codes were not rejected, they were disregarded; voices other than those using received pronunciation became acceptable and were heard on broadcast media; and domestic consumption took on new forms, paradigmatically, the new modern designs sold by Terrence Conran's Habitat stores.

As the impact of affluence rolled through the social world, commentators noted changing attitudes in respect of politics. Social scientists picked up on these changes and began to speak of class de-alignment: sociologists looked at the weakening of old class identities and looked at the impacts on hitherto relatively settled communities;[5] political scientists looked at patterns of voting and found signs of shifting allegiances so where one person might vote Labour because of a self-identification as working class, another might vote Conservative because of a self-identification as wanting to get on. So, for social scientists, what had seemed settled in the early post-war years and in pre-war days, that is, relatively stable communities, now seemed more fluid, and whilst there were some changes that could be quantified (various measures and social indices), other changes could only be picked up qualitatively (issues of identity and desire). Moreover, class seemed to matter less in general as new lines of social differentiation emerged. One unexpected development in the late 1950s and early 1960s was the rise of youth culture. As prosperity and welfare worked to undermine inherited social hierarchies, many commentators remarked upon the emergence of young people as an identifiable social category. There were also signs that these people understood themselves to be distinct, thus a social group, where the mix included their youth, the experience of prosperity and their being acknowledged. They were identified and provided for by the corporate world. They became a consumption category, first in America, then later in Britain, Europe and elsewhere in the liberal market sphere; they were labelled 'teenagers' and 'young people'. At this point, post-war social change had helped create a novel and identifiable social group, youth.

Thereafter, as the 1960s unfolded, there were further novel lines of social cleavage, again centred on the USA but variously replicated in Europe and Britain. In the USA young people found reason to distinguish themselves from their parents and the rest of society: in particular in respect of war, where they found themselves at risk of being drafted into the armed forces in order to participate in the war in Vietnam. There was widespread resistance. This rejection was part pragmatic, part idealistic. The response was class and race differentiated and so, roughly speaking, the more educated the prospective draftee, the more likely was there to be a rejection of that fate. This rejection of received ideas was echoed in the Civil Rights Movement. Here the issue was race prejudice; the movement garnered widespread support. Thereafter, the rejection of received ideas was also echoed by the burgeoning sphere of popular music, which, in turn, in part, overlapped with the practice of recreational drug use and the combination produced a distinctive subculture, which was variously tagged, for example, as 'the alternative society'. It was partly carried by commerce (radio stations, theatres, record companies and fan magazines), partly carried by an illegal network of recreational drug smugglers and users (networks, shops selling relevant paraphernalia, magazines). All these elements were jumbled together to create a novel albeit internally differentiated social group comprising the young, blacks[6] and other assorted social activists, together, active critics of the status quo.

Changing mass media

Changing social mores were facilitated by new forms of media: broadcast and print. The number of television channels was increased – it remained a duopoly with the BBC and independent television (ITV) but now there were more channels (BBC2 and ITV2). In popular music the long-established Radio Luxembourg was joined by a number of pirate radio stations, all serving the burgeoning youth music scene. In print there were new youth magazines amongst a host of niche-targeted publications, whilst at the same time mainstream newspapers began to decline.

There were new audiences. As rising prosperity meant more people with disposable incomes, they were the available audiences for established consumption forms and for new ones – overseas holidays – or car ownership or new styles of cooking – and more channels meant more chances to acknowledge these new groups. And, in broadcasting, there were new editorial and commercial lines; in part, the decline of the Reithian ethos of high-minded provision; and in part, simply flowing from the fact of more diversity in the products offered.

Contingent circumstances

Tracking changes in political culture is not straightforward and one temptation must be resisted, the inclination to see progressive patterns, for many of the changes were occasioned by concatenations of circumstances, that is, there was no essential logic, merely contingent events:[7] the Vietnam War, the Civil Rights Movement and the youth or democratic movement. Many commentators have marked generational change, picking out those born shortly after the Second World War as the post-war baby boomers. All the social changes noted above are routinely summed in terms of the idea of the baby-boom generation. The term designates those born in the late 1940s and early 1950s in those countries materially untouched or relatively untouched by the war, the sphere of liberal market capitalism. A cultural coherence is imputed to this demographic set. This generation was lucky, enjoying peace, welfare, money and burgeoning life chances (not just increased consumption) and as the imputed identity would have it, they were ill disposed to the passive receipt of established ideas, preferring personal and cultural experimentation. And whilst these claims need unpacking, for they are contested, thus whilst some looked to personal or cultural experimentation, it might be guessed that more looked merely to enjoy what one theorist in the 1960s tagged as 'high mass consumption', it remains the case that this demographic was associated with significant material and moral change.

One area of change was sought by the Civil Rights Movement in the USA. Its concern was with the practical emancipation of black Americans; nominally equal they had been subject to routine discrimination, in particular in the Southern States. The movement was constructed around the leadership of Martin Luther King and sought through mass peaceful protest to upgrade the status of black Americans. It was met with violence in some Southern States but it also drew support from young people across the United States. It became an example of the possibilities and costs of direct social action oriented towards a compelling goal and one that demanded no more than that the country's constitution to be respected with equality before the law. And, at the time, the USA was the cultural model for much of the West. Not merely a Cold War bloc-leader promulgating bloc-think, but a genuine model of a rich, creative, democratic society. Consequently, the Civil Rights Movement had a very wide audience. Thus the example was widely influential around the West and it encouraged a concern for social activism. It was copied in Northern Ireland in the late 1960s where Catholics sought to use the model as a vehicle to secure an analogous acknowledgment of their rights as citizens of Britain and – as in the Southern States – these peacefully presented demands provoked a hostile reaction from the established Protestant ascendency. The Northern Ireland Civil Rights Movement occasioned a series of reactions, including riots, house burnings, population relocations, the use of the British military, the reinvention of armed republican paramilitary forces, the British security services' collusion with Protestant paramilitaries and – in all – a 30-odd year low-level dirty war. It was mostly confined to Northern Ireland, but also spilled over onto the main island where republican bombing campaigns caused something of a mixed reaction: first, state condemnation, widespread hostility towards those responsible for planting bombs coupled to stereotyping resident Irish; plus, second, a countercurrent of opinion routinely vilified by the state, which called for negotiations with the paramilitaries and their political masters with a view to a long-term settlement, including an indication that the British state was not irrevocably committed to maintaining its juridical sovereignty over the territory.[8]

Wars of colonial withdrawal figured strongly in the 1950s and 1960s: notably, the British, French, Belgians, Portuguese and, crucially, the USA. In all, these wars marked the slow final disintegration of the European state empires. The earliest withdrawals were in Asia, later Africa. Many withdrawals were accompanied by violence. This was true of the withdrawal of the British from their extensive overseas territories. The British left India in short order at the end of the 1940s, a precipitous withdrawal that left the communal violence of Partition in its wake. Similarly, the British left Burma, which promptly collapsed into civil war. The British fought two counterinsurgency wars in Southeast Asia, which ran on from the mid-1940s to the mid-1960s in Malaya (against erstwhile Communist Party allies) and Malaysia (against an Indonesian claim to territories on the island of Borneo). All these events were wrapped up in a strand of the national past, which presented the shift from empire to Commonwealth as smooth and agreed. Compulsory national service ended in 1960 and these low-level wars drifted out of mainstream public consciousness.

All that said; the violence that attended British withdrawal was mild compared to the disasters, which overcame first the French and then the Americans in Vietnam. These wars remained firmly in the public eye, in the United States and Europe. The French fought two catastrophic wars of colonial retreat: first, in Vietnam, until the mid-1950s, and then, later, in Algeria in the 1950s and early 1960s. The damage caused to the participants in Vietnam, Algeria and metropolitan France was considerable: material losses, many casualties and an experience of ordered violence that marked all three societies. In the mid-1950s the French withdrew from Vietnam only to be followed by the deployment of US power in the form of money, influence, arms and eventually an army of 0.5 million men. So far as the West in the 1960s was concerned, it was to be the American's war in Vietnam that was to dominate the public sphere.

It was a major preoccupation in the USA from the mid-1960s onwards and given the role of the USA in the Western alliance, it was a major public issue for many other countries. In the United States young people, in particular those eligible for the draft, reacted strongly against the war and notwithstanding an army of 0.5 million deployed in Vietnam the protests did have an impact. In the media images were available in uncensored print and broadcast photojournalism,[9] and film material was available in broadcast media. The war was made a topic of popular music and the occasion for criticism of politicians as dishonest – a novel theme then, familiar now – and the episode also encouraged a more general political activism, and this in turn created further images, thus, for example, photographs of students shot dead by the National Guard at Kent State University, and later, in time, it produced a number of fine exercises in film.[10]

Finally, these social changes had one more contemporaneous expression in the youth-cum-democracy movement. Broadly speaking, social activism became familiar during this era. It marked it out from the 1950s with its largely acquiescent populations enjoying their novel prosperity and the more fraught and eventually subdued periods that followed, with populations increasingly sceptical about mainstream politics, inclined to join single-issue groups and turn to populist parties or individuals. One aspect of burgeoning youth culture of the 1960s was an emphatic affirmation of the ideal of democracy: in the USA, for the poor and blacks; in Germany, via critiques of the politics of Chancellor Adenaeur's government and the many silences about the National Socialist period; and in France, in the guise of reactions against an analogous patrician conservatism associated with the figure of de Gaulle.

All this was echoed in Britain albeit in a veiled, distorted fashion, as the two main parties dominating the formal political landscape were both conservative but nonetheless carried on a vigorous schedule of ritual public squabbling. Thus the patrician conservatives saw no need for democratic reform (institutions were best tested over the years, not designed by enthusiasts and so the received machineries of the British state were broadly speaking fine).[11] On the other hand, the subaltern conservatives agreed, seeing only the need to turn extant machineries towards the needs of the respectable lower/middle classes, so political reform was understood in terms of ameliorist welfare provision. Arguments for democratization found little purchase in the political mainstream and at the margins the socialist/communist left were weak, so too the rump of the old liberal party, too weak to force change, as was, at this time, the market-liberal wing of the conservative party, which, in the 1980s, was to drive through a thoroughly market-liberal agenda as once again arguments for democracy were set aside.

Themes in the public sphere: Criticism and calls for action

The experience of post-war affluence provided many not only with a sense of security and comfort in their own lives but also disposed them to involvement in debates within the public sphere. Further impetus to such involvement was provided by the sequence of more specific episodes noted above – civil rights, war, youth and the like. At this time, a number of general themes emerged, some of which found subsequent expression and which run on down into the present – these are ideas that became part of a popular tradition – available for subsequent use and reuse.

General themes: Doubt, criticism, change and action

One counterpart to the decline in deference was an increase in available social doubt: it flowed from an appreciation amongst significant sections of the population that it was no longer clear that the old established elite knew how to plot a route to the future. Familiar claims in respect of the polity, its character, its direction, were called into question. This could be specific, hence the Doors singing 'tell me lies about Vietnam', some was more general, thus baby boomers looked at the world of welfare and consumption, which they took for granted, and opined that going forwards it was not enough, that is, they insisted that life had to mean more than basic security and material ease.

The fading of deference towards established elites was paralleled by a rise in public criticism: there was a clear understanding amongst broad swathes of the subaltern classes that the social world need no longer be approached in deferential mode; not politically, not socially, not in terms of personal ethics and crucially not intellectually. Numerous groups offered critiques of extant states of affairs: some were to become influential (feminists); others were to become significant (social reformers); some were an irrelevance (the hippies, much loved by the media); whilst others were to become influential years later (ecologists – greens). One group, widely disregarded at this time, came to dominate the latter decades of the century, namely the market-liberals with their plans for rolling back the state, freeing enterprise, letting the market rule and so on.

Somewhat more broadly, there was a widespread celebration of change; thus the media insisted that economic advance had precipitated social and cultural change and so now change was a defining characteristic of the era. Illustrations were quickly found: in the United States, in January 1961, J.F. Kennedy became president and many invested their hopes for the future in his presidency; in Britain, in October 1964, Harold Wilson became prime minister and spoke of progressive change being driven by advances in science and technology. All celebrated, one way or another, promise for the future carried on economic success. Change was read optimistically.

And finally there was an oft-stated preference for action: numerous groups in society evidenced a widespread appreciation of the possibilities of action and there was a corresponding inclination amongst individuals towards becoming involved. Self-conscious critical social groups sought to do something: feminism began as intellectual critique and became the creed of a political movement; social reformers were active and effective in regard to poverty, domestic and international;

hippies sought an alternative lifestyle, thereby providing the majority with entertainment (mostly via a frisson of low-level fear as the current folk devils (earlier incumbents of that role had ridden motorcycles or motor scooters, adopted distinctive styles of dress and staged mass brawls along Brighton beach)).[12]

Symbolic episodes read into the public sphere

As the decade unfolded a number of events were read into the public sphere which came to have a symbolic quality. These events/stories were taken to exemplify the condition of England or played an equivalent role in some other country, thereafter reported in Britain.

(i) In Britain

The 1960s saw a mixture of deep-seated advance – the continuation of the post-war long boom together with a series of signal events – occasions when economic or social or cultural or political change was widely remarked.

(a) The Beatles' first LP. It was released in early 1963.[13] The album changed popular music. It signalled the rise of new domestic variants of American blues-derived popular music. It gave rise to a new social prominence for popular music itself as the media invented a style of response tagged 'Beatlemania'. Hanif Kureshi[14] later commented that the significance of the Beatles was that they taught their audiences to write their own songs, that is, popular music was in effect directed towards some sort of authenticity in treating the local scene – places, people, their preoccupations. The contrast was with the inauthentic production line of imported US music and its local copies. Jenny Diski[15] remarks in her memoir of the 1960s that the music was good even if much else later became tarnished one way or another. The music drew in other figures: the actor Peter Sellers[16] doing a spoken version of a Lennon-McCartney song; John Betjeman releasing a music-backed version of his own poetry; Philip Larkin[17] using the date to bookend the putative discovery of sexual intercourse in his poetry.

(b) Cathy Come Home. The BBC broadcast *The Wednesday Play* and Ken Loach's 1966 play tells the story of a young couple with children who through no fault of their own lose their house, thereafter slowly sliding down the housing/welfare ladder until they end up sleeping rough. The play caused a political sensation. It provoked the establishment of charity groups oriented towards helping the destitute

124 Britain After Empire

and it provoked the state into reviewing and updating its welfare provisions. It was a cathartic tale, provoking effective action and long remembered.

(c) Abortion Law reform. David Steel's private members bill to reform the law on abortion was in retrospect one of the two most significant parliamentary secured reforms of the 1960s for abortion law reform, together with technical improvements in contraception (in particular, 'the pill') and shaped by changing social mores, gave women power over their own fertility. The Abortion Act 1967 was seen then as socially progressive and it was disputed by religious conservatives. The impact was great and it reinforced a political-cultural environment favouring reforms.

(d) Homosexual Law reform. Leo Abse's sponsorship of the Sexual Offences Act 1967 which decriminalized homosexual relationships was the second significant reform; decriminalization freed a significant element of the population from fear of persecution – and perhaps prosecution – and in turn it paved the way for ideas of 'gay liberation' – the call for equality of respect for gays.[18]

(e) Student rebellions. There were sit-ins and demonstrations in 1968 at Hornsea College of Art and in 1969 at the London School of Economics. Borrowing ideas and action from the mainland, students at these and other colleges of higher education staged demonstrations and sit-ins aimed at their institutions – demands for reforms to structure of governance were made – roughly, an end to top-down management and presumptions of in loco parentis authority, which thereafter were to be replaced by voluntary classes (and other forms of autonomously determined learning) and the development on the part of the college authorities of a habit of regarding and treating its students as adults. These demands were dressed in the rhetoric of wider social change, and although these demands were often mild they were usually resisted by college authorities.

(f) Feminist critiques of the gender status quo. The publication of Germaine Greer's 1970 book *The Female Eunuch* opened up to a wide public gaze the ideas of feminism and the claim to female repression and the demand for equality. A number of other books were published around the same time, including Kate Millett's 1970 *Sexual Politics*, Erica Jong's 1973 *Fear of Flying* and a little earlier Doris Lessing's 1962 *The Golden Notebook*,[19] and all spoke, one way or another, to the theme

of female experience as a species of human experience conjoined to the demand for equality. These texts entered the mainstream, that is, they were not books relegated to the ghetto of women's books and they picked up on long familiar themes. Simone de Beauvoir had reopened debates begun earlier in the century and reaching back into the earliest years of the modern period, but this time around they had affluence and fertility control available to buttress/cushion their arguments, and they fed into legislation for equal pay and they fed into legislation outlawing discrimination on the basis of gender.

(ii) In the USA

The Civil Rights March: the campaign for black equality reached one climactic moment in the march held in Washington in 1963, it was a major social/political movement in the 1960s and it drew in many reformers. The Reverend Martin Luther King gave a speech, which contained a number of resonant phrases, including: 'I have a dream...'.

Violence overseas: the experience of military violence suffused the international activities of the American state during the 1960s, crucially the foreign war in Vietnam. American troops landed in numbers at Da Nang in March 1965 and as they marched up the beach they were greeted by serried ranks of news photographers and thereafter news photographers were given free rein to move around the country as they pleased. They produced a flow of startling uncensored images of the war in Vietnam. The basic frame was set early and became a cliché: verdant green landscapes splashed with the yellows and reds of exploding ordnance as a very beautiful country is subject to the savagery of high-tech weapons. These sorts of images showed the domestic American population something of the nature of the war and it contributed to a growing revulsion against the war. There were some key images: a young girl burned by napalm,[20] the summary execution of Vietcong,[21] photographs of bodies scattered amongst ruined buildings or damaged plantations or despoiled farmland and numerous shots of napalm and other ordnance exploding against backdrops of beautiful tropical green landscapes.[22]

Violence at home: the American polity was suffused with political violence during this period and there were a number of political assassinations: J.F. Kennedy in November 1963, Martin Luther King in April 1968 and Robert Kennedy in June 1968. The first was a significant political event as it brought L.B. Johnson to the presidency. And it was a reverberating politicalcultural shock: that a US president could be assassinated in the late twentieth century; that a president as seemingly gifted as JFK could be the target of an assassin; and that the judicial authorities could handle the aftermath so poorly (thus the assassination of the chief suspect[23] and the popular doubts about the report of the Warren Commission).

Urban violence: the period also saw a sequence of urban riots, notably, in the Watts district of Los Angeles (August 1965), at the Democratic Convention in Chicago in August 1968 and at Kent State in May 1970 when four students were shot dead by national guardsmen.

The impact of these episodes of violence, which figured prominently in the media, was to begin a slow transformation of the popular image of the United States held in Europe. The country had been a cultural model in the post-war period, but from the 1960s onwards, for a great number of people that ceased to be the case. This situation obtained until the high tide of the 1980s/1990s neo-liberal era when a US centred on finance became a model, albeit for a small segment of the population, in particular, financiers and politicians in London.[24]

(iii) In Europe

France and Paris May 1968: student protests brought the country to the edge of a revolutionary change of government. In the early months of the year there were a number of student-centred demonstrations but these were subdued by the efforts of the labour movement (demanding pay rises) and President de Gaulle (calling an election). Other commentators have said that the key to the end of the events was the arrival of summer, when the students went home or on holiday.

Germany and Bader-Meinhof (1967–72): German politics in the 1950s had been dominated by the conservative figure of Konrad Adenauer and his successors followed in his tracks. Dissenting groups styled themselves an extra-parliamentary opposition and began a low-level campaign of violence for which there was some sympathy amongst sections of the population. Nonetheless, the state reacted as might be expected with suppression and over time the members of the group were imprisoned or killed.

Italy and the Red Brigades: Italian society in the 1950s saw rising prosperity and it also saw the establishment of a seemingly permanent conservative right-wing government. The political party was the Christian Democrat Party and they had links to business and the Catholic Church and they were backed by the USA. The left wing was marginalized. In time, as in Germany, an extraparliamentary opposition was formed and the conservative right responded not only with the machinery of the state but also with right-wing terrorist attacks. The end of the Cold War coupled to judges uncovering the scale of corruption in the mainstream conservative parties meant the 'years of lead' were at an end and a more familiar liberal democratic parliamentary politics was thereafter pursued.[25]

Idea of alternatives: Press, music and film

There were many political and social groups during this period which offered lines of analysis or diagnosis or practice that were at variance to mainstream ideas and procedures – that these ideas were different was reflexively embraced – difference was good itself – the idea that summed this attitude as that of the 'alternative'. It came in many varieties: claims were made in respect of economics (that the market-based pursuit of ever-rising levels of consumption was criticized as neither possible nor desirable); claims were made in respect of society (that consumerism plus the nuclear family had undermined both community and individual moral/creative autonomy); and claims were made about culture (that vacuous consumerism veiled widespread alienation). The most all-embracing variant was a claim to an 'alternative society'.

In respect of the business of livelihood, the period saw the rise of environmentalism where ideas taken from natural scientists and social activists fed the nascent public environmental agenda. At first a concern for a small group of social critics but later these ideas spawned an influential political movement: political parties devoted to environmental issues were established and their thinking (and policy proposals) became widely acknowledged. As the sciences of environmental impact and climate change developed, it became clear that these alternative critics had been correct in their general diagnosis.[26]

In the matter of alternative society, the period was sympathetically disposed to experimentation. Some of the experimentation was evident in social behaviour: in social forms (communes), social mores (liberal attitudes to sex) and social styles (fashions). Some of this caught the attention of the mainstream, but it was easily ignored. Some of the experimentation looked to alternative states of consciousness. And here two strands can be identified: respectable and non-respectable. First, a more or less respectable line involving psychiatry, where in some cases recourse was made to the therapeutic use of psychotropic drugs and as a spin-off work was pursued in the realm of anti-psychiatry where the proposed alternative was not a drug-induced state but a change in social attitudes towards those persons exhibiting non-standard behaviour; in this last noted, the figures of R.D. Laing, Thomas Szasz and Michel Foucault.[27] Then second a non-respectable line which involved the use of psychotropic drugs not only for therapeutic reasons in the context of psychiatric dialogues between doctors and patients but much more widely within the general social world as a means to facilitate moral and aesthetic growth in people; in this last noted, Timothy Leary.[28]

In the realm of culture there was an alternative press: activists established grass-roots newspapers and magazines. Sometimes these were produced by social activists engaged in community work. Some magazines focused on the popular music scene. One distinctive form of grass-roots magazine looked to serve the alternative society, mixing music, politics and recreational drug use (thus, *International Times* and *Oz*). There was also alternative music: the period saw a self-conscious reaction against the mainstream music industry. New small-scale record labels appeared. Artists insisted on using their own material. Some labels succeeded,[29] many bands succeeded and many others failed. And some directors could be labelled alternative in film:[30] the period saw film directors offering self-conscious critiques of society and a number of people made their names around this time: Ken Russell,[31] Michelangelo Antonioni,[32] Lindsay Anderson,[33] Nicholas Roeg – and others.

In the end, the general claims to an alternative society did not survive the 1960s; they faded into the collective memory of the baby-boom generation and were more generally forgotten or if remembered then dismissed. However, some strands of alternative thinking did survive although the form might be rather different from any original utopian expectations.

Idea of the New Left

The idea of the New Left developed in the 1950s. It was a strand of Marxist analysis and opinion. The magazine of that name developed out of the *New Reasoner* and the *Universities and Left Review*.[34] The magazine rooted its work in the traditions of Marx but it was independent of any established political party and was therefore free to explore various strands of thinking. The intellectual curiosity embraced by the magazine meant that it was often engaged with ideas at the cutting edge of social and political thought. During the 1950s and 1960s there were a number of major thinkers working in or with reference to this tradition.[35] These, in turn, informed its broad political commentary. Stefan Collini[36] comments on the work of the New Left, in particular those surrounding the journal *New Left Review*. Noting the Anderson-Nairn thesis (the failure of British-based intellectuals to adequately and critically theorize their society as a result of the failure of the bourgeoisie to remove the pre-modern social forms (landed power)) and its left-wing critics such as E.P. Thompson, he unpacks the subsequent debates, diagnosing a preoccupation with the ability of the elite to sustain itself in power.

Stuart Hall[37] tracks the emergence of the journal in 1960 from earlier journals produced in the 1950s, when the Cold War was raging, with the aim of providing a space for informed, principled left political analysis (not the Labour Party and not the Communist Party, both variously discredited in the eyes of New Left supporters). The magazine has been intellectually influential. It introduced the work of mainland European thinkers to an otherwise somewhat insular audience amongst the left in Britain. Others followed – in publishing and journalism[38] – with, for example, *Marxism Today*'s discussion of Post-Fordist 'New Times'.

Wider issues: High culture, popular culture and the state/corporate sphere

The 1960s saw significant changes in general public discourse. A disparate spread of novel issues were addressed. Some of these were narrowly political, thus the softening of elite attempts at explicit top-down control and the concomitant recognition of subaltern lives; others more abstract, thus the issue of authenticity or the proliferation of images throughout the public sphere.

End of elite censorship of high culture

The 1960 trial of the D.H. Lawrence's novel *Lady Chatterley's Lover*[39] and the later abolition of theatre censorship (Theatres Act 1968) ended attempts by a patrician elite to regulate what the masses could and could not see. The abolition of censorship in the theatre plus a related relaxed attitude towards sex/violence on the part of the film-censorship board meant that the contribution to public discourse of these art forms was – at least in principle – much richer as themes otherwise too awkward to deal with were successfully presented, but of course the abolition of censorship opened the way not merely to the arts but also to violence and pornography.[40]

Celebration of subaltern lives and art

The opening for a positive treatment of the lives of subaltern classes had been made in the 1950s by the plays and novels of the so-called angry young men. New work was also done by social scientists. It is true that work had always been done – reaching back to Friedrich Engels – on the condition of the working classes, but now the focus changed, not just their poverty (anyway mitigated by the impact of welfare-state provisions) but more generally their form of life, now acknowledged, described, here and there celebrated and here and there routinized.

One strand of such work was found in 'community studies'; thus, famously, Young and Willmott[41] on the working classes in the East End of London, whose ethnographic approach was repeated for communities in many other cities. This work continues and it sits easily with the overall evolutionist and ameliorist tone of much of the social science produced in Britain. Another strand of work was intellectually more radical. The invention of cultural studies presented an idea, which subsequently gained wide international recognition and whilst the starting point was similar, the line of travel was quite different. The work of Richard Hoggart and Stuart Hall focused on the lives of subaltern classes and the ways in which such local cultures intersected with the demands placed upon them by the wider social system. It opened up a new area of enquiry – the intellectual and moral resources of the local community could be detailed and their complex intersections with the demands of wider systems unpacked; the field of cultural studies was concerned to map these shifting patterns of power and understanding.

In Hoggart's case the work was suffused with a distinctive moral sensitivity, as the work was both ethnographic and critical in that the moral worlds of the subaltern classes were valued and judged, not in their own terms, for Hoggart was writing as a middle-class university professor, but in subaltern radical terms[42] and not the moral schedules of the elite. Hoggart[43] looks at the commercial popular press and identifies both entertainment (people buy and enjoy them) and cultural degradation (simplification, cliché and thus loss of meaning) but the traffic is not all one way, local communities do generate authentic experience, so the commercially carried dross does not sweep all before it. In this analysis, Hoggart opens up the area of cultural studies. It points to the realms of ordinary life, which both generate their own meanings and through which meanings prepared by the powerful (political or corporate) flow, to interact with locally generated ideas, producing what might be termed an 'acquiescent little tradition'.[44] Stefan Collini[45] discusses the work of Richard Hoggart, mentions F.R. Leavis and Raymond Williams, identifies a common thread in a concern for the value of literature and finally tags Hoggart not as a cultural analyst (as they have on the mainland) but rather as working within a long tradition of English moralists concerned with the state of the population (along with Ruskin, Lawrence, Cobbett and Orwell). Then, finally, in contrast, in Hall's case there is a more explicit recourse to Marx and to the experience of inward migration and race. Hall's work was more overtly engaged with political life, characterizing elite political projects, unpacking their impacts upon ordinary people and looking for ways in which the subaltern classes might reply.[46]

And, if the work above was positive, the more liberal style of the public sphere of the late 1950s and 1960s made space for negative work: tabloid journalism and tabloid television looked at that same area of social life – subaltern classes – and produced banal material (soap opera, thus the long-running *Coronation Street*), distracting material (newspapers devoted to scandals amongst celebrities of one sort or another) and in due course straightforwardly exploitative material (reality television shows of one sort or another). In all these, one way or another, the subaltern class were an object – a mere audience segment.

Issue of authenticity

One issue that derived from wider changes was that of authenticity. It is an old theme in studies of the media-carried public sphere where there are concerns for promise/performance measured against an abstract model of a democratic polity. In the 1960s these established concerns were revisited and there were a number of contributions to the overall issue: the angry young men had introduced doubts about the ideas and ethics of the elite; working-class novelists had insisted that subaltern thought was worth attention; young people, exercised by overseas wars and domestic problems, were sharp in their criticism of the alleged hypocrisies of elites and other figures of authority; and intellectuals and commentators discovered mainland authors, thus Kierkegaard or Sartre.

So authenticity became an issue. A few examples can be mentioned: first, economic prosperity plus change plus war generated political engagement amongst subaltern groups – middle class and working class – a concern for 'getting on' or 'protecting one's position' and this was authentic, if self-interested and occasionally unseemly; second, the media plus indulgent consumption generated 'hippies'; a wholly inauthentic confection contrived by lazy journalists, irresponsible editors and passed on to a gullible readership (a contemporary variant of the media irresponsibly amplifying anxieties would be all the talk of 'terrorism' and 'radical Islamists' – in this case the initial anxieties were created by the political classes); third, the media plus popular music generated both authentic and inauthentic work; plus there was one influential deployment of the concern for authenticity to be found in the fashion for satire,[47] readily available in the late 1950s and early 1960s, the key instance being the BBC's *TW3*.

An image-drenched social world

As images are as old as humans, thus cave paintings from 20,000 or 30,000 years ago, a history of images could be sketched. It would be a record of the evolving social construction of images – manufacture, distribution and consumption: in Europe, the oldest images are the cave paintings found in southern France; thereafter, moving from pre-history into history (when written records became available), in the pre-industrial era, image-making would be a matter of elite concern, domestic decoration aside, in a public role, particularly associated with religious institutions and themes (thus sacred texts for the clergy or churches filled with images designed to instruct the non-literate masses); then as the industrial era unfolded, image-making and use expanded (cheap printing plus new colours from chemists and a growing reading public); and today image-making is available to anyone with a cameraphone.[48]

The modern world is now an image-drenched environment: newspapers and magazines, television and our private domestic accumulations of photographs, paintings, prints and the like. Images today are available in multiple forms. Images can be created in various ways (lots of different media and techniques). Images can be deployed in various ways (means of dissemination). And images can be deployed with various intentions in mind, for example, to argue, to entertain, to inform, to deceive, to persuade, to advise, to exhort and so on. One film released during the 1960s encapsulated this aspect of the period – the film *Blow Up*[49] – the movie recorded a photographer accidentally capturing a murder – after some time he elects to leave matters as they are – that is, the murder is left merely as an image – thus it is proposed that the period was drenched in images and that images were both important and could substitute for action, in this case, simple neglect of moral duties.

In the collective social environment of political communities, self-conscious images can be placed in the public sphere (making argument) and they can shape the public sphere (impact, repetition and habituation). These processes are not straightforward. First, most images are top-down, that is, elite groups of one sort or another make and deploy the images (states, corporate world or organized groups such as political parties) and such elite groups have an ambiguous relationship with the creators of art, that is, artists. Then, second, the status of artists shifts and changes from craftspeople, to the individual genius (perhaps working alone in a garret room – the romantic variant) or as players involved in the art market (dealers and galleries and patrons). And third, typically, the mass of ordinary people are not invited to join in the production and dissemination of images – often they are merely audience – however, ordinary people do construct their own images – thus folk art, or naïve art, or graffiti – subaltern messages deployed in the public sphere. Then, fourth, there is a further realm of image-making – corporate world messages directed towards the consumer market: technical and manipulative images can be used to constitute a quasi-public sphere or a parallel-public sphere – the imaginary realms conjured by pervasive advertising imagery – life as it should be lived (consumption); related images are built into 'brands' – the companies promote themselves and their products; and generally, the social impact is profound – the replacement of repression by seduction means that these images are significant to the economic/political system.

So, in the public sphere, images mix – top-down, grass roots and commercial – and a balance is struck, typically, but not inevitably, favouring the elite. Nonetheless, images deployed in the public sphere can be unpacked and analysed in terms of the trio of elements: *context* – what was the context within which the image was made – social (what was the real-world situation) – political (what issues concerned players) and – technical (what were the available media (how could images be made/deployed)); *theorist* – what ideas about aesthetics did the theorist have, what skills (technical issues of handling the media in question) and what ideology (ideas about the social/political world); and *audience* – what audiences were addressed, as reading publics or viewing publics and how they understood and responded to the proffered messages (accept, reject, misread or reread).

The political intent/result of such images varies:[50] images can serve a positive political purpose, thus, in a familiar example, they can serve to *construct a national idea*; and, contrariwise, images can serve a *critical political purpose* when they are produced or used by various dissenting groups in order to undermine the world-taken-for-granted of their community, where the implication of such activity is that there must be other ways in which social and political arrangements could be organized. And – running alongside – the corporate world feeds in a plethora of images – designed, in total, to manipulate the population, celebrating consumption.

A number of examples of positive work are available. First, in fine-art painting, using images of dead soldiers and sailors as heroes in the process of the creation of the British Empire where they take the form of pietas: Nelson at Trafalgar or Woolf at Quebec. In a similar fashion, using Canaletto's paintings to represent London-as-Venice,[51] thereafter celebrating the empire. Many images of newly acquired territories were reproduced for metropolitan core consumption.[52] Second, later, with new techniques of photography further image production/distribution was possible: recording events, early on, in still images, the American Civil War, later, in moving images, the First World War, then the Second World War. The images distributed at the time were shaped to carry messages of optimism (the archives became available later, and looking at this material now misleads as to what was available to masses at the time). And, third, the equivalent today, might be the film from embedded journalists covering wars (recently, Falklands, Iraq or Afghanistan).[53] All these images run through a simple sequence – impact, repetition and habituation – and the messages carried in the images become part of the mental furniture of their audiences. If they function, then they function in this way; habituation is read as legitimation, and if the images don't work, then they simply fade into the cultural background.[54]

A number of examples of critical work are available. First, the use of political satire where there is a long tradition of image making: two examples in Britain, James Gillray and Gerald Scarfe. Gillray worked during the during the late eighteenth and early nineteenth century and made prints that appeared in magazines and sold directly to the general public: two targets, first, the upper classes and the Royal Family around George III who are depicted generally as dissolute, and second, Napoleon who is depicted as dangerous. And then Gerald Scarfe, who belongs to the mid twentieth and early twenty-first century, also made prints with multiple targets: politicians, individuals, social habits and so on. These images run through a simple sequence – impact and repetition – satire cannot work if the messages it presents become habituated (retelling the same joke does not work, rather target and audience are degraded – routine and familiarity absorb the moral and aesthetic force and clarity, and undermine the spontaneity and genuineness of any response). Again, messages can be accepted, rejected or modified as neither positive nor critical messages translate neatly into practical action by addressees. Second, the use of satire in fine art: two examples from Germany, Georg Grosz and Otto Dix. Thus Grosz, working in the early/mid-twentieth century, made paintings offering critiques of modern society (disorganized, corrupt and failing) and conservative political figures (presented as useless or worse). And Otto Dix, again working in the early/mid-twentieth century, produced work offering critiques of the effects of the First World War (contrasting war-wounded with content bourgeoisie) and critiques of contemporary society (depicted as class divided).[55] And then third, the later use of photojournalism, thus the iconic photograph of the burned girl in Vietnam. Or, fourth, mainstream film, for example, a number of films treat colonial life, war and Cold War in Southeast Asia,[56] or, again, the making of critical films for public television (BBC's *The War Game* – and as film is an industry-based activity, so many people are involved – some have veto powers – this film was not shown).

A number of examples of corporate world images might be mentioned. Corporate world images are produced in great quantity, producing thereby a densely filled quasi-public sphere oriented towards consumption. Advertising images are oriented towards the creation of wants and contemporary lived-experience is flooded by such imagery. Formally, consumption is engineered in a variety of ways: blurring images (living/consuming); blurring messages (choice/freedom); blurring genres (commerce/art); blurring truth (enquiry/brands). Substantively, schematically, a trajectory can be sketched: in the nineteenth century there are the beginnings of consumer life and the creation of advertisements; in the twentieth century consumer life is established and celebrated – advertising is used to create brands, sophisticated imagery blurs the distinctions between art and commerce (thus: London Underground posters, both commerce and art; Andy Warhol's use of advertising material as art, contributing to the creation of pop art; recently, the United Colours of Benetton's use of art-house photographs as advertisements). And now, in the twenty-first century the proliferation of images continues – now digital, now carried by the internet and networks of mobile devices.

In sum, now, the current situation sees a multiplicity of image-makers placing material in the public sphere: elite images are presented in the public sphere; subaltern messages are presented in the public sphere; and corporate messages are presented in the public sphere. The public sphere is now image drenched, perhaps saturated.

Running down to the present: Legacies and repetitions

There are many debates about the period of the 1960s and disentangling transient youthful self-advertisement ('counterculture') or equally transient media confections ('hippies') from local activist achievement (the Civil Rights Movement or recovery of historical memory in Germany[57] or reforms to universities) and enduring social changes achieved within the mainstream (abandonment of censorship or abortion law reform in Britain) is not straightforward as these various strands of argument, image-making and action were all intertwined. Tony Judt[58] notes the demographic change, the rise in the number of young people amongst the population, notes their rebellion in style (clothes, music and so on, adding that it wasn't just trivial)[59] and their rediscovery of radical politics (amongst intellectuals and students, where the actual working class were typically union or church organized, welfare oriented and politically quiescent). Judt notes that their disparate calls for political reform did have merit in that they helped remove the political generation that had come to power immediately after the war years. These characteristics were repeated in various mixtures throughout Western Europe. And, at the same time in the East, there was modest prosperity and there were also rumblings of discontent with a political system imposed after the war years. The suppression of the Prague Spring in 1968 ended hopes of reform for 20-odd years, until the autumn of 1989. Overall, the legacy of the 1960s was a broad social liberalization: figures in authority were no longer so readily accepted by the mass of the population; and a number of crucial specific legal reforms were made in which the situation of women in particular was significantly improved (even if the matter of equality remains in some respects an ongoing project).

Against these achievements, which are taken for granted at the start of the twenty-first century, there is one area of failure, that is, that little was achieved in terms of institutional reform and dissenting groups – from utopian proponents of alternative societies to natural science-based rational groups of environmentalists – remained shut out.[60] The notion of an alternative society flagged the existence of an oppositional subculture with its distinctive arts and social mores; one aspect of which was the increasing use of recreational drugs, a mix of hedonism and mysticism. The recreational drug use within these circles could be directed towards either pole – hedonism and/or mysticism – and these orientations unpacked differently down the years. The hedonism was no great threat to the status quo (state authorities outlawed the trade in recreational drugs and sought to suppress their use whilst the existing and politically influential alcohol industry eventually replied to the threat to its markets with 'alcopops', 'shot-bars' and 'happy hours' with the mass media happy to run scare stories about recreational drugs in order to secure markets and advertising revenues). Perhaps surprisingly, the mysticism was, in places, more of a threat, overlapping with the early environmental movement and modulating into today's green movement, it called attention to the place of people in the natural world and urged the creation of an appreciation of this deep-connectedness. It thus contributed to the development of an effective critique of mass-consumer capitalism (and it was helped by one marvellous image produced by a NASA spacecraft of a very beautiful blue-green earth hanging in the darkness of space). It might also be added that in other places it became one more sphere of consumer tat, thus health/healing products, candles, bath salts, crystals, massage oils and so on; much of it now available in local supermarkets.

Jenny Diski[61] presents a memoir of the period, detailing the optimism and the hedonism; she rues the collapse of the decades' rhetorical preoccupation with 'freedom' into the neo-liberal market-ism of Thatcher. But Diski celebrates the music and suggests that the generation that participated in the events were lucky for on the one hand they inherited the benefits of the long boom and on the other they escaped the worst of the economic/social stress of the following neo-liberal years. In sum, she suggests, the 1960s generation enjoyed a very long gap year.

8
Corporate World, Media and Politics

The post-war boom ran out of steam in the early 1970s as the coalition of political groups that had sustained the economic and social progress fractured and the corporate world, trade unions and the state dissolved their hitherto successful corporate-style habits of cooperation such that what had been a contested compromise was no longer a compromise as contestation came to the fore. The 1970s experience of stagflation created a political space for new players and the long building forces of the New Right took their chance, secured power and unrolled their neo-liberal project and the public sphere was filled with novel celebrations of enterprise, profit-making and calls for individual self-responsibility. Formal politics were drawn into the ambit of the corporate world both in terms of policy stances (privatization, deregulation and so on) and in terms of style thus politicians became celebrity figures, parties vote-getting machines. The established British elite prospered, other social groups managed as best they could and the general population bought into debt-fuelled consumerism, an engagement that was to deepen through most of the remaining years of the century.

The 1960s came to an end in the early 1970s. In Britain a mixture of ill-informed Keynesian economic policies plus complacent managements plus self-indulgent trades unions plus external shocks in the form of sharp rises in the price of oil all combined to usher in an era of 'stagflation' – a mixture of economic stagnation, that is, no or low economic growth plus price inflation (driven in part by raw material costs and in part by wage demands). Available economic theory said this wasn't possible and accordingly a new economic theory was sought. One group had arguments available and they moved to take their chance, unpacking their ideas both in technical terms (monetarism) and also in political terms (neo-liberalism). At the back of their proposals was a steadfast belief in the power of the uncluttered marketplace: given the chance to operate cleanly it would maximize a range of benefits for its participants, not merely material goods but also moral and intellectual benefits as individuals took responsibility for their own lives, lives now seen more clearly.

In Britain these theorists and their related networks of think-tanks, media commentators and political agents were tagged the New Right and from the late 1970s, after the Conservative Party government had defeated the discredited proto-monetarist government of James Callaghan, their neo-liberal project unfolded in a range of policy initiatives. However, it did not unfold in a smooth or unproblematic fashion – as subsequent commentators have been quick to point out – indeed, the reverse was the case for the early experiments in economic policy failed and the government was only rescued from deep unpopularity by the fortuitous accident of foreign military aggression against an obscure remnant of the now defunct state-empire system. After this episode the government was secure. Thereafter the state was deployed to weaken the post-war welfare settlement and strengthen the power of the corporate world with the changes legitimated in authoritarian populist terms (which noted the demands of the economic arithmetic, celebrated the power of entrepreneurial drive and targeted the resistance of the various enemies within). The proponents of the project drove it forwards energetically. Corporate world players saw a coincidence of interest between the possibilities for their businesses and the line of advance of the neo-liberals in government; state assets were sold off cheaply; and corporate media players fell in behind the neo-liberal political agents and the already energetic project was thereby further reinforced/energized.

Episode: The deployment of the neo-liberal project

The neo-liberal project directly challenged the post-war contested compromise, that particular mix of Keynesian-informed corporatism coupled to the ethos of welfare that had helped to order post-war recovery, both in respect of economic and social policy and with regard to overarching schemes of legitimation. The goals of state-secured full employment and extensive welfare transfers organized for the benefit of society in general were repudiated. In place of the collective pursuit of better lives for all, the neo-liberals called for rolling back the state and celebrating individual responsibility in the expectation that all would benefit. The free market would maximize a range of benefits;

material, moral, social and intellectual.[1] The proponents of this iconoclastic package happily accepted the inevitable consequence of greater social inequality.

These arguments were not new, indeed they were rooted in the late nineteenth century, and had been around in their contemporary guise since the wartime period, but by the early 1970s the post-war settlement, with its particular mix of ideas and social forces, was looking increasingly tired, the cohesion of its adherents was fraying (disputes within a social bloc embracing patrician reformers, cautious social democrats and assorted dissidents) and so too was the plausibility of its core message in respect of the managerial role of the state (claims to expertise and ethic looked intellectually insecure). So the economic and political difficulties of the mid-1970s offered critics an opportunity and a spread of ideas were presented in the public sphere by academics, think-tanks, newspapers, corporate lobby groups and party politicians, in which the liberal market figured centrally. All the ideas revolved one way or another around the proposition that the liberal marketplace needed to be reanimated in order to move the economy, society and polity forwards. Viewed positively, these ideas amounted to a celebration of individual freedoms, which in turn would encourage individual and collective benefits, but seen negatively, the same ideas amounted to little more than a celebration of selfishness,[2] which in the 1990s would modulate into a fashion for unrestrained greed.[3]

The dissolution of the post-war contested compromise

The political project of the elite in the years following the end of the Second World War comprised a mix of denial and confection, where the former dismissed the empire, casting that which had been lost as of little concern whilst the latter took the residual core of empire and reimagined it as the legatee of a long-established nation-state, or continuing Britain. The project's domestic concerns, that is, reconstruction, welfare and for a whilst the New Elizabethan Age, required a successful economy and in this regard policy became associated with the work of the political economist John Maynard Keynes.[4]

The intellectual and policy work undertaken in the 1930s by Keynes and others sought to rescue liberal market capitalism both from problems inherent in the system (specifically, in his terms, depression equilibrium) and from errors made by the policy-makers (government spending cuts, balanced budgets and corporate sector retrenchment). Keynes showed, contrary to neo-classical theory with its core notion of the self-regulating system, that economies could go into depression equilibrium, that is, assume a stable configuration which left both capital and labour underutilized. And he also showed, contrary to standard economic policy advice, which insisted that the state should balance its books, that is, not spend more than it raised in taxes, that deficit financing whereby the state raised debt in order to fund spending activities could be used to raise the general level of operation of an economy. Thus was Keynesianism born. It became the intellectual spine of a variant form of social democracy.

In Britain these ideas were put into practice in a particular context. The war years had seen the creation of a command economy oriented towards the production of goods for war fighting and this system had been organized not by market players but by the state. Thus the machinery of the state, plus private business plus trades unions were brought together in an integrated system of planned production.[5] With this recent experience a particular habit of thought grew such that whenever there were problems – economic or social – arguments were made that the state should take action and that state spending should be deployed. Moreover, as both major political parties bought into this pattern of thinking a kind of vulgar-Keynesianism emerged: state spending became a sovereign remedy for a multiplicity of policy problems. In the terms of later social science, it was an elaborate discourse. It presented a version of corporatism, where tripartite agreements at the elite level could serve the interests of the wider population. The whole endeavour was ordered around the activities of the state: in planning, financing and extensive activity in various sectors of production;[6] and thereafter it found expression within the public sphere and the social world more broadly.

However, the contested compromise was not stable. The state, employers and trade unions had different agendas: the former attempting to deal with the unacknowledged collapse of the state-empire system in which it had played a central role, or, in brief, find a role; the second noted group concerned to sustain an economic system which had in significant measure taken shape in the late nineteenth century (thus, major sectors of the economy were based in coal, steel, railways and ship-building, which were vulnerable to competition underpinned by technological advance, and the pattern of industrial location was similarly shaped by that period with particular areas of the country dominated by heavy industries and old established domestic and international markets were changing rapidly); and the final group, the trade unions, made powerful by the functional requirements of a war economy, sustained by a strong worker ethos, and by virtue of their association with the Labour Party, inclined to claim a privileged place in respect of the business of building and running the welfare state, were unprepared for changes in the economy which undermined their core areas of strength in heavy industries. Over time the ability of the system to deliver state-level rational policy slowly faded.[7] And, further, this domestic unclarity was then severely impacted by outside pressures: competition in hitherto safe export markets; competition from newly powerful economies; plus the impact of the early 1970s rise in oil prices.

The first noted was predictable for as the state-empire system dissolved away and as the US-inspired and centred global liberal trading sphere began to take shape, those trading relationships which the British metropolitan core had enjoyed with various peripheral territories were bound to come under pressure. Newly independent states could buy wherever they wished and so too could those countries that had been part of the broad swathe of informal empire, territories, for example, in Latin America that now turned to their powerful northern neighbour. Of course, patterns of trade did not change over night, but within a marketplace quality and price will over time displace habit secured in sentiment; thus, in particular, the Commonwealth was never going to substitute in this regard for empire. Then, the second noted, was perhaps more of a surprise and perhaps the greater failure. In 1945 the British economy was pre-eminent in Western Europe, it had to be as it had endured six years of command economy, buttressed by US and empire resources, with much of the British war effort going into high-tech weapons systems, in particular, aircraft (which, in turn, demand a spread of supporting high-tech light industries),[8] where, in contrast, mainland economies had endured the ravages of occupation, forced labour, blockade, several years of allied bombing plus, finally, the impact of armies fighting their way across the Continent[9] (and note the situation in Eastern Europe was much worse). However, the mainland economies recovered quickly and in Germany commentators spoke of an economic miracle economy. The same was true of the Japanese economy. In 1945 it was in a devastated condition but with the SCAP reverse course, which attended the development of the Cold War in the region plus the economic demands flowing from the US prosecution of the war in Korea, the Japanese economy began a trajectory of growth, which was to continue for decades. And, as with West Germany, traditional habits of thought and organization were deployed not merely to rebuild shattered infrastructure but also to build new industries based on new technologies or management styles. These two economies, plus the other members in Europe of the nascent European Union, recovered from the impacts of war and advanced rapidly and the British economy was rather quickly overtaken, its problems mounting. And, finally, the third external problem was occasioned by the hike in oil prices that attended one more war between Israel and its neighbours. The Arab states received assistance from the Gulf oil producers in the form of a series of price rises designed to pressure Western governments into taking some sort of action in respect of the ongoing problems surrounding Israel and the Palestinians. The oil price rise had a series of disastrous effects: it raised the prices of production in Western oil-consuming countries, depressing economic activity; it generated a flood of money, as oil was paid for at new higher prices (in oil-dependent economies demand could only be reduced at the margins), which was put into the international money markets which in turn recycled it in the form of loans for development in Latin America and Africa, in the event unsustainable, leading to a third-world debt crisis; and it made Western governments sensitive to the political demands of the Gulf states so that diplomatic support was forthcoming, that is, these autocracies were spared the criticisms meted out to other governments not so well placed in regard the West – so too was defence support – an ambiguous relationship developed which saw oil profits being recycled back to the West in the guise of purchases of high-tech weapons systems (and down the years, this aspect of the relationship of the oil-producing and oil-consuming countries attracted accusations of routine corruption).

Confronted with these problems of internal incoherence and international pressures, the standard vulgar Keynesian response of yet more state spending did not help and the system shifted into a configuration that available economic theory said was not possible, that is, stagnation plus inflation or 'stagflation'. So the post-war contested compromise frayed: its component social groups drew apart, the institutional machineries of cooperation weakened and the integrative ethos of post-war social democracy faded in the face of events and critical attacks. The symbolic end-point of the package – alliances, ideas and policy – was found in the actions of Chancellor Denis Healey who famously, in 1976, was obliged to turn back from London Heathrow in order to attend to another economic crisis. The shift in elite-level political and policy opinion was made explicit at a Labour Party conference in the same year when Prime Minister Jim Callaghan advised delegates that it was no longer possible to 'spend our way out of trouble'.

Neo-liberal alternatives presented

The ideas underpinning neo-liberalism were not new. Cast in terms of the intellectual history of economics in Britain they could be traced back to the late nineteenth-century neo-classical revolution and the shift of intellectual and policy attention away from political economy (with its inherent concern for the politics of the social creation of wealth) to the competitive liberal marketplace (which focused on the aggregative logic of individual choices in the marketplace with the issues of the social production of wealth simply set aside). A conservative perspective on economic policy-making continued until the crises of the 1930s provoked change: a new conventional wisdom was established – with difficulty – around the proposition that active state involvement in managing the economy was appropriate and effective. These ideas in turn ran on into the post-war period but they had always been opposed and arguments in favour of liberal markets were presented during the war years and affirmed over the long period of Keynesian policy hegemony that followed. But the moment of political opportunity, the passing context within which such ideas could be presented to an audience wider than long-established bands of enthusiasts was provided in the late 1970s by the experience of stagflation. At this point Keynesian-informed policy-making had run into the sand and alternative voices were able to offer alternatives policies. In Britain these thinkers and activists constituted what was tagged the New Right and drawing on work done in Austria and Chicago,[10] abstract theories of the marketplace were recast as a series of proposals for reform, at first modest suggestions for the sale of state assets, later more ambitious schemes designed to remake the political-economic culture of the country such that state-centred habits of thought were replaced by market-centred thinking; it was the slate of ideas that were to find expression in the neo-liberal package of privatization, deregulation and financial liberalization.

One aspect of this situation is of note in the present context; that is, the intermingling of calls made by enthusiasts for sweeping somewhat utopian marketplace reform, the much narrower instrumental interests of politicians in securing power in Westminster and thereafter Whitehall and the coincidental emergence of powerful corporate media groups anxious to secure their unfettered continued development. So politicians and media acted to reinforce the otherwise often somewhat general theoretical proposals for reform. The traffic of ideas in the public sphere quickly became mostly one way, that is, ideas celebrating the marketplace became central to public politics; at first in insurgent mode, later as a settled consensus and finally as unremarked common sense.

The effective promulgation of the package of ideas/practices within the realms of politics and policy took a relatively short period of time. Say from 1976 when Denis Healey and James Callaghan flagged changing ideas amongst the elite through to 1983 when Margaret Thatcher's Conservative Party won its second general election victory and embarked on a programme of reforms. It was a short period of some six or seven years. It was also a period of economic, social and political upheaval for the proto-monetarism of Healy and Callaghan was resisted by the left of their party along with large sections of the trade-union movement until the government was finally doomed by the long 'winter of discontent', a series of public sector strikes. Thereafter the first government of Margaret Thatcher saw 'punk-monetarism' tried out with the result that large swathes of manufacturing industry went bust, unemployment soared and protests and riots accompanied these policy failures. These troubles continued until the government was fortuitously rescued through prosecuting a victorious war in the South Atlantic after which, secure in parliament, it inaugurated a programme of reforms – many not planned in advance – that saw hitherto utopian free-market ideas translated into practice. The changes in ideas and practice involved a number of elements: changes in power relations within society, novel ideas about policy and a relentlessly active core elite. As one analyst memorably cast it, the objective was to use the 'strong state to create a free economy'.[11]

(i) The rise of corporate power[12]

The disintegration of the post-war contested compromise saw the union movement significantly weakened/discredited as the corporate world asserted its interests directly. There were significant clashes with the union movement (Grunwick, Wapping, Miners), legislation was brought in restricting their range of activities and then relatedly but more broadly a number of pressure groups advanced the cause of the corporate world in the public sphere such as the Institute of Directors or the Adam Smith Institute and behind the scenes there were influential lobby organizations like the Bilderberg Group, Montperlin Society, Davos Meetings and so on. The direction of political travel was clear. The corporate world was asserting its importance and this was cast in neo-liberal terms; the stress was not on advancing corporate power, rather on the more anodyne and neutral and even reassuringly non-political realm of the competitive marketplace, thus it was claimed that power was to be dispersed and placed in the hands of everyman via the marketplace[13] – an absurd claim that gained wide acceptance.

(ii) The preference for market solutions

It is possible to date the intellectual/policy collapse of Keynesianism to 1976 when the Callaghan/Healey government changed its policy stance in the light of domestic failures and international pressures. The government was replaced in 1979 and the shift to a new monetarist policy was made explicit. The new government of Margaret Thatcher adopted a variant of monetarism which – it was claimed – would purge the economic system of inflationary tendencies and all the associated deleterious effects and allow the economy to reboot itself with the market operating cleanly once again – the policy involved curbs on government spending, restrictions on credit and together these produced high unemployment and economic recession. In the first Thatcher government the theory/policy was tried and it failed. However, the government was rescued as a result of success in a foreign war and thereafter new policies were adopted ad hoc, in particular, privatization and financial liberalization. The second phase of the experiment was a success: economic recovery plus widespread popular support. The ideological rhetoric of liberal markets began to pervade British public life: it slowly spread through the machineries of government; it slowly spread through the public sphere (theorized as new public management);[14] and the claims of the neo-liberals to the evident superiority of the untrammelled marketplace slowly became a species of common sense amongst the population.

(iii) The privatization of state assets

The early failure of monetarist experiment was followed by further initiatives. These were initiated in an ad hoc fashion, only slowly turning into the package subsequently tagged Thatcherism. The early initiatives involved the privatization of state assets in manufacturing industries and utilities and stocks of social housing. The programme had several benefits for the incumbent government: it raised windfall income for the treasury, it got rid of several troublesome industries, it weakened the trade unions and in turn weakened the income stream of the Labour Party, it provided a steady supply of electoral bribes whereby the population was enjoined to buy cheap shares (most were sold, those that were kept were mostly kept in small quantities) and it showed that the government's ideological commitments to the liberal marketplace were being translated into practice. The privatization programme was presented in popular form via two aspects: shares were made available to ordinary people who profited from a market rigged so that offer prices were always less than the market price when the newly distributed shares were first traded and social housing was sold off at heavily discounted prices. The programme was a success as steel, electricity, water, coal, railways and so on were all sold into the private sphere plus the sale of housing marked a major transfer of wealth to an hitherto asset poor group. An elderly Harold Macmillan described all this as 'selling off the family silver'[15] – but he belonged to another generation and along with other critics was disregarded – one failure, at least in terms of the ideological declarations that attended these programmes, was the reluctance of the population to join in the 'share owning democracy' – shares or housing at heavily discounted prices was one thing, overnight conversion to the ethos of neo-liberalism was something else – but it did come later – albeit in a number of unsustainable housing bubbles and a final catastrophic financial scandal.[16]

(iv) The privatization of state functions

After the first phase of privatizations, later exercises turned away from assets that could be transferred to functions that could be contracted out. In this new phase various state functions, for example, prisons or hospitals or government organizations (ordnance survey, meteorological office and the like), were offered either in part or whole on contract to private suppliers or management companies. Such schemes were further developed as core state functions were identified for contracting out, for example, in the field of defence where, by the early twenty-first century, private military companies were routinely used by the state.[17] A related scheme saw government inviting private suppliers to build major infrastructure that the state then leased, for example private finance initiative (PFI) hospitals,[18] in effect this was the state buying on the never-never and unsurprisingly it was a controversial process.

(v) The deregulation of the economy

Institutional economics[19] points out that all economies are everywhere embedded within societies and ordered, inevitably, by the moral and cognitive resources of their broad culture.[20] Or, in brief, all markets are rule bound. The rules are lodged in the general social world (they specify what is and is not proper behaviour in respect of the business of livelihood) and thereafter codified by the state.

The schedule of codified rules associated with the post-war corporatist welfare state settlement was superseded during the late 1970s and early

1980s by an accumulative process of revision: regulative regimes were relaxed so that the legal and regulative environment within which corporate business operated were slowly adjusted in line with both the demands of abstract theory (for example, the celebration of competition) and the requirements of real-world business (which rarely involved competition unless it was unavoidable); corporate taxation was revised; trade-union law was revised; and through the 1980s and 1990s governing parties and their allies in the corporate world and public sphere (commentators, journalists, theorists and so on) unleashed a sustained barrage of argument in favour of liberal competitive markets, in which it was claimed that the discrete, autonomous individual was the fundamental asocial basis of a marketplace-secured spontaneous social order. The argument was incoherent (markets are both social constructions, via contracts, and natural givens, via their base in discrete autonomous individuals), self-aggrandizing (the social construct of liberal rational economic man is represented as asocial, timeless and thus general) and after a whilst widely accepted.

(vi) The programme of financial deregulation

In 1986 the financial industry of the City of London was deregulated and foreign firms moved in and the industry grew rapidly as new products were invented as the process of creating what turned out to be a bubble economy began. The crash came in 2008/10;[21] it was triggered in the USA, but spread quickly, and a number of major British banks were nationalized as banks throughout Europe came under pressure. Banks were bailed out by taxpayer monies and these monies in turn were placed on the balance sheets of states and a number of these states then came under pressure from the global financial markets. Thus a private debt crisis was transmuted into a public debt crisis and the response of states, individually and collectively, was twofold: they had to protect themselves against the global financial markets, hence 'austerity,' and more positively, there were moves towards reregulating the banks and the parallel informal banking system. All in all, it was a slow process. Predictably, it was resisted by the very banking industry that had caused the crisis in the first place and had only been rescued by state-provided taxpayer funds.[22] Unsurprisingly, the bubble years, the subsequent crash and bailouts plus austerity have proved to be highly contentious.[23]

(vii) The celebration of consumption

The period saw the slow rise of an unrestricted celebration of consumption and whilst for neo-liberals this was the point of the system and its celebration a practical justification of their arguments, for those remaining adherents of the old contested compromise the celebration of consumption looked like an undignified, that is, infantilizing, celebration of banal greed.[24] Somewhat more ambitiously, consumption also came to be characterized in terms of the idea of postmodernism.[25] Proponents celebrated what they took to be a new sphere of individual autonomy and collective benefit, arguing that knowledge-based economies produce so many riches that any individual could construct a pattern of life from these proffered materials; critics were more wary and spoke of a system substituting seduction for coercion for those within its sphere leaving the poor to be controlled via bureaucratic welfare systems; and a related line looked back to the proponents and diagnosed intellectual and moral bad faith in the response of otherwise politically defeated groups, a species of self-deceiving accommodation.[26]

Smoothing Thatcher's route to power

The Conservative Party under the leadership of Margaret Thatcher fought the 1979 election campaign using techniques which hitherto had not been seen in Britain, specifically a modern sophisticated commercial-style advertising campaign. This was associated with the advertising company Saatchi and Saatchi. Their involvement flagged a strand of media-carried populism, which was to continue throughout her period in office and that of her successors, reaching, perhaps, an apogee in the media-dominated activities of the Labour government led by Tony Blair.

Saatchi and Saatchi was a London-based advertising company and it served the world of commerce. In the 1979 election campaign its skills were deployed in order to sell the Conservative Party and to denigrate its opponents, the Labour Party. One memorable advertisement[27] – used before the campaign – printed and published on huge roadside hoardings showed a long queue of people winding their way to the employment office and carried the tag-line 'Labour isn't working'. It was a sophisticated piece of work – it drew attention and criticism – but, to the point, it made the Labour Party look very old-fashioned. The Saatchi brothers were successful in the advertising business and subsequently Charles Saatchi[28] contributed to the emergence of 'Brit Art' via his funding of young artists, such as Tracy Emin and Damien Hirst.[29] The Saatchi brothers also contributed – one source amongst others – to the rise of the twin artefacts of the media world, spin and celebrity. These were to mark the ever-closer involvement of the media with the political world as their ideas/practices contributed to the development of celebrity politics; politicians and media celebrities became overlapping categories of actors in the public sphere, substance gave way to image.

More generally, the corporate media world has helped create an image-drenched social world. Print media have made extensive use of images using illustrations made by artists and images made by photography. The latter technology gave rise to a specialist role of photojournalist;[30] later the use of lightweight hand-held news cameras and recently cameraphone footage uploaded onto the internet so that the audience can vicariously share time, place and experience. In all this, Simpson[31] considers the role of photography, looking at 'iconic' photographs, asking how they run within the public sphere. Simpson is sceptical about the impact of such photos, suggesting that they are quickly absorbed into the stream of events, available later as stylized forms of memory. Kennedy[32] picks up on the issue of the relationship of US photojournalism and the foreign-policy stances of the American state – author finds a correspondence – the photojournalism parallels the official position – US foreign policy is for the good of others and for the further development of a liberal world. And, generally, Campbell[33] pursues the issue noting that photojournalism offers multiple lines of meaning: factual (this is what the situation in question looks like); aesthetic (this is how it can be seen as exemplifying something beyond itself, that is, the claims of art); and political (this is what we, the audience, might want to do about the situation thus revealed). So reading the resultant image is not straightforward, nor will its impact within the public sphere be simple to predict.

Media conglomerates[34]

The 1980s and 1990s saw the rise to public prominence of a number of corporate media figures; these included, for example, Rupert Murdoch, Conrad Black and Silvio Berlusconi.[35] Their media operations blurred the distinctions between the world of politics and the world of the media. All three were for a period very successful. They were also subject to severe criticism. It was alleged that corporate power was made available to elite-level politicians in return for favours (collaboration). The scandals surrounding Murdoch[36] and Berlusconi[37] later opened up a window on such exchanges.

Gillian Doyle[38] discusses the rise of the corporate media and she looks at the economics, regulation and political interests of such organizations. So first the economics of media firms and the logic of the media marketplace: reviewing how firms operate (cooperation and competition) she notes that as the media is a marketplace like any other then the same logic bears down upon media firms – concentration (integrated firms), consolidation (fewer firms) and cartels and/or monopolies. These are routinely policed by the state in respect of all corporate activities – however, the media are especially important in certain respects. Thus second she looks at government regulation of the industry – same as any other – plus, importantly, a concern to defend (more or less intermittently) an idea of the importance of pluralism in the media in regard to their role in the public sphere (so, a preference for diverse voices and diverse suppliers). All of which, third, is mediated by politicians, who, of course, have their own concerns. Doyle comments that the recent history of British government regulation of the media industry has been consistently to favour the interests of the industry – concerns for the impact of the media on pluralism (and thus 'democratic debate') have been secondary. One good point in this last regard is the existence of public service broadcasting where the BBC continues to enjoy both a high reputation amongst its media peers and the general public and sustained attacks from media moguls anxious about the competition it offers to their corporate interests. Doyle concludes that media concentration may make good market sense but it does not serve the ideal of democratic debate. The exchange between corporate world and government regulators will continue to shape the media – so too will be the rise of novel media mechanisms and here the rise of the internet does seem to offer a route into the public sphere for a new diversity of voices.[39]

Media themes: Political and corporate ideologies in action

The effective deployment of neo-liberal ideas and practices required change both in the policy ideas affirmed by the elite, a mix of novel ideas, argument and the ever-shifting demands of contingent circumstances, and the sets of ideas running through the wider population. The mass media figured in both areas. The press acted as a vehicle for making pro-market ideas intelligible and acceptable to the population and as a means to the distribution of specific exercises in elite-sponsored policy. This relationship between politicians and media is not new but the novelty of the current period resides in the direct way in which commercial techniques were embraced by politicians. At first, there were spin-doctors, public relations and advertising copy; thereafter, as the decades wore on, these techniques came to be supplemented by several varieties of lying, instrumental, adventitious and systemic.[40]

Thatcher's authoritarian populism

Such was the novelty of the policies of the government of Margaret Thatcher that they acquired a label; commentators spoke of an ideology, Thatcherism. The core of the ideology, the package of ideas and policy, was a preference for liberal markets, taken to be efficient and taken also to be definitively anti-socialist. The governments of Margaret Thatcher used the machinery of the state to advance the cause of the free market. This was no mere rebalancing of inherited policy; it was a broad sea change in thinking. It was not a simple shift from state-oriented policy to market-oriented policy; rather the state was used to rejig the web of law and regulation facilitating the liberal competitive marketplace. One commentator captured this relationship in the thesis of the strong state creating a free economy,[41] whilst another commentator, looking to the cultural aspects of the programme, the way it presented itself in the realms of ordinary life, summed the package of ideas and action as 'authoritarian populism'.[42]

The ideology found expression in a number of ideas/styles: marketism, nationalism and individualism. First a market orientation was stressed: the government was self-declaredly pro-market and anti-state thus comments, proposals and sometime policy initiative were cast in the form of a radical competitive market liberalism. In the context of a now-fading Keynesian-centred consensus, these public statements were shocking, thus famously, Margaret Thatcher remarked that there was 'no such thing as society' and almost as noted was the phrase 'there is no alternative' or Tina, the claim she made about her own policy choices. Second, nationalism/jingoism was affirmed: the government and its ardent supporters tended to be anti-European and anti-foreigner; the former was not a notable trait until late in her premiership (she signed the Single European Act, just as her successor John Major was to sign the Maastricht Treaty – and indeed, just as her predecessor as conservative prime minister, Edward Heath, had signed the treaty taking Britain into Europe) and after she had stepped down as prime minister, she became a rallying point for conservative anti-Europeans.[43] It is perhaps here that the broader anti-foreigner sentiment begins to have effect. Moreover, Thatcher and her supporters were also concerned with 'the enemy within' – trade unions being a particular bug-bear – Thatcher reportedly routinely divided the political world in a Manichean fashion by asking whether someone or other was or was not 'one of us'. And third, individualism within popular culture was affirmed: members of the government routinely stressed individual responsibility, with one senior figure, Norman Tebbit, famously advising the unemployed to 'get on their bikes and look for work'. There was a corresponding celebration of the self in respect of consumption, the celebration of shopping, in all a period of excess.[44]

Corporate media populism

The populist tone of political ideas was echoed in the corporate media realm – two aspects came to the fore: hostility towards public service broadcasting and a preference for cheap, populist programming.

Commercial broadcasters along with their neo-liberal think-tank and political allies showed unreserved hostility towards public service broadcasting. The BBC was subject to repeated attacks and alongside these attacks a role was sketched for the broadcaster centred on niche programming for cultural minorities.[45]

Commercial print and broadcast media used low-quality materials; noted here, they include: football; sex; gambling; and sensation.

Corporate world, media and politics in review

The neo-liberal project unrolled vigorously over the last couple of decades of the century and ran on until the debacle of 2008/10. The ideological package offered a celebration of freedom and the overall ethos of the polity was remade. Public policy included amongst other things, privatization of state assets and deregulation of the marketplace. The post-Second World War Keynesian-theorized social democracy was wound back and in its place emerged a vigorous liberal individualism – individual freedom – individual responsibility – individual consumption.

The neo-liberal era was represented in the mainstream media: the mainstream media in the main went along with this reorientation – they reported the changes – politically right-wing sections of the press acted as cheerleaders.

Public intellectuals went along with the changes: one group celebrating post-modernism (the arts, humanities and social sciences)[46] whilst another group celebrated globalization (favoured by economics/business commentators). Offshoots sprang up – 'post-modernist architecture'[47] and here there is a wider debate here about the role of cities, the nature of urban forms and the role of urban renewal. There are various strands: first, modernists, working post-Second World War – welfare state modernism – 1950s – (noted by Owen Hatherley)[48] – celebrates design-for-masses; second, heritage, post-Second World War reaction against architectural and social loss – National Trust – anti-welfare state, celebrates heritage; and third, post-modernists, 1980/1990s celebration of the possibilities of market carried consumption – anti-welfare state – in cities celebrates profit, speculation and pastiche.[49] And sharp criticisms were made – globalization was dismissed[50] whilst post-modernism was tagged the disappointed consciousness of hitherto left intellectuals.[51]

The neo-liberal era saw the development of a politically influential right-wing populist press, the tabloids and they evidenced two distinctive traits: first, writing for effect so that an audience was both entertained (the tabloids were very popular, that is, they sold copies in the marketplace) and manipulated; and second, obliging political agents to acknowledge their power (symptomatically, the Murdoch press' access to government). Specialist commentators have pursed these issues at length: thus, John Street looks at the media, tracks the changes, tracks their techniques and stresses the relationship of politics and media: it is about power; where it lies, how it is exercised.[52] Gillian Doyle[53] also looks at the economics and politics of the media and argues that the media's market-driven inclination to concentration must be challenged as it works against democratic debate, thus the government must regulate to sustain pluralism in the media, owners and voices.

Wider issues: Liberal versus democratic polity

The media have long been considered as a vehicle for a number of lines of argument – simple reportage, entertainment and all those debates which together help constitute the public sphere – this last comes from Jurgen Habermas who argues, in his many writings, that language-based communication can in appropriate circumstances uncover lines of action oriented towards a democratic polity. The debate has run down the tradition of the Frankfurt School. A variant is found in the liberal political philosophy of John Rawls with the notion of public reason. These arguments propose, in brief, that the media can be a servant of public debate and thus societal dispositions towards democracy.

Thereafter, many commentators have looked – in all sorts of circumstances – at whether or not the media were doing their job, that is, reporting accurately on the life of the polity in question. One strand of debate has considered media conglomerates versus public service broadcasting.[54] Thus corporate world media – in particular broadcast, in particular those associated with News International, have run a long campaign against the BBC; accusing it of being elitist, accusing it of being unreasonably subsidized, accusing it of not offering anyone a choice about whether or not they wish to fund the organization, and accusing it of being left-wing. But, on the role of BBC, surveys show that the BBC is trusted by the British population. It can be seen to have a dual role – one noted, the other not. The public service broadcaster role is noted, thus the BBC is upmarket, its audiences diverse and these should be served appropriately; the second role is more subtly articulated for the organization is part of 'invented nation of Britain', both its simple existence (an icon of Britain) and a useful propaganda weapon (disseminating a distinct package of ideas).

Finally, commentators have considered the exchange between the manipulative impact of political advertising and familiarly affirmed aspirations towards democracy (again, promise and performance). Here one novelty has been the emergence of overt political advertising; techniques from the realm of public relations and advertising have been borrowed and they have been put to work in selling parties, politicians and policies.

Running down to the present: Legacies and repetitions

The political elite of Britain has pursued a neo-liberal project for 30-odd years and that being so it would be a surprise if it were not influential. And so it proves. The core claims of the neo-liberal project are now assiduously reiterated by political leaders, commentators and – via the doctrine's pervasive reach within society – ordinary members of the community. The ethos of the neo-liberal project now pervades the public sphere in Britain.

These intellectual/moral, or more simply ideological, claims can be broken down into a number of subsets: consumption, enterprise and the public sphere.

The neo-liberal ethos offers widely accepted celebrations of consumption, affirming in turn: the central importance of consumption; the equivalence of wants (consumer desires are equal); and the inevitability and propriety of debt.

The neo-liberal ethos embraces the marketplace, affirming in turn: the crucial role of enterprise (the protective ideology of the rich, 'because we're worth it', and, by implication, 'you are not'); the distinction between 'wealth creators' in the corporate world and those who either create nothing very much (public sector) or nothing at all (welfare recipients); an undisguised celebration of the role of finance, bankers and the City of London (and the 2008/10 counterpart, the insistence upon state action to underpin a minimally reformed system at the expense of the wider tax-paying general public); an acceptance of inequality (commentators speak of a new 'gilded age', such is the difference in income/wealth between the elite and the masses – ' the ninety-nine per cent' in one protest formulation);

The ethos embraces the public sphere, affirming in turn: the role of celebrity in public sphere; a pervasive anti-intellectualism (present in the demotic tone of the mass media, a spurious claim to equality of opinion); a celebration of a banal individualism (available to the masses in 'choices made in the consumer marketplace');[55] and in upmarket guise, the ideas of postmodernism (where self and choice and consumption find mutual implication).[56]

However, all that said, these doctrines revolve around the existence – actual or anticipated – of a vigorous liberal marketplace, but, unfortunately for the celebrants of neo-liberalism the financial crisis of 2008–10, with its origins in debt-fuelled consumerism in the USA, has blunted the appeal of this package, nonetheless, it must be granted that whilst neo-liberalism is intellectually discredited,[57] it runs on in political and policy-making circles and amongst the wider population.

9
Amongst the Bullshit Industries

The corporate media realm expanded dramatically over the 1980s and 1990s and what had been separate companies dealing with say newspapers, or radio, or television, or film, or books were reworked as multimedia conglomerates. In commercial matters, one strand of the business could repeat and resell work from another strand with expressive consumption celebrated, arguably fine in the commercial consumer marketplace. However, cross-platform holdings also developed in the news arena and this was potentially disastrous in the realms of politics for media concentration and cross-platform holdings could allow companies to garner extensive influence over the realms of formal political life either through running a line in the media or suborning politicians with flattery, or offers of support or contrariwise threats. The era of neo-liberal excess enfolded within its moral envelope much of the media world. In the consumer realm, expressive consumption was celebrated, with critics of such practices routinely denigrated. Bullshit industries burgeoned and their messages were broadcast indiscriminately, variously addressed to all social groups: 'because you're worth it' justified an open-ended indulgent consumerism. In the news realm, where politics and media met, just as in the world of investment banking where operatives were enjoined to 'eat what they killed', so in the realms of journalism. One simple characterization of the styles of the political media in this period would be to note its aggression: aggression in popular tabloids, aggression in popular television, aggression in films (and later the burgeoning games industry) and such aggression was turned towards unfavoured politicians or parties or ideas or countries or ordinary people.

Once more, the shock of the new,[1] this time in the guise of the rolling impact of the burgeoning world of corporate media with all the gaudy output of a system centred on the pursuit of market share and profit: for some, an occasion for vocal dismay (critics speaking of the degradation of the public sphere); for others, an occasion for celebratory abasement (those hitherto critical, now post-modernist);[2] plus for many, an occasion for simple pleasure (amongst the new audiences, whether, novel sports presentation or afternoon television or reality programming – all popular); and, crucially, for the corporate world, an occasion for profit. And in recent years, the media world of print and broadcast plus related industries like advertising and fashion and design grew to such an extent that one commentator tagged London as a major centre for the 'bullshit industries'.[3]

The output of decades can be summed, a clichéd way of recording the passage of time: thus, the respectable 1950s, the declamatorily engaged 1960s, the anxious 1970s and – in these terms – the increasingly gaudy 1980s and 1990s. The core concern of the neo-liberal era mainstream mass media of print and broadcast was consumption: nominally individual, nominally expressive and nominally life-enhancing, but better seen as the individualized output of a system fuelled on debt. The ethic/orientation found expression in the news realm as politics was read in neo-liberal terms; aggressively pro-market, intolerant of other voices, with media outlets thus oriented outnumbering and outselling those turned towards the more traditional British or European left.

The system experienced crisis in 2008/10[4] with financial sector collapse, state rescues and thereafter an elite-level political battle which shifted the burdens of failure from investors and shareholders onto the tax-payer and framed public debate not in terms of reforming a corrupted banking sector (tagged 'banker bashing') but in terms of reducing expenditures within the public sector. In some cases the pro-liberal market propaganda became more virulent (the right-wing press warning against Keynesian backsliding) and in some cases there were anxious debates about the future (in the financial press, for example), but in the main the new styles and audiences simply continued: as household budgets were cut, television programmes oriented towards domestic consumption continued; as the financial world was revealed to be systemically corrupt, newspaper pieces oriented towards domestic saving/investment continued; as the housing market became quiet and prices fell, television programmes devoted to property improvement and speculation continued.

In the period one novelty emerged, based on a new technology; the use of digital technology for the dissemination of materials in radio, television, music and text. The internet served as both symbol and crucial mechanism/medium. The *former* role served to advertise diverse hopes for the future – early enthusiasms for novel commercial operations in the marketplace produced the dot-com bubble of the early 2000s – other styles of enthusiasm for novel political activity helped produce what was tagged the 'Arab Spring'.[5] The *latter* provided opportunities for extant forms in commerce and politics to rework themselves as the internet became widely available: old forms of communication were reworked (thus, online newspapers)[6] and entirely new forms emerged (thus, social networks); and some of this spilled over into politics in an unexpected way with both government and corporate world surveillance and popular organization and protest. But these belonged to the later 2000s, in the 1980s and 1990s older forms continued but the styles adopted and the audiences addressed were new – gaudy, popular, cynical – one expression of the system's shift from control to seduction.[7]

Episode: The rise of corporate media

Down the years many groups have presented arguments within the public sphere, but the social and institutional make-up of that sphere is not fixed, it changes; the participants within that sphere are not settled, they change; so too do audiences, those variously addressed; and so too do the technical means whereby arguments are made and disseminated. In the science-based modern era, such technical changes have flowed from scientific advances, including radio, telegraph, film, telephone, FM radio, television, cable and now internet.[8] And in each case the introduction of these new technologies has provoked conflict: participants would include copyright-holders or patent-holders, small innovative firms, established large firms, state regulatory bodies, politicians and assorted groups within the otherwise largely passive general public. Or, in brief, novel technologies do not translate into practice smoothly and their adoption and use are the outcome of political processes.

In the 1980/1990s changes in political, regulatory and technical environments facilitated corporate media advance and satellite, cable and digital technologies allowed new business models to be developed, which in turn placed pressure upon existing models, both corporate and public sector.

Corporate media advance

In the 1980/1990s a confluence of forces came together: novel digital technologies, an ascendant pro-market political constellation and a recently deregulated finance industry anxious to create income-generating debt. One aspect of this episode was the rise of market-based, profit-oriented cross-platform international media conglomerates.

The corporate broadcast media advanced slowly in a period of free-to-air transmission. In Britain independent television was organized rather like the BBC[9] and a full range of programmes was offered and delivered via regional broadcasters. It was funded not by a licence fee but by paid advertisements. In general, there were no radical changes notwithstanding some patrician anxieties about the deleterious impact of advertisements.[10] But satellite and cable offered the chance to build subscription channels. Now the audience were providing two streams of income: they paid subscriptions and they were an audience available for sale to advertisers; for example reports[11] surrounding the 2011/12 scandal at News International indicated that the group's newspaper interests were marginal to its other media interests in film and television. The income streams from subscription channels allowed corporate media expansion and there were major media tie-ups in the USA (for example, Time Warner and America Online[12]). In Britain the exemplar of such media expansion was Rupert Murdoch's News International (Sky television, the *Sun* and the *News of the World*).

Public service broadcasting retreat

As the market-oriented corporate media advanced, public service broadcasting experienced a loss of audience share: sometimes because they were slow to appreciate trends amongst their audiences, thus pop music (current formats begin with Radio Luxembourg and later pirate radio stations); sometimes because they lagged in innovation, thus, ITV opened up new soap operas such as *Coronation Street*; and sometimes they were outbid, thus Sky bought rights to screen football. However, that said, the BBC remained the premier news channel and a major player in the arts.

The BBC had been a monopoly broadcaster until the middle 1950s when ITV was given a licence. The ITV licence required it to offer a spread of programming something like the BBC and so competition between the two broadcasters quickly came to adopt a familiar pattern: the ITV companies drifted towards using a more popular schedule of programming whereas the BBC retained a wider spread of materials including news and arts. This is not to say that the BBC never produced popular material or that ITV never produced quality news, but it was possible to distinguish the two channels in these terms. Later the duopoly was altered, first with more free-to-air channels and then with cable and satellite.

These last noted meant that there were now hundreds of channels and competition for audiences began. At first the BBC continued with a restricted set of channels, although some were now directly popular whilst others focused on the arts or news and then later the BBC did open up further free-to-air channels and one novel distribution route via the internet; the BBC iPlayer. The iPlayer made all BBC free-to-air material available plus all the preceding week's output. The website was of a very high quality and also very popular. These developments attracted the hostility of the corporate world, which complained of unfair competition.[13] Overall, throughout this period, public sector broadcasting lost audience share.

The BBC's formal status is that of a corporation established by royal charter. It is funded by a compulsory licence system. It is quasi-independent. And this being the case, its work is subject to political pressures by politicians, lobbyists and the general public who can offer comments about how it is organized and run and whether or not it should be changed. The licence system is reviewed every five years and this gives the incumbent government a powerful weapon. During the period of neo-liberal ascendency the ideological celebration of the competitive marketplace and the denigration of the state sector produced fading elite-level political support but the weapon of control of money cannot be wielded freely as the BBC notwithstanding falling audience share commands widespread support from the general public. The corporation commands widespread admiration for its news coverage – when major stories break the public prefers to listen to the BBC – and its arts programming, indeed, the corporation is a major sponsor of the arts in Britain. Moreover, the BBC has an international reputation and sells programmes worldwide.[14]

Media themes: Corporate demands, new technologies and novel products

The corporate world placed a number of demands on the media. The fundamental concern of media corporations was with market share and profit otherwise their businesses failed. This preoccupation with market share encouraged the embrace of new technologies where these could cut costs or increase efficiency or create new income streams. It also encouraged a search for new audience and in place of the socially inclusive mass audience of the public service broadcasters, a new audience was created and this audience was both a mass (and thus could be addressed via familiar inexpensive fashion) and differentiated (with various subgroups receiving programming aimed at their particular interests); the paradigm case being imported shows from Hollywood with multiple variations on a few basic themes. All these changes – technological, regulatory and financial – meant that media corporations routinely offered novel products as they sought market share in the form of audience (twin sources of money – as subscribers and as audience to sell to advertisers).

New technology, new working practices, new audiences, new styles

A number of technology-related factors contributed to the growth of the corporate media: first, new technologies included lightweight cameras and recording equipment, small-scale editing equipment and digital and satellite distribution systems; second, new working practices cut costs (symptomatically, in Britain, News International relocated from Fleet Street to Wapping); and third, established content manufacturers became more efficient (Hollywood – responsible for a vast output of standardized entertainment products[15]). Corporate media used novel technologies and practices to shift from craft production to mass production; the earlier form looks to produce a series of one-off products whereas the latter form looks to produce an endless flow of marginally distinguished products. Corporate media were now able to revisit their relationships with their audiences; revising the ways in which their product was created and made available: first, segmentation coupled to massification and second, popularization. The former saw audiences disaggregated into ever-smaller segments, which could be addressed via targeted product design and marketing,[16] whilst at the same time material could be bought in from mass producers. The latter saw audiences offered the familiar spread of commercial mass culture including football, sex, sensation, celebrity talent shows and the like. The resultant pattern is now instantly recognizable in the routine output of television in Britain.

(i) Market segmentation plus mass

The development of new technologies for production (lightweight cameras and recording equipment) and distribution (cable, satellite and internet) meant that the available audience could be disaggregated with programme material aimed at ever-smaller market segments whilst at the same time the costs of production and the broad spread of distribution channels meant that the audience could be treated in financial terms as a mass audience. Channels proliferated, content was easily obtained and cheap specialist subjects could be supplemented by the output of Hollywood and its clones. It created cheap production-line television. The result has been a multiplicity of narrowly focused material presented in popular format: any sport, or reality television, or gardening, or cooking, or home improvements, or shopping, or god and so on, all of which are generated by a media production line, that is production is standardized. And, recalling cross-platform holdings, such products are available in broadcast and print versions and also available in commercial tie-ins (that is, related themed products such as games, souvenirs spin-offs and the like[17]).

(ii) Popularization: Corporate money, sport and nationalism in the example of football

The aspect of popularization is crucial as it allows commercial media companies to secure large subscription/audience numbers; these are their income stream; and two aspects of this might be schematically identified, gaining an audience and keeping it. Gaining an audience requires that you provide something new (thus mobile phones, novel, a new market, so new users and new social practices such as emailing or texting or tweeting) or provide something established in a new format (thus News International buying up football in order to foster the rise in the marketplace of Sky television where exclusive rights plus extensive coverage gained Sky a high reputation and a vast high-paying subscriber audience). Keeping the audience is the next task. The greater the numbers of subscribers or users, the greater the potential income stream, hence the preoccupation of managers. This would have held in the past for popular media depend upon their audience, however, the modern corporate world is able to monitor and adjust its product very rapidly so as to keep its audience.

Broadcast and print media utilize sports in order to sell their products. In Britain, the major sport was football. It had been broadcast by the BBC until it was comprehensively outbid by Sky television. The audience for football is now large (numbers) and segmented (sports fans, ordinary people who cannot escape its coverage so come to have a passive interest/opinion (one can talk to strangers about the weather or football) and public figures who are obliged to have an interest/opinion).[18] As a consequence of these factors, football has spread as a particular cultural phenomenon throughout the wider political culture of the country.

* * * * *

Everyone has an identity. Identity can be unpacked in various ways.[19] One way is to consider: first, locale – the place where a person lives and inhabits a dense social network (family, community, workplace and so on); second, network – the contacts a person has in other places (family, friends and so on); and third, memory – the ways in which experience is actively sifted and selected – some things are carefully forgotten whilst others are carefully remembered. The same procedure can be used for political identity – the way in which people come to belong to an organized political community with common ideas, institutions and leaders. A political identity is learned and there are symbols (flags, parades and anthems), sacred sites (places exemplifying the collective life of the community), official truths (the view of the community presented by the elite), folk memory (the view of the community passed down through informal stories); and the national past. This is crucial: substantively it is a contested compromise between elite and popular memory that tells an inclusive story about the community – who we are, where we came from and where we are going. Identity and political identity once learned are psychologically powerful. Identity is who we are. It is our membership of our group. This means that if our identity is threatened we can respond with hostility. And in the case of the working classes (and others) in Britain, football has come to be a carrier of identities – personal, local, national.

Football developed in England amongst the working classes in the nineteenth century. The game had quite definite characteristics: it was organized at a local community level; it was run by local business figures who held the shares in the limited companies that organized and ran teams; supporters turned up each week and bought tickets; and supporters formed 'supporters clubs' and were passionate about 'their' local team. These organizations became known as 'football clubs'[20] and in time they organized competitions and formed a league but the game retained its working-class character as the English middle and upper classes played other sports (cricket,[21] rugby, rowing, horse-riding, shooting and so on).

As the game became more and more popular national teams were formed and international competitions were held. The original ways of understanding football where the local team competed against the team of a neighbouring town now changed: the local teams provided players to make up the national teams and a broader collective endeavour grew; national teams were distinctive – they had their own style and ethos and developed their own identities – these identities were taken to express the characteristics of the nation from whose ranks they recruited their players. So two ideas come to be run together: the national football team comes to stand for the nation itself. This fusion of two ideas is picked up and amplified in the popular media: in newspapers; on television and more recently in film.[22] And the fate of the national team in international competitions becomes more and more important as it is routinely discussed in the media. All the national teams are seen to have an ethos and a style. The England team have an ethos of 'hard work' and 'character' and a 'workmanlike' style: first, 'hard work' means the team members are required to demonstrate effort (they must run about a lot); second, 'character' means the team members are expected to be physically tough, not very intelligent and a little bit violent; and third, 'workmanlike' means a simple and direct style of play which is unsophisticated in technique and tactics.

These issues are discussed in the media and the role of the media gets larger and larger: local newspapers carry football reports; national newspapers carry football reports; the BBC carries reports; and crucially, News International cable television is devoted to sport and to football. The new role of the media adds a further element to national team and national identity. It adds large amounts of money and celebrity. The national team is now made up of highly paid celebrities. The team exemplifies the nation. When there is a match all the media report it. If the team are successful general happiness follows and media pundits reflect on the greatness of the nation. If the team are unsuccessful general unhappiness follows and media pundits reflect on the sad decline of not merely the football but also the nation. And when there are no matches the activities of the celebrity players are folowed: commercial activities (the brands they sell, the merchandise they sell); personal activities (where they go and who they are with); and media appearances. In all this, one key figure becomes 'the England manager'.

In 2008, after the England national team failed to qualify for the international competition called Euro 2008, the manager was sacked. The outgoing manager, Steve McClaren, an Englishman, was widely characterized as hopeless, with the tabloid press tagging him 'the wally with the brolly' under a photograph of him sheltering from the rain during his last match. A great media debate about his replacement began. After a few weeks the new manager was announced: Fabio Capello, an Italian. Another debate began. Some commentators mourned the fact that the English game could not produce an England manager (no one was good enough) and read this in terms of football and national decline; some commentators invoked identity and said that an Italian would not be able to understand the English game (ethos/style); and some commentators insisted that Fabio Capello should have an English assistant (so that in time the assistant could take over after his contract was ended). However, other commentators pointed to his excellent record and said what mattered was football knowledge; and more critical commentators said that his appointment was a good idea because the record showed that mainland European teams were more successful than English teams.

Capello's record was good but in 2012 he resigned after a dispute with his employer. A new manager was appointed, an English man Roy Hodgson[23] and the media circus began with familiar themes being recycled. These debates reveal the popular cultural importance of the game and also the media interest. The sport commands a large audience and this is what corporate media have to sell to their clients in the advertising world. In total, the money involved in the game is now very large and these sums have been augmented, as the game more recently has become an object of interest to the corporate world.

Corporate world involvement in football has produced winners and losers. Football originates as a working-class game. Football clubs were typically private limited companies with shares controlled by a small group and not traded on the stock market. The club had a board of directors and shareholders and they were often the same group of people. Supporters were legally paying customers. Clubs encouraged supporters but the relationship was social or cultural, it was not legal. Club and supporters were mostly local: local businessmen financed and ran the club; local people in a town or city were the support base; and local media reported on the club. There was little money in the game: local businessmen put in the money, the wages of players were capped, and the supporters paid small entrance fees to watch each week. All this has changed. The rise of media conglomerates in Britain has been crucial.[24] The key company has been News International's Sky television: it is well connected politically; it has access to corporate finance; the company has invested heavily in expanding its operation; it needs subscribers to its services in order to grow revenue streams; it needs lots of content; and it targeted sport – in particular football. In Britain, football was popular; it had the correct demographic; the game suited television (90 minutes every week with opportunities for spin-off celebrities and commentary and marketing); and Sky television has grown along with its showing football. Today there are now vast amounts of money in the game[25] with corporate finance and wages not capped so that elite players receive huge salaries, whilst supporters pay much higher fees (entry tickets for stadiums, cable television charges and costs of merchandising). But the money that flows into football does not flow in a single stream: there has been competition amongst clubs for access to corporate money; the most successful clubs receive the most money; the best clubs split away from the rest and this led to the formation of the Premier League; and all the changes have been significant for the clubs, their fans and the game itself.

Clubs are public limited companies with shares that can be bought and sold on the stock market. There are usually major shareholders, for example, US media companies, Russian billionaires or Arab billionaires. Many become involved as market investors. Supporters are only one income stream amongst others. The clubs encourage supporters but the relationship is commercial and ordered via the media (the supporters have no status). Clubs and supporters are dispersed: corporate world owners; a global television audience; and global television and media commentary. Football is no longer a domestic working-class game. Internationally, there is a global television/media audience, domestically, the game is becoming more middle class and ticket prices are rising. They rise because stadiums are rebuilt and this is expensive, the costs of running the clubs are rising rapidly as wages rise and ownership has moved into the corporate world and leveraged buying requires that assets be sweated. Global football club brands prosper, but others fail and go to the wall.

The corporate media have reworked the social role of sport: what was local, small scale and often amateur or where professional not highly paid, is now a managed product for a large maybe global audience. Within this frame, the corporate world has changed football. The corporate ethos is distinctive: finances and business plans, cash flows, corporate-inspired restructuring and very large rewards for key participants. First, corporate-style finance: money is raised in the financial market and so debt can be taken on in order to buy a club and thereafter the new owners take fees for management. The club must find the income to service the debt and some flows from television rights and some from global marketing operations and the costs of ticket rises for ordinary fans. These operations are part and parcel of corporate-style business plans: these are substituted for local businessmen supporting their local club from their own pocket; finance is sourced in the financial markets, business plans are written and income streams identified. Second, high cash flows: there are very large amounts of money flowing through the elite-level game and in respect of Britain, the sums per annum are in the neighbourhood of £1 billion.[26] There are large rewards for participants as owners and shareholders extract hefty management fees and professional footballers extract huge incomes plus there are assorted hangers-on. In order to fund these expenditures, large income streams are necessary and the contemporary game depends on these: from television, from marketing and from ticket sales. The present pattern is unsustainable without these money flows. And, third corporate involvement entails change and large rewards for the elite: the Premier League is now very rich and remote from ordinary clubs and ordinary players. The lower divisions have much less money as money coming into the game from television is skewed towards the elite levels. The elite-level clubs have the funds to buy in talent, lower level clubs do not and the divide between top and bottom is unbridgeable. Corporate football is like other corporate sport: it is part of the realm of the corporate media entertainment sector; it is a media-supplied spectacle for the masses of television audiences; and it now has a global audience measured in billions.

(iii) Popularization: Celebrity

Celebrity, now widely remarked upon as a novel form of social identity. Generally, individuals and media cooperate in order to make the celebrity product and once the brand is up and running it can be sustained only with a regular supply of media stories. In its purest form celebrity refers to people who are famous for being famous, but a wide spread of people can be subject to the process, that is, made into celebrities for one reason or another. But, in the end, they all find themselves in the same place, whatever they might have been, they become famous simply for being famous.

That celebrity is a media construct is a familiar comment, but an extension to this claim can uncover the aggression involved as an individual is accorded celebrity status. There is a simple sequence: the creation of the celebrity, the use of the celebrity and finally the business of discarding the celebrity, at which point the individual is returned to ordinary life or otherwise quits the celebrity stage. The figures involved are quite varied, they have in common that they either put arguments into the public sphere (a politician) or they constitute 'arguments deployed', that is, they carry a latent claim (a member of the Royals);[27] here, a rough collection including a professional politician, a public figure, an institution, an actor and – one of the progenitors of the role – an artist.

A celebrity could be a politician, for example Tony Blair: the party leader was consciously marketed, like any other commercial product, and the party he led was explicitly rebranded New Labour. In the event it turned out that there was little behind the labels and unlike Margaret Thatcher whose political career in Downing Street generated the label

'Thatcherism' along with much analysis, Blair, for all the talk about the New Labour project produced no similar characterizations or discussion. In time Blair came to be called (amongst other things) an actor manager, implying that his public self was a self-conscious act,[28] a social style turned towards the public and serving only to keep him in the business. Something that was also said, rather more generally, about New Labour, identified as a catch-all party run by professional politicians, that is, the party served merely as the electoral machinery of professional politicians with no ideological orientation.[29]

A celebrity could be a public figure, for example Princess Dianna: she was quickly taken up by the press which first presented her as a fairy-tale princess, an innocent embraced by the Royal Family, part encouragement, part exemplar. She was presented as a distant exemplar of what any woman could become if the gods smiled on her and now, as princess, she became an aspirational model for all women, stylish and rich. Later she was reimagined as a tragic figure, rejected by her husband (she was photographed sitting alone in front of the Taj Mahal)[30] and neglected by the Royal Family. Then, in death, she was reimagined once again and embraced by the ordinary population, with Tony Blair tagging her 'the people's princess'.

A celebrity can be an institution, for example, the Royal Family: this group of people are celebrated for being royal, that is, the present carriers of a venerable institution. Both family and institution sit at the centre of an elaborate public relations apparatus. They sit at the centre of an equally elaborate media-carried apparatus of admiration. Tom Nairn[31] writes of the invention of tradition (pageantry), royal work (patronizing charities, opening buildings, being seen in public by appreciative crowds, waving and so on), the media rituals (the sycophantic respect accorded 'senior royals') and the media's construction of endless stories about the royals.

A celebrity could be an actor, thus Marilyn Monroe: celebrated for her on-screen beauty and her on-screen sexuality, taken up by the press such that professional role and private life become somewhat intertwined and then, in death, taken up as a symbol of the ways in which the corporate media world could embrace, use and destroy an otherwise ordinary women.

A celebrity could be an artist, for example Andy Warhol: one of the inventors of pop art; one of the inventors of artist-as-brand;[32] one of the inventors of artist's studio as production facility, thus 'the factory'; and the figure who gave us the comment in respect of the future of contemporary culture where 'In the future, everyone will be famous for fifteen minutes' and whose work was characterized, in one piece by Robert Hughes, as an exemplar of 1980s 'supply-side aesthetics'.[33]

Thus far, it might be said that celebrity is just one more product of an extraordinarily productive industrial capitalist system and in that sense unremarkable, if otherwise regrettable (yet more media rubbish). But celebrity has spilled over into Westminster politics. Now politicians can become quasi-celebrities. Now parliamentary politics can be reported in terms used for celebrities: personalization, scandal, tales about families and friends, trivial disputes blown up into media events and so on. Now politicians and parties can be marketed in just the same way as media celebrities: Labour as 'New Labour', the Conservatives as 'compassionate'. And none of this, to note, is relevant to parliamentary politics as it is commonly represented, that is, as being the deliberative core of political life, and none of it comes close to issues of power in the deeper sense where the core issues are which groups wield power, to what end, legitimated how.[34]

(iv) Rolling news and infotainment

One supplement to this diet of entertainment in both commercial media and public service broadcasting was the invention of rolling news. This was a distinctive way of reporting events. In some ways arguably providing a genuine service, but in terms of offering a variant on familiar half-hour or one-hour news bulletins, a marked shift towards the trivialization of what was already a stylized format linking events and audiences. Thus novelty was crucial, in-depth analysis secondary and the news values embodied in such programming contributed to a more general blurring of the line between information and entertainment; these products became tagged 'infotainment' – arguably, a better place to start when considering rolling news; and matters became more awkward as state broadcasters joined the marketplace, adding to the brew, propaganda (of varying quality).

Rolling news programmes begin with Ted Turner and CNN. The idea was dismissed at first as critics asked who could be expected to watch an endless news programme. It has proved successful and there are now numerous rolling news programmes, some commercial, some state and some public service broadcasters: they are repetitive, superficial and given to gimmicks. They are interesting to compare as they all reflect the environment within which they are produced: it is not possible to confuse BBC World with CNN or Al Jazeera or Russia TV or China Central Television and so on. Finally, a relative of rolling news is infotainment, a mix of information and entertainment, blurring the distinction. One specimen dealing in political material is Fox News. It serves up a diet of right-wing opinion, prejudice and propaganda. It is produced by News International but could as easily have emerged from the comic imaginations of the Monty Python team.

Wider issues: Corporate culture and the idea of a democracy

Critics of the media have often mentioned its alleged disregard of the ethic of democracy. In Habermasian terms, discourse in the public sphere is the core of a democratic polity and it requires appropriate institutional mechanisms to carry such debates: newspapers, clubs, societies, films and so on. It is an arena of debate independent of the state, which rests on the vigour of the wider civil society. If Habermas's diagnosis is at all accurate, then the institutional vehicles of the public sphere are crucial – no vehicles, no public sphere – and the popular media are one such institutional vehicle. These arguments open up a large area of debate in respect of the media's role in a democratic polity: what is necessary, what is harmful and what is the role of the state?

Corporate media exchange with politics: Power/celebrity

The nature of political life in liberal democratic systems in which regular elections play a role obliges the established politician – and aspirants – to maintain, or seek to maintain, good relationships with media companies, for they, as noted, are one element of that public sphere with reference to which, at least in part, the politician must orient themselves as they pursue their own or their party's projects. Their relationship with the media corporation is thus quite intimate. They need a good press. They have a range of tools at their disposal: gifts of access to decision makers; gifts of legal or regulatory accommodation to the needs of the corporate world; gifts of turning a blind eye to corporate wrongdoing, and so on. Sometimes force can be used – the law, the regulators – but these exchanges are not made public and they emerge, if at all, only much later, as commentators and historians conduct their interviews or comb through files newly released. Running the argument the other way, media corporations wield great power: they can offer or withhold the support of their various newspapers or television channels; they can parley their power for political access and seek legal or regulative accommodation on the part of the politicians.

Contemporary parliamentary life is suffused with the demands of the media world and this includes the creation and use of celebrity. The media can make or break a politician by treating them or not treating them as a celebrity. In recent years, the contrast between the mainstream treatments of Tony Blair as opposed to Gordon Brown stands as a good example of the power that can be wielded by the press. The former politician was for many years lionized, whereas the latter was, after a brief media honeymoon, mercilessly denigrated and eventually disappeared from domestic public view.

In both cases, the media, a crucial institutional vehicle of the public sphere, is subject to sectional or private concerns, pursuing their own agendas, undermining, thereby, its role within the democratic polity.

Corporate versus public service broadcasting

The culture of the corporate world media is determined by commercial pressures as key income streams are provided by subscribers (cable or satellite) and audience (whose availability is sold on to advertisers). There are sets of regulations in place to govern print, broadcast and satellite or cable sources; free-to-air television has to maintain a mix of programmes (news and arts as well as popular programming) and in respect of politics print media are relatively free to say what they like, whereas broadcast media are obliged to maintain some sort of balance. Some corporate media organizations have chafed at these restrictions; News International has been vocal in its criticisms of the BBC and – politics aside – it is a reasonable speculation that the core objection is in respect of costs – public service broadcasting, especially in Britain, is of a high standard – this pushes up costs, not just for the public service broadcaster but also for corporate world media bound by regulation to adopt some of the same quality standards.

The culture of public service broadcasting is quite different. Some aspects will be the same, for example, all the technical detail of making programmes, but other aspects will be quite different: the BBC began with a charter oriented towards a commitment to educate, inform and entertain and this implies a broad spread of programming in order to serve a broad audience (all those compelled to buy the licence fee). The BBC also plays a key national role as a funder of arts programmes. On the other hand, the BBC also operates like commercial television under a requirement to provide in respect of politics coverage that is balanced. And, in more recent years, the BBC has proved able to sell its programming overseas.

The corporate world continually pressures the public broadcaster with repeated demands that the BBC be downgraded, reduced to a niche broadcaster, whilst the corporate world expanded and hence increased its income and its profits.

Celebrity politics and mass sphere: Personalization/popularization

Personalization means that politics is reduced to the clash of individual figures and whilst this lets the audience secure some sort of grasp of the issues in question it is at the cost of any deeper engagement; thus, for example, in recent years, the wide-ranging conflicts of the Middle East have been summarily presented in terms of two discourses, Israel plus Palestine and al Qaeda plus terrorism.

Populism relies on the strategies of simplification, stereotyping, rabble-rousing (upmarket[35] and down) and the like. For example (again) the issues relating to Israel plus Palestine are simplified into the claims made on behalf of the two groups, where supporters of Israel present the country as the only democracy in a rough neighbourhood, whilst supporters of Palestine present that people as oppressed by a quasi-apartheid state. Such simplifications ensure that newspapers sell and they also ensure that the status quo in terms of the domestic understanding of this issue remains in place; the same can be said about al Qaeda plus terrorism as the terms are used to frame almost any report of violence in the Middle East, and as the contrast is usually made, implicitly or explicitly, with the West and the United Nations, where both are taken to evidence an automatic concern for human rights, this in the end produces not rational reports but banal strategies of dismissal. Against this, the same strategy of simplification can be used for ostensibly humanitarian purposes – that is, actions which would claim to address a general concern – Kate Nash[36] looks at the success/failure of a campaign to offer aid to the poor, noting the ways in which show-business celebrity and aid donation were run together in a grass-roots campaign to require governments to attend to millennium development goals; it raised some money, little else, showing the limits of such mobilization.

On celebrity in general there are various aspects to the phenomenon along with various opinions amongst commentators; Street[37] offers a defence of celebrity arguing that it is a new style of political life so it is worth studying on its own terms.

The face of the new public media considered

The style and flavour of the media shifts and changes down the years, for example in the 1950s, saucy seaside postcards were freely available, today online porn is equally freely available; or again, in the 1950s politicians appeared as remote formal figures, today they go out of their way to be reported in the context of informal, domestic settings; then, in the 1950s, violence in films was stylized, today it is graphic; and finally in the 1950s, newspapers were oriented towards hard news, today, human interest stories and commentary are more prominent. In all this, one trend, evident during the years of neo-liberal excess has been the emergence of the habit of aggression – always present in human communities, but recently evident as a media style (of both operation, the way they work, and presentation, how they present their material to their audiences).

The habit of aggression

The character of the new corporate media world involved more than a rise in the provision of popular and commercial programming or print material, it was also flagged in a shift from Reithian-style patrician good manners to a distinctly aggressive style of broadcast/print material; two loosely related aspects can be noted: attack journalism and spillovers.

Attack journalism in politics has been widely remarked upon, as it is a novel form of political broadcasting and reporting. In politics the ideal-typical role of journalism is that of providing a space for rational discourse and around this ideal-type actual journalism can be ranged and judged, better or worse. However attack journalism makes no pretence to conformity with such models, instead it is precommitted to a given line of criticism and all reporting is organized around this prior decision; thus American 'shock-jocks' and Fox News.

Aggressive journalism also targets non-politicians as private individuals are investigated and made the subject of stories (for example, the numerous cases from the *News of World*[38] or the materials published by the *Daily Mail*[39]). One recent cause celebre involved Max Mosley whose private activity was made the subject of sensational press coverage. Mosley sued the offending paper and won and has continued a now public political campaign to curb the power of the press in this regard; that said, he himself notes that he has the money to go to law, most private individuals are not in this position – in other words, for the media, they are soft targets.

Aggression in the media can generate responses in society, that is, instead of entertaining or persuading or shocking the intended audience, members of that audience can react directly. Three recent examples have involved violence: first, the Dutch politician Pym Fortuyn was assassinated in May 2002 following his theatrical populist campaigns against the established political order in general and migrant communities more particularly; second, the Dutch film-maker and populist provocateur Theo van-Gogh was murdered in November 2004 following the making of a film, *Submission*, attacking the religion of Islam; and third, in January 2011 American politician Gabrielle Giffords was shot and severely wounded and the shooting was linked to the attack-journalistic political style of the Tea Party Movement.

Bosmand and d'Haenens[40] looked at the Pym Fortuyn case and noted that the mainstream press demonized him, that is, he was not accurately or fairly reported. Alexander and Eyerman[41] looked at the murder of Theo van Gogh and invited the unpacking of the narratives of killing, how diverse groups told the story. The issue is pursued by Buruma,[42] who reads the two killings as flagging a deep-seated unease amongst the majority population about pace of change, inward migration and cosy elite agreements in regard to multiculturalism. In these cases, as with Giffords, media activities meshed catastrophically with individual motivations, as more generally protests are an important phenomenon, long part of the broad democratic sphere, and today they are rather self-conscious as demonstrating groups try to manage their reception.[43]

* * * * *

Looking to the future, Davies[44] 2009 offers an insider's view on the newspaper industry and it is somewhat pessimistic. The author diagnoses a severe falling away from hitherto affirmed ideas of professional journalism centred on accurate reporting. The causes are easy to specify: the commercialization associated with the general absorption of newspapers into larger corporate organizations as the resultant focus on profit skews the work of newspapers, producing a concern to cut costs, avoid trouble and serve up what the target audience wants and expects. All of this shapes contemporary journalism, degrading it. Davies reports that newspapers largely recycle material from the wire or from PR firms or from government press releases and so reporting gets 'thin', many groups are excluded,[45] and the older ethic of reporters getting the story straight is no longer central. Maybe 20 per cent of reports in the press originate with in-house reporters, the rest is variously bought in[46] and the result is 'knowledge chaos'.[47] It is probably unreformable but the internet does offer new possibilities, both for sources (although the web is full of chaotic nonsense) and for existing newspapers as it could let them cut the costs of hard copy by shifting to digital and recycling savings into journalism.

Running down to the present: Legacies and repetitions

Corporate media are a major presence in contemporary public life. The development of digital media offers more routes for them to disseminate their products. The creation of mixed platforms – print, broadcast and cable – makes them more influential by virtue of their ubiquity within the broad public sphere. Commentators suggest that some corporate groups have pursued clear political agendas in addition to their more fundamental concern for marketplace success, that is, running a profitable business. In recent years, in Britain, the influence of major newspaper proprietors has been noted but agendas can be pursued in general and diffuse ways. The media are just part of the overall political/cultural scene and their basic concerns are commercial (selling newspapers,[48] selling television, selling video, selling games), whilst thereafter they register a cultural impact (celebrating consumption, liberal market individualism and so on) and a political impact (offering routine support to this or that political party or ideology or spread of prejudices).

In recent decades – from the 1980s until around now – the substance of these messages has been suffused with the neo-liberal agenda of free markets and so debt-fuelled consumption has been encouraged in part by the media offering celebrations of such patterns of life: the aggressive individualism of reality television and game shows; the celebration of profit to be found in otherwise banal programmes devoted to antiques or upgrading houses in order to sell on; and the world of overseas long-haul holidays. In these realms the products of the bullshit industries enter common culture unnoticed, their influence drifting down through the channels of unremarked routine.

10
Familiar Utopias: New Technologies and the Internet

Digital technologies are changing the public sphere. Novel technologies of data-gathering, transmission, storage, analysis and distribution are remaking the scope of the public sphere. The technology is in its infancy so any commentary is directed to a work in progress. Quite where the new technology will take the public sphere is anyone's guess but several strands can be picked out as the state, corporate world and ordinary people interact with the new technology: thus, digital surveillance, digital government, digital data-mining and digital social media. In respect of political life, celebrants have advertised the imminent arrival of a new age of popular democracy; doubters have called attention to the increased powers of surveillance provided to the machineries of the state and the corporate world. In the case of British political culture these technologies are feeding into a complicated scene, in which a highly centralized state machine coupled to a party political scene dominated by a dual-conservative party hegemony interacts with a populace that is diverse, internet-savvy, and in significant measure disenchanted with mainstream politics.

Digital technologies have been driven by basic scientific research, innovator dreams, corporate concerns, government agendas and the evolving practical interests of end-users; state, corporate and private.[1] These technologies are very new and there is no sign that they are becoming a mature sphere. They are still developing. Digital technologies are the latest in a long line of innovative changes in means of communication. But these technologies do have novel characteristics: carrying capacity, speed of use and ease of distribution. However, a novel technology does not determine its own pattern of social use, such patterns are socially determined and the technology can be put to use by states, corporate firms and ordinary people, so the use of a novel technology depends upon who is involved, at what stage of the technical game and with what intentions in mind.

In respect of political culture in general the development of digital technologies has altered the public sphere, some commentators respond positively, seeing new opportunities, for example, the libertarian possibilities of the internet, whilst others offer warnings, seeing, for example, a risk for printed materials or internet land-grabs by big technology firms.[2] Moreover, relatedly, the development of digital technologies has altered some patterns of social interaction. Social media have encouraged new forms of community amongst consumers, activists, protestors and so on. At the same time, the use of digital communications has made it easier for the corporate world to collect information in respect of its customers and it has also made it easier for the state to spy on its citizens. Thus, in respect of Britain, these new technologies are being made available within a particular environment: in brief, a soft-oligarchic structure of power, a highly centralized state machine, a party political scene dominated by a dual-conservative party hegemony, engaged thereafter with a diverse, internet-savvy population, which is, in some measure, disenchanted with mainstream politics.

Episode: Digital promise and performance

Digital technologies are new, but new technologies are not for there have been many earlier communications systems and their introduction has attracted corporate and political attention plus often exaggerated claims in respect of their ongoing impact.[3] Digital is novel in respect of capacity, speed and reach, and it is these characteristics that have provoked so much enthusiasm.

The enthusiasm attached to claims for the speed and reach of the technology were seen first, in the 1980s the dot-com bubble, when the world of corporate finance looked to internet-based businesses as a new opportunity for profit and invested heavily, producing thereby a bubble on the stock market which in due course burst. A second example of corporate world enthusiasm was revealed in the run-up to the 2008/10 financial crisis when problems were caused in stock prices by computer-based high-speed trading. These procedures were impossible without digital and they proved dangerous to marketplace stability, it turned out that computers could create very rapid fluctuations in prices, which in themselves unsettled the market players. A final example, from recent years, is available in the enthusiasm for social media (networking sites, file-sharing sites, mobile communications) where one subset of these activities was used in political protests, thus commentators claimed a role for social media in the 2011/12 'Arab Spring'.

The preliminary task for scholarly commentary is that of looking at the claims asserted, their coherence and thereafter, as appropriate, evaluating the performance achieved with respect not merely to the claims of the various participants but to the wider traditions of the European social sciences – in which case, the crucial question for the present purposes is the nature of the impact of digital upon the public sphere. In all this, to recall, it is necessary to acknowledge both that these technologies are new (and thus both novel and rapidly developing so tomorrow's debates might have a different focus) and that recent years have seen a blizzard of enthusiasm amongst commentators, ordinary users (thus social media) and more practically amongst the corporate world and it may be that the enthusiasm has been overdone. It might also usefully be remembered that the agency with the most to gain from digital communications might just be the state – not for the purposes of upgrading democratic forms (something the British elite have assiduously avoided) but for the purposes of surveillance and control.

Characteristics of digital systems

Digital communications and the rest depend upon a number of high-technology developments and whilst these can be traced to the late 1930s and 1940s it is only in the last couple of decades that these technologies have attained the sophistication with which end-users are now familiar. A number of elements can be listed.

First, high-speed computer processing: this had developed from around the time of the Second World War and recent advances in technology have been rapid. The heart of the technology is machine processing of coded data. For the ordinary end-user the ensemble of science-based technological advance is summed in the idea of the silicon chip. The technology has developed dramatically such that processing capacity that took a room-sized machine in the 1940s now fits into a mobile phone and where processing capacity was scarce and expensive it is now treated as a commodity, that is, a non-specialized, basic resource in a science-based industrial capitalist system.

Second, high-capacity data storage: machine processing requires access to data, as high-speed processing is pointless without high-capacity storage. The development of this aspect of digital technologies has gone hand in hand with processing. The capacity of digital storage technologies is now enormous and for the ordinary office or domestic end-user these advances in technology make themselves available in a number of ways perhaps and an obvious example is available in the form of the near-ubiquitous thumb-drive – a small piece of magic plastic, carried in a purse or trouser pocket or pencil case which can hold large bodies of data (books, datasets, photographs, music and so on).

Third, software packages: the hardware is run according to the instructions placed in software packages. There are coding systems designed to run the machines (operating systems) and coding systems designed to run on the machines (applications). These technologies have developed alongside processing/storage and their use is now as ubiquitous as the computer hardware in which they sit and which they run. For the ordinary end-user these advances are available in the seemingly annual upgrades of operating systems for home computers and in the multiplicity of application software packages available to run on these machines; the early twenty-first century acme of such provision being found in Apple Computers' 'app shop'.

Fourth, transmission: the construction of systems cable, wireless and satellite have enabled data to be moved around the planet and moving data around is the final element of this new digital technological set. Once again the technologies have advanced in terms of capacity such that they cover the planet: satellite systems – major powers have either constructed such systems or are in the process of making them (USA – European Union – Russia – China); undersea cables extend around the planet; and the coverage offered by wireless systems is rapidly expanding. In rich countries transmission systems are available to most of the population and for the ordinary domestic end-user they present themselves in the form of a contract for their mobile phone or a cable running into their home plugging them into the internet.

Fifth, the internet: all these technological elements can be run as discrete units but a further advance was made when natural scientists realized that discrete systems could be linked together, both for convenience and to increase the overall capacity of the system. The internet has since burgeoned and it carries a vast amount of traffic: state, corporate and private, and for the ordinary end-user it presents itself as an individual means of access to a plethora of websites: information, education, commentary and entertainment (plus a vast avalanche of miscellaneous rubbish).

Changing the character of communication systems

Digital technologies have changed the territory of electronic media.[4] The core of the technology is the use of digital means to record and transmit data and there have been parallel developments in computing, data storage and transmission mechanisms. In recent years these technologies have developed very rapidly and the upshot is that it is now technically possible for machines to record, process, store and transmit very large amounts of digital data. These technological changes have been the occasion of a wave of innovation in the modes of communication utilized by agents in the state, the corporate world and those in the public sphere. Digital data systems exhibit novel characteristics: high capacity for processing information, the use of advanced technologies and for end-users the curious experience of product omnipresence (the devices are everywhere) combined with cognitive inaccessibility (the internal workings of these devices are incomprehensible to all but trained specialists).

(i) Information capacity

The digital world revolves around the technical business of the recording/transmission of text or image or sound (including voice) using binary code. It has its basis in simple electrics – thus a circuit can be on or off – '0' or '1' – the technical basis of digital code, which in turn is the basis of all digital equipment. In contrast to analogue recording, which it superseded, it is both flexible (it can record anything once in binary code) and very high capacity.

The use of analytical programmes permits data to be processed so that text, image and sound can be altered and presented in new forms. Digital is relatively easy to manipulate, unlike analogue systems where altering a recording or image or text is relatively difficult. With digital media texts can be revised, images can be altered, sounds can be changed. In the arts, for example, these characteristics have been embraced: film directors can use digital imagery or computer-generated images (CGI) and soundtracks of great complexity can be created using voices and instruments or without the need for these resources.[5]

The use of analytical programmes permits data to be interrogated such that user-required information can be pulled out of available datasets or raw data can be analysed for specific features. These features of digital have been of particular interest to states and the corporate world. The former can utilize them to monitor all digital traffic using the internet (if material is sent over the internet then it flows through a complex network of cables, satellites and computer servers and this is monitored by state security services).[6] The state can also use digital technologies to monitor flows of people (ID cards, CCTV). It can maintain extensive personal records (tax, health, insurance, television and so on) and all these can be linked – creating profiles of populations or certain elements or particular places[7] or individuals. The state can also variously access the resources of the corporate world.[8] The latter can use digital technologies to monitor stocks and create lean-production systems; loyalty cards can be used to allow individual shopping patterns to be recorded and such data can be used to build up profiles of consumers with the information made available to other companies for marketing or planning purposes; and more recently (with experimental systems) aggregated data – from credit card or mobile phone use or CCTV with face-recognition software – can be used to predict behaviour.[9]

(ii) High-technology

The basic machinery of the digital world is high-tech: research scientists, product designers, production engineers and finally high-tech factories, in style ranging from Boeing or Airbus aircraft assembly hangers through to the workers on the line in consumer-electronics factories in southern China.[10] This high-tech world operates in a complex environment: market competition with other firms (hence the drive for new products, spying (today, digital) and the use of patent law and copyright law to secure control of intellectual property); and state regulation as many high-tech products are potentially dual use, that is, they might have a military application and in this case access is controlled.

The digital world is not a product of familiar craft-derived metal-bashing engineering; instead the apparatus is the output of science-based industry so that research laboratory work and factory work are intertwined. It is also fragile: computers can be damaged (material issue), computers can be corrupted (social issue), mobile phones can be lost (social issue) and domestic consumer-durables can break down (material/social issue). Against that, digital products/applications are usually characterized by multiple redundancies so that it is unsurprising to find domestic machines continuing to function long after they have been made technologically redundant (or redundant by virtue of corporate commercial decisions – vinyl gives way to CDs give way to downloads – and then vinyl reappears as an upmarket niche product).

The processing is high tech and speeds increase such that what took a room-full of machines in the 1940s now fits into a mobile phone.[11]

The technical data-storage capabilities are high: data can be stored in very large quantities; digital data is easy to store; and technological advance has made such storage devices inexpensive. These devices carry programs which help run many machines (in automated factories and in end-user products such as cars or washing machines or cameras and so on) and when states or corporate agents generate datasets on populations or other phenomena (say, weather), these can be made available in appropriately processed form to subsequent users (official, commercial or private).

(iii) Opacity

Given their base in high technology, digital mechanisms/programmes are generally opaque to end-users (state,[12] corporate and domestic). The technology has a built-in asymmetry of power, where producers know how it works and end-users do not. Earlier technologies were accessible to large numbers of people. Thus, say, engineering where the basics of levers, pulleys, slab beams and the like can be comprehended easily. A trained engineer commands a specialism which in outline is intelligible to a wide audience and that audience can perform very simple tasks: fixing the car, or mending simple household appliances or assembling a garden shed. Contemporary digital technology is different: digital processors and memories come embedded in plastic or arrays of coloured plastic and whilst many people will be able to recognize a silicon chip only specialists will have any idea about how it works; recall Arthur C. Clarke, who remarked that a modern technology to a primitive people will look like magic – the argument also works for different social groups within our contemporary world.

Somewhat paradoxically, digital data is intrinsically insecure. Analogue data was not easy to copy or transmit whereas in contrast digital data can be copied and transmitted to new locations at the touch of a button – digital data relies on the operation not merely of sophisticated hardware but also of software – this is intrinsically insecure.[13]

Digital technologies: Products/uses

Digital technologies now find uses in very many areas of modern life, for example, in management systems in government and corporate worlds, or in regulatory systems running anything from power stations to jet liners to individual car engines plus the plethora of consumer digital electronic products.[14]

(i) The state

Public record-keeping using digital means is in principle both more exhaustive (as vast amounts of data can be kept and various state record systems can be interlinked and historical archives can be digitized thus together further increasing the available digital record), more reliable (as materials don't get misplaced and computers don't go on strike or off sick (provided systems are robust and backed up)), more useable (that is, many state operatives can access the data directly from their office desks or other workplace) and more efficient (as the cost per byte is much lower than using paper equivalents).

Computer-based management systems can be used to routinize many otherwise specialist tasks: high-level professionals are replaced by expert systems, mid-level office staff have their responsibilities transferred to specified and monitored routines and low-level office staff are simply replaced by machines (whose servicing in turn might be contracted out). And the general simplification of tasks increases the ability of levels within management hierarchies to monitor subordinates and thus the effectiveness of the particular activity: simplification of tasks allows responsibility for any particular task to be made specific to given personnel; simplification allows for increased top-down oversight of personnel and activities; and all these innovations serve to shift power upwards in the machinery of the state.

Population-surveillance systems[15] can utilize digital technologies. Modern digital technologies permit extensive routine surveillance of populations. The individual use of a digital device can be recorded and this record passed to a central recording and analysis centre. Many everyday activities involve using such digital devices: bank cards, swipe cards, loyalty cards, emailing or visiting social media sites or other websites – all these individual exchanges are recorded, logged and either can be or are passed on to central recording and analysis centres. Many everyday activities involve individuals making themselves known to the surveillance systems: CCTV systems are ubiquitous in Britain – their use is extensive in all public areas (roads, buildings, transport links and so on) and these systems continue to extend their reach within the target population (more cameras, better imaging, more sophisticated software and wider distribution of these materials throughout the machinery of the state).

(ii) Corporate world

Head-office functions – record-keeping – production functions – distribution functions – are more efficiently handled using digital technologies and in the corporate world many of these functions are now outsourced – head office manages a series of subcontractors in order to deliver its advertised products and the system can only work with reliable record-keeping.

As regard management systems: as with the state, so with the corporate world, digital enables effective power to move up the hierarchy.[16]

Corporate customer surveillance is a burgeoning field: here state surveillance of the population is replicated by the corporate sector albeit with significant differences: the corporate world is interested in customers (not citizens or dissidents or masses or mobs); the corporate world is concerned with consumer monitoring (what sells, what does not); consumer research (what particular groups or individuals buy); and stock control (the logistics of just-in-time-production systems); moreover, the corporate world is bound by law (that is, it cannot just spy on people and nor can it just make up the rules as it goes along).[17]

(iii) Private arena

In the private arena the usage is rather different as in place of standard tasks (management, data-gathering and analysis and so on) there is a more ad hoc collection of consumer uses. Digital machines are consumer durables and like other durables their usage is specific, so there is no overall pattern, but there are very large markets.

Desktop, laptop and tablet computers enable effective office work in the domestic environment, that is, people can work from home: employees of corporate world firms, small firms or independent one-person operations. Digital systems allow general information to be accessed via the internet – it allows specialist information on the payment of subscriptions.

Mobile phones are ubiquitous in developed economies – they provide ease of contact – they enforce permanent contact (cannot stay out of contact without flagging that choice to callers – including employer superiors) – mobile phones are a developing technology – in the second decade of the twenty-first century such phones were internet enabled – that is, they could function in many regards like a laptop computer.

GPS devices are hand-held or easily portable devices which record fairly accurately the machine's position on the planet – information is superimposed on a standard map of the local area – thus the user can know their location – used in ships, used in planes, used in cars and so on (also available for sports – thus GPS rangefinders for use on your local golf course) – the positional information is derived from a network of satellites – the GPS system is American (which is to say, the US government controls the on/off switch) and others are building their own systems: European Union, Russia and China.

Entertainment websites and social media websites: the internet allows vast stock of entertainment products to be accessed (and these can be displayed on new high-definition television) – it also allows social media websites to flourish whereby people with particular interests can link up and pursue their common concerns.

Themes in the public sphere

The new digital technologies have been put to use by the state, the corporate world and ordinary people. The resultant patterns of use are extremely varied and are determined by institutional concerns, particular agent agendas and changing social mores. Or, put another way, available technology does not translate into social practice in any simple mechanical fashion. As patterns of use can be varied, this suggests that any simple declaration of the benefits or disbenefits of the technology should be set aside in favour of looking at how actual practice is unfolding.

All that said, there is a long history of collective reflection upon the nature of the media both informal and scholarly and one aspect of this, rooted in the concerns of the late nineteenth and early twentieth centuries, the period of the emergence of mass societies, modern cities and large reading publics, was the nature of the relationship between an ever more visible media and the ideal models of political life sketched out in models of democracy. Or, in brief, were the mass media unpacking their latent promise (more debate, better informed leading to rational and democratic decisions) or were they somehow failing (serving special interest groups or playing to the lowest common denominator in pursuit of profit)?[18]

Digital technology – promise and performance
The development of digital technology has produced a rash of claims about its potential benefits in the social sphere: in regard to the state and democracy, in regard to the corporate world and its responsiveness to its customers and in regard to the public sphere with new forms of engagement available.

(i) E-democracy
Recent anxieties about apparently fading citizen involvement in formal political life has led to some speculation about e-democracy;[19] the idea points to using the internet to encourage 'citizen participation in the democratic process',[20] that is, participating in consultations through online surveys, participating in elections with online voting, or participating in formulating agendas via online petitions and proposals.

Thus, for example, 10 Downing Street boasts a petition centre on the government website. It went live in August 2011 and if an e-petition gains enough signatures then the proposal will be considered for debate in parliament. Some of the petitions are predictable (bringing back hanging); some are optimistically eccentric (establishing an English parliament); some gather support as they are topical (punishing rioters); and some address long-standing local grievances (Hillsborough tragedy reports).[21]

To date, the problem with all these lines of argument is that they address issues relating to electoral processes and to participation/consultation exercises. But the *former* does not address the core of the ideal of democracy (the idea, requisite institutions and desired practice), that is, the effective distribution of power/responsibility around the polity and judged in these terms the British political system is highly centralized and elite-dominated and as a type of polity is best tagged 'soft-oligarchic'. Whilst the *latter* is rather foolish as such exercises leave all power with those running the participation/consultation exercises. Thus far proposed e-democracy initiatives do not address these matters, the system is left unreformed, the agenda of democracy untouched and unadvanced.

(ii) E-government

In respect of the role of the state, there are websites offering information and online services; in respect of the role of political parties, they make extensive use of e-services to maintain contact with members and to identify potential supporters during pre-election periods, in respect of the work of Whitehall e-administration is a routinely affirmed aspiration.

In Britain, the various departments of the state machine have set up websites where basic official information can be accessed, forms downloaded and some issues can be dealt with online, thus, submitting a tax return and paying the resultant bill. All well and good, but marginal; the state withdraws a little into web-land.

(iii) E-state surveillance

It is a commonplace that the population of Britain is subject to a regime of routine surveillance, which is in some respects the most severe of any developed country. The standard story points to the proliferation in recent years of CCTV cameras in public, corporate and private places. This most likely understates the extent of the state surveillance of its population.

In addition to CCTV the state monitors internet-carried digital communications directly and also has access to the records of companies making available digital services: thus, all internet-carried communications traffic is monitored/recorded by state listening stations; in Britain, GCHQ in Cheltenham and Menwith Hill in Yorkshire;[22] internet service providers log internet site use and email traffic and such information can be made available to the state; all mobile phone records are kept by companies and can be made available to the state; all commercial transactions, such as credit or debit card use, are recorded and can be made available to the state. In recent years, the state has moved to integrate the computer-based records of various agencies, such as the police, other uniformed services and health and welfare organizations.

The state now can gather and process a wealth of information about its population. The drive to increase the amount of surveillance continues with new technologies, new law and a burgeoning security sector, state/private.[23]

(iv) E-corporate surveillance

Corporate world organizations gather a vast amount of data on those with whom they deal; this includes, for example: loyalty cards, credit cards and debit cards (all of which record patterns of use – where, when, what); or websites visited, product details consulted and any advertisements checked (all of which, again, is recorded); plus every user's web traffic (which sites, times, dates, places).

All this commercial data, once gathered can be mined in order to extract information about patterns of consumption or other activities amongst the population. Such processed information can be sold on, for example to advertisers, and can be made available to agencies of the state.

The corporate world can now gather and process a wealth of information about its customers/users.

(v) E-activism/networking

The internet has allowed the development of social network sites, which are available to all those who sign up for them. They were intended for social use, hence social networks, but they have also proved useful for political organizing, popular and elite.

In the first place, social network sites allow grass-roots organizations to flourish. The sites allow information to be uploaded and images to be uploaded; mobile phones allow gatherings to be organized and as mobile phones now usually include a camera, images can be quickly made and uploaded and distributed. A species of public sphere has been created. These social media have been credited with enabling significant social dissent to crystallize into the phenomenon tagged the 'Arab Spring'. All that said, social media are like any other internet-based exchange, that is, the material is unedited, its provenance unknown and its quality indeterminate.

In the second place, strategies of e-activism can be used by the state and the corporate world. The elite-sponsored variant of activism can be either passive, for example, via state provision of alternatives sources to corporate source, or it can be active, for example, through promoting or constructing social groups sympathetic to the state. In these cases the intention of the authorities is to combat and control critical voices in the e-network sphere. The corporate-sponsored version of activism can use PR firms to run covert campaigns in social media.[24] Once again, the intention is to discreetly influence otherwise public and open debate.

(vi) E-entertainment

Finally there is the familiar realm of popular entertainment: familiar media represented (commercial film, music and words); less familiar material made widely available (pornography); familiar practices reinvented (e-shopping); and novel practices created (e-games either self or group). Many of these activities have migrated happily to the web and it is a growing area of activity.

One particular problem associated with this sphere is the uneasy relationship between content providers, websites and end-users. The development of the web has created novel problems for established businesses: issues of intellectual property have been raised (how to keep copyright control over easily copied digital material); social practices reconsidered (sharing materials with friends or other enthusiasts); and business models have had to adapt (control and sell versus rent or give away free) – an ongoing area of conflict.

Wider issues: Some of the impacts noted

Digital technologies are now ubiquitous and their use is still developing, consequently numerous issues attend this process, here three are noted: the impress of ever more available information upon individuals and various social systems; the business of forgetting, something familiar to humans, sometimes a nuisance, sometimes a benefit, but a subjective/social process cut against by digital technologies as they do not decay; and finally, the issue of power/control – who is watching whom and who (if anyone) has control of the on/off switch.

The impress of information overload

The notion of information overload has been used to point to one aspect of the contemporary human situation: expressed passively, individuals now have access to more information than they can comprehend; or expressed more actively, individuals are now subject to a relentless flow of information which is impossible to assimilate.

Various lines of commentary flow from noting the flow of information: first, that individuals and communities are subject to stress (thus a psychological response is posited – bombarded with information, individuals lose their bearings and become anxious); second, that individuals and communities are encouraged to become passive (thus a social response is posited – bombarded with information, individuals disengage and withdraw into more private realms); third, that individuals bombarded with information become habituated to its receipt (thus an intellectual response is posited that the flow of information overwhelms critical faculties and the population experiences 'dumbing-down'); or fourth, that individuals and communities are subject to irritation (thus a political response is posited – too much junk mail provokes an angry response).

It is true that individuals are now subject to a relentless flow of information – websites, broadcasts, print – junk mail, circulars and the never-ending cascade of advertisements but the notion of overload might be too simple; agents are not passive, they respond, the traffic is not all one way.[25]

The business of forgetting[26]

The issue of privacy has been raised by commentators as the state and the corporate world collect vast amounts of data and process it: the former in the context of e-state activities (surveillance, control and also provision of services); and the latter in the context of making available e-consumerism (supplying and creating consumer wants). So, in respect of the activities of both state and corporate worlds the issue arises of the rights of individuals (or organizations, thus, say, NGOs) to privacy; that is, to freedom from e-surveillance or e-data gathering.

Viktor Mayer-Schonenberger[27] offers a discussion centred on the idea of forgetting. The author notes that humankind both remember and forget and that these are both intrinsic to our humanity. The latter is not simply an inconvenience; it is, cast in information terms, a mechanism for screening and weeding memory, thinning out what is remembered so that we can deal with the present day. The development of digital technologies has permitted powerful organizations such as the state and corporate world to increase their e-surveillance and e-data gathering so that both state and corporate world now gather and process vast amounts of data about individuals and groups. Mayer-Shonenberger argues that this cuts against the business of forgetting and it introduces new difficulties for humankind as individuals and groups can be burdened by too much 'past'. Add to this the attentions of the state and corporate sector and the problem becomes acute: society is in the process of creating a 'digital panopticon[28]'. In answer to the question – so what is to be done? – the author rehearses some standard moves[29] (regulation, minimize use or just live with it) and adds to these a proposal for time-limiting digital records, that is, they should have expiry dates, a technical reinvention of forgetting.[30] All of which is fine but the author does not consider the world of politics and no argument is advanced as to why the state or corporate world would wish to give up its power and nor is there any suggestion as to how they might be made to surrender the new powers that the new technologies are making available.

Digital data can be kept; it accumulates at a rapid rate; analytical software advances at the same time. In respect of the state and polity the business of remembering and forgetting has been long debated by historians. One aspect of the claim to legitimate authority made by all states is the creation of a national past – a careful mix of active remembering and equally active forgetting – a set of statements that tells the particular political community where it came from, where it is now and where, ideally, it should seek to be in the future. It may be that digital records will burden the state and the polity, making the business of updating agreed national pasts all that more difficult.

State and corporate control: Oversight?
Digital technologies enable relatively small groups of people to subject relatively large groups to extensive and intrusive surveillance. In the past, amongst specialists, the British state has been routinely criticized for being secretive and via the notion of the Crown in parliament answerable only to itself (no written constitution overseen by a constitutional court). The polity and its core armature, that is, the machinery of the state, are best characterized as a soft oligarchy: power is restricted and public involvement or oversight is neither needed nor sought nor permitted. Digital technologies work to reinforce this sharp hierarchical

bifurcated set-up: elite power is reinforced, the possibilities of subaltern power correspondingly weakened.

An analogous situation obtains with respect to the corporate world. Clearly, the corporate world works differently: it wields less political power, it has less reach within the population and it is bound by law. But it has connections to power-holders via either membership of the networks or lobbying and it can protect some in-house data from scrutiny by deploying the notion of commercial sensitivity.

New technologies: Possible lines to the future

The development of digital systems has polarized debates. Substantive debate often seems divided between celebrants and sceptics: celebrants represent digital as key to the future in many areas of human social life, private and public; where sceptics either don't believe a word of it or do believe it but see a nightmare (state control or corporate intrusion). The recent track record of digital offers no clear evidence: search engines and social network sites are very popular; but IT projects for state and corporate world have failed expensively.

(i) Enthusiasm and disappointment

Tim Wu[31] tracks the patterns of enthusiasm and disappointment that have attended the arrival of novel technologies: the arrival of new technologies, the conflicts over their exploitation and control, plus the likely position of digital on this model sequence.

So, first, Wu invokes Schumpeter on creative destruction to grasp the dynamics of the arrival in the marketplace of novel technologies. The disruptive technology produces a variety of responses: it is often celebrated by those inclined to libertarian utopianism (wide communication and new communities); it is dealt with pragmatically by businessmen (how to profitably develop an industry); and it is viewed as threat/opportunity by those already providing similar services (thus existing telegraph owners tried to block new telephone companies).

Then, second, Wu looks at the successive careers of telegraph, telephone, radio, feature films, television, cable and notes the recent arrival of the internet. Wu tracks the mix of creative technology, existing firms and the activities of new firms looking for new industries along with the role of the state via licensing or copyright law or patent law/lawyers. The move from new technology to new consumer industry is anything but direct. The mix of technology and media is contingent: thus the AM radio industry blocked the superior FM system for many years; and

Sony Betamax tape failed when confronted with the technically inferior VHS tape produced by JVC. Government regulators can determine success or failure by awarding or withholding licences to broadcast frequencies; large companies can bankrupt smaller innovative firms with lengthy courtroom battles over patents, and so on.

Finally, third, Wu speculates that the internet is now entering a phase of consolidation; that is, the early utopian phase is over, but it is not clear what will follow. The open network nature of the internet makes it difficult to control but commentators said that about all the other systems and each was brought under commercial and statutory control; neither state nor corporate world have any interest in an unregulated internet.

(ii) Against net enthusiasts

Evgeny Morozov[32] is sceptical about the claims made by net enthusiasts: four arguments are made, against cyberutopianism, against net centrism, against the technological fix and for cyber-realism.

First, against cyber-utopianism: the internet is not a guaranteed way to encourage and facilitate liberal-democratic style politics, the argument is silly, the internet is just as useful for repression as it is for emancipation. Three errors are noted: one temptation to this error is a false argument about the 1989/91 changes in the Soviet bloc but this was a matter of structural problems not the availability of smuggled fax machines and so on; an interesting error is to suppose that polities can only be legitimated via liberal-democratic politics – not so – try jingoism or material benefits or familiarity; and finally an interesting comparison can be made between Orwell and Huxley[33] – repression versus seduction, Huxley has won as the web is mostly used for recreation ('soma').

Second, against net centrism: the focus on the geek world of internet apparatus is a mistake, it misdirects attention towards the machineries and away from the inevitable and varied social context of its use so this geek focus is foolish. Four points are noted: one temptation is to believe everything Google tells you – geeks run it – but social change has deep roots (and where it does not, digital technology is neither here nor there); the web is full of spin (misleading information); the web is full of rubbish (not activism but slacktivism); and finally the web is full of mad people (conspiracy theories etc.).

Third, against the technological fix: technological reductionism is old stuff and as an argument strategy it is poor because technology itself does not automatically produce anything and nor is it neutral between any end. It offers possibilities for use and how such possibilities are actually used depends on who and where and when. All the usual business of social context; three arguments are noted: web-based postings can be read by anyone and state machines are very good at reading and analysing web traffic so posting instructions on how to make the revolution merely announces your presence to the state plus the state can post on its own behalf plus the state can offer sites on which people can post; the web can facilitate discussion and the web can facilitate the dissemination of prejudice with sectional interest groups running intolerant lines and so the net does not point to inevitable modernization of political life for context is crucial; and net libertarianism is crazy, as liberal democracy requires a strong state.

And, finally, fourth, for cyber-realism: the sensible strategy is to look at how a novel technology fits into given social practices, then spot any changes and then decide how to react/judge.

Running down to the present: Legacies and repetitions

Recent decades – including the 2000s – have seen the state; the corporate world and ordinary people embrace digital technologies. They have become ubiquitous, part and parcel of the ordinary routines of life. But various groups have dealt with them in different ways, they run into established patterns of life in different ways.

The state has embraced digital technologies: various governments have invested in computer-based management systems; various governments have invested in digital-based surveillance systems; various governments have invested in public information systems and the results have been patchy.

The corporate world has embraced digital technologies: in finance (digital trading platforms – quantitative models running on computers – high-speed trading on computer systems); in production (computer-aided design and computer-controlled production – robots); in services (thus logistics or marketing data analysis, for example, supermarkets); and in the media, where, in film, music, television and newspapers, digital has undermined pre-digital ways (from corporate strategies down to particular craft skills).

Against this, the ways in which digital has run into the realms of public politics (state, parliament and parties) is much less clear for technology is not a panacea. Any new technology implies reworking existing relationships, yet whilst digital technologies have strengthened elite control mechanisms, they have also offered something to the wider populations that looks like mass empowerment through participation in election campaigns and participation in civil rebellion. And these technologies have been embraced by social network users – new online communities have come into being – their status remains unclear (fad or genuine novelty). The outcome is not clear and where enthusiasts point to new forms of politics, sceptics are dismissive of such claims, seeing familiar power relationships adapting to marginal mass-media novelties.

Pleasure in technical advance is familiar in post-war British political culture and whilst it is true that technology can and does open up new fields – advertising, entertainment, networking and a novel variant of the public sphere – all that said, in Britain, the suspicion must be that technological novelty serves as a substitute for institutional/cultural democratic reform, for no conceivable spread of digital channels of information, entertainment and commentary can substitute for reform of the soft-oligarchic structure of the British polity.

11
Continuing Britain: Contemporary Political Culture Unpacked

The political system of Britain in its current form took shape in the years following the Second World War when the elite were obliged to respond as best they could to the collapse of the state-empire system in which they had been embedded. The response was creative and involved a mix of denial and confection as any explicit recognition of profound structural change was elided in favour of an idea of 'continuing Britain', an old nation, recently victorious in a virtuous war, a bridge between Europe, the United States and the Commonwealth, a country which punched above its weight, a model for other states/nations. Upon this political-cultural base further additions were made as the post-war period unfolded and events provoked their own reactions. Unhappily, the elite's initial response was a fantasy and their vision of the future of the political-cultural project of Britain was untenable moreover their vision entailed accommodation to the demands of the USA in respect of a global liberal trading sphere and prompted them to turn away from Europe where the first steps towards union were being made. In recent decades this has meant an enthusiastic affirmation of model of liberal-market democracy, however the recent financial crisis and consequent collapse of the neo-liberal package has underscored the scale of the errors made by the elite in those days. Neither European, nor American nor plausibly independent, the British polity turns this way and that, celebrating a stylized past and trumpeting its self-proclaimed status whilst casting around for a plausible tale to tell about its future. All this implies a rather urgent reconsideration of the character and direction of the polity. And as the present situation combines an established base plus various accretions, it is from within this repertoire of ideas that plans for the future must be fashioned. So looking to the future, downstream from crisis, the polity confronts a choice: poodle-hood, muddle-through or Europe.

The British polity is – like others – enmeshed within global structures of power.[1] Here change is a given. The state acts as a transmission mechanism. It is the institutional means whereby elites can read and react to enfolding structures, where the resources of inherited culture provide the reservoir of intellectual, moral and imaginative resources that inform action. The incumbent elite are crucial in determining how the machinery of the state will be deployed and what sorts of developments will be sought. The exchange of structural circumstances and state elite projects will – over time – sketch out an unfolding trajectory, a distinct line of development and this means that each polity has its own internal make-up, its own logic. The political system of Britain is best characterized as a soft oligarchy: power is concentrated in a narrow elite, which has strong links to the USA through finance, defence and political nostalgia;[2] it is served by a core executive based in the machineries of the state; this, in turn, is fronted by party-based governments, whose activities are legitimated by the popular resources of the national past and the rituals of a largely decorative parliament, which, finally, is oriented towards ordering an acquiescent population broadly content with welfare-buttressed consumerism.

The system attained its current form, for it is a thoroughly contingent achievement,[3] in the years following the Second World War. The elite responded to the catastrophe of the loss of empire by first denying that the hitherto peripheral territories had ever been vital and thereafter by assiduously working to secure as best it could an advantageous economic and political position within the new liberal sphere centred upon the USA whilst wrapping defeat and the new settlement in the political-cultural rhetoric of 'continuing Britain'. This Britain was presented as the legatee of thousands of years of history,[4] the recent victor in a virtuous war and a model for other states and nations. The episode of war provided a new foundation myth, and the basic themes found in the public sphere were put in place: the enduring British, the war, welfare and the special relationship.

Looking at the post-war period we can see that the polity slowly changes its character. *First, power relations change*: domestic relationships between class groups in society are not fixed, rather any balance represents a contested compromise, and such compromises can shift (as new groups emerge, one group or other successfully asserts its wishes and old groups disappear), and international relationships are not fixed either, so structures change, and local elites must respond to new constellations. *Second, institutional mechanisms change*: the institutional structure, which buttresses any particular pattern of power relations, is not fixed; it is contingent. Institutional arrangements are shaped by the relations of power within a polity, so some institutions are more powerful than others and such centres of power change; as some rise in influence, others decline. Amongst these shifts the public sphere alters its character: new participants, new media and new arguments deployed. And *third, ways of understanding the resultant pattern also change*: the location, structure and direction of the polity-in-general is captured in the national past and it is continually updated; in Britain, often it seems the updating is done very subtly, change is smoothed out, potential challenges anticipated and disarmed.

Overall, the structural location of the polity has changed surprisingly little in the intervening period: the subordination to the USA continues, modified to some extent by a partial engagement with the European Union and whilst events down the years have presented further ideas to be added to the confection of 'continuing Britain' the basic pattern remains intact. But the international and domestic environment of the state and the demands placed upon the elite are not fixed; change is a given. And as noted, the political system of Britain in its current form took shape in the years following the Second World War when the elite were obliged to respond to the collapse of the state-empire[5] system in which they had been embedded. The response included a mix of denial and confection as any explicit recognition of profound structural change was elided in favour of an idea of continuing Britain. In this way, the elite accommodated themselves to the new power/authority of the USA. This Atlanticist stance was pursued within domestic politics in terms taken from Keynes and a modestly ameliorative role was granted to the state, but in the 1980s there was a change of tone as the elite turned to embrace the fashionable neo-liberal package of ideas. These ideas informed political practice for some 20-odd years. They were not sustainable. Thus the still unfolding 2008/10 financial crisis has underscored not only recent policy mistakes but also the scale of the political errors made by the elite in those early post-war days for the polity is now neither attached to the USA nor to Europe and claims to a robust independence are implausible.[6]

The arguments made in this text have sought to unpack the layers of identity, which make up the contemporary ideas of what it is to be British: they specify a foundation myth, note a stylized deep history, review the gradual accretion of elements and reveal that the elite responded to the loss of empire with a mixture of *denial* (rather than confront directly the consequences of the loss of their state-empire system) and *confection* (in their insistence in the existence of a 'continuing Britain'). This strategy of denial/confection underpins contemporary political culture; the sets of ideas that run through the public sphere and work to restrict discussion of alternative images or futures for the polity.[7] Yet in the wake of the recent financial crisis such discussion is necessary for presently the polity going forwards confronts distinct alternatives and three scenarios can be posited: 'poodle-hood', 'muddle-through' or 'Europe'; the choice is important and debate must start with the critical apprehension of the resources to hand, the sets of ideas running through received political culture.

Enquiries into contemporary culture

The idea of continuing Britain is central to public politics. The polity is represented as a long-established nation-state, recently victorious in a virtuous war[8] and in total something of a model for other countries to emulate. Thereafter, events have produced further accretions of ideas – from subaltern protest to the celebration of individual greed – whilst the basic imagery remains securely in place. As it happens, the proffered story is nonsense. The post-war disintegration of the state-empire system severed the link of metropolitan core and various peripheries; the latter secured independence and sought development, the former, sought solace in a confected past as a long-established nation-state whilst accommodating itself to the demands of the dominant power of the USA. Yet now, as the second decade of the twenty-first century opens, this settlement, redolent of the politics of the mid-twentieth century and harking back to earlier years, seems overdue for reform.

A number of ideas can be deployed to order critical substantive enquiry: the public sphere, the elite, subaltern groups, an accumulative process in respect of the ways in which events feed ideas into the common stock, which stock, finally, is summed in the idea of the national past.

Arguments in the public sphere

There is a long-established concern for the public sphere itself; that is, it should exist and not be shut down; and for the nature of argument deployed within the public sphere, which, ideally, should be oriented towards an enlightened and engaged citizenry. Those disposed to use the idea of the public sphere would wish to ground it, one way or another, in familiar human social practice. In the case of Jurgen Habermas the idea is grounded in language, the medium of human communication and the locus of a minimum ethic;[9] or cast in rather different terms, open debate is part and parcel of an open society. These two interrelated ideas become the measure against which current circumstances are judged.

In Britain, the political community in general has long experience of participation within a public sphere, however, notwithstanding that eighteenth-century Britain provided Habermas with the materials for his ideas, it is not clear that this sphere can discharge these responsibilities. Two reasons, first, the character of the broad media realm itself, then second and more importantly, the nature of the political system in Britain. The media is limited in its aspirations. Print media is flourishing, diverse but heavily skewed towards entertainment, whilst broadcast media comprises a significant public broadcast operation, the BBC plus spillover, whose output in respect of politics is conservative, and a corporate sector concerned with audience share and thus oriented towards whatever is popular. This impoverished public sphere confronts a political system that is in essence oligarchic in structure, thus power is remote from a public sphere, which is itself weak. This does not add up to a functioning Habermasian public sphere. Cast in general terms, a better characterization of the situation comes from Alasdair MacIntyre who writes of a public culture where spurious claims to individual rights to property and welfare confront equally spurious official claims to bureaucratic expertise, exemplifying thereby a political culture adrift from an appreciation of the role of community, lost to the intellectual and moral nonsense of liberal individualism.[10]

Elite fractions

All political systems have key groups; they are central to the make-up and reproduction of the polity in question. Recruitment to these positions can vary and here these matters are cast in terms of the notion of elites.[11] Elite groups must secure their livelihoods and these have their foundations within definite locations within the overall productive sphere. Elites are made up of fractions. Such groups can exist in various combinations but whatever their differences they have in common that their interests are best served by sustaining the overall coherence of the elite in relation to subaltern groups.

Elite groups promulgate ideas in order to legitimate their power and there are various ways of grasping these sets of ideas; here, the notion of a great tradition, the sum total of the overarching ideas in respect of claims to knowledge, ethics, expertise and practice that work to promulgate elite ideas and thereby secure order. In Britain, nominally a liberal democracy, better described as a soft oligarchy, key elite fractions include sections of the machinery of the state (monarchy, army and church), the realms of financial businesses, defence-related multinational business, and a penumbra of related businesses (media, property and the like (influence and money)). The coordinating committee for these powerful factions is the core executive lodged in the heart of the machinery of the state, the permanent government in Whitehall/Westminster. And thereafter, we find parliament, parties and the familiar realms of public political life, the point at which arguments based in ideas of liberal democracy can misleadingly begin.

Subaltern groups

The claims of the elite are embedded in institutional practices, social mores and the formal statements of explicit ideology, the realms of official truths and subaltern class groups operate in terms of a variety of responses: after Frank Parkin, deferential, aspirational or oppositional. Subaltern groups can submit to the status claims of the elite and thereafter turn away to the resources of the local environment, the little tradition; or they can acknowledge and embrace elite-status claims, seeking to emulate them, to catch up and maybe join in; or finally, they can reject the claims of the elite in favour of explicit alternatives.

Whatever response is deployed, subaltern ideas will be involved in a subtle exchange with elite ideas and the ideas of the more powerful group will inform the responses of the weaker, the result being some sort of fusion or contested compromise. In Britain subaltern class groups command a small share of available societal wealth and income, and the asymmetry in access to resources shows up in differential life chances.[12] Cast in simple terms subaltern groups can be divided on wealth/income grounds: thus professional, business and service middle classes (either independent figures in the employment market or employees of the state); skilled working classes (either independent craftspeople or employees of market-based forms or employees within the state sector); unskilled working classes (with insecure employment in market or state sector); along with a significant unskilled underclass (insecure employment, welfare and black economy). Sets of ideas promulgated by the elite will perforce interact with a diversity of local or little traditions, producing a diverse pattern of thinking amongst subaltern groups.

Accumulation of arguments

The exchange between elite and subaltern groups is ongoing, it is never fixed, it never reaches an end-point. Relationships change as the power of various constituent groups within both these broad groupings waxes and wanes and all the whilst such changes are accompanied by a steady flow of running commentary, one part of the substance of the public sphere. Such commentary will be reiterative, as available resources are recycled but there will also be accumulations, as new resources are created. Here we turn to events, ideas and residues: social life is eventful, things crop up,[13] some of them are given a significance and read into collective ways of thinking and their influence runs down through time, they leave residues. The stock of ideas whereby members of a polity might read and react to their circumstances is not fixed; it is continually augmented as novel practice-derived ideas are added, whilst others fade.

In Britain, after Linda Colley, there was the contingent process of creating the British state-empire system and associated spreads of ideas in both metropolitan and peripheral areas and amongst a multiplicity of identifiable groups. Such ideas included, centrally, the idea of Britain and the British. After the Second World War the state-empire system disintegrated and a new round of domestic debate followed and in the event the collapse was met with elite denial and the construction of a 'continuing Britain', whilst subaltern classes were rendered content with welfare and consumption. But these matters are never settled, debate is open ended, and whilst generally not much happens, ideas do accumulate and sometimes there are shifts and changes.

National past – contested

Elite ideas and those of subaltern groups exist in tension, the one pushing, the other variously accommodating or resisting. Such exchanges, over time, at a general level produce an agreed version of the polity, its history, present-day and ideal future, that is, a 'national past'.[14] It is never finally agreed as it exists in tension and carries the divergent wishes of assorted class groups. It is always a contested compromise about power/legitimacy and both sides of the equation are liable to disturbance. Critical commentary can address the later part, what those working within and with reference to the work of the Frankfurt School would tag as 'emancipatory critique'. In Britain the national past encompasses continuing Britain and a contingent accumulation of bits and bobs, the fruits of post-war events and the ways in which they were read into common culture.

Collapse, denial and confection

A number of commentators have challenged the received national past offered by official Britain, the mix of denial and confection discussed throughout this text, and what these writers have in common is their concern for the ways in which the polity reads its own past.[15] Thus contemporary ideas of Britain and the British can be unpacked. The identity comprises a number of layers: in brief, a foundation myth supplemented by an accretion of further elements. The key to unlocking the set is the collapse of the state-empire system. The elite responded with a mixture of denial and confection: first, *denial* – the loss of peripheral territories was simply disregarded, the event was read out of the national past; and second, *confection* – the residual metropolitan core of the former state-empire was reimagined as the long extant nation-state of Britain; so continuity was affirmed and the lost territories reimagined as of only transitory interest; the package can be tagged 'continuing Britain'. The complex of ideas making up this package is found not only in elite-level practice but they also run through the common sense of contemporary political culture, and that being so, they exhibit the familiar trait of invisibility-by-virtue-of-familiarity, in other words, the ideas are hegemonic. But the ideas – at the same time – are found in the public sphere and so they can be approached in a critical fashion and unpacking these ideas encourages debate.

Denial and confection

The collapse of empire was the crucial structural change for the British polity. As the state-empire system within which it had been embedded disintegrated, elite reaction was pragmatic in that they sought to protect their interests as best they could. But their response was also one of denial; that the empire had never been that significant, that it had in any case been succeeded by the Commonwealth and that the baton of leadership had been passed to the USA for whom the British were number-one ally. Paralleling the strategy of denial was one of confection as the diminished former metropolitan core of the state-empire system was reimaged as a long-established nation-state. This putative nation-state had for thousands of years found its home on the geographical territory of the British Isles,[16] had recently been victorious in a virtuous war and it was now a model for other countries to emulate.

Remembering and forgetting

It is, of course, perfectly possible to offer critiques of received political culture. Collective historical memory is a mix of active remembering and equally active forgetting.[17] In Europe, the task of establishing an official/popular memory of the Second World War was difficult. Much of the resultant official/popular memory is very poor history. There was no simple end to the war and the period saw a spread of local civil wars develop with many people and groups simply accommodating themselves to unfolding events. Yet the business of rebuilding demanded some sort of political-cultural settlement and the process of remembering and forgetting did serve to establish crucial foundation myths for contemporary Europe; what one scholar[18] characterizes as 'the allied scheme of history', where the Russians were heroic, the Americans determined, the British virtuous, with, in contrast, the Germans being those responsible for the catastrophe.[19] But the impacts of war went deeper, shaping the self-understanding of Europeans: the subtle appreciations of loss (the dead, the damage), shame (as the crisis was, so to say, home-made) and learning (the impulse towards cooperation, plus the reluctant/enforced abandonment of empires).

Tony Judt has looked at the process of establishing an official/popular memory of the Second World War and argues that much of the official/common memory is very poor history. There was no simple end to the war and the period end saw a spread of local civil wars develop with many people and groups simply accommodating themselves to unfolding events. Yet the business of rebuilding demanded some political-cultural settlement (the more awkward as there was neither a peace treaty process nor harmony, the Cold War soon began to build) and the unsatisfactory process of remembering and forgetting did serve to establish crucial foundation myths for contemporary Europe. The war provides key themes in Britain's national past.[20] Patrick Wright has written extensively on political identity in the United Kingdom and the work is intellectually rooted in the writings of Agnes Heller, a follower of Georg Luckacs. Wright recalls that Heller attends to the realm of everyday life, the mundane sphere of ordinary living, as it is within this sphere that people encounter both history (the ways in which their lives are slotted into unfolding time – personal, familial, community and polity) and culture (the ways in which their lives are informed by a repertoire of concepts carried in tradition). Heller insists that everyday life is situated; that is, it is always precisely located and imbued with the intellectual/moral resources of tradition, which presents itself in stories. It is with reference to these stories that people lodge themselves in communities and in turn tie these into wider schemes of history. Such exercises can also be done critically. Wright takes these ideas and puts them to work to unpack British political culture,[1] to unpack the key themes in the national past. First, there is nostalgia for a pre-industrial and/or empire past, a time when social arrangements were clear and unproblematic, matters of place and hierarchy. The pre-industrial theme can be unpacked into claims about rural life:

imaginary (happy farmers/farm workers) or aesthetic (the enchanted landscape), or fanciful (ley lines and Arthur's realm), or planned (urban reformers), or reassuring (heritage – great houses or television serials). Then the empire theme points to the civilizing mission of the British: heroes, heroines, victories plus some scoundrels. Second, there are auratic sites/objects. These are places/objects of great significance, the unique place or building or painting and these places/objects are taken to exemplify the essence of the political culture (Runnymede for Magna Carta, Cenotaph for Great War, White Cliffs of Dover for Vera Lynn for England, or monarchy/church/parliament for official Britain). And third, there is remembered war: wars against revolutionary powers, America and France; wars against assorted foreigners in the pursuit of empire;[21] and wars against European competitors, recently Germany, with the Second World War read as victory in a morally virtuous war.

Contemporary political culture: Events, readings and legacies

The long history of Britain in the modern world has been folded into a stylized history and made a part of today's national past. It is a kind of deep history.[22] The more recent episode of significance was the Second World War and it is here that we find a species of foundation myth for Britain, with thereafter, in the post-war period, further accretions, constituting, in sum, of the contemporary political culture of Britain.

Reading the political culture of Britain in the post-war period

The political culture can be grasped as a series of 'layers'; the metaphor points to the accumulations of practices/ideas that constitute a live unfolding tradition.

(i) Deep history: Great tradition and little tradition

The British state-empire system had been accumulated over several centuries yet it dissolved away over a couple of decades, leaving the domestic core elite confronting a political-cultural catastrophe. Their project of empire was over and they had perforce to fashion a response; pragmatically, they accommodated themselves to the power of the USA and the loss of empire was sidelined and the war years were invoked, provided the basis for a new national myth, which in turn was a part of the confection of a 'continuing Britain,' nominally, a long-established deeply rooted country.

(ii) The layers noted

The end of the Second World saw the institutional vehicles and rhetorics of wartime and welfare put in place and they were to serve as the political-cultural foundations of 'continuing Britain', a victory in a virtuous war appropriately rewarded. The 1940s/50s saw the rhetoric of wartime revisited time and time again: themes of heroic victory, remembered war, nostalgia for empire, along with superiority to mainland countries, variously occupied or defeated. The 1940s/50s also saw the regular affirmation of ideas associated with welfare: fairness, equality, cradle-to-grave care, planning and rights. All these ideas moved into mainstream public discourse. Thereafter, these basic themes were supplemented by other ideas as events provoked reactions amongst elite and mass, some of these episodes passed without leaving much of a trace, others left a deeper mark and were read into common culture; a sequence, repeated – events, ideas and residues.

So, building on the memory of wartime, first by the late 1940s the European mainland was in process of being reorganized as two great military powers occupied the territory, in the west the USA, in the east the Soviet Union. These powers constructed a bloc system: an institutional apparatus was created, an overarching rhetoric was deployed, which served to institutionalize Manichean politics, doctrines of military exterminism (weapons of mass destruction) and domestic paranoia giving rise to spies, dissidents, fellow travellers and the like. The rhetoric of Cold War became pervasive. Then, second, in the late 1950s the standard tale was challenged by a dissenting counter-rhetoric; the rhetoric of complaint with angry young men, youth rebellion, experimentation in the arts, the end of deference and the discovery of the working classes, all within the environment of full employment. And, third, in the 1960s/70s, there was the rhetoric of social differentiation and protest; thus there were new social groups and new media with advertising directed more precisely at new groups, hence the rise of consumers; and on the other hand, there was the rhetoric of crisis, the mix of affluence, violence, rebellion and progressive social change. But postwar enthusiasms for change met their match in the late 1970s as state, market and the organized working classes drifted apart. New ideas were deployed. So fourth, in the 1980s/90s there was the novel rhetoric of corporate advance provided by the new right when a spread of ideas was presented: the market, liberalization, deregulation and the enemy within. These were further supplemented by the rhetoric of corporate success: corporate world, corporate power, corporate media and business efficiency. And in the decades of the new centuries, there was a new rapidly evolving rhetoric of digital revolution: e-government, e-surveillance, and an e-democracy of citizen/consumers. And in each of these schematic phases, events generate ideas, which leave their mark, ideas laid down over time; and received culture is passed on as an available layered resource; tradition.

In sum, these ideas encompass the political culture of contemporary Britain. A mixture of elite ideas and subaltern ideas; at any one time, what is accepted – claims about who we are – represent a contested compromise between these two groups (with all their subdivisions). There is no enduring core to the political culture of the polity. Against those familiar nationalist readings, which posit an enduring polity, 'Britain', it can be asserted that there is only the presently available living stock of ideas, those currently informing those practices, which in total constitute the polity. These layers of meaning underpin contemporary debates within the public sphere; they are an available repertoire of concepts – they allow novel events to be grasped and taken into debate. The set is diverse. It is carried in a variety texts and text-analogues. And, crucially, it is contingent.

(iii) The layers critiqued

In the realms of politics, modernity can be unpacked around the interrelated ideas of states, nations and public sphere; the last noted a broad arena of debate with many contributors, many conflicts, many novelties, and many reiterated themes. In all, the public sphere is fluid, popular and democratic. The various contributors place their arguments into the public sphere and many of these will be presented in written form (statements, commentaries, manifestos, declarations and the like), but many are also presented in a non-discursive fashion: ideas can be embedded in quotidian routines and simply taken for granted; ideas can be embedded in concrete and walked past in everyday life (buildings, statues, memorials, etc.); and of course ordinary social routines are infused with political-cultural meanings (thus discourses of race, or class, or religion, plus liberal markets produce unequal societies so the social world is not 'flat', rather hegemonic ideas legitimating such distinctions infuse the social world, they work 'behind our backs'). Together these disparate contributions constitute an unfolding tradition, a set of ideas about the polity. The set is not fixed (ideas wax and wane in influence): the set is not definitive (ideas are introduced into discourse and they can fall away); the set is not agreed (there are many ongoing arguments about which ideas could/should be utilized); and many arguments are never resolved (events move on, participants change). These ideas are both constitutive, thereby establishing the polity in discourse, and a resource, providing the means to the critique of established ideas/practices and a way of grasping the unfolding changes impacting the established ideas/practices of the polity).

Substantive enquiry focused on post-Second World War Britain can track the shifting nature of discourse within the public sphere; uncover the layers of meanings that underpin contemporary debates. This process of excavation can be ordered around a trio of ideas – *events, ideas and residues* – whereby incidents within the general flow of life are read by participants in terms of the idea of 'events', not just something or other happening, but something of significance, which are grasped in terms of definite 'ideas', new formulations serving to grasp and underscore the significance of those episodes in question, and which, thereafter, in greater or lesser measure leave a permanent 'residue' within the political culture, they become a part of tradition, of collective memory or the national past.

As noted, the resources presently available can be grasped as a series of layers: the base is laid down by the events of the Second World War, subsequent layers include welfare and the Cold War and thereafter further events lay down more ideas; together, comprising a number of phases, roughly tracking the decades. So, first, in the 1940s/50s, the rhetoric of wartime with themes of heroic victory, nostalgia for empire and remembered war;[23] the rhetoric of welfare with themes of fairness, equality, cradle-to-grave care and social planning; and the Manichean rhetoric of Cold War, the institutionalization of military exterminism,[24] together with a panoply of domestic enemies in the guise of critics, dissenters and spies. Then second, in the 1960s/70s, the rhetoric of complaint, with angry young men, youth rebellion and the end of deference; an environment of full employment, novel social differentiation and the discovery of the working classes; later the rhetoric of new popular media, advertising, the rise of consumers, along with violence and widespread social/political rebellion. And third, in the 1980s/90s, the rhetoric of corporate advance, market liberalization, deregulation and enemies within and without (class victory/defeat and Cold War II); the rhetoric of corporate success, corporate power, business efficiency and the bottom line; plus corporate media aggression, its populism and commercialism; and in the decades of the new century, the rhetoric of a digital revolution for citizen/consumers, with e-government, e-democracy and e-surveillance.

The layers of meaning are carried in a variety of media, and they are contingent: there is no essence to the culture of the polity, rather there is only the presently available living stock of ideas, those currently informing those practices, which in total constitute the polity. And cast in these terms, the contemporary British polity comprises an entrenched enlightened elite, a soft oligarchy, not closed, adjusting to the loss of empire, in thrall to the USA via finance, defence and ideological nostalgia, ordering a demobilized acquiescent mass content with welfare-buttressed consumerism. The national past is grounded in the era of the Second World War, in reality, a political-cultural catastrophe, but now read as a founding myth, victory in a virtuous war, and thereafter, various amended by subsequent events/themes – welfare, class, protest, popular consumerism and so on. Domestically, the structural framework of the polity is resilient, the passing detail fluid and the possibilities of internally generated reform seemingly, slight. However, the demands of the wider world have to be met and so whilst the overall pattern might well remain the same, the detail, the precise character of the unfolding elite-sponsored political-cultural project might be more open to question. As the unfolding 2008/10 financial crisis has shown, events are unpredictable, so the future is not closed, and alternative scenarios can be envisaged;[25] and in the event that they are developed they will be so on the basis of the intellectual-cultural resources available to the elite and mass – the contingent sets of ideas that presently make up the British polity.

Further unpacking received wisdom

The tale offered by official Britain is a simple nationalist story: the country is a coherent entity with a long history, which, if tracked back, disappears into the mists of time; the country has a particular character, which can be unpacked in terms of land and people (official British-England[26]); and the long history of the country plus its particular character implies definite ways of reading change, as lines to the future are inscribed in the otherwise unchanging present. However, this complex, familiar, elegant and reassuring tale cannot sustain scholarly criticism: there is no single polity; there is no simple record; there is no simple story; and there is no simple political-cultural logic.

First, contingency – *there is no single polity*; the idea can be approached in general philosophical terms;[27] in which case, human language-carried social life is radically contingent, it has no overall shape or purpose. And closer to the more familiar concerns of the social sciences, it can and has been argued that polities subsist within wider structural contexts, polities exist in relationships, their boundaries are not fixed, nor are their internal logics and what is present to the observer at any one time is simply the contingent out-turn of dynamic social processes. Thus the geographical territories making up the British Isles have been home to a number of quite different polities: on occasion the territory has been home to many small polities whilst at other times the territory has been subsumed within much wider political units. A simple sketch recalls this: in 1707 Scotland and England were united; in 1926 Eire was established; and over the period 1945–60 (say) the state-empire system centred on the home island was dissolved into a plethora of new nation-states. What is presently available on the home island – 'Britain' – has no single coherent past and it has no single guaranteed future.

Second, memory – *there is no simple record*; the history of the polity reveals contingency, a matter of ever-shifting economic, social and political relationships; and the tales told by members of the polity about their history also reveal contingency as the historical trajectory of the polity is grasped in the tales told by members of that community, official and popular. The collective memory of a polity is a subtle social construction and setting aside the detailed mechanisms it can be said in general to involve a mixture of active remembering and equally active forgetting.[28] Collective memory is a stylized statement and in the narrower sphere of the national past the stylization is more pronounced. The current set of claims comprising the national past revolve around a claim to continuity: the disintegration of the state-empire system within which the core unit had been located for several centuries has been disregarded; and a claim made to the essential continuity of the core unit informs. A related claim centres on the war years themselves: an affirmation of victory in a virtuous war, a part of the allied scheme of history, and thereafter the various layers of ideology contained therein can be unpacked, the tale to which all will give assent, if reluctantly and provisionally.

Third, storytelling – *there is no simple story*; the presently familiar national past is a fairly recent confection and it can be unpacked. The key moves are denial and confection but these moves are supplemented by an elaborate characterization of the collectivity, that is, a national identity is affirmed with lists of traits, making up the English/British. But these political-cultural traits are no more fixed than any other set of social relationships; they are a social construction, matters of learning within definite institutional contexts; again, contingent with their post-war occasion specifiable, their present post-crisis status in doubt.

Fourth, futures – *there is no simple political-cultural logic*; the contemporary pattern does have a logic but it is the contingent out-turn of social processes and in the absence of tensions or pressures it might be expected to carry the polity into the future. Inertia, what was done yesterday is repeated today and will be repeated again tomorrow. The polity over time describes a trajectory, but such trajectories are contingent and if patterns of power change so will the trajectory. The financial crisis and collapse of neo-liberal explanatory/justificatory schemes might just be the shock that will disturb the system, redirecting it into new channels.

So, against the claims of conservative nationalists of whatever party political or ideological stripe, the future is open, and there are alternatives; the question is, which will be pursued?

The present settlement: Power/legitimacy

The present political settlement in Britain can be summarized in a few broad claims. First, power is concentrated domestically. The polity is a soft oligarchy; the population acquiesces in welfare plus consumerism plus tolerance; but a public sphere is available and individuals and groups can speak their minds; and there are minority groups, these are vigorous, along with many pressure groups. Second, the system is stable at present. Third, there are possible challenges: domestic social disturbances as financial crisis spills over into the real economy with sustained economic recession, increasing inequality and some groups experiencing relative deprivation; domestic political disturbances as nationalist pressure from constituent nations of the union (Scottish nationalism, English nationalism plus rising Welsh self-awareness); international disturbances as financial crisis causes further problems in the eurozone and the European Union. Fourth, there are few expectations of change in the future. The British elites are solidly entrenched and they have a track record of adjustment so without any international or domestic surprises there is little reason to expect significant structural, institutional or cultural change.

Yet current debates within the public sphere show that many people – individuals, pressure groups, political parties and scholars – do see change in structural patterns long taken to be more or less fixed. For citizens in Britain these can be read as a series of concentric circles, bearing down and running through the polity and requiring a response from elite and mass: thus, at a distance, changing relationships within the global system (East Asia, Latin America, India and the USA seem to be shifting relative economic positions – rising/falling); more immediately, changing relationships within Europe (Germany's increasingly salient lead role, France's diminished position and the British elite's seeming choice for relative marginalization); and more domestically, the implications of changing relationships within the polity (thus, the influence of peripheral nationalisms, in particular, Scotland). Add to this the corrosive effects of scandals in Whitehall/Westminster, plus the corrosive effects of a financial crisis, which had its origins in the deregulated casino capitalism of the City and Wall Street,[29] and all these processes/events point in the direction of change: the polity is under pressure to adapt/renew.

Some 30 years ago Tom Nairn[30] revisited the idea of nation in order to argue for the importance of identity within contemporary political life, characterized the extant British polity as moribund and so offered a diagnosis of the break-up of Britain. These debates reappeared in the end-time of New Labour with the resurgence of nationalist sentiment in Scotland.[31] A further impetus to debate was given by the 2008/10 debacle of neo-liberal globalization. The collapse of the neo-liberal settlement offers critics a moment of opportunity; it is likely that the political elite will recover their balance; but it is not likely that they will be able to reconstruct the status quo ante. Circumstances will impress change upon the polity. Looking to the future it is possible to contrive a number of scenarios: first, a defence of the status quo, the 'poodle option'; second, a strategy of modest reforms, the 'muddle through option'; and finally, a programme of much deeper reforms, the 'Europe option'.[32] Each of these scenarios can be unpacked but they are only up-market guesses, nonetheless, that said, it would be surprising if some variant of greater Europeanization were not on the cards.

The poodle option: The status quo affirmed (variously)

(i) Change rejected

This response centres upon a studied refusal to consider matters, a turning away or turning inwards, the embrace of a species of elite-level instrumental privatism; the elite refuse to engage prospectively with these issues, preferring ad hoc adjustments to unfolding events; and domestic reform is minimal.

The relatively successful position of core groups[33] (that is, the fundamental power networks and the related core executive), plus the difficulties of engineering widespread change, plus available celebrations of the current situation (thus conservative philosophers and less sophisticated polemicists, think-tankers and other hangers-on), all point to this being a well-regarded option. It is an option that seems to sit well with an increasingly significant sector of the British electorate; not only are sections of the long-established Conservative Party relentlessly hostile to the European Union but there are signs of a more populist anti-European party gaining electoral strength.[34] The strands of opinion seem to most commentators to be populist, that is, to be pandering to superficial readings of the current situation of the British polity, but, again, it reduces any domestic pressure on the elite.

(ii) Further engagement with the USA

This response points to a continuation in revised form of the post-Second World War elite preference for the status of number-one ally; the existing financial linkages of the City with Wall Street remain; the financial system is not significantly reformed; defence/security linkages (state and corporate) are unreformed; and public policy statements from parliament continue to speak of the special relationship and the sphere of Anglo-Saxon capitalism and/or the sphere of the English-speaking peoples.

All this assumes reciprocity from key agents in the USA; this is moot. The American elite might represent themselves as internationally minded but this is merely the style of their nationalism; American nationalism claims the country is exceptional and a model for all others.[35] Engagement with others is – predictably – on American terms and in line with American interests. Now commentators report that Washington increasingly looks towards East Asia; China is a major trading partner, it runs a trade surplus with the USA and it is upgrading not merely its domestic economy – known for years, admired more recently – but also its military. Much American public commentary seems somewhat hysterical – redolent of the 1990s writings about Japan – but that said China is on the way to becoming a great power. In contrast, when Washington looks towards Europe, it is the wider membership of the European Union that concerns them and consequently they have no particular use for a number-one ally in Europe. However, notwithstanding the problems associated with this line of thinking, its great advantage is that it requires little change; the comfortable, well-situated British elite continues in power, domestic reform is minimal.

(iii) Reinventing the past

Many commentators offer the elements of more dramatic scenarios; there is a body of opinion amongst the City and Wall Street financial community to the effect that the euro currency area is unsustainable; there are speculations about the break-up of the euro currency area and there are speculations one step further to the effect that it is not impossible to imagine the European Union dissolving back towards its constituent state units, a sort of return to the nineteenth-century status quo ante. In this case the British elite would not be engaging with the European Union but with some successor arrangement, for example, a variant of the nineteenth-century concert of Europe with many states and many alliances, or more modestly, a variant of the European Free Trade Association (EFTA) II[36] which it has long sought.

The speculations about the euro are familiar. They were first raised when the currency was formed. They have been voiced since the start of the financial crisis. These speculations have multiple strands – some technical, others political. Most generally, they are represented as being informed by the confidence of the Anglo-American financial community in respect of its grasp of economic, financial and political matters: the argument (in summary form) claimed that the member economies were too disparate, the governing machinery too weak and that national commitments would inevitably override community interests. These debates have waxed and waned as the 2008/10 financial crisis has dragged on and various break-up scenarios have been sketched,[37] but two comments might be made: first, after the debacle of 2008/10 – created by the financial industry – it might be thought that their intellectual credibility was low, and second the members of the currency have continued to lend it their support, thus allowing the European Central Bank to move towards acting as a central bank, notwithstanding issues relating to its charter and simultaneously moving towards eurozone- and European Union-wide new banking regulations. Or, in brief, thus far, political commitment has been unwavering. The Anglo-US financial community has misread the strength of the commitment of mainland elites to the project of 'ever closer union'. Also familiar are the desires of the British elite to construct an EFTA II but this was never on offer and it is difficult to see why it should be on offer now. Nonetheless, this strategy does offer the British elite a version of the status quo.

The muddle through option – status quo evolution

This response points to a process of rebalancing in order to maintain a post-empire global role: linkages with the USA are maintained but the sentimental nostalgia is played down; linkages with Europe are maintained but the hostile rhetoric is played down; linkages with former empire territories within the organizational frame of the Commonwealth are maintained with residual nostalgia for empire eschewed; the utility of the world's business language being the same as the national language is exploited; and the City of London remains a large-scale offshore banking centre, a circumstance implausibly veiled by the claim that 'London is a world city'. Domestic reform is minimal.

Overall, it is a strategy of muddle through, changing only when unavoidable. It is a species of low-level realism. In respect of the opening pair, the former is inevitable as the USA is turning towards East Asia and – if the idea of 'going it alone' is rejected – so is the second. Here, it is worth recording that the British and French elites do evidence a common nostalgia for days of empire – hence the 2012/13 Franco-British military interventions in Libya and Mali – these are instances of a cooperation long recommended by defence specialists. The Commonwealth is less significant, sometimes invoked, at others forgotten and in any case requiring independent states scattered around the planet to buy into schemes hatched in London seems deeply implausible. The last noted arguments are perhaps the most interesting – it is true that English is one major global language, thanks, over the last 60-odd years to the great power status of the USA, but the British also benefit and here it facilitates the international offshore financial role of the City – post-2008/10 a dubious proposition, as is the way in which inward migration has been interpreted, thus London is presented as a 'world city', suggesting that its citizens are looking outward to the world's global system rather than inward to the nation. It is spurious, the elite do not look outwards to the world, which, contra the neo-liberal's ideology is not a unitary liberal marketplace, rather they look to the USA whilst casting around for a role. Nonetheless, the search for Britain's role in the world is longstanding, a kind of itch that remains forever unscratchable.

The Europe option – domestic reforms and international rebalancing

This response posits a change of heart on the part of the British elite. It would seem to be the most implausible scenario. The elite have dragged their feet in respect of engagement with the European Union; essentially they have played a defensive game in pursuit of EFTA II. Indeed, the British have been surprisingly successful within the machinery of the European Union, for example, helping to drive forward the project of the Single Market, with its nominal commitment to neo-liberal ideas.

However, the core mainland members of the European Union remain wedded to the project (as do other members) and this is essentially political; hence 'ever closer union'. This is something it seems the British elites have never fully grasped. Looking to the future, it is easy to envisage further foot-dragging. Yet an alternative future is possible: the shock of 2008/10 has disturbed the British elite and two important elements are under pressure, finance/banking and military/security (the one discredited and in process of inevitable reform, the other wedded to expensive high-tech kit in an era of fiscal conservatism coupled to an absence of any plausible available enemies), and as both have worked to tie Britain to the USA their weakening opens up novel possibilities. One possibility would be greater integration in the European Union: this might be opened up under the pressure of events, such as the financial crisis, or in the wake of chronic domestic policy failures such that mainland models are considered (German technical education, Scandinavian welfare systems, French elite education for policy-makers and so on). In utopian mode a radical reform agenda could be envisioned, built around an interlinked trio of reform programmes: Europeanization, democratization and modernization. Again, this assumes reciprocity from European Union member states; it may be forthcoming, but it may be that notwithstanding mainland elite commitment the chance is passing for drawing the British into closer relations with the European Union.[38]

Britain: An unstable settlement

The current situation of the British elite is paradoxical: they have successfully managed the dissolution of state empire, the hitherto core area has been reimagined as a long-established nation-state, the hitherto peripheral areas allocated to the Commonwealth and the population has acquiesced in welfare-buttressed consumerism; but the settlement is failing. In politics, change is a simple given and global structures are reconfiguring: the USA is in slow relative decline; East Asia and other BRICs are attaining a greater salience in international affairs; and closer to home the European Union continues its haphazard progress.

The empire habit in the present

The issue of Europe bubbled up within British politics with the decision of Prime Minister Cameron to veto a formal treaty revision at the Euro summit of early December 2011. The action was greeted with widespread dismay; various commentators pointed out that the veto would not stop mainland European Union members from going ahead, was unlikely over the medium term to protect the speculative operations of the City from further accumulatively achieved regulation and would carry a political price-tag in respect of the British government's diminished influence within current European Union networks.[39] The issue refused to die down, indeed, Conservative Party back-benchers became ever more vocal until, in early 2013, the prime minister was obliged to offer the promise – somewhat vague and long-dated – of a referendum on British membership of the European Union.

As the inquests, recriminations and readjustments unfolded a measure of truth was found in all these lines of commentary, but none of them addressed perhaps the most startling aspect of the whole business, namely, the deep-seated, profound hostility revealed during these months by sections of the Conservative Party and general public towards the political-cultural project of the European Union. It might be asked: what are the roots of this seemingly unreasoning hostility? One answer to this question can be found in the habits of thought of these irreconcilables and this points to matters of political culture, where the preoccupation with 'sovereignty', the concern for 'independence', the antipathy towards 'Brussels' and the invocation of 'the bulldog spirit' all evidence a deep-seated historical amnesia; specifically, a failure to understand that the British Empire and the cultural baggage of that apparatus is long gone and that the polity is deeply enmeshed in wider political and economic networks. A reluctance to confront the implications of that loss feeds the repetitive-compulsive habit of harking back to the supposed intellectual, moral and political resources of that period. Viewed in these terms, those well disposed to the project of the European Union can look to the future with a measure of confidence – as the generations turn over it will become more and more difficult to sustain these anachronistic ideas, more and more difficult to avoid confronting the reality of an increasingly integrated European present and more and more difficult to ignore the practical experience and learning of younger people – those who travel, live and work in Europe and for whom the ingrained idiocy of the British anti-Europeans offers nothing.

Contingency: The inevitability of change

Structural changes cannot but impact the British elite. The project of 'continuing Britain' seems ever more implausible, reason enough to attend to the process of manufacture, reason also to speculate about future lines of development and reason enough to sketch alternative scenarios; the elite might elect to cleave ever more tightly to the USA, they may choose not to choose, to muddle through, or they may finally decide to accommodate themselves to the idea of Europe.

Notes

1 After the Empire: Establishment Designs, High Arts and Popular Culture in Britain

1. The text treats the 'British Empire' as an integrated unit, comprising economy, society, culture and polity (including the military), hence 'state-empire'. The idea is not especially new. Indeed, it draws freely on the work of established scholars (I. Wallerstein, E. Hobsbawm, J.M. MacKenzie, B. Porter, D. Cannadine, C. Bayly and a host of other scholars who have written about East Asia). Their work is noted in other texts, but the idea is worth a declaration. First, because post-1945 British political culture has denied the nature of this system by affirming a sharp distinction between core and periphery, adding the claim that the latter was of no great moment. Second, this in turn allowed the consequences of the collapse to be veiled or ignored or misread, but that collapse demanded a response from the elite. Their response has been unpacked down the subsequent years and finds expression in today's ideas of 'Britain'.
2. This text is one of a sequence looking at political-cultural identity and at Englishness in regard to Europe. See P.W. Preston 1994 *Europe, Democracy and the Dissolution of Britain*, Aldershot, Avebury; P.W. Preston 1997 *Political/Cultural Identity: Citizens and Nations in a Global Era*, London, Sage; P.W. Preston 2004 *Relocating England: Englishness in the New Europe*, Manchester University Press; P.W. Preston 2012 *England after the Great Recession: Tracking the Political and Cultural Consequences of the Crisis*, London, Palgrave.
3. P.W. Preston 2009 *Arguments and Actions in Social Theory*, London, Palgrave.
4. A fairly conventional position, available in numerous versions. See, for example, Sidney Pollard 1971 *The Idea of Progress*, Harmondsworth, Penguin; G. Himmelfarb 2005 *The Roads to Modernity: The British, French and American Enlightenments*, New York, Vintage; on England, see Liah Greenfeld 1992 *Nationalism: Five Roads to Modernity*, Harvard University Press; J. Passmore 1970 *The Perfectibility of Man*, London, Duckworth; Pollard 1971; and on the 'British Enlightenment' see Roy Porter 2000 *Enlightenment: Britain and the Creation of the Modern World*, London, Allen Lane.
5. A familiar take on the shift to the modern world in Europe. For a text which argues that much of the non-European world was dynamic, see C.A. Bayly 2004 *The Birth of the Modern World 1780–1914*, Oxford, Blackwell; for texts which ask why Europe and not the rich territories of East Asia, see A.G. Frank 1998 *Re-Orient: Global Economy in the Asian Age*, University of California Press; J.M. Hobson 2004 *The Eastern Origins of Western Civilization*, Cambridge University Press.
6. E. Gellner 1983 *Nations and Nationalism*, Oxford, Blackwell; see also D. Cannadine 2011 *Making History Now and Then*, London, Palgrave, Chapter 7.

Notes 219

7. B. Anderson 1983 *Imagined Communities*, London, Verso.
8. J. Habermas 1989 *The Structural Transformation of the Public Sphere*, Cambridge, Polity.
9. Ibid.
10. The notion of the public sphere makes political life broad, so too contributions to debate. It can be contrasted with a perhaps more familiar way of speaking of the relationship of politics, understood as parliament and politicians, and media, understood as print and broadcast journalism. Throughout this text the broad use is preferred as it opens up a much richer agenda (and, of course, it subsumes the narrower).
11. See, in brief, S. Crichley 2001 *Continental Philosophy: A Very Short Introduction*, Oxford University Press. The term is often taken to be one used on the west side of the English Channel – continental philosophy is contrasted with analytic philosophy where the former asks general questions about the nature of humankind whilst the latter is more preoccupied with the technical machineries of argument-making (in particular as exemplified by natural science).
12. See Peter Winch 1958/90 2nd ed. *The Idea of a Social Science and Its Relation to Philosophy*, London, Routledge and Kegan Paul.
13. H-G. Gadamer 1979 *Truth and Method*, London, Sheed and Ward, presents a philosophical hermeneutics where language enfolds all specific substantive claims, thus 'Being that can be understood is language' (p. 432).
14. P.W. Preston 2009 *Arguments and Actions in Social Theory*, London, Palgrave.
15. H.P. Rickman 1976 *Wilhelm Dilthey: Selected Writings*, Cambridge University Press.
16. Gadamer 1979.
17. F. Saussure 1990 *Course in General Linguistics*, London, Duckworth.
18. Winch 1958/90 2nd ed.
19. G. Grass 1959 *The Tin Drum*, London, Secker and Warburg; G. Grass1999 *My Century*, London, Faber and Faber; G. Grass 2002 *Crabwalk*, London, Faber and Faber.
20. Including J.G. Ballard 1996 *Cocaine Nights*, London, Flamingo; J.G. Ballard 2001 *Super Cannes*, London, Harper Collins; J.G. Ballard 2004 *Millennium People*, London, Harper Collins.
21. J.G. Ballard 1988 *Empire of the Sun*, London, Grafton Books; J.G. Ballard 1991 *The Kindness of Women*, Toronto, Harper Collins; J.G. Ballard 2008 *Miracles of Life: From Shanghai to Shepperton, An Autobiography*, London, Fourth Estate.
22. Lars von Trier 1991 *Europa*.
23. Ridley Scott 1982 *Blade Runner*.
24. Peter Greenaway 1982 *The Draughtsman's Contract;* Peter Greenaway 1985 *Zed and Two Noughts;* Peter Greenaway 1986 *The Pillow Book*.
25. Recently, for Britain, see, for example, Owen Hatherley 2010 *A Guide to the New Ruins of Britain*, London, Verso.
26. E.D. Weitz *Weimar Germany: Promise and Tragedy*, Princeton University Press.
27. Tom Nairn 1988 *The Enchanted Glass: Britain and Its Monarchy*, London, Hutchinson Radius.
28. See, for example, Chua Beng Huat 2007 'Introduction: Political Elections as Popular Culture' in Chua Beng. Huat ed. 2007 *Elections as Popular Culture in Asia*, London, Routledge.

29. G. Tett 2009 *Fool's Gold*, New York, Little Brown.
30. Z. Bauman 1987 *Legislators and Interpreters*, Cambridge, Polity distinguishes between legislators, who understand themselves to be producing reliable objective knowledge in respect of the social world, where such knowledge can be authoritatively deployed by appropriate agents (for example, the state), and interpreters, who understand themselves to be producing commentaries upon the existing social world which they present to the public sphere.
31. B. Fay 1975 *Social Theory and Political Practice*, London, Allen and Unwin, after the style of Jurgen Habermas, identifies three forms of engagement: positive – empirical analytic sciences which inform instrumental policy science; interpretive – historical and hermeneutic sciences unpack patterns of meaning within the social world; and critical – critical work looks to the conditions of meanings and offers engaged commentary.
32. A. MacIntyre 1985 *After Virtue*, London, Duckworth, argues that the Enlightenment project of reason failed to replace pre-existing religious-based ethics leading to the unintended construction of an emotivist culture where claims to rights are deployed against the claims of bureaucratic managerialism (and the later are buttressed by the claims to expertise of positivistic social sciences which habitually misrepresent subtle social relations in terms of putative objective facts).
33. These have appeared recently. Quite what they are intended to convey is unclear but they effectively flag on the part of the denizens of the state machine a collective anxiety with respect to foreigners (and they are an embarrassment to those not so afflicted).
34. Henry Porter 'Privacy from state snooping defines a true democracy' in the *Guardian* 3 April 2012; see also Editorial in the *Guardian* 4 April 2013.
35. A point picked up years ago by J.K. Galbraith 1958 *The Affluent Society*, Harmonsdsworth, Penguin, on the role of advertising in the creation of wants.
36. F. Inglis 1993 *Cultural Studies*, Oxford, Blackwell.
37. L. Colley 1992 *Britons: Forging the Nation 1707–1837*, Yale University Press.
38. R. Metzger 2007 *Berlin in the Twenties*, London, Thames and Hudson.
39. Others noted the model and joined in – in particular, the United States (notwithstanding any contemporary self-understandings) and imperial Japan. The clash of these two state-empires in Northeast Asia contributed directly – but not exclusively – to the later collapse of the system.
40. In respect of the empire in the East, Chris Bayly and Tim Harper get the point nicely – they refer to the 'arc of empire' running from Northeast India down to Singapore – a distance of several thousand miles and, at one point, all part of the same state-empire system. See C. Bayly and T. Harper 2004 *Forgotten Armies: The Fall of British Asia 1941–45*, London, Allen Lane; C. Bayly and T. Harper 2007 *Forgotten Wars: The End of Britain's Asian Empire*, London, Allen Lane.
41. P.W. Preston 2010 *National Pasts in Europe and East Asia*, London, Routledge.
42. See Preston 1994.
43. Thus, internationally, Ernest Bevin's 'Churchill option' locating Britain between the three spheres of Commonwealth, the United States and Europe (on this generally, John Saville 1984 'Ernest Bevin and the Cold War 1945–50' in *Socialist Register*), and domestically, the welfare state, the

new Elizabethan age of science-based progress, new towns, public housing, motorways and so on – the moves which tied the polity into the American-centred 'West'.
44. Preston 1994.
45. In respect of Kenya the tale has been disinterred (see C. Elkins 2005 *Imperial Reckoning: The Untold Story of Britain's Gulag in Kenya*, London, Weidenfeld) and reviewed (see B. Porter 'How did they get away with it?' in *London Review of Books* 27.5, 3 March 2005).
46. On this see Rainer Metzger 2012 *London in the Sixties*, London, Thames and Hudson. The author gets the vapid 'style' but misses the deeper creativity, especially in music. See also Jenny Diski 2009 *The Sixties*, London, Profile.
47. On the scene in the United States, see Richard Rorty 1998 *Achieving our Country: Leftist Thought in Twentieth Century America*, Harvard University Press, on old left/new left split, and Anthony Woodiwiss 1993 *Postmodernity USA*, London, Sage, on the consumer consolations available to the defeated. In Britain the debates revolved around the failures of the Callaghan government – splits, internecine squabbles and so on, culminating in the rise of New Labour.
48. A nationalist take would look to find an essence – in stylized history, or purported psychological traits or some culturally specific resource – which worked to evade contingency. They don't work; and on contingency see R. Rorty 1989 *Contingency, Irony and Solidarity*, Cambridge University Press.
49. Preston 2012.
50. Dating the crisis is not straightforward and as it continues (in early 2013), any dating is going to be arbitrary. For this text the start date is 2008, when the crisis broke in New York, the second date is 2010, when the crisis began to unfold in Europe. Again, it must be noted that the crisis continues to unfold. See Preston 2012.
51. Preston 2004, 2011.

2 Foundation Myths: The War, Wartime and 'Continuing Britain'

1. The term has been popularized by Joseph Nye but a better source is Susan Strange's structures of power, including 'knowledge' – both science and culture – S. Strange 1988 *States and Markets*, London, Pinter.
2. After the style of Norman Davies geographical territory and political unit should be distinguished – thus the geographical territory of British Isles have has been home to a number of polities – the most recent dramatic change was the collapse of empire – what was left was the pursuit of statehood in the peripheries (what is familiarly known as decolonization) and the creation of a post-empire state in the hitherto core – this is usually veiled by speaking of a 'continuing Britain' which once did not have colonies, but then did, and a bit later did not – the claim to continuity is false – the business of reconstruction in the core was as significant as it was in the peripheries – see Norman Davies 1997 *Europe: A History*, London, Pimlico; Norman Davies 2000 *The Isles: A History*, London, Papermac.
3. Cf. Alan Milward 1992 *The European Rescue of the Nation State*, London, Routledge.

4. Tony. Judt 2005 *Post-War: A History of Europe since 1945*, London, Allen Lane, see especially the annex on historical memory – a mix of active remembering and equally active forgetting.
5. In respect of 'finding a role' David M. McCourt 2011 'Rethinking Britain's "Role in the World" for a New Decade' in *British Journal of Politics and International Relations* 13, offers a Wittegensteinian-informed critique of the elite's preoccupation with 'Britain's role in the world' and notes that academe is disposed to reflect back to the elite this same preoccupation – McCourt notes that all this does not help useful thinking or policy-making; and whilst one might expect foot-dragging from an essentially conservative elite, the same is true of the Labour Party, discussed in Mathew. Broad and Oliver Daddow 2010 'Half Remembered Quotations from Half forgotten Speeches' in *British Journal of Politics and International Relations* 12.
6. Arguably – 'decline' is a tricky issue – the end of empire was not decline, it was a radical collapse necessitating reconstruction – thereafter, the track record of various industries might be discussed.
7. On this, see D. Urwin 1997 *A Political History of Western Europe Since 1945*, London, Longman; British elite opposition to the nascent European Union (EU) was deep-seated.
8. These 'white dominions' also had to 'relocate and reimagine' themselves – on shifting identities within the Australian population, see G. Whitlock and D. Carter eds. 1992 *Images of Australia*, University of Queensland Press.
9. A slow business, not especially wanted in Canada, particularly given a giant neighbour to the south; see David. Cannadine 2011 *Making History Now and Then*, London, Palgrave, Chapter 8 'Dominion: Britain's Imperial Past in Canada's Imperial Past'.
10. There are many texts of the Second World War – one that summarily grasps the catastrophe which Europeans contrived for themselves is offered by M. Mazower 1998 *Dark Continent: Europe's Twentieth Century*, London, Penguin; see also T. Garton-Ash 1998 'Can Europeans Really Find a Way of Living together in Democracies other than Living Apart' in *London Review of Books* 20.18, 17 September 1998.
11. There were debates as to how – Edgerton 2011 (p.31) reviews options – 'appeasement plus military upgrade' looked to accommodate Germany – a rational strategy (recall E.H. Carr 1939 [2001] *The Twenty Year Crisis*, London, Palgrave) – other strategies ranged from pacifist through to 'rearmament and resistance' – Edgerton, focusing on science and the economy, argues that the British Empire was very strong – early defeats were read back into time as unpreparedness – this is wrong, they were prepared, they just got defeated – the myth of unpreparedness continues down to the present day, obscuring the actual strength – that said – origins and character of the Second World War are not concern of this text – there are well established debates – pursued in P.W Preston 2010 *National Pasts in Europe and East Asia*, London, Routledge – what happened was a general crisis, the collapse of the system of state empires.
12. See David Edgerton 2006 *Warfare State: Britain 1920–1970*, Cambridge University Press; David Edgerton 2011 *Britain's War Machine: Weapons, Resources and Experts in the Second World War*, London, Allen Lane.

13. Precipitating the eventual collapse of the empire – see C. Bayly and T. Harper 2004 *Forgotten Armies: The Fall of British Asia 1941–45*, London, Allen Lane; C. Bayly and T. Harper 2007 *Forgotten Wars: The End of Britain's Asian Empire*, London, Allen Lane.
14. On the lines of metaphor and their plausibility/implausibility, see S.O. Rose 2003 *Which People's War: National Identity and Citizenship in Wartime Britain 1939–1945*, Oxford University Press.
15. W. Webster 2005 *Englishness and Empire 1939–1965*, Oxford University Press.
16. Davis 1997.
17. George Orwell's critical novel *Nineteen Eighty-Four* showed how, yet, paradoxically, Orwell was a contributor to the reversion to type of elite characterizations of the erstwhile war time ally, the Soviet Union, in the late 1940s, a matter to be discussed later in regard to the Cold War.
18. Webster 2005.
19. Correctly in regards to military science and production according to Edgerton 2011.
20. Minimal impact thesis – argues, roughly, that the empire was accumulated haphazardly and disposed of largely indifferently – that is, empire was always incidental to Britain (Webster 2005, p.2) – the position has been called 'rightwing propaganda' – see J.M. MacKenzie 2001 'The Persistence of Empire in Metropolitan Culture' (p.23) in Stuart Ward ed. 2001 *British Culture and the End of Empire*, Manchester University Press.
21. A point made – perhaps without grasping the significance – by Edgerton 2011.
22. Tony Judt 2002 'The Past is another Country: Myth and Memory in Post-War Europe' in J-W Muller ed. *Memory and Power in Post-War Europe*, Cambridge University Press; Tony Judt 2008 'What have we Learned, if anything?' in *New York Review of Books* 55.7; Tony Judt 2008 *Reappraisals: Reflections on the Forgotten Twentieth Century*, London, Heinemann; Norman Davies 1997 *Europe: A History*, London, Pimlico.
23. Webster 2005, pp.6–8.
24. On this see Rose 2003 who points out that the idea of nation-as-home was strongly presented – related idea was community – these ideas fed into later (subaltern) nostalgia (Chapter 1).
25. Relations with the generally anti-colonial USA had to be managed carefully – not only empire but also the issue of race – race in colonies and race as an issue in the United States and with its armed forces stationed in the United Kingdom (Webster 2005 – Chapter 1).
26. Webster 2005, pp.55–8.
27. P.H. Hausen 2001 'Coronation Everest' in Ward ed. 2001.
28. And some groups did care – thus empire loyalists and so on – see A. May 2001 'Empire Loyalists and Commonwealth Men' in Ward ed. 2001.
29. MacKenzie 2001.
30. Webster 2005 chapters 5 and 6.
31. Webster 2005 Chapter 7; see also D. Rebellato 2001 'Looking Back at Empire: British Theatre and Imperial Decline' in Ward ed. 2001; also S. Ward 2001 'No Nation Could Be Broker' in Ward ed. 2001.
32. Webster 2005 Chapter 3.
33. Ironically reworked by Tom Nairn as 'Ukania'.

34. The creation of an identity 'Canadian' along with a country 'Canada' seems to have been slow and not entirely what the locals wanted – taking shape after the Great War – with tensions between anglophone and francophone plus in the recent post-war era the inflow of new migrants from Asia.
35. Thus, as a rough example, in East Asia, British commercial interests in China; thus, in Latin America, where American concerns had extended their interests.
36. Webster 2005.
37. One line of criticism granted these claims, denied their benign character and cast them as neo-colonialism – but it now looks as if both agent and critics over-estimated the success of this aspect of managing the dissolution of empire.
38. Best recent example – Margaret Thatcher referring to Nelson Mandela as a terrorist.
39. On India/Pakistan, see Salman Rushdie 1981 *Midnights Children*, London, Jonathan Cape; Salman Rushdie 1983 *Shame*, London, Jonathan Cape.
40. On Malaya – see Anthony Burgess 1981 *The Long Day Wanes*, London, Penguin.
41. Webster 2005.
42. Cast in those terms, it is difficult to see why this should be so – Israel is a part of the Middle East – Britain imports oil from Arabia and the Gulf (with some monies recycled as arms sales) – and the key Western power in the region is the USA.
43. On decolonization, see M. Shipway 2007 *Decolonization and Its Impact*, Oxford, Blackwell; on sub-Saharan Africa see Doris Lessing's *Martha Quest* novel series.
44. J. Paxman 2011 *Empire: What Ruling the World did to the British*, London, Viking, pp.6–7; recall also David Cannadine 2001 *Ornamentalism: How the British Saw their Empire*, London, Allen Lane; also Tom Nairn 2011 2nd ed. *The Enchanted Glass: Britain and Its Monarchy*, London, Verso.
45. On the exchange see Robert Skidelsky 2004 *John Maynard Keynes 1883–1946*, London, Macmillan.
46. On Bevin, see David Marquand 1989 *The Progressive Dilemma*, London, Fontana.
47. On the relationship see C. Hitchens 1990 *Blood, Class and Nostalgia: Anglo-American Ironies*, London, Vintage.
48. Stephen George ed. 1992 *Britain and the European Community: The Politics of Semi-Detachment*, Oxford University Press.
49. Finally, it seems, to be withdrawn fully in 2019 in the context of the 2013 government cuts – see M. Hastings 'It is Rash to Blunt the UK's Fighting Edge' in *Financial Times* 8 March 2013.
50. In retrospect presented as the most successful period of Labour government – Prime Minister Clement Atlee is revered as a key figure – an iffy judgement – see P. Addison 1986 'Darling Clem' in *London Review of Books* 8.7 17 April 1986.
51. An argument challenged by Edgerton 2011 – again, invoking science and production, he insists that the early post-war years saw no absolute decline,

merely relative – in particular the rise of the USA – 'declinists' who point to a loss of scientific and productive expertise are wrong, however, Edgerton's 'relative decline' involves the loss of a global empire – and he does grant that post-war the polity turned inwards.

52. And, the history of the islands is recalled as clearly separate – all the myths attacked by Normal Davies 1997, 2000.
53. Jokes in circulation – those at the expense of Germans and Italians could refer back to the war – so too the French – all these groups could be characterized in stereotypical terms – one way in which the elite preference for distancing found parallel expression in common conversation – the cliché joke 'fog in channel, Continent isolated'.
54. See Patrick Wright 1985 *On Living in an Old Country*, London, Verso; see also review Paul Addison 'Getting on' in *London Review of Books* 8.17, 09 October 1986.
55. On the scale of the battle as revealed in casualty numbers, Norman Davies 2006 *Europe at War 1939–1945: No Simple Victory*, London, Macmillan.
56. Davies 2006.
57. Memoirs of the events offer clearer insight, for example: Paul Richey 2001 *Fighter Pilot*, London, Cassel; Irene Nemirovsky 2007 *Suite Francais*, London, Vintage; Anonymous 2006 *A Woman in Berlin*, London, Virago; and Vasily Grossman 2006 *A Writer at War: With the Red Army 1941–45*, London, Pimlico; on the camps see Gita Sereny – Also available in the arts; for example: Kazuo Ishiguro 1989 *The Remains of the Day*, London, Faber (also film); Joseph Heller 1964 *Catch22*, London, Corgi (also film); Kurt Vonnegut 1969 *Slaughterhouse Five*, New York, Delacorte Press (also film); and Jonathan Littel 2009 *The Kindly Ones*, London, Chatto.
58. Davies 2006; W.I. Hitchcock 2008 *The Bitter Road to Freedom: A New History of the Liberation of Europe*, New York, The Free Press.
59. This characterization is from Patrick Wright 1885 *On Living in an Old Country*, London, Verso; on this see William Boyd 'In the Days before Bond' in the *Guardian* 22 October 2011 which argues that Ian Fleming's early death from banal excess – booze and cigarettes – was symptomatic of a life which never recovered from the war years – action had made a difference, the rest was by comparison, of little account.
60. Edgerton 2011, p.31.
61. Ibid., pp.70–1.
62. See D. Edgerton 'Declinism' in *London Review of Books* 18.5, 07 March 1996 – plus the subsequent exchanges with Corelli Barnett.
63. Edgerton 2011, p.272.
64. Ibid., p.282.
65. J. Paxman 2011 *Empire: What Ruling the World Did to the British*, London, Viking, p.286.
66. Mostly indirectly, via collective memory of earlier wars, or from broadcast or print images (of contemporaneous wars) and for a few professional military personnel, directly.
67. A. Leftbridge 2011 *Losing Small Wars*, Yale University Press.
68. Noted by many, see, for example, the Preface to B. Porter 2004 *The Absent Minded Imperialists*, Oxford University Press.

3 Grand Designs: Patrician Reformers, Subaltern Demands and the Ideal of Welfare

1. On European systems, see Gosta Gasping-Anderson 1990 *The Three Worlds of Welfare Capitalism*, Cambridge, Polity, on varied welfare regimes; in a different vein, Peter Hall and D. Soskice eds. 2001 *Varieties of Capitalism: The Institutional Foundations of Comparative Advantage*, Oxford University Press.
2. Commentators spoke of 'the post war consensus' as if it described a situation rather than declaring a political objective or hope – the project of the welfare state was always contested. On this see R. Toye 2012 'From "Consensus" to "Common Ground": The Rhetoric of the Post war Settlement and its Collapse', *Journal of Contemporary History* 48.1.
3. One way of grasping the issue is to distinguish between 'welfare' and 'welfare-ism' – anecdotally, in Singapore, when in power, Lee Kuan Yew used to regularly bemoan 'welfare-ism', seeing it as a pernicious doctrine, undermining personal responsibility and national performance – dismissed as a reactionary then, but now, Singapore's gross national product per capita has surpassed that of the United Kingdom. On the sapping effects of welfare-ism, see the conservative commentator Ferdinand Mount 2012 *Mind the Gap: The New Class Divide in Britain*, London, Short Books.
4. Colonial Welfare and Development Act 1940. On early 'growth theory', see P.W. Preston 1981 *Theories of Development*, London, Routledge and Kegan Paul.
5. Reformers took their chance in the state empire's domestic sphere, so too did reformers in the peripheral areas; these were not exclusive groups, the dissolution of the state-empire system was just that – a unit dissolving – not domestic reform plus external decolonization, the standard 'continuing Britain' view – reformers could work in both areas – thus the pre-war work of J.S. Furnivall 1939 *Netherlands India: A Study of Plural Economy*, Cambridge University Press. On Furnivall, see Julie Pham 2004 'Ghost Hunting in Colonial Burma: Nostalgia, Paternalism and the Thoughts of J.S. Furnivall' in *South East Asia Research* 12.2.
6. P. Addison 1977 *The Road to 1945*, London, Jonathan Cape.
7. For some images from the period see Robert Kee 1989 *The Picture Post Album: Fiftieth Anniversary Collection*, London, Barrie and Jenkins; Tom Hopkinson 1970 *Picture Post: 1938–50*, London, Allen Lane The Penguin Press.
8. D. Kynaston 2008 *Austerity Britain 1945–51*, London, Bloomsbury, p.19.
9. W. Beveridge – J.M. Keynes – C. Atlee – and so on.
10. Karl Mannheim – G. Myrdal – and so on; on USA and New Deal, see Preston 1982; on reformers travelling to the Soviet Union and getting the story wrong in part, see Patrick Wright 2007 *Iron Curtain: From Stage to Cold War*, Oxford University Press.
11. On the groundswell of arguments for reform, see Peter Hennessey 1992 *Never Again: Britain 1945–51*, London, Jonathan Cape; Addison 1977.
12. Contemporary popular (media vehicled) memory has it that the war effort was a mix of heroic improvization (thus 'Dad's Army' or 'the few' plus technical wonders – 'Spitfire' or 'Bletchley Park') but the reality was rather different, a state-empire was mobilized and this empire was a global

economic and scientific power – on these last, see D. Edgerton 2005 *Warfare State*, Cambridge University Press.
13. Addison 1977.
14. Robert Skidelsky 2004 *John Maynard Keynes 1883–1946*, London, Pan Macmillan; reviewed by Paul Addison 1993 'How Left was he?' in *London Review of Books* 15, 1, 7 January 1993.
15. The term belongs to Karl Popper, who offered it as a contrast to what he dubbed 'historicism', that is large-scale predictions about the future, which he associated with Marxism; Popper was a social reformer in pre-war Vienna but became increasingly reactionary in post-war Britain. See M.H. HaCohen 2000 *Karl Popper: The Formative Years 1902–1945*, Cambridge University Press.
16. On all this, see C. Bayly and T. Harper 2004 *Forgotten Armies: The Fall of British Asia 1941–45*, London, Allen Lane; C. Bayly and T. Harper 2007 *Forgotten Wars: The End of Britain's Asian Empire*, London, Allen Lane.
17. Addison 1977.
18. In film – Alexander Mackendrick 1951 *The Man in the White Suit*; John and Roy Boulting 1959 *I'm All Right Jack*; BBC TV Rudolph Cartier 1953 *The Quatermass Experiment*.
19. For the Soviet Union, 'the great patriotic war' – for Imperial Japan, 'the thirteen year war' – for Communist China, 'the anti-Japanese war' – for Germany, the Second World War is slotted into the history of 'the brown years' or the record of 'a criminal regime' – different participants, different places and different memories.
20. Skidelsky 2004.
21. Preston 1982, see 'neo-institutionalists'.
22. On post-war European social democracy, see Tony Judt 2005 *Post War: A History of Europe since 1945*, New York, Penguin.
23. Skidelsky 2004 – the usual story in respect of economic governance is that Keynes lost out to Harry Dexter White, representing the United States, so the final institutional design was less ambitious (for example, Keynes's proposals would have blocked states from running up huge trade surpluses – a contemporary source of imbalance in global system).
24. Associated with Herbert Morrison – hence 'Morissonian socialism'. On Morrison, see David Marquand 1989 *The Progressive Dilemma*, London, Fontana.
25. L. Mumford 1966 *The City in History*, Harmondsworth, Penguin; less optimistically, Mike Davis 2002 *Dead Cities and Other Tales*, London, The New Press.
26. In 1945, rural areas in Britain and in Europe were still significant; in Eastern Europe the condition of rural areas was parlous; for Western Europe, this situation was one root of the European Union's Common Agricultural Policy.
27. The romantic reading of rural life is available from Laurie Lee 1962 *Cider with Rosie*, Harmondsworth, Penguin; for a take on urban working classes, Terence Davies 1988 *Distant Voices, Still Lives* (film); for the lower middle classes, George Orwell 1936 *Keep the Aspidistra Flying*, London, Gollancz; for this period directly, that is one group of artists working at the time, see Alexandra Harris 2010 *Romantic Moderns: English Writers, Artists and the Imagination from Virginia Woolf to John Piper*, London, Thames and Hudson.

28. See R. Williams 1980 *Keywords*, London, Fontana; Peter Gay 2008 *Modernism: The Lure of Heresy*, New York, Norton.
29. In Glasgow – Rennie Mackintosh – in London, Hoover Building, and the graphics for London Underground.
30. Two early examples – Letchworth and Welwyn Garden City.
31. H.M. Stationary Office 1963 *Traffic in Towns: The Specially Shortened Edition of the Buchanan Report*, Harmondsworth, Penguin.
32. Cadbury Bros 1931 *The Bournville Story*, Bournville, Cadbury Bros. Ltd.
33. Thus the garden suburb of Kowloon Tong in Hong Kong, or Singapore advertising itself as a garden city – another idea exported was that of a large central urban park – from Birkenhead on the River Mersey to New York's Central Park, noted by Peter Worsley 2008 *An Academic Dancing on Thin Ice*, Oxford, Berghahn Books.
34. On this, for and against, see Patrick Wright and Raphael Samuel – see the exemplary television film series Granada Television 1981 *Brideshead Revisited*.
35. Notably, opposing a proposal by Peter Palumbo to build a design made by Mies van der Rohe; on architecture more generally, see HRH The Prince of Wales speech at the Corporation of London, Mansion House, 1 December 1987; HRH The Prince of Wales speech at the 150th Anniversary of RIBA, Hampton Court Palace, 29 May 1984.
36. F. Jameson 1991 *Post-Modernism, Or the Cultural Logic of Late Capitalism*, London, Verso; D. Harvey 1989 *The Condition of Postmodernity*, Oxford, Blackwell.
37. Owen Hatherley 2011 *A Guide to the New Ruins of Great Britain*, London, Verso; see also review by Patrick Wright in *Architecture Today*.
38. N. Foster 1984 *Norman Foster: Architect, Selected Works 1962/84*, Manchester, Whitworth Art Gallery; on Foster, see Jonathan Meades 2012 *Museum Without Walls*, London, unbound.
39. G. Smith 2006 *30 St. Mary Axe: A Tower for London*, London, Merrell.
40. David Kynaston 2007 *Austerity Britain 1945–51*, London, Bloomsbury; Peter Hennessy 1992 *Never Again: Britain 1945–51*, London, Jonathan Cape.
41. It emerges in the 1930s as a technocratic non-political approach (a non-political politics) – tendency is reinforced by the demands of the war economy in the 1940s – ideas flow into the post-war period. On PEP, see Keith Middlemas 1981 'Facing the Future' in *London Review of Books* 3, 24, 7 December 1981.
42. A. MacIntyre 1985 2nd ed. *After Virtue: A Study in Moral Theory*, London, Duckworth.
43. Bauman 1988 *Freedom*, Milton Keynes, Open University Press.
44. Many examples from the health service – as science-based medical technology advances, costs soar – an example in *Daily Telegraph* 31 July 2012 cited a new designer drug for some cystic fibrosis sufferers at a cost of £200,000 p.a.
45. Successive British governments dealing with rising numbers of unemployed – consequence of neo-liberal occasioned deindustrialization – concentrated in particular locations – by shifting them onto the long-term disability register.
46. See *Daily Mail* and *Daily Telegraph* – scroungers – chavs, etc.
47. Judt 2005.
48. Wright 2007.

49. Earliest signs of 'youth' – LPs 1948 – singles 1949.
50. Paul Addison 1977 *The Road to 1945*, London, Jonathan Cape.
51. Addison 1977.
52. In retrospect not well regarded – however, rational. See E.H. Carr.
53. Stefan Collini 2006 *Absent Minds: Intellectuals in Britain*, Oxford University Press.
54. Thus the 2008–10 financial crisis has revealed, amongst other things, the routine moral corruption of the finance industry in general – more recently the revelations about corporate tax cheating where a spurious distinction between evasion and avoidance is deployed – these attitudes may be summed up as 'fuck you politics' ('I am powerful, I can get away with it, so fuck you!') – occasionally the intellectual collapse is even more dramatic – one financial commentator defended tax evasion as moral because it stops the state from taking and using other people's money – this may be tagged the 'parasite-idiot argument' – these examples could be multiplied.
55. HaCohen 2000.
56. Wright 2007.
57. MacIntyre 1985.
58. Robert Hughes 1993 *Culture of Complaint: The Fraying of America*, Oxford University Press.
59. Z. Bauman 1988 *Freedom*, Milton Keynes, Open University Press.
60. Thus, F.V. Hayek 1944 *Road to Serfdom*, London, Routledge; M. Freidman and R. Freidman 1980 *Free to Choose*, London, Secker.
61. Intellectually and ethically straightforward, as these interlinked exercises in liberal ideology are readily dismantled; but in practice, during the era of Mrs Thatcher these ideas did gain traction and downstream from her period in office the attacks both public and legislative have been relentless.

4 Making Enemies: The Cold War

1. The orthodox tale is available from J.L. Gaddis 1997 *We Know Now: Rethinking Cold War History*, Oxford University Press; J.L. Gaddis 2005 *The Cold War: A New History*, London, Penguin; on all this it is possible to distinguish elite and mass where the former were anti-Soviet in orientation and thereafter the masses were fed propaganda, a situation pithily summed up in respect of the present day by Simon Jenkins 'We are fighting Islamism from ignorance, as we did the Cold War' in *The Guardian* 1 March 2012 – noting that no serious historian now thinks that Stalin had designs on Western Europe, rather the problem lay with 'bombastic American leaders' – the last point parallels remarks from Anatole Lieven in a sharp review of Gaddis's work where he diagnoses a US nationalism blind to its own part in events – and where the end of the Cold War 'confirmed in the minds of most Americans deeper nationalist myths about the inevitable triumph of American power and goodness' see A. Lieven 2006 'US/USSR' in *London Review of Books* 28.22, 16 November 2006.
2. Patrick Wright 2007 *Iron Curtain: From Stage to Cold War*, Oxford University Press; favourably reviewed by Tom Nairn 2008 'Where's the Omelette?' in *London Review of Books* 30.20, 23 October 2008.

3. There were communist revolutions in Europe in 1918, which were defeated, thereafter domestic communist parties were viewed with suspicion; there were anxieties about communists amongst colonial powers that saw local parties as opponents of colonial rule; the nature of the Soviet Union became a topic for debate (Wright 2007 notes study visits made by intellectuals to the Soviet Union); the Spanish Civil War became a cause célèbre (and had Soviet and fascist involvement) – and so on.
4. Begins with a currency reform – 1948 introduction of D-Mark in West – soon the division into two areas solidified – see D. Urwin 1997 *A Political History of Western Europe Since 1945*, London, Longman.
5. R. Aron 1973 *The Imperial Republic: The US and the World 1945–73*, London, Weidenfeld.
6. Wright 2007.
7. Neal Ascherson 2009 'Wedgism' in *London Review of Books* 31.14, 23 July 2009 offers an insight into the atmosphere of the late 1940s – official policy was anti-Soviet, seeing either a Russian empire or international communism – elite propaganda and popular media were hysterical (recall George Orwell) – the notion of 'totalitarian' was advanced, blurring distinctions between fascism and communism – Ascherson nods to the Bush-era neo-conservatives and their propaganda in regard to the Middle East.
8. Bruce Cummings 2010 *The Korean War: A History*, New York, Modern Library, offers a discussion of the place of the Korean War in the developing process of the US construction of the Cold War, suggesting that prior to the war there was no disposition to construct a worldwide network of military bases, the war gets the military-industrial complex going; on empire, see Chalmers Johnson 2004 *The Sorrows of Empire*, London, Verso; and on US nationalism, see D. Lieven 2004 *America Right or Wrong: An Anatomy of American Nationalism*, London, Harper Collins; on the background to policy, see G. Kolko 1968 *The Politics of War: US Foreign Policy 1943–45*, New York, Vintage.
9. For the standard story, see J.L. Gaddis; for the 'revisionists', see D.F. Flemming 1961 *The Cold War and Its Origins*, New York, Doubleday; Kolko 1968; and Carolyn Eisenberg 1996 *Drawing the Line: The American Decision to Divide Germany 1944–49*, Cambridge University Press.
10. S.L. Carruthers 2009 *Cold War Captives: Imprisonment, Escape and Brainwashing*, University of California Press – see the Introduction – the author notes the vast numbers of displaced persons, the wide experience of camps (people in uniform, people in prison camps) and thus the urgent issue of what to do with all these people – control of people thus became one root of the conflict between the powers – later, as the author notes, the image of 'camps' mutates into a general idea of 'captivity', which, later is simply applied to the Soviet bloc – a realm of captivity, of unfreedom.
11. Eisenberg 1996, p.446.
12. The cynicism is breathtaking – the war in Europe ended in April 1945 – VE Day was 8 May 1945 – the official end of the war – so Churchill made his speech only nine months later – this after the Soviet Union lost around 26 million dead in a series of exchanges which left the bulk of German war dead on the Eastern Front (N. Davies 2006 *Europe and War 1939–1945: No Simple Victory*, London, Macmillan; T. Judt 2008 'What have We Learned, if Anything?' in *New York Review of Books* 55.7, 1 May 2008

[VJ Day was 15 August 1945; the famous surrender ceremony on the *Missouri* was 2 September 1945]).
13. Wright 2007.
14. Eisenberg 1996, pp.289–301.
15. See Jackson Lears 2012 'Beware Biographers' in *London Review of Books* 34.10, 2012.
16. Guy Burgess and Donald Maclean defected in 1951; Kim Philby in 1963; Anthony Blunt was identified/questioned in 1964. At the time and subsequently, these, and others, have attracted a vast amount of commentary. Neal Ascherson 1980 'What Sort of Traitors?' in *London Review of Books* 2.2 offers a defence of the spies – in the middle of the war the British/Americans withheld information from the Russians who at the time were dying in large numbers – so the spies were not just bored dilettantes or drunks, rather, they had a point – the article is followed by a number of letters, which, for today, perhaps flag something of the political/emotional character of the period; see also Tim Fywell 2003 *Cambridge Spies* (BBC film).
17. Subsequently much debated – the standard US official line is that it helped save lives by shortening the war – grotesque nonsense – on this see T. Hasegawa 2005 *Racing the Enemy: Stalin, Truman and the Surrender of Japan*, Cambridge University Press.
18. Eric Hobsbawm 2011 'Everybody Behaved Perfectly' in *London Review of Books* 33.16.
19. Ethel and Julius Rosenberg.
20. See Richard Wilkinson and Kate Pickett 2009 *The Spirit Level*, London, Allen Lane; and Ferdinand Mount 2012 *Mind the Gap: The New Class Divide in Britain*, London, Short Books.
21. A key symbolic site – suffused with meanings – glorious public relations for anti-Soviet West – on the history of the wall, see Neal Ascherson 2007 'The media did it' in *London Review of Books* 29.12, 12 June 2007.
22. David Caute 1978 *The Great Fear: The Anti-Communist Purges Under Truman and Eisenhower*, London, Secker and Warburg; Carruthers 2009; T. Doherty 2003 *Cold War, Cool Medium: Television, McCarthyism and American Culture*, Columbia University Press.
23. On this, David Caute 2003 *The Dancer Defects: The Struggle for Cultural Supremacy During the Cold War*, Oxford University Press; David Caute 1978 *The Great Fear: The Anti-Communist Purges Under Truman and Eisenhower*, London, Secker and Warburg; Lillian Hellman 1976 *Scoundrel Time*, New York, Little Brown; and on the ambiguous spill-over into Hollywood movies, David Bromwich 2012 'My Son has been Poisoned' in *London Review of Books* 34.2, 26 January 2012.
24. The political elites of both Cold War blocs encouraged intellectuals to rally to their support – within each block intellectuals were recruited to celebrate the local form of life and criticize that of the other bloc – across the divide dissidents were supported – thus Western support for Eastern bloc writers and poets – thus Eastern bloc support for Western Communist Party publications such as the Communist Party of Great Britain's (CPGB's) *The Daily Star* – groups in the West received covert funding from the CIA via support for ostensibly non-partisan cultural journals (Tony Judt comments on one strand of such work, that of 'Cold War liberals', asking, disingenuously, what

232 Notes

was wrong with this – see Tony Judt 2012 *Thinking the Twentieth Century*, London, Heinemann, pp. 228–9).
25. Paradigmatic 'story' from G. Orwell 1949 *Nineteen Eighty-Four*, London, Secker.
26. Web search gives many sources for these stories – most to UK press publications – see, for example, www.bilderberg.org/mi5.htm (accessed 11 March 2012).
27. Susan L. Carruthers 2009 *Cold War Captives: Imprisonment, Escape and Brainwashing*, University of California Press.
28. Artists were dragged into this conflict – see David Caute 2003 *The Dancer Defects: The Struggle for Cultural Supremacy During the Cold War*, Oxford University Press – see, for example, pp.271–305 on Bertholt Brecht.
29. Thomas Doherty 2003 *Cold War, Cool Medium: Television, McCarthyism and American* Culture, Columbia University Press.
30. Doherty 2003, pp.49–59.
31. Doherty 2003 also notes (Chapter 12) that after the HUAC witch hunts, elements of the media – film and television – acknowledged their role and indicated regret but this was *after* the event.
32. Len Deighton 1962 *The Ipcress File*, London, Hodder and Stoughton; John Le Carré 1968 *A Small Town in Germany*, London, Heinemann; John Le Carré 1986 *A Perfect Spy*, London, Hodder and Stoughton; John Le Carré 1974 *Tinker, Tailor, Soldier, Spy*, London, Hodder and Soughton; on Le Carré, see Ian Hamilton 1980 'Smileyfication' in *London Review of Books* 2.5; Christopher Tayler 2007 'Belgravia Cockney' in *London Review of Books* 29.2; and John Sutherland 1986 'Carré on Spying' in *London Review of Books* 8.6, who focuses on Le Carré's 1986 *A Perfect Spy*, London, Hodder, and unpacks the biographical and political elements, praising the author, whose work offers both upmarket engage thrillers and a species of 'condition of England' text.
33. John Irvin 1979 (BBC television series) *Tinker, Tailor, Soldier, Spy*; Thomas Alfredson 2012 (film) *Tinker, Tailor, Soldier, Spy*. See Michael Wood 2011 'At the movies' in *London Review of Books* 33.19; also satirical – Stanley Kubrick 1964 *Dr Strangelove*; Sidney Lumet 1964 *Failsafe*; and recently the critical film by Phillip Noyce 2002 *The Quiet American*. In respect of the USA, Jacqueline Foertsch 2008 *American Culture in the 1940s*, Edinburgh University Press, suggests that memories of the period focus on the early 1940s, the war years, with the later 1940s dropping out of sight – the Cold War announces the arrival of post-war and the 1950s.
34. In a review of David Caute's *The Dancer Defects* 2003, A. Huyssen 2004 'Degeneration Gap' in *London Review of Books* 29.19, 7 October 2004, looking at the Cold War culture wars makes the point that 'Cold War culture' needs unpacking – by country, by period and by groups involved – fair comment – in this text the phrase 'bloc-think' will continue to be used in order to flag the elite-sponsored top-down nature of the enterprise, but, thereafter, its impact would be as nuanced as Huyssen suggests.
35. Afual Hirsch 'Islamists hold over Mali threatens Europe, diplomat warns' in *The Guardian*, Friday 13 July 2012 – one person responded 'God almighty, when will this scare mongering stop? Orwell couldn't have been more prescient. We're hearing a lot from MI6 lately. Is it funding time?'

36. Alec Leemas is lied to – George Smiley is lied to – Magnus Pym lies all the time – in recent times the habits of the British state have been summed in terms of one civil servants phrase – 'economical with the truth' (in the context of the *Spycatcher* trial in Australia).
37. On the expansion of NATO eastward, see Stuart Croft, John Redmond, G. Wyn Rees and Mark Webber. 1999 *The Enlargement of Europe*, Manchester University Press.
38. The BBC and ITV recycle these themes in an apparently inexhaustible supply of costume dramas – they are formulaic – historical events provide a backdrop against which cardboard cut-out characters run through a standard repertoire of moves – in respect of the very popular television series *Downton Abbey*, see Jeni Diski 'Making a Costume Drama out of a Crisis' in *London Review of Books* 34.12, 21 June 2012.
39. Debated by Patrick Wright and Raphael Samuelson – the former is particularly critical of the National Trust – but it now has the largest membership of any organization in Britain – nostalgia might be a part of it, but not all – Samuelson, in contrast, celebrates popular history-making (even if it is a bit out of focus?).
40. Paul Gilroy writes about melancholia – the half acknowledged loss of empire transposed into hostility towards migrants from the former periphery arriving in the equally former core – see Paul Gilroy 2010 'Has it Come to this?' in S. Howe ed. 2010 *The New Imperial Histories Reader*, London, Routledge – the extract is from Paul Gilroy 2004 *After Empire: Melancholia or Convivial Culture*, London, Routledge.
41. John Lanchester 2002 'Bond in Torment' in *London Review of Books* 24.17 suggests that the ennui that pervades the Bond books has its roots in changes in the class position of the author – more freedom recalled earlier constraints, the upshot being a pervasive boredom – as with Evelyn Waugh and Graham Greene – in Ian Flemming's case it seems he drank/smoked himself to death – dying aged 56 – see also John Bayley 1993 'Snug' in *London Review of Books* 15.17, 9 September 1993 who reads the character of James Bond as a late middle-aged confection – part fantasy, part adventure story – a salve for boredom.
42. A later, glossier and more violent example of this genre revolves around alleged systemic wrong-doing by the CIA: in thriller mode, the movies around the character Jason Bourne (Doug Liman 1980 *The Bourne Identity* (film), Paul Greengrass 2004 *The Bourne Supremacy* (film), Paul Greengrass 2007 *The Bourne Ultimatum* (film)), or with reference to Middle East, Ridley Scott 2008 *Body of Lies* (film).
43. Blair tried a number of pen-names before settling on George Orwell – a respectful biography is available from Bernard Crick 1980 *George Orwell*, Harmondsworth, Penguin.
44. Orwell was hostile towards the Communist Party and underenthusiastic about the Labour Party – late in life and ill he handed over a list of 'fellow travellers' to the authorities in the Foreign Office.
45. Stefan Collini 2006 *Absent Minds*, Oxford University Press; see also Crick 1980; S. Lucas 2003 *Orwell*, London, Haus; Beatrix Campbell 1984 *Wigan Pier Revisited: Poverty and Politics in the Eighties*, London, Virago.

46. E.P. Thompson in Raymond Williams ed. 1974 *George Orwell: A Collection of Critical Essays*, Englewood Cliffs, Prentice Hall, p.82.
47. There are earlier specimens of spy novels – thus Erskine Childers 1903 *The Riddle of the Sands*, London, Smith, Elder and Co.; thus Dashiell Hammett 1930 *The Maltese Falcon*, New York, Alfred Knopf; then for the 1930s and immediate post-war, Graham Greene (see John Bayly 1991 'John Bayly writes on Graham Greene' in *London Review of Books* 13.8, noting to the Catholicism, pointing to the mannered realism, and remarking that Le Carré is his 'most faithful disciple'); see also Stefan Collini 'On the Lower Slopes' in *London Review of Books* 32.15, 5 August 2010.
48. William Boyd – now a thriller writer – offers a nice comment on the book, see William Boyd 2010 'Rereading: The Spy Who Came in from the Cold by John Le Carré' in *The Guardian* 24 July 2010.
49. E. Hobsbawm 2002 *Interesting Times: A Twentieth Century Life*, London, Allen Lane; he discusses other recollections of the CPGB in E. Hobsbawm 2007 'Cadres' in *London Review of Books* 29.8, 26 April 2007; in a similar if sadder vein, see V.G. Kiernan 1998 'The Unrewarded End' in *London Review of Books* 20.18, 17 September 1998; and more generally, P. Anderson 2002 'The Age of EJH' in *London Review of Books* 24.19, 30 October 2002.
50. Recalling days as a student researching in the Soviet Union – S. Fitzpatrick 2010 'A Spy in the Archives' in *London Review of Books* 32.23, 2 December 2010.
51. Peter Wright 1987 *Spycatcher: The Candid Autobiography of a Senior Intelligence Officer*, New York, Viking – the book was subject to scandal as British government tried to block its publication – a court case in Australia gave us the phrase 'economical with the truth' (Cabinet Secretary Robert Armstrong) – subsequently taken to mean that officials of the British state are happy to mislead when it suits.
52. On the matter of spies, Christopher Hitchens bluntly suggests that the tittle tattle of retired spies and the like needs to be replaced by some reliable history of this marginal, grubby aspect of great power competition, Christopher Hitchens 1995 'Lucky Kim' in *London Review of Books* 17.04.
53. These were the two areas where US-led opposition to state-socialist regimes was focused – the core opponents being, respectively, the Soviet Union and the People's Republic of China, but, thereafter, the Cold War was exported around the globe – thus, in particular, in Latin America, in the Middle East and in Southeast Asia.
54. An idea developed by Frankfurt School, running together Marx and Freud.
55. W. Kornhauser 1960 *The Politics of Mass Society*, London, Routledge.
56. Say, Clint Eastwood *Firefox* or Sean Connery *The Hunt for Red October*.
57. Say, John Wayne *The Green Berets*, or Sylvester Stallone *Rambo*.
58. Kolko 1968.
59. Tony Judt 2005 *Post-War: A History of Europe Since 1945*, New York, The Penguin Press; on Judt's work overall, see Dylan Riley 2011 'Tony Judt: A Cooler Look' in *New Left Review* 71 September/October – the body of work is unpacked – criticized, often sharply – not very good on *Post-war* – as regards the later work, Riley, writing before the Judt 2012 collection, misses the role embraced by Judt of 'public intellectual'.
60. Judt 2005, p.104.

61. Ibid., p.117.
62. Ibid., p.137.
63. Judt 2012, p.228 (see also, for example, Graham Greene 1955 *The Quiet American*, London, Heineman, and Phillip Noyce 2002 *The Quiet American* (film)).
64. Judt 2012, p.227.
65. Wright 2007, pp.1–51.
66. Hobsbawm 2002 recalls the interwar period and points out that the political choice was between communism and fascism and an enfeebled liberal sphere (post-First World War plus Great Depression) – the immediate post-1917 period was optimistic for the left – Hobsbawm recalls that he became involved with the Communist Party in Weimar Germany – in other words, the 1920s and 1930s saw active political exchanges, whereas the Cold War was in comparison an elite-level confection serving to discipline populations in Europe, East and West.
67. At the risk of pointing to the obvious – in March 2013, the tenth anniversary of the invasion of Iraq, there were a number of reports and broadcasts and their overall tenor was of fractions of the elite granting that the episode had been a gross error; now routinely tagged as the worst foreign policy decision since Suez and – obviously enough, at the time and in retrospect, one involving routine instrumental lying by elite-level agents of the state directed towards the general population.

5 Voices of Complaint, Voices of Assertion

1. See Wendy Webster 2005 *Englishness and Empire: 1939–1965*, Oxford University Press, who suggests that the angry young men could have been angry because the elite – to which they had looked – had failed, that is, it had lost the empire and now it lacked vigour and this quality they found in the working classes.
2. After, Frank Parkin 1972 *Class Inequality and Political Order*, London, Paladin.
3. Later the new sentiment was to find intellectual and political expression in the 'new left'.
4. D. Kynaston 2008 *Austerity Britain 1945–51*, London, Bloomsbury, p. 19.
5. P. Hennessy 2006 *Having It So Good: Britain in the Fifties*, London, Allen Lane, notes the record of the Atlee years – successful – and, stepping back to look at the political whole, remarks 'A case could easily be made for mid-century Britain as the most settled, deferential, smug, un-dynamic society in the advanced world' (p.435).
6. Stefan Collini 2006 *Absent Minds: Intellectuals in Britain*, Oxford University Press.
7. D. Edgerton 2005 *Warfare State*, Cambridge University Press.
8. The French were left in the lurch, resolving not to trust either the Americans or the British in the future, hence their independent stance in diplomacy and military matters; the Israelis noted the power of the USA, later after a subsequent war, a coincidence of interests would take shape; and the British elite drew a particular lesson – that their diplomatic and defence stance would be one of deep alliance with the USA.

9. Frank Kermode cites Edward Heath referring to TW3 as the occasion for this idea (Frank Kermode 2002 'Snarling' in *London Review of Books* 24.23, 29 September 2011).
10. Patrician tone is unsettling in today's Britain, but Macmillan's politics were of his day, that is, his constituency was in the North and he was a social reformer.
11. The domestic scene was stable – the Conservative government did not dismantle the new welfare state – nationalized industries (except for steel) were left alone – tripartite Keynesian bargaining continued successfully – and internationally, the Korean War was over and the series of small-scale conflicts in the periphery could be safely kept at an imaginative distance – the Cold War was a general worry, but such matters were anyway dominated by the Americans, the only problematic event was the last spasm of pre-war great power activity, that is, the invasion of Suez.
12. Allan Sillitoe 1958 *Saturday Night and Sunday Morning*, London, W.H. Allen.
13. Rattigan's 1952 play was revisited recently in film, see Terence Davies 2011 *The Deep Blue Sea*.
14. Frank Kermonde 2002 'Snarling' in *London Review of Books* 24.23, 29 September 2011.
15. Kermonde in *London Review of Books* 24.23.
16. John Osborne 1956 *Look Back in Anger* (play).
17. John Braine 1957 *Room at the Top*, London, Eyre and Spottiswoode.
18. Sillitoe 1958.
19. Shelagh Delaney 1958 *A Taste of Honey* (play).
20. Ian Haywood 'Stan Barstow obituary' in *The Guardian* 1 August 2011.
21. Later picked up around this time by Nell Dunn 1963 *Up the Junction*, London, MacGibbon and Kee.
22. Copied by the BBC – *Eastenders*.
23. One of a sequence of plays on BBC – series called The Wednesday Play – a seriousness which later faded from the mainstream schedules.
24. Terence Davies 1988 *Distant Voices, Still Lives* (Film); Terence Davies 1992 *The Long Day Closes* (Film); in similar vein Terence Davies 1995 *The Neon Bible* (Film).
25. Caroline Aherne *The Royle Family*, BBC television series, 1998/2012.
26. Sidney Pollard on the 'hopes of labour' – S. Pollard 1971 *The Idea of Progress*, Harmondsworth, Penguin.
27. Friedrich Engels to George Orwell to Peter Townsend; on ameliorative social science see P. Abrams 1968 *The Origins of British Sociology*, Chicago University Press; for a specimen, see M. Young and P. Wilmott 1957 *Family and Kinship in East London*, London, Routledge.
28. Titus Salt – Lever Brothers – Cadury Brothers and so on.
29. A position under pressure since the 1980s – neo-liberalism – class conflict continues – after turn of twenty-first century a new term emerged – 'chavs' – aimed at the working classes, now characterized as welfare-dependent parasites – see Owen Jones 2011 *Chavs: The Demonization of the Working Class*, London, Verso.
30. Politics – the welfare state – the arts, noted – in scholarship – three lines might be noted – first, the area of 'community studies', which were often of working class communities – classic example, Wilmott and Young

1957 – second, the area of what became known as cultural studies – the strategy of attending directly to the intellectual and moral resources of particular local communities (rather than measuring their failure against some elite model) – thus Richard Hoggart 1958 *The Uses of Literacy*, Harmondsworth, Penguin – and third, related, the rise of a group who came to be tagged 'the British Marxist Historians' – in their camp, Edward Thompson 1968 *The Making of the English Working Class*, Harmondsworth, Penguin.

31. Thus – theatre – classical music – opera – art galleries – and so on.
32. Thus, says, the BBC Home Service – example – long running radio soap *Mrs. Dale's Diary* – or in the press, a profusion of magazines.
33. Stefan Collini writes on Larkin and Amis – the former perhaps genuine (dull, provincial but maybe with insight), the latter probably just a selfish bigot (except maybe for Kingsley Amis 1986 *The Old Devils*, London, Hutchinson, which won the Booker Prize). See Stefan Collini 2009 'Self Positioning' in *London Review of Books* 31.12, 25 June 2009; Stefan Collini 2006 'Do You Think He didn't Know' in *London Review of Books* 28.24, 14 December 2006. (In my terms – Amis could write, but had nothing to say).
34. Phillip Larkin 1955 *The Less Deceived*, The Marvell Press.
35. Their relationship has been subject to numerous essays in the *London Review of Books* – much is known about their lives and their work – in summary style, Larkin is regarded as an occasionally first-rate poet, Amis, probably overall a failure.
36. Subsequently made into a wildly successful television series – slow, pretty, languid – later a film, less well received.
37. Target for Patrick Wright – on James Lees-Milne see D. Canadine 1983 'Brideshead Revered' in *London Review of Books* 5.5, 17 March 1983.
38. On the nineteenth-century novels which often inform these 'classic serials', see Raymond Williams 1963 *Culture and Society 1780–1950*, Harmondsworth, Penguin; he reads them as apologetics at the time – recycled they are exercises in mystification – on the issue of 'authenticity' compare with say Peter Greenaway's *The Draughtsman's Contract* or Hollywood's *Pirates of the Caribbean* – Greenaway's work has the authenticity of art – neither classic serials nor Hollywood have this characteristic – at best they have 'high production values'.
39. As advertised in the late 2012 and early 2013 Westminster activities that drew from the prime minister the promise (distinctly ambiguous) of a referendum on membership of the European Union.
40. Dennis Potter 1981 *Pennies from Heaven*; Dennis Potter 1986 *The Singing Detective*; Dennis Potter 1993 *Lipstick on your Collar* – all BBC television films.
41. Alan Bennett 2004 *The History Boys* (play), later Nicholas Hytner 2006 *The History Boys* (film).
42. Frederick Rafael 1976 *The Glittering Prizes* – BBC series.
43. On cultural studies, see Fred Inglis 1993 *Cultural Studies*, Oxford, Blackwell.
44. Famously, Ralph Milliband 1969 *The State in Capitalist Society*, London, Weidenfeld; also with John Saville the series on socialism entitled *The Socialist Register*.
45. On the 2008–10 financial crisis, see P.W. Preston 2012 *England After the Great Recession*, London, Palgrave.

238 Notes

46. Recently, Richard Wilkinson and Kate Pickett 2009 *The Spirit Level*, Harmondsworth, Penguin, gained a brief splash of attention, then it was back to the government's neo-liberal agenda of austerity, deregulation and privatization.
47. Parkin 1972.
48. Celebrated in film – Tony Richardson 1959 *Look Back in Anger* (film); Karel Reisz 1960 *Saturday Night and Sunday Morning* (film); Tony Richardson 1961 *A Taste of Honey* (film); John Schlesinger 1962 *A Kind of Loving* (film); or later, in a similar vein, Terence Davies 1988 *Distant Voices, Still Lives* (film); or Denis Potter 1993 *Lipstick on Your Collar* (BBC TV film).
49. Tony Judt 2005 *Post-War: A History of Europe Since 1945*, New York, The Penguin Press.
50. Corporate interests resisted – settler colonies produced strong local opposition – in particular, Kenya, later Southern Rhodesia – plus the long-running problem of apartheid South Africa.
51. Thus in 1945 mainland Europe still had significant peasant farming sectors – in France and the Mediterranean areas and in Eastern Europe, where standards of living were low – on this, see Norman Davies 1997 *Europe: A History*, London, Pimlico; Norman Davies 2007 *Europe: East and West*, London, Pimlico.
52. Judt 2005, p.337.
53. Stefan Collini 2006 *Absent Minds*, Oxford University Press, Chapter 7, on the 1950s.
54. Collini 2006 Chapter 8, on *New Left Review* and New Right.
55. On the distinction between 'Anglo-Saxon' and 'Continental' philosophy, see S. Critchley 2001 *Continental Philosophy: A Very Short Introduction*, Oxford University Press.
56. Collini 2006.
57. Ibid.
58. Ibid.
59. A theme picked up by Tony Judt 2012 *Thinking the Twentieth Century*, London, Heinemann; the division was repeated in the USA – see Richard Rorty – in Judt's case the hostility towards the Marxist left seems to have been a fixed feature of his thought; for a cordial review/obituary, see Robert Zaretsky 'Frequent bouts of wisdom' in *Le Monde Diplomatique*, 16 May 2012.
60. Summer 2012 – begins in London, copied around Britain.
61. In respect of the USA, Robert Hughes 1993 *Culture of Complaint*, Oxford University Press.
62. Kingsley Amis 1986 *The Old Devils*, London, Hutchinson.
63. An alternative position is that his reputation was contrived so as to have a local reply to the work of modernist poets – a group was identified, 'the movement'.
64. Owen Jones 2011 *Chavs: The Demonization of the Working Class*, London, Verso.
65. Alasdair MacIntyre 1985 2nd ed. *After Virtue*, London, Duckworth – argues that contemporary liberal democracies see spurious claims to bureaucratic expertise confronting equally ungrounded claims to moral rights – all contrasted with a communitarian ethic.

6 Patrician Retreat: Quickening Change in the 1950s and Early 1960s

1. On the thinking of economists, see Roger Backhouse 2002 *The Penguin History of Economics*, Harmondsworth, Penguin.
2. Clark Kerr, J.T. Dunlop, F.H. Harbison, C.A. Myers. 1960 *Industrialism and Industrial Man*, Harmondsworth, Penguin – for a critical response, see Alasdair MacIntyre 1971 *Against the Self Images of the Age*, London, Duckworth.
3. On this, see Peter Kerr 2001 *Postwar British Politics*, London, Routledge.
4. On the distinct national traditions, see Geoffrey Hawthorn 1976 *Enlightenment and Despair*, Cambridge University Press.
5. A point made by Denis Potter in conversation with Alan Yentob – from BBC TV *Arena* 1987 [rebroadcast via iPlayer 7 February 2012].
6. Television showed images – more impact – in the domestic sphere television required that it be watched (unlike radio which could be listened to whilst doing other things) – radio had several stations – television at first had only one – it could draw audiences measured in the millions.
7. Denis Potter makes it clear, in the above-noted interview, that television in Britain in the late 1950s was seen as an exciting new medium. It subsequently became more diverse, popular and commercial – on the sequence of innovation, commercialization, regulation and cultural decline of information media (with particular reference to the experience of the USA), see Tim Wu 2010 *The Master Switch: The Rise and Fall of Information Empires*, London, Atlantic.
8. Quite directly in some instances: thus news broadcasters eventually discontinued the pre-war practice of reading the news whilst wearing dinner jackets; later, received pronunciation was joined by regional accents; it was a process not of slow democratization (the BBC is still a part of the establishment), but of acceptance of the habits of mind and tastes of the great mass of the population; and the commercial stations followed.
9. A prosperity picked up by the London Underground in its famous pre-war series of posters.
10. Frank Parkin 1972 *Class Inequality and Political Order*, London, Paladin, who pointed out that subaltern class self-consciousness could take various forms.
11. Arthur Seaton had a disposable income in part because he still lived at home – so did teenagers – they too were to acquire disposable income and they too found ways to spend it.
12. These expectations are unpacked by Frederic Raphael 1976 *The Glittering Prizes*, BBC TV film series.
13. D. Edgerton 2011 *Britain's War Machine: Weapons, Resources and Experts in the Second World War*, London, Allen Lane, argues economy was strong; see also D. Edgerton 'Declinism' in *London Review of Books* 18.5, 7 March 1996 plus subsequent exchange of letters.
14. Wendy Webster 2005 *Englishness and Empire, 1939–1965*, Oxford University Press.
15. The phenomenon tagged by Alasdair Campbell as the two-week media 'shitstorm', adding that if attacks were still under way at the two-week mark, then the politician in question was doomed.

16. Where these might in the past have been one more set of stories in the media, noticed but not pursued, now they became major scandals – they were pursued over days and weeks – relations were shifting – newspapers, politicians and reading publics – thus 'social construction of a scandal'.
17. The trial was significant for human rights – effectively asserting them against the cultural and class prejudices of the patrician elite – Geoffrey Robertson QC 'The Trial of Lady Chatterley's Lover' in *The Guardian* 22 October 2010.
18. A further 'high society' scandal was provided by the divorce case of the Duke and Duchess of Argyll, see David Randal 'The Scarlet Duchess of Argyll: Much more that just a Highland Fling' in *The Independent* 17 February 2013.
19. I. Gilmour 2006 'Dingy Quadrilaterals' in *London Review of Books* 28.20, 19 October 2006.
20. Later the subject of a film – Michael Caton-Jones 1989 *Scandal* (film).
21. Politicians were not afraid to pontificate on television – Lord Hailsham criticized Profumo's sexual activities and was rebuked by Lord Balfour who noted: 'When a man has by self-indulgence acquired the shape of Lord Hailsham, sexual continence requires no more that a sense of the ridiculous' (noted on Wikipedia – http//en.wikipedia.org/wiki/Quintin_Hogg_Baron_Hailsham_of_St_Marylebone accessed 9 February 2013).
22. See David Runciman 'Take a Bullet for the Team' in *London Review of Books* 35.4, 21 February 2013.
23. Leveson Inquiry.
24. Wu 2010.
25. Ibid., pp.40–4.
26. Ibid., pp.136–42.
27. See Stefan Collini 2006 *Absent Minds*, Oxford University Press.
28. See J.K. Galbraith 1958 *The Affluent Society*, Harmondsworth, Penguin, who makes a criticism of the advertising industry as a 'wants creation apparatus' – thus fundamentally manipulative of its audiences and inimical to the pursuit of the wider public good.
29. Stefan Collini 2006 *Absent Minds*, Oxford University Press.
30. There were extensive police enquiries into News International during 2012 – these were extended to encompass the Metropolitan Police themselves – by early 2013, the time of writing, a number of prosecutions were ongoing – the newspaper at the heart of the scandal, *The News of the World*, was closed down by the owners.
31. 'The Future of the Murdoch Dynasty' in *Financial Times*, 20 October 2011.
32. For example: A. Briggs and P. Cobley eds. 2002 *The Media: An Introduction*, London, Longman; Raymond Kuhn 2007 *Politics and the Media in Britain*, London, Palgrave; Graham Burton 2005 *Media and Society: Critical Perspectives*, Open University Press; John Street 2010 2nd ed. *Mass Media, Politics and Democracy*, London, Palgrave.
33. Attributed to R.H Thomson – later Lord Thomson – a Canadian newspaper owner who acquired the franchise for the commercial station Scottish Television in 1957–.
34. See Wu 2010 on the difference between public service broadcasting and commercial television – the latter is concerned with making available an audience to advertisers – entertainment is crucial.

7 Affluence Attained, Affluence Doubted

1. Jenni Diski cites the music as enduring, J. Diski 2009 *The Sixties*, London, Profile.
2. On the British contribution to the United States' wars in Iraq and Afghanistan, see F. Ledwidge 2011 *Losing Small Wars: British Military Failure in Iraq and Afghanistan*, Yale University Press; on the anniversary of the invasion of Iraq, expressed more bluntly by Seamus Milne 'Iraq War: Make it Impossible to Inflict such Barbarism again' in *The Guardian*, 16 March 2013.
3. These last noted begin with the declaration of war aims made after Churchill and Roosevelt met in Newfoundland – the Atlantic Charter – they feed into San Francisco meetings which set up the United Nations – key elements of post-war international organization.
4. In hindsight, the elite were slow off the mark – their relative position offered a brief space in which the advantage might be secured and plans for the future laid – but complacency reigned, elite figures looked back to the 1930s and to empire and sought continuity where it was not available – the detail is given by Peter Hennessy 1992 *Never Again: Britain 1945–1951*, London, Jonathan Cape, see the last chapter.
5. Lots of work on community studies – change was taking place – often read as some sort of threat to community – never quite clear what that was – one suspicion was that it was middle class romanticism in respect of the lives of the working classes – relatedly, that these communities were settled was open to question – many of these areas of urban development dated from the nineteenth century – historically recent – opened up the issue of how long a community has to be in place to become settled? Nonetheless, social scientists diagnosed significant change.
6. Polite terminology shifts – here from 'negro' to 'blacks' and later to 'African-Americans', in the 1960s, the second term was favoured.
7. On contingency – in political life, Harold Macmillan's one-liner – 'events dear boy, events' – in philosophy, the idea is taken seriously by Richard Rorty 1989 *Contingency, Irony and Solidarity*, Cambridge University Press.
8. Harold Wilson and then Edward Heath sought to resolve the problem – it was made worse by the government of Margaret Thatcher – progress was made by John Major – a solution was finally engineered under the government of Tony Blair – a power-sharing government was put in place in Northern Ireland's parliament (Stormont Castle, a bombastic building worthy of Nicklaus Ceausescu) – it has endured – albeit with occasional problems – thus Protestant riots in late 2012 over the issue of flag flying – on the political sociology of the colony, see Colin Kidd 2013 'On the Window Ledge of the Union' in *London Review of Books* 35.3, 7 February 2013.
9. One noted figure was Tim Page – he is noted in Michael Herr 1977 *Dispatches*, New York, Alfred Knopf – he has also published collections of his work – Tim Page 1984 *Tim Page's Nam*, London, Thames and Hudson.
10. For example, see Francis Ford Coppola 1979 *Apocalypse Now* (film).
11. R. Scruton 2001 *England: An Elegy*, London, Pimlico.
12. Stan Cohen 1972 *Folk Devils and Moral Panics*, Oxford, Martin Robertson.

13. The Beatles 1963 *Please Please Me (L.P)*.
14. Kureshi's observation is good and today bands usually write their own stuff.
15. Jenny Diski 2009 *The Sixties*, London, Profile.
16. Peter Sellers 1965 in a television show devoted to The Beatles recites a *Hard Days Night* in Shakespearean mode.
17. Philip Larkin's poem 'Annus Mirabilis'.
18. In social action – Gay Liberation – later Stonewall – and one prizewinning television film – *The Naked Civil Servant* – a life of Quentin Crisp – autobiography published in 1968 – television film made by Thames Television and shown in 1975.
19. Diana Athill 'Doris Lessing's Golden Notebook 50 years on' in *The Guardian*, 6 April 2012.
20. Photo by Nick Ut June 1972 – girl was called Kim Phuc – and she survived.
21. Photo by Eddie Adams 1968.
22. See, for example, Page 1984.
23. Lee Harvey Oswald was in police custody when he was shot dead in a melee by Jack Ruby – the official report was doubted because some witnesses reported a second assassin – the report discounted this idea.
24. See P.W. Preston 2012 *England After the Great Recession*, London, Palgrave.
25. Marco Giordana 2003 *The Best of Youth* (film).
26. In Germany, in 1980, the Greens were formally established as a political party and the model has been copied in other polities.
27. See, for example, R.D. Laing 1967 *The Politics of Experience and the Bird of Paradise*, Harmondsworth, Penguin; Thomas Szasz 1961 *The Myth of Mental Illness*, New York, Harper; M. Foucault 1973 *The Birth of the Clinic*, New York, Vintage.
28. A manifesto was made available: see Timothy Leary, R. Metzner, R. Alpert 1964 *The Psychedelic Experience*, New York, Citadel Press.
29. Island Records – Motown – and the like.
30. Criticism of contemporary society came up repeatedly – Lindsey Anderson 1968 *If* (film); Michelangelo Antonioni 1966 *Blow Up* (film); Ken Russell 1970 *The Music Lovers* (film); Nicolas Roeg 1970 *Performance* (film); and F.F. Coppola 1979 *Apocalypse Now* (film).
31. Ken Russell made a series of television films dealing with music for the series *Monitor/Omnibus* – including *Elgar* (1962) and *Song of Summer* (1968 – focused on Frederick Delius) – later he made film – notably, *Women in Love* 1969.
32. Many films in his native Italian – made *Blow Up* (1966) in English – a success.
33. Made movie *If* (1968).
34. Discussed by Stefan Collini – see also G. Hawthorn 1992 'Post-nationalism' in *London Review of Books* 14.23, 3 December 1992.
35. Hence – the British Marxist Historians – see Harvey Kaye 1984 *The British Marxist Historians*, Cambridge, Polity.
36. Stefan Collini 1999 *English Pasts: Essays in History and Culture*, Oxford University Press.
37. Stuart Hall 2010 'The Birth of the New Left Review' in *New Left Review* 61 January/February.
38. Ross McKibbin 'The Way we Live now' in *London Review of Books* 12.01, 11 January 1990.
39. Noted earlier in connection with 'Patrician Retreat'.

40. An unlooked for consequence noted by Richard Hoggart.
41. M. Young and P. Willmott 1957 *Family and Kinship in East London*, Harmondsworth, Penguin.
42. Stefan Collini 1999 *English Pasts: Essays in History and Culture*, Oxford University Press, pp.219–30.
43. Richard Hoggart 1992 *The Uses of Literacy*, Harmondsworth, Penguin.
44. John Corner 1991 'Studying Culture: Reflections and Assessments', in *Media, Culture and Society* 13 records an interview with Richard Hoggart who recalls the book *Uses*, the establishment of the Centre for Contemporary Cultural Studies (CCCS) and then a little of the subsequent changes in British popular culture.
45. Stefan Collini 1999 *English Pasts: Essays in History and Culture*, Oxford University Press.
46. See Stuart Hall 1988 *The Hard Road to Renewal: Thatcherism and the Crisis of the Left*, London, Verso; for a sceptical note on some later work, Ross McKibbin 1990 'The Way we Live now' in *London Review of Books* 12.1, 11 January 1990.
47. On Peter Cook, see Paul Foot 1997 'Half Bird, Half Fish, Half Unicorn' in *London Review of Books* 19.20, 16 October 1997.
48. The long historical process could be schematically mapped: *fine art painting* (frescoes offering religious images for elite/mass) (oil on canvas offering religious/secular images for elite); *graphics* (prints, posters, advertising images placed in broad public sphere); and *photography* (as record (American Civil War, nineteenth-century traders/explorers, colonial officials or photojournalists)), as art form (Andre Bresson, Annie Leibovitz, Helmut Newton), and as entertainment (cheap and easy to use cameras or recently camera-phones for everyone).
49. Michelangelo Antonioni 1966 *Blow Up* (film).
50. Patrick Wright 1985 *On Living in an Old Country*, London, Verso, after Agnes Heller, distinguishes particularity and individuality – the former inhabits the world-taken-for-granted, the latter is self-conscious.
51. The image uses are discussed by Linda Colley – the political model is discussed by Tom Nairn.
52. J.E. Crowley 2011 *Imperial Landscapes: Britain's Global Visual Culture*, Yale University Press.
53. The process of 'embedding' stops the production of genuine photojournalism of the sort produced by – say – Tim Page's Vietnam photography and generates propaganda, which can be more or less subtle, but which generally excises or softens the violence of war (that is, obscures its core activity).
54. Thus, today, we see few groups announcing that they are 'backing Britain' or selling Union Jack tea-towels.
55. Rainer Metzger 2007 *Berlin in the Twenties: Art and Culture 1918–1933*, London, Thames and Hudson.
56. The film *Indochine*, directed by Regis Wargnier, released in 1992, deals with the colonial world in the 1930s – the film details the experiences of a family caught up in the events – it ends with the country portioned in 1954; the film *The Scent of Green Papaya*, directed by Ahn Hung Tran, released in 1993, deals with life in Vietnam in the 1950s showing the beauty of nature and tracking the life of one young women – offers idyllic images of the country; the film *The Quiet American*, directed by Phillip Noyce, released

244 Notes

in 2002, deals with the intervention of foreigners in Vietnam – the cynical humanism of the Europeans involved is contrasted with the destructively naïve behaviour of a young American – the entry of the Americans into the incipient war is recorded; the film, *Apocalypse Now*, directed by Francis Ford Coppola, released in 1979, deals with the nature of US power in Vietnam – a descent into madness.

57. Maude Anne Bracke 'One Dimensional Conflict: Recent Scholarship on 1968 and the Limitations of the Generational Concept' in *Journal of Contemporary History* 47.3, 2012, argues that to speak of the '68 generation is to privilege the recollections of one student movement originating group of 'witness historians' to the neglect of others in the public realm.
58. Tony Judt 2005 *Post-War: A History of Europe Since 1945*, New York, The Penguin Press.
59. Or, see Rainer Metzger 2012 *London in the Sixties*, London, Thames and Hudson, who records, precisely, the style.
60. One instance – the legalization of cannabis – rejected by the authorities in the 1960s and on subsequent occasions as various reports were published – in early 2013 Home Secretary Theresa May announced that her department would look at recent experiences in mainland Europe and in the USA of decriminalization – a mere 50 years later.
61. Diski 2009.

8 Corporate World, Media and Politics

1. See P.W. Preston 1994 *Discourses of Development*, Aldershot, Avebury.
2. Ted Honderich 1990 *Conservatism*, London, Hamish Hamilton, offered an excoriating critique which reduced the ideas to a celebration of selfishness – in retrospect, refocused on neo-liberalism, prescient.
3. Hence Gordon Gecko in *Wall Street* (film) – 'greed is good'.
4. Robert Skidelsky 2004 *John Maynard Keynes 1883–1946*, London, Pan Macmillan.
5. On the war and science and production, see D. Edgerton 2006 *Warfare State: Britain 1920–1970*, Cambridge University Press; D. Edgerton 2011 *Britain's War Machine: Weapons, Resources and Experts* in the Second World War, London, Allen Lane.
6. Production – coal, steel, railways, water, domestic electricity and gas; finance – government fiscal policy, that is, state spending; planning – state involvement in supporting industries, some strategic, thus defence, some semi-automatically, thus with the NHS the state was a major purchaser of goods from pharmaceutical industry, and some for political reasons, thus, monies to say the car industry to sustain jobs in this or that region (on this, see Peter Hennessy 2006 *Having It So Good: Britain in the Fifties*, London, Allen Lane, and generally Tony Judt 2005 *Post War: A History of Europe Since 1945*, New York, Penguin Press).
7. Peter Hennessy 1992 *Never Again: Britain 1945–1951*, London, Cape, discusses the post-war elites and diagnoses 'complacency' – it seems a little ungenerous as the structural problems they faced were severe but if one criticism could with justice be made it was the gross error of recoiling from

the early construction of what in time became the European Union where 'complacency' understates the perversity of this mistake.
8. Edgerton 2006, 2011.
9. M. Hitchcock 2008 *The Bitter Road to Freedom*, New York, The Free Press.
10. Key players included Friedrich von Hayek and Milton Freidman.
11. Andrew Gamble 1988 *The Free Economy and the Strong State*, London, Macmillan.
12. Some films addressing the ethos of the era: Oliver Stone 1987 *Wall Street* (film); Barry Levinson 1997 *Wag the Dog* (film); Roman Polanski 2010 *The Ghost Writer* (film).
13. An argument satirized by Jospeh Heller in the character of Milo Minderbinder who privatized war and advertised that 'everyone has a share' – see Joseph Heller 1964 *Catch 22*, London, Corgi.
14. NPM – a political-cum-management theory, which argued that the performance of the public sector could be improved by deploying private sector regimes – it unpacked in practice as top-down management plus targets – see Kate McLaughlin Ewan Ferlie, and Stephen Osborne eds. 2002 *New Public Management: Current Trends and Future Prospects*, London, Routledge.
15. Wikiquotes (accessed 29 February 2012) sources this to a speech given to Tory Reform Group, then reported in *The Times*, 9 November 1985 – actual words are rather different, but this is now the popular memory version.
16. The first housing bubble plus crash of the neo-liberal era was in the mid-1980s – the next one in the early 2000s – the financial crisis arrived in 2008 – on the latter, see P.W. Preston 2012 *England After the Great Recession*, London, Palgrave.
17. One discussion is available from Clive Walker and Dave Whyte 2005 'Contracting Out War: Private Military Companies, Law and Regulation in the United Kingdom' in *International and Comparative Law Quarterly* 54.03.
18. On the issue/record of PFI, see Denis Campbell, James Ball and Simon Rogers 'PFI will Ultimately Cost UK300bn' in *The Guardian*, 5 July 2012; see also the work of Allyson Pollock, for example, A. Pollock 2005 *NHS PLC: The Privatization of Our Health Care*, London, Verso.
19. G. Hodgson 1988 *Economics and Institutions*, Cambridge, Polity.
20. Stephen Gudeman 1986 *Economics as Culture*, London, Routledge.
21. Some of the implications are pursued in P.W. Preston 2012 *England After the Great Recession: Tracking the Political and Cultural Consequences of the Crisis*, London, Palgrave.
22. There is a rich and growing literature. On the public debates, see, for example, Simon Jenkins writing in *The Guardian* for a polemic sustained over many months aimed at crooked bankers; recently, S. Jenkins 'Ban bonuses. They are mad. Discretionary gifts from top executives from company funds should be considered a malpractice' in 'With a Ban on Bonuses, Fred Goodwin could have Kept his Knighthood' in *The Guardian*, 31 January 2012; or S. Jenkins 'In any other business such bonuses would be regarded as theft from the firm' in 'Ignore the Howls. If Bankers Leave, it would be no Loss', in *The Guardian*, 6 March 2013.
23. For a witty overview of the madness, see John Lanchester 2010 *Whoops: What Everyone owes Everyone and No One Can Pay*, London, Penguin.

246 Notes

24. For a popular celebrant, see T.L. Freidman 1999 *The Lexus and the Olive Tree*, New York, Farrar, Straus and Giroux.
25. Various strands in the arts, in economics, in epistemology; all arguments with merit, however, they were run together in a package version that was intellectually incoherent but briefly fashionable; on the various strands, see David Harvey 1989 *The Condition of Postmodernity*, Oxford, Blackwell; F. Jameson 1991 *Postmodernism: The Cultural Logic of Late Capitalism*, London, Verso.
26. Anthony Woodiwiss 1993 *Postmodernism USA*, London, Sage.
27. Ivan Fallon 'Saatchi and Saatchi the Agency that Made Tory History' in *The Independent* 17 September 2007.
28. Charles Saatchi has been a major benefactor of young British artists – championing their work, buying it and displaying it in galleries.
29. Brit Art was viewed with contempt by Robert Hughes – he dismissed Damien Hirst – see 'Robert Hughes on Art' in *The Guardian*, 7 August 2012; Robert Hughes 2012 'The Mona Lisa Curse' (television film) *Channel Four* 21 September 2012; Michael McNay 'Robert Hughes Obituary' in *The Guardian*, 7 August 2012.
30. On the social production and processing of death, in particular images of the dead, see D. Faust 2008 *This Republic of Suffering: Death and the American Civil War*, New York, Alfred Knopf.
31. D. Simpson 2007 'Iwo Jima versus Abu Graib' in *London Review of Books* 29.23.
32. L Kennedy 2008 'Securing Vision: Photography and US Foreign Policy' in *Media, Culture and Society* 30.3.
33. P. Campbell 2009 'The Lens of War' in *New Left Review* 55 January/February.
34. Gillian Doyle 2002 *Media Ownership*, London, Sage; R. Kuhn 2007 *Politics and Media in Britain*, London, Palgrave.
35. Thus, for example, tabloids, with their distinctive contribution – J. Thomas 2007 'Bound by History: The Winter of Discontent in British Politics' in *Media, Culture and Society* 29.2; John Lanchester 2008 'Riots, Terrorism etc' in *London Review of Books* 30.5; M. Hampton 2007 'Book Review: Martin Conboy, Tabloid Britain' in *Media, Culture and Society* 29; H. Wasserman 2009 'Book Review: Sofia Johansson, Reading Tabloids' in *Media, Culture and Society* 31.
36. News International employees were accused of illegal snooping, suborning state officials and perjury – for a taste of the scandal, see Dan Sabbagh 'Power, Corruption and Lies' in *The Guardian*, 28 February 2012; Dan Sabbagh 'The Son also Sets: James Murdoch Quits News International' in *The Guardian*, 1 March 2012; it might be added that in early March 2013, employees and ex-employees of the Mirror Group were also alleged to be implicated in similar illegal activities, see *The Guardian*, 11 March 2013.
37. On Berlusconi, see *The Economist*.
38. Gillian Doyle 2002 *Media Ownership*, London, Sage.
39. Tim Wu 2010 *The Master Switch: The Rise and Fall of Information Empires*, London, Atlantic, notes that new technologies have often been welcomed – but the realization of their apparent promise is by no means straightforward.
40. *Instrumental* – knowing presentation of falsehoods or partial truths to secure a specific goal; *adventitious* – knowing presentation of falsehoods or partial truths in a political emergency so as to avoid an issue for the moment;

systemic – the deployment of taken for granted untruths via ordinary state machinery.
41. Gamble 1988.
42. Stuart Hall's 'authoritarian populism' pointed to the package of ideas, actions and prejudices which served as the ideological counterpoint to Gamble's 'strong state and free economy', all the ideas deployed in the public sphere which smoothed the way of a neo-liberal elite and their allies in the media and the corporate world.
43. Scepticism in respect of the European Union dates from earliest post-war years and by the time of the Thatcher government the press had become generally hostile – on this see Benjamin Hawkins 2012 'Nation, Separation and Threat: An Analysis of British Media Discourses on the European Union Treaty Reform Process' in *Journal of Common Market Studies* 50.4; see also Oliver Daddow 2012 'The UK Media and "Europe": From Permissive Consensus to Destructive Dissent' in *International Affairs* 88.6, who argues that Thatcher opened a space for Murdoch and thereafter politicians let him (and others) get away with it – however, for Murdoch the baseline is money.
44. Gordon Gecko, or in a subtler comment, P.J. Harvey, track 12 of album *Stories from the City, Stories from the Sea* (2000, Universal Island Records).
45. One high point of these attacks was the speech of James Murdoch at the Edinburgh Festival – shortly before scandal engulfed News International.
46. Jameson 1991.
47. There is a wide debate here: see Jameson 1991, Harvey 1989.
48. Owen Hatherley 2010 *A Guide to the New Ruins of Great Britain*, London, Verso.
49. See the work of Patrick Wright – for a comment on his work, N. Ascherson 1991 'Down Dalston Lane' in *London Review of Books* 13.12, 27 June 1991.
50. P. Hirst and G. Thompson 1992 2nd ed. *Globalization in Question*, Cambridge, Polity.
51. Woodiwiss 1993.
52. J. Street 2011 2nd ed. *Mass Media, Politics and Democracy*, London, Palgrave.
53. Doyle 2002, see Chapter 11.
54. See Dai Yong Jin 2008 'Neo-liberal Restructuring of the Global Communications System' in *Media, Culture and Society* 30.3; N. Just 2009 'Measuring Media Concentration and Diversity' in *Media, Culture and Society* 31.1; J. Bardoel and L. d'Haanens 2008 'Reinventing Public Service Broadcasting in Europe' in *Media, Culture and Society* 30.3.
55. An observation taken from F. Jameson 1991 *Postmodernism, Or the Cultural Logic of Late Capitalism*, London, Verso.
56. Woodiwiss 1993; Jameson 1991; A. Callinicos 1989 *Against Postmodernism: A Marxist Critique*, Cambridge, Polity.
57. Preston 2012.

9 Amongst the Bullshit Industries

1. A borrowing from R. Hughes 1991 2nd ed. *The Shock of the New*, London, Thames and Hudson.
2. A. Woodiwiss 1993 *Postmodernity USA*, London, Sage.

3. On these industries and the contrast with manufacturing, see L. Elliot and D. Atkinson 'Talk is Cheap' in *The Guardian*, 18 May 2007 – 'The Germans may have engineers, the Japanese may know how to organize a production line, but the Brits have the barristers, the management consultants and the men and women who think that making up jingles and slogans in order to flog Pot Noodles and similar products is a series job.'
4. P. W. Preston 2012 *England After the Great Recession*, London, Palgrave.
5. For an introductory survey, see Michelle Pace and Francesco Cavatorta 2012 'The Arab Uprisings in Theoretical Perspective: An Introduction' in *Mediterranean Politics* 17.2.
6. The internet is a problem for the traditional press, see John Lanchester 2010 'Let us Pay' in *London Review of Books* 32.24, 16 December 2010.
7. Z. Bauman 1988 *Freedom*, Milton Keynes, Open University Press.
8. T. Wu 2010 *The Master Switch: The Rise and Fall of Information Empires*, London, Atlantic.
9. Law made in 1954, ITV began broadcasting in autumn 1955.
10. S. Collini 2008 *Common Reading: Critics, Historians, Publics*, Oxford University Press, essay 21.
11. The News International scandal received extensive coverage in mainstream British broadsheet press – see *Guardian, Independent, Financial Times* and *Daily Telegraph* – autumn 2011 to spring 2012 – in 2013 the Mirror Group was drawn into the scandal, see *The Guardian*, 12 March 2013.
12. T. Wu 2010 *The Master Switch: The Rise and Fall of Information Empires*, London, Atlantic.
13. Revenues – the BBC from the licence fee and commercial from subscriptions and advertisements – the implied claim is that the BBC has an unfair advantage by virtue of either unlimited money or no reason to pay attention to costs or both somehow run together – in the case of BBC iPlayer it is notable that it is very high quality and very popular.
14. That said, one of its biggest sellers in the 2000s was the comedy motoring programme *Top Gear*.
15. A number of points might be made here, thus this author: (i) is not buying into an elitist notion of what is good and bad, (ii) is happy to grant that whilst much of the output of Hollywood and its emulators is rubbish, that such rubbish can be entertaining, and (iii) accepts that individual tastes in such rubbish are likely to be entirely idiosyncratic (and thus not easily subject to definitive expressions of approval/disapproval) but (iv) believes, nonetheless, that the rubbish can be criticized – there is a point at which popular rubbish becomes socially or morally offensive – thus, for example, many/most daytime television 'reality' shows – or the violence pornography of some mainstream Hollywood directors.
16. Thus programmes on fishing or surf boarding or any other minority hobby.
17. Significant income streams – thus protected – see, for example, the case of the London Olympics 2012, where the organizing committee and commercial sponsors were anxious to block the local population from using the Olympic theme in their merchandise – see also Euro 2012 football competition – in Thailand a local dispute between broadcasters and rights-holders restricted access – see again the case of the British pub landlady who bought access to football matches via a non-British satellite company and was taken to court by British broadcasters.

18. Hence – New Labour politicians, it is said, were encouraged to take an interest.
19. P.W. Preston 1997 *Political/Cultural Identity: Citizens and Nations in a Global Era*, London, Sage.
20. As the corporate world has become more involved in football, the distinction between those who own the 'clubs' and those who are 'supporters' has become clearer – the point was made by the son of the American owners of Manchester United when he somewhat ill-advisedly made it clear that the owners did not care what the members of the supporters club thought – in other words 'football clubs' are private companies, players are employees and those who watch are paying customers – older paternalistic ideas, where the owner did pay attention to local opinion belong in the past.
21. Mike Marquese 1994 *Anyone But England: Cricket and the National Malaise*, London, Verso.
22. Gurinder Chada 2002 *Bend It Like Beckham* (film); there are also popular novels about football – Nick Hornby – criticized by Mary Dejevsky 'The cult of football is a blight on our national life' in *The Independent*, 10 February 2012 for encouraging the middle classes to become involved via a species of social 'slumming it'.
23. Who spent much of his managerial career on the mainland and speaks four or five languages.
24. For a succinct summary see David Conn 'Follow the Money' in *London Review of Books* 34.16, 30 August 2012 – who points out that the key changes were made in the early 1990s as corporate money flowed into clubs reorganized along corporate lines – there is an interesting contrast with the situation in Germany where regulations have ensured that the clubs are controlled by club members, that is supporters – Conn adds that this is clearly to the benefit of the sport and the supporters.
25. The financial accountants Deloitte and Touch report each year on football, see *Annual Report on Football Finance* available on the firm's website.
26. Deloite and Touche.
27. Royal female celebrity is deconstructed by Hilary Mantel 'Royal Bodies' in *London Review of Books* 35.4, 21 February 2013.
28. Originally the tag was applied to Harold Macmillan.
29. See Colin Hay 1999 *The Political Economy of New Labour*, Manchester University Press.
30. L. Brauer and V. Rutledge Shields 1999 'Princess Diana's Celebrity in Freeze Frame: Reading the Constructed Image of Diana through Photographs' in *European Journal of Cultural Studies* 2.5.
31. T. Nairn 1988 *The Enchanted Glass: Britain and Its Monarchy*, London, Hutchison Radius.
32. An approach deployed by Charles Saatchi in successfully creating 'Brit-art' – for a rare partial defence of Damien Hirst, see Marina Walker 'Once a Catholic...' in *London Review of Books* 34.13, 2012.
33. Robert Hughes 'The Rise of Andy Warhol' in *The New York Review of Books*, 18 February 1982; see also Robert Hughes 1991 *The Shock of the New*, London, Thames and Hudson.
34. An old issue, recent contributions, for/against: John Street 2012 'Do Celebrity Politics and Celebrity Politicians Matter?' in *British Journal of Politics and International Relations* 14, argues that something is going on, not

sure what, politicians ape style to get votes (instrumental), some celebs join in politics/media to support 'good causes', people are drawn in, but rational debate?; Mark Wheeler 'The Democratic Worth of Celebrity Politics in an Era of Late Modernity' in *British Journal of Politics and International Relations* 14, notes Frankfurt School inspired critics, but wonders if media could not be a new form of involvement, in a 'network society'.
35. Symptomatically – the absurd and dangerous stereotyping of Muslims as liable to violent fanaticism – 'Islamo-fascism' – see, for example, Christopher Hitchens.
36. Kate Nash 2008 'Global Citizenship as Show Business: The Cultural Politics of Make Poverty History' in *Media, Culture and Society* 30.2.
37. John Street 2004 'Celebrity Politicians: Culture and Political Representation' in *British Journal of Politics and International Relations* 6.
38. The Leveson enquiry plus Metropolitan Police enquiries have uncovered numerous examples of poor practice or law-breaking.
39. Nick Davies 2009 *Flat Earth News*, London, Vintage, details some of the aggressive work of the *Daily Mail* – it produces from some replies in the courts – a list of damages paid out by the *Daily Mail* is given (pp.368–9) – the overall tendency is related back to commercialization – newspapers as business targeting audiences and making them available to advertisers – key is profit.
40. J. Bosman and L d'Haenens 2008 'News Reporting on Pim Fortuyn' in *Media, Culture and Society* 30.5.
41. J.C. Alexander 2010 'Eyerman, R., The Assassination of Theo van Gogh: From Social Drama to Cultural Trauma (Book Review)' in *British Journal of Sociology* 61.2, p.385.
42. Ian Buruma 2007 *Murder in Amsterdam*, London, Penguin.
43. S. Cottle 2008 'Reporting Demonstrations: The Changing Media Politics of Dissent' in *Media, Culture and Society* 30.6; see also Lisa Leung 2009 'Mediated Violence as Global News: Co-opted Performance in the Framing of the WTO' in *Media, Culture and Society* 31.2.
44. Davies 2009.
45. K Karppinen 2007 'Against Naïve Pluralism in Media Politics: On the Implications of the Radical Pluralist Approach to the Public Sphere' in *Media, Culture and Society* 29.3.
46. Davies 2009 – see Chapter 3, where he discusses 'suppliers' of news.
47. Davies 2009, p.154.
48. On money/finance, see John Lanchester 'Let Us Pay' in *London Review of Books* 33.24, 16 December 2010.

10 Familiar Utopias: New Technologies and the Internet

1. Tim Wu 2010 *The Master Switch: The Rise and Fall of Information Empires*, London, Atlantic.
2. Evgeny Morozov 2011 *The Net Delusion: How Not to Liberate the World*, London, Allen Lane.
3. Wu 2010.

4. M. Featherstone 2009 'Ubiquitous Media: An Introduction' in *Media, Culture and Society* 31.
5. By way of illustrations of the range of users – the 2009 movie *Avatar* directed by James Cameron and using CGI or the artist David Hockney using an iPad to make sketches of his native East Yorkshire, see David Hockney 2012 *David Hockney: A Bigger Picture*, London, Royal Academy of Arts.
6. In Britain – GCHQ in Cheltenham and Menwith Hill.
7. One attempt went awry in an area of Birmingham, when a number of digital CCTV cameras were set up to monitor the population in a predominantly Muslim area.
8. Issues of legal authority crop up here – the state can make excuses for interlinking its own datasets but other arguments have to be made in order to access private sector data – for example, the police may request access to film and television recordings of public demonstrations.
9. See Ryan Gallagher 'Software that Tracks People on Social Media Created by Defence Firm' in *The Guardian* 10 February 2013 – see also Dan Schiller 'Masters of the Internet' in *Le Monde Diplomatique* 13 February 2013 on the conflicts for control of the 'political economy of cyberspace'.
10. See L.T. Chang 2010 *Factory Girls: Voices From the Heart of Modern China*, London, Picador.
11. See 'Gordon Moore's Law' on capacity doubling every 18 months.
12. For example, British government and imported US helicopters – the suppliers would not release key computer code and so the utility of the machines was compromised – see D. Hencke 'Chinook Blunders Cost MoD £500m' in *The Guardian* 4 June 2008; see also National Audit Office 'Ministry of Defence: Chinook Mk3 Helicopters' 4 June 2008.
13. Hence 'mal-ware' or 'computer viruses' – difficult to imagine a vinyl or print equivalent (except, perhaps, for the rituals of old hot-metal print setters employed by the Grauniad).
14. Creating a vast amount of e-rubbish – for some facts and figures see Electronics Take Back Coalition 'Facts and Figures on E-waste and Recycling' on http://www.electronicstakeback.com/wp-content/updoads/Facts_and_Figures_on_Ewaste_and_recycling.pdf. accessed 15 February 2013.
15. State surveillance is extensive – a list of techniques is given by BBC News 'Britain is a "Surveillance Society"' see http://newsvote.bbc.co.uk accessed 19 July 2012. See also John Kampfner 'Liberal Values have never Been more Important or less Popular' in *The Independent* 19 July 2012 – on why the political left should be worried about this. See also John Kampfner 'Finally Ed Miliband could Recalibrate Labour as the Party of Liberty' in *The Guardian* 19 July 2012 – same point.
16. One example – Amazon – see Sarah O'Conner 'Amazon Unpacked' in *Financial Times* 8 February 2013.
17. One caveat – the big corporate IT companies are making it up as they go along in one crucial area – that of intellectual property rights – thus, Google street view (never asked anyone's permission) or Google digitizing libraries (never asked any author's or publisher's permission) or Google linking up to other sites and thus using their material (never asked permission) – all these have been subject to debate and challenge – but these debates are in the nature of various small groups debating one by one land-grabs by

252 *Notes*

a large powerful landowner minded to take over whatever they can get away with.
18. On this John Street 2011 2nd ed. *Mass Media, Politics and Democracy*, London, Palgrave.
19. A. Kelso 2007 'Parliament and Political Disengagement: Neither Waving nor Drowning' in *Political Quarterly* 78.3 July–September.
20. Use of scare quotes for two reasons – the phrases are widely used but are clichés offering a stylized image of Western political processes, including those of Britain – the phrases offer a stylized image which is implausible, that is, it is quite easy to argue, say, that the last thing Whitehall/Westminster wants is the citizens of Britain to get involved, rather, what they want, is for the citizens to *believe* that their involvement is wanted, recognized and respected.
21. S. Ward, R. Gibson and W. Lusoli 2003 'Online Participation and Mobilization in Britain: Hype, Hope and Reality' in *Parliamentary Affairs* 56; L. Miller 2009 'E-petitions at Westminster: The Way forward for Democracy', in *Parliamentary Affairs* 62.1.
22. Inverse of covertly gathering information is covertly distributing misinformation – on state-sponsored propaganda see the stories presented by Nick Davies 2009 *Flat Earth News*, London, Vintage, Chapter 6, 'The Propaganda Puzzle' in *Particular* pp.225–8.
23. This text was written before the news about Edward Snowden broke his revelations about the scale and scope of state digital spying can be found in the *Guardian* news paper over the summer months of 2013.
24. Some PR company activity is discussed by Davies 2009.
25. And you can just switch off all the stuff, see Jim Holt 'Smarter, Happier, more Productive' in *London Review of Books* 33.5, 3 March 2011.
26. Victor Mayer-Schonberger 2009 *Delete: The Virtue of Forgetting in the Digital Age*, Princeton University Press.
27. Mayer-Schonberger 2009.
28. Ibid., p.11.
29. Ibid., p.168.
30. Ibid., Chapter 6.
31. Tim Wu 2010 *The Master Switch: The Rise and Fall of Information Empires*, London, Atlantic.
32. Morozov 2011.
33. George Orwell's authoritarian dystopia *1984* and Aldous Huxley's benign dystopia *Brave New World*.

11 Continuing Britain: Contemporary Political Culture Unpacked

1. Spelled out with exemplary lucidity by Susan Strange 1988 *States and Markets*, London, Pinter.
2. One critic writes of the 'Anglo-sphere' – a consolation for an elite that lost its empire – see Andrew Gamble 2007 'Hegemony and Empire: British Exceptionalism and the Myth of Anglo-America', paper presented to the Political Studies Association Conference, University of Bath, 11–13 April

2007; see also James Meek 'Short Cuts' in *London Review of Books* 35.6, 21 March 2013.
3. On contingency in general, see Richard Rorty 1989 *Contingency, Irony and Solidarity*, Cambridge University Press; on the contingency of European states, see Norman Davies 2011 *Vanished Kingdoms: The History of Half-Forgotten Europe*, London, Allen Lane.
4. There is a 'deep history', which read in stylized form, provided the core elements of an elite great tradition. So there are two stands in these discussions: synchronic, detailing the logic of the system – here the elite's deep history of Britain finds expression in a 'Great Tradition' centred on the monarchy, parliament and claims to liberal democracy and it has informal extension, thus a little tradition; and diachronic, unpacking the history in a chronological fashion, noting the configurations of groups and their ways of grasping and ordering their situations; see P.W. Preston 1994 *Europe, Democracy and the Dissolution of Britain*, Aldershot, Avebury; P.W. Preston 2004 *Relocating England: Englishness in the New Europe*, Manchester, Manchester University Press.
5. Inelegant – but it points to the integrated nature of the British Empire – arguments to the effect that the empire was accumulated absentmindedly and discarded easily is right-wing propaganda – see J.M. MacKenzie 2001 'The Persistence of Empire in Metropolitan Culture' in Stuart Ward ed. 2001 *British Culture and the End of Empire*, Manchester University Press; see also Wendy Webster 2005 *Englishness and Empire 1939–1965*, Oxford University Press.
6. Doesn't mean they aren't made, see R.J. Evans 'The Wonderfulness of Us: The Tory Interpretation of History' in *London Review of Books* 33.6, 17 March 2011.
7. These alternatives are readily sketched – poodle-hood, muddle or Europe – see P.W. Preston 2012 *England After the Great Recession*, London, Palgrave.
8. Hence, surely, in part, the British publishing trade's output of histories of Nazi Germany and Adolf Hitler – the available negative against which the positive glows more brightly.
9. On arguments from language, see P.W. Preston 2009 *Arguments and Actions in Social Theory*, London, Palgrave.
10. A. MacIntyre 1985 2nd ed. *After Virtue: A Study in Moral Theory*, London, Duckworth.
11. The idea of elites is taken from William Case 2002 *Politics in Southeast Asia: Democracy or Less*, London, Routledge Curzon – the source of the ideas lies in the interwar 'New Machiavellians' – Mosca, Michels and Pareto.
12. Long tradition of ameliorative welfare research in British social science – all the way back to Friedrich Engels and other reform-minded patrician businessmen – later William Beveridge – later still Richard Titmuss and Peter Townsend – recently R. Wilkinson and K. Picket 2009 *The Spirit Level: Why Equality is Better for Everyone*, London, Allen Lane.
13. An idea noted by Harold Macmillan in his famous one-liner, and pursued by Joseph Heller – see Thomas Powers 'Comedy is Murder' in *London Review of Books* 34.5, 5 March 2012.
14. For notes on the debate amongst historians, see Linda Colley 2010 'Little Englander Histories' in *London Review of Books* 32.14, 22 July 2010,

Linda Colley 2001 'Multiple Kingdoms' in *London Review of Books* 23.14, 19 July 2001.
15. Thus in particular – Linda Colley, Tom Nairn, Perry Anderson, Stuart Hall, Richard Hoggart, Patrick Wright, Norman Davies and Tony Judt.
16. See Norman Davies 2000 *The Isles: A History*, London, Papermac.
17. Tony Judt 2002 'The Past is another Country: Myth and Memory in Post-war Europe' in J-W Muller ed *Memory and Power in Post-war Europe*, Cambridge University Press; Tony Judt 2008 'What have we learned, if anything?' in *New York Review of Books* 55.7; Tony Judt 2008 *Reappraisals: Reflections on the Forgotten Twentieth Century*, London, Heinemann.
18. Norman Davies 1997 *Europe: A History*, London, Pimlico.
19. Tony Judt 2005 *Postwar: A History of Europe Since 1945*, London, Penguin, see Epilogue.
20. Patrick Wright 1985 *On Living in an Old Country*, London, Verso; Wright's discussion is intellectually rooted in the writings of Agnes Heller, a follower of Georg Luckas, and Wright recalls that Heller attends to the realm of everyday life – the mundane sphere of ordinary living – it is within this sphere that people encounter both history (the ways in which their lives are slotted into unfolding time – personal, familial, community and polity) and culture (the ways in which their lives are informed by a repertoire of concepts carried in tradition). Heller insists that everyday life is situated – that is, it is always precisely located and imbued with the intellectual/moral resources of tradition – it presents itself in stories – it is with reference to these stories that people lodge themselves in communities and in turn tie these into wider schemes of history – such stories focused on the polity can be tagged 'the national past' – Wright has looked at both urban and rural – see, for example, Patrick Wright 1993 *A Journey through the Ruins: A Keyhole Portrait of British Postwar Life* and Culture, London, Flamingo; Patrick Wright 1995 *The Village that Died for England*, London, Jonathan Cape.
21. Richard Gott 2011 *Britain's Empire: Resistance, Repression and Revolt*, London, Verso.
22. The past was made available as 'deep history' – a stylized summary of the history of the polity – cast in formal terms – a great tradition – unpacked and infusing a subaltern little tradition.
23. Thus, internationally, Ernest Bevin's 'Churchill option' locating Britain between the three spheres of Commonwealth, the USA and Europe (on this generally, John Saville 1984 'Ernest Bevin and the Cold War 1945–50' in *Socialist Register*); domestically, the welfare state, the new Elizabethan age of science-based progress, new towns, public housing, motorways and so on – the moves which tied the polity into the US-centred 'West'.
24. With military strategies built around weapons of mass destruction – the destruction of whole cities and populations was built into military/industrial planning.
25. Preston 2004, 2012.
26. One coherent statement is made by Roger Scruton – England as home, rooted in the land and the local folk-ways whereby life is ordered – R. Scruton 2001 *England: An Elegy*, London, Pimlico.
27. Rorty 1989.
28. Judt 2002.

29. On this see John Lanchester 2010 *Whoops: What Everyone Owes to Everyone and No One Can Pay*, London, Penguin; P.W. Preston 2012 *England After the Great Recession: Tracking the Cultural Consequences of the Crisis*, London, Palgrave; John Lanchester 2009 'Bankocracy' in *London Review of Books* 31.21, 5 November 2009; John Lanchester 2010 'The Great British Economy Disaster' in *London Review of Books* 32.5, 11 March 2001.
30. Tom Nairn 1977 *The Break-Up of Britain*, London, New Left Books, reprinted with a new Preface in 2002 – Nairn distances himself from the economistic elements of the work, insists that the arguments for nation and democracy remain good, so too the diagnosis of the moribund nature of the British polity.
31. There is a European aspect to these debates – rebalancing power and authority within nation-states, hitherto considered to be institutionally unproblematic, is a Europe-wide issue – in conventional terms, the European Union moves power both upwards and downwards – but there is also a local aspect – the Labour Party in Scotland has combined a generic subaltern conservatism with a determined celebration of the union and thus British-ness – it has failed to grasp the logic of the rise of the Scottish National Party – which addresses itself to Scotland qua Scotland – on this see T. Nairn 2010 'Triumph of the Termites' in *London Review of Books* 32.7, 8 April 2010.
32. These 'scenarios' are taken from speculations made in Preston 2004 and Preston 2012 and the comments have been updated – events in the interim have seen the euro crisis drawn out to an extraordinary length plus domestically the apparent return of that 'nasty' Conservative Party which many had supposed that David Cameron had been anxious to bury – early 2013 saw the promise – deeply ambiguous it must be said – made of a referendum on British membership of the European Union.
33. Since the 1980s, the neo-liberal era, the distribution of income and wealth has moved in the direction of the richer groups in society.
34. In early 2013 a parliamentary by-election in the constituency of a disgraced coalition member of parliament saw his party retain the seat but also saw a spectacular advance for a populist anti-Europe party called the United Kingdom Independence Party.
35. Anatole Lieven 2004 *America Right or Wrong: An Anatomy of American Nationalism*, London, Harper Collins.
36. See D. W. Urwin 1997 *A Political History of Western Europe Since 1945*, London, Longman, Chapter 9.
37. Thus – the exit of Greece – the division of the eurozone into a hard northern bloc and a soft southern bloc – the withdrawal of Germany – and so on – for details, presented in contrasting tones, see *Financial Times* and *The Economist*.
38. Lots on Britain/Europe: for a specimen sensible pro-Europe work see, say, Anand Menon 2008 *Europe: The State of the Union*, London, Atlantic; Robert Cooper 2012 'Britain and Europe' in *International Affairs* 88.6; the rise of Euroscepticism is addressed by Simon Usherwood and Nick Startin 2013 'Euroscepticism as a Persistent Phenomenon' in *Journal of Common Market Studies* 51.1 (who argue it should be addressed directly); and also Julie Smith 'Introduction' (Britain in Europe Special Edition) in *International Affairs* 88.6 (who notes that the British elite were latecomers and never really signed up for the core member's project).

39. As a sample from the immediate commentary, which was mostly highly critical: Philip Stephen 'Was this the Moment the UK Stumbled out of Europe' in *Financial Times* 12 December 2011; Jonathan Powell 'Cameron's Catastrophic Decision on EU' in *Financial Times* 11 December 2011; Quentin Peel 'A Case of Different Mindsets' in *Financial Times* 11 December 2011; Andrew Rawnsly 'Now it's Three-Speed Europe. And We're Left on the Hard Shoulder' in *The Guardian/Observer* 11 December 2011; Charlemagne 'Europe's Great Divide' in *The Economist* 9 December 2011; Bagehot 'Britain's not Leaving, but Falling out of the EU' in *The Economist* 9 December 2011; Charles Grant 'Britain on the Edge of Europe', *Centre for European Reform* 9 December 2011; Gideon Rachman 'The Summit will Prove a Footnote' in *Financial Times* 12 December 2011; Peter Mandleson 'David Cameron is no Bulldog. Even Thatcher never Left the European Table' in *Guardian* 11 December 2011; David Owen 'High-Handed Approach that has Exposed the Coalition's Faultline' in *Independent* 12 December 2011; and Norman Tebbit 'David Cameron has Taken the First Steps in Solving Euro Crisis' in *Guardian* 11 December 2011.

Bibliography (Readings/Viewings)

Abrams, P. 1968 *The Origins of British Sociology*, Chicago University Press.
Addison, P. 1977 *The Road to 1945*, London, Jonathan Cape.
Aherne, C. *The Royle Family*, BBC television series, 1998/2012.
Ahn Hung Tran 1993 *The Scent of Green Papaya* (film).
Alasdair, M. 1971 *Against the Self Images of the Age*, London, Duckworth.
Alexander, J.C. 2010 'Eyerman, R., The Assasination of Theo van Gogh: From Social Drama to Cultural Trauma (Book Review)' in *British Journal of Sociology* 61.2.
Alfredson, T. 2012 (film) *Tinker, Tailor, Soldier, Sp.*
Amis, K. 1986 *The Old Devils*, London, Hutchinson.
Anand, M A. 2008 *Europe: The State of the Union*, London, Atlantic.
Anderson, B. 1983 *Imagined Communities*, London, Verso.
Anderson, L. 1968 *If* (film).
Anonymous 2006 *A Woman in Berlin*, London, Virago.
Antonioni, M. 1966 *Blow Up* (film).
Aron, R. 1973 *The Imperial Republic: The US and the World 1945–73*, London, Weidenfeld.
Ballard, J.G. 1988 *Empire of the Sun*, London, Grafton Books.
Ballard, J.G. 1991 *The Kindness of Women*, Toronto, Harper Collins.
Ballard, J.G. 1996 *Cocaine Nights*, London, Flamingo.
Ballard, J.G. 2001 *Super Cannes*, London, Harper Collins.
Ballard, J.G. 2004 *Millennium People*, London, Harper Collins.
Ballard, J.G. 2008 *Miracles of Life: From Shanghai to Shepperton, An Autobiography*, London, Fourth Estate.
Bardoel, J. and d'Haanens, L. 2008 'Reinventing Public Service Broadcasting in Europe' in *Media, Culture and Society* 30.3.
Barthes, R. 1973 *Mythologies*, London, Paladin.
Bauman, Z. 1987 *Legislators and Interpreters*, Cambridge, Polity.
Bauman, Z. 1988 *Freedom*, Open University Press.
Bayly, C.A. 2004 *The Birth of the Modern World 1780–1914*, Oxford, Blackwell.
Bayly, C. and Harper, T. 2004 *Forgotten Armies: The Fall of British Asia 1941–45*, London, Allen Lane.
Bayly, C. and Harper, T. 2007 *Forgotten Wars: The End of Britain's Asian Empire*, London, Allen Lane.
Bennett, A. 2004 *The History Boys* (play).
Bosman, J. and d'Haenens, L. 2008 'News Reporting on Pim Fortuyn' in *Media, Culture and Society* 30.5.
Boulting, J. R. 1959 *I'm All Right Jack* (film).
Boyle, D. 1996 *Trainspotting* (film).
Bracke, M.A. 'One Dimensional Conflict: Recent Scholarship on 1968 and the Limitations of the Generational Concept' in *Journal of Contemporary History* 47.3.

Braine, J. 1957 *Room at the Top*, London, Eyre and Spottiswoode.
Brauer, L. and Rutledge Shields, V. 1999 'Princess Diana's Celebrity in Freeze Frame: Reading the Constructed Image of Diana through Photographs' in *European Journal of Cultural Studies* 2.5.
Briggs, A. and Cobley, P. eds. 2002 *The Media: An Introduction*, 2nd ed. London, Longman.
Broad, M. and Daddow, O. 2010 'Half Remembered Quotations from Half forgotten Speeches' in *British Journal of Politics and International Relations* 12.
Burgess, A. 1981 *The Long Day Wanes*, London, Penguin.
Burton, G. 2005 *Media and Society: Critical Perspectives*, Open University Press.
Buruma, I. 2007 *Murder in Amsterdam*, London, Penguin.
Cadbury, B. 1931 *The Bournville Story*, Bournville, Cadbury Bros. Ltd.
Campbell, B. 1984 *Wigan Pier Revisited: Poverty and Politics in the Eighties*, London, Virago.
Campbell, P. 2009 'The Lens of War' in *New Left Review* 55 January/February.
Canadine, D. 2001 *Ornamentalism: How the British Saw their Empire*, London, Allen Lane.
Cannadine, D. 2011 *Making History Now and Then*, London, Palgrave.
Carr, E.H. 2001 [1939] *The Twenty Year Crisis*, London, Palgrave.
Carruthers, S.L. 2009 *Cold War Captives: Imprisonment, Escape and Brainwashing*, University of California Press.
Case, W. 2002 *Politics in Southeast Asia: Democracy or Less*, London, Routledge.
Caton-Jones, M. 1989 *Scandal* (film).
Caute, D. 1978 *The Great Fear: The Anti-Communist Purges Under Truman and Eisenhower*, London, Secker and Warburg.
Caute, D. 2003 *The Dancer Defects: The Struggle for Cultural Supremacy During the Cold War*, Oxford University Press.
Chada, G. 2002 *Bend It Like Beckham* (film).
Chang, L.T. 2010 *Factory Girls: Voices From the Heart of Modern China*, London, Picador.
Childers, E. 1903 *The Riddle of the Sands*, London, Smith, Elder and Co.
Chua B.H. ed. 2007 *Elections as Popular Culture in Asia*, London, Routledge.
Cohen, S. 1972 *Folk Devils and Moral Panics*, Oxford, Martin Robertson.
Colley, L. 1992 *Britons: Forging the Nation 1707–1837*, Yale University Press.
Collini, S. 1999 *English Pasts: Essays in History and Culture*, Oxford University Press.
Collini, S. 2006 *Absent Minds*, Oxford University Press.
Cooper, R. 2012 'Britain and Europe' in *International Affairs* 88.6.
Coppola, F.F. 1979 *Apocalypse Now* (film).
Corner, J. 1991 'Studying Culture: Reflections and Assessments' in *Media, Culture and Society* 13.
Cottle, S. 2008 'Reporting Demonstrations: The Changing Media Politics of Dissent' in *Media, Culture and Society* 30.6.
Crichley, S. 2001 *Continental Philosophy: A Very Short Introduction*, Oxford University.
Crick, B. 1980 *George Orwell*, Harmondsworth, Penguin.
Croft, S., Redmond, J., Rees, G.W. and Weber, M. 1999 *The Enlargement of Europe*, Manchester University Press.

Crowley, J.E. 2011 *Imperial Landscapes: Britain's Global Visual Culture*, Yale University Press.
Cummings, B. 2010 *The Korean War: A History*, New York, Modern Library.
Daddow, O. 2012 'The UK Media and "Europe": From Permissive Consensus to Destructive Dissent' in *International Affairs* 88.6.
Dai Yong Jin 2008 'Neo-Liberal Restructuring of the Global Communications System' in *Media, Culture and Society* 30.3.
Davis, M. 2002 *Dead Cities and Other Tales*, London, The New Press.
Davies, N. 1997 *Europe: A History*, London, Pimlico.
Davies, N. 2000 *The Isles: A History*, London, Papermac.
Davies, N. 2006 *Europe at War 1939–1945: No Simple Victory*, London, Macmillan.
Davies, N. 2009 *Flat Earth News*, London, Vintage.
Davies, N. 2011 *Vanished Kingdoms: The History of Half-Forgotten Europe*, London, Allen Lane.
Davies, T. 1988 *Distant Voices, Still Lives* (film).
Davies, T. 1992 *The Long Day Closes* (film).
Davies, T. 1995 *The Neon Bible* (film).
Davies, T. 2011 *The Deep Blue Sea* (film)
Deighton, L. 1962 *The Ipcress File*, London, Hodder and Stoughton.
Delaney, S. 1958 *A Taste of Honey* (play).
Diski, J. 2009 *The Sixties*, London, Profile.
Doherty, T. 2003 *Cold War, Cool Medium: Television, McCarthyism and American Culture*, Columbia University Press.
Doyle, G. 2002 *Media Ownership*, London, Sage.
Dunn, N. 1963 *Up the Junction*, London, MacGibbon and Kee.
Durham, M.G. and Douglas, K.M. eds. 2006 *Media and Cultural Studies: Key Works*, Oxford, Blackwell.
Eco, U. 1987 *Travels in Hyperreality*, London, Picador.
Edgerton, D. 2006 *Warfare State: Britain 1920–1970*, Cambridge University Press.
Edgerton, D. 2011 *Britain's War Machine: Weapons, Resources and Experts in the Second World War*, London, Allen Lane.
Eisenberg, C. 1996 *Drawing the Line: The American Decision to Divide Germany 1944–49*, Cambridge University Press.
Elkins, C. 2005 *Imperial Reckoning: The Untold Story of Britain's Gulag in Kenya*, London, Weidenfeld.
Faust, D. 2008 *This Republic of Suffering: Death and the American Civil War*, New York, Alfred Knopf.
Fay, B. 1975 *Social Theory and Political Practice*, London, Allen and Unwin.
Featherstone, M. 2009 'Ubiquitous Media: An Introduction' in *Media, Culture and Society* 31.
Flemming, D.F. 1961 *The Cold War and Its Origins*, New York, Doubleday.
Foertsch, J. 2008 *American Culture in the 1940s*, Edinburgh University Press.
Fosse, B. 1972 *Cabaret* (film).
Foucault, M. 1973 *The Birth of the Clinic,* New York, Vintage.
Frank, A.G. 1998 *Re-Orient: Global Economy in the Asian Age*, University of California Press.
Freidman, M. and Freidman, R. 1980 *Free to Choose*, London, Secker.
Freidman, T.L. 1999 *The Lexus and the Olive Tree*, New York, Farrar, Straus and Giroux.

Furnivall, J.S. 1939 *Netherlands India: A Study of Plural Economy*, Cambridge University Press.
Fywell, T. 2003 *Cambridge Spies* (BBC film).
Gadamer, H-G, 1979 *Truth and Method*, London, Sheed and Ward.
Gaddis, J.L. 1997 *We Know Now: Rethinking Cold War History*, Oxford University Press.
Gaddis, J.L. 2005 *The Cold War: A New History*, London, Penguin.
Galbraith, J.K. 1958 *The Affluent Society*, Harmonsdsworth, Penguin.
Gamble, A. 1988 *The Free Economy and the Strong State*, London, Macmillan.
Gamble, A. 2007 'Hegemony and Empire: British Exceptionalism and the Myth of Anglo-America', paper presented to the *Political Studies Association Conference*, University of Bath.
Gasping-Anderson, G. 1990 *The Three Worlds of Welfare Capitalism*, Cambridge, Polity.
Gay, P. 2008 *Modernism: The Lure of Heresy*, New York, Norton.
Gellner, E. 1983 *Nations and Nationalism*, Oxford, Blackwell.
George, S. ed. 1992 *Britain and the European Community: The Politics of Semi-Detachment*, Oxford University Press.
Giddens, A.1990 *The Consequences of Modernity*, Cambridge, Polity.
Gilroy, P. 2004 *After Empire: Melancholia or Convivial Culture*, London, Routledge.
Giordana, M. 2003 *The Best of Youth* (film).
Gott, R. 2011 *Britain's Empire: Resistance, Repression and Revolt*, London, Verso.
Grass, G. 1959 *The Tin Drum*, London, Secker and Warburg.
Grass, G. 1990 *Two States, One Nation*, London, Secker and Warburg.
Grass, G. 1999 *My Century*, London, Faber and Faber.
Grass, G. 2002 *Crabwalk,* London, Faber and Faber.
Greenaway, P. 1982 *The Draughtsman's Contract* (film).
Greenaway, P. 1985 *Zed and Two Noughts* (film).
Greenaway, P. 1996 *The Pillowbook* (film).
Greenfeld, L. 1992 *Nationalism: Five Roads to Modernity*, Harvard University Press.
Greengrass, P. 2004 *Bourne Supremacy* (film).
Greengrass, P. 2007 *Bourne Ultimatum* (film).
Grossman. 2006 *A Writer at War: With the Red Army 1941–45*, London, Pimlico.
Gudeman, S. 1986 *Economics as Culture*, London, Routledge.
H.M. Stationary Office 1963 *Traffic in Towns: The Specially Shortened Edition of the Buchanan Report*, Harmondsworth, Penguin.
Habermas, J. 1989 *The Structural Transformation of the Public Sphere*, Cambridge, Polity.
HaCohen, M.A. 2000 *Karl Popper: The Formative Years 1902–1945*, Cambridge University Press.
Hall, P. and Soskice, D. eds. 2001 *Varieties of Capitalism: The Institutional Foundations of Comparative Advantage,* Oxford University Press.
Hall, S. 1988 *The Hard Road to Renewal: Thatcherism and the Crisis of the Left*, London, Verso.
Hall, S. 2010 'The Birth of the New Left Review' in *New Left Review* 61 January/February.
Hammet, D. 1930 *The Maltese Falcon*, New York, Alfred Knopf.
Hampton, M. 2007 'Book Review: Martin Conboy, Tabloid Britain' in *Media, Culture and Society* 29.

Harris, A. 2010 *Romantic Moderns: English Writers, Artists and the Imagination from Virginia Woolf to John Piper*, London, Thames and Hudson.
Harvey, D. 1989 *The Condition of Postmodernity*, Oxford, Blackwell.
Harvey, P.J. 2000 *Stories from the City, Stories from the Sea* (CD).
Hasegawa, T. 2005 *Racing the Enemy: Stalin, Truman and the Surrender of Japan*, Cambridge University Press.
Hatherley, O. 2010 *A Guide to the New Ruins of Britain*, London, Verso.
Hawkins, B. 2012 'Nation, Separation and Threat: An Analysis of British Media Discourses on the European Union Treaty Reform Process' in *Journal of Common Market Studies* 50.4.
Hawthorn, G. 1976 *Enlightenment and Despair*, Cambridge University Press.
Hay, C. 1999 *The Political Economy of New Labour*, Manchester Univerisity Press.
Hayek, F.V. 1944 *Road to Serfdom*, London, Routledge.
Heller, J. 1964 *Catch 22*, London, Corgi.
Hellman, L. 1976 *Scoundrel Time*, New York, Little Brown.
Hennessy, P. 1992 *Never Again: Britain 1945–51*, London, Jonathan Cape.
Hennessy, P. 2006 *Having It So Good: Britain in the Fifties*, London, Allen Lane.
Herr, M. 1977 *Dispatches*, New York, Alfred Knopf.
Himmelfarb, G. 2005 *The Roads to Modernity: The British, French and American Enlightenments*, New York, Vintage.
Hirst, P. and Thompson, G. 1992 *Globalization in Question*, 2nd ed. Cambridge, Polity.
Hitchcock, W.I. 2008 *The Bitter Road to Freedom: A New History of the Liberation of Europe*, New York, The Free Press.
Hitchens, C. 1990 *Blood, Class and Nostalgia: Anglo-American Ironies*, London, Vintage.
Hobsbawm, E. 2002 *Interesting Times: A Twentieth Century Life*, London, Allen Lane.
Hobsbawm, E. and Ranger, T. 1983 *The Invention of Tradition*, Cambridge University Press.
Hobson, J.M. 2004 *The Eastern Origins of Western Civilization*, Cambridge University Press.
Hockney, D. 2012 *David Hockney: A Bigger Picture*, London, Royal Academy of Arts.
Hodgson, G. 1988 *Economics and Institutions*, Cambridge, Polity.
Hoggart, R. 1958 *The Uses of Literacy*, Harmondsworth, Penguin.
Holub, R.C. 1991 *Jurgen Habermas: Critic in the Public Sphere*, London, Routledge.
Honderich, T. 1990 *Conservatism*, London, Hamish Hamilton.
Hopkinson, T. 1970 *Picture Post: 1938–50*, London, Allen Lane The Penguin Press.
Howe, S. ed. 2010 *The New Imperial Histories Reader*, London, Routledge.
Hughes, R. 1991 *The Shock of the New*, 2nd ed. London, Thames and Hudson.
Hughes, R. 1993 *Culture of Complaint*, Oxford University Press.
Hytner, N. 2006 *The History Boys* (film).
Inglis, F. 1993 *Cultural Studies*, Oxford, Blackwell.
Irvin, J. 1979 (BBC television series) *Tinker, Tailor, Soldier, Spy*.
Ishiguro, K. 1989 *The Remains of the Day*, London, Faber.
Jameson, F 1991 *Postmodernism: The Cultural Logic of Late Capitalism*, London, Verso.
Jameson, F. 1991 *Post-Modernism, Or the Cultural Logic of Late Capitalism*, London, Verso.

Jennings, J. and Kemp-Welch, A. 1997 *Intellectuals in Politics: From the Dreyfus Affair to Salman Rushdie*, London, Routledge.
Johnson, C. 2004 *The Sorrows of Empire*, London, Verso.
Jones, O. 2011 *Chavs: The Demonization of the Working Class*, London, Verso.
Judt, T. 2005 *Post-War: A History of Europe since 1945*, London, Allen Lane.
Judt, T. 2008 *Reappraisals: Reflections on the Forgotten Twentieth Century*, London, Penguin.
Just, N. 2009 'Measuring Media Concentration and Diversity' in *Media, Culture and Society* 31.1.
Karppinen, K. 2007 'Against Naïve Pluralism in Media Politics: On the Implications of the Radical Pluralist Approach to the Public Sphere' in *Media, Culture and Society* 29.3.
Kaye, H. 1984 *The British Marxist Historians*, Cambridge, Polity.
Kee, R. 1989 *The Picture Post Album: Fiftieth Anniversary Collection*, London, Barrie and Jenkins.
Kennedy, L. 2008 'Securing Vision: Photography and US Foreign Policy' in *Media, Culture and Society* 30.3.
Kerr, C., Dunlop, J.T., Harbison, F.H. and Myers, C.A. 1960 *Industrialism and Industrial Man*, Harmondsworth, Penguin.
Kerr, P. 2001 *Postwar British Politics*, London, Routledge.
Kolko, G. 1968 *The Politics of War: US Foreign Policy 1943–45*, New York, Vintage.
Kubrick, S. 1964 *Dr Strangelove* (film).
Kuhn, R. 2007 *Politics and the Media in Britain*, London, Palgrave.
Kynaston, D. 2008 *Austerity Britain 1945–51*, London, Bloomsbury.
Laing, R.D. 1967 *The Politics of Experience and the Bird of Paradise*, Harmondsworth, Penguin.
Lanchester, J. 2010 *Whoops: What Everyone owes Everyone and No One Can Pay*, London, Penguin.
Larkin, P. 1955 *The Less Deceived*, The Marvell Press.
Lash, S. and Urry, J. 1987 *The End of Organized Capitalism*, Cambridge, Polity.
Le Carre, J. 1986 *A Perfect Spy*, London, Hodder.
Leary, T., Metzner, R. and Alper, R.T. 1964 *The Psychedelic Experience*, New York, Citadel Press.
LeCare, J. 1968 *A Small Town in Germany*, London, Heinemann.
LeCare, J. 1974 *Tinker, Tailor, Soldier, Spy*, London, Hodder and Soughton.
LeCare, J. 1986 *A Perfect Spy*, London, Hodder and Stoughton.
Lee, L. 1962 *Cider with Rosie*, Harmondsworth, Penguin.
Leftbridge, A. 2011 *Losing Small Wars*, Yale University Press.
Leung, L. 2009 'Mediated Violence as Global News: Co-opted Performance in the Framing of WTO' in *Media, Culture and Society* 31.2.
Levinson, B. 1997 *Wag the Dog* (film).
Lieven, D. 2004 *America Right or Wrong: An Anatomy of American Nationalism*, London, Harper Collins.
Liman, D. 1980 *Bourne Identity* (film).
Little, J. 2009 *The Kindly Ones*, London, Chatto.
Lucas, S. 2003 *Orwell*, London, Haus.
Lumet, S. 1964 *Failsafe* (film).
MacIntyre, A. 1985 *After Virtue, A Study in Social Theory*, 2nd ed. London, Duckworth.

Mackendrick, A. 1951 *The Man in the White Suit* (film).
Mannheim, K. 1960 *Ideology and Utopia*, London, Routledge and Kegan Paul.
Marquand, D. 1989 *The Progressive Dilemma*, London, Fontana.
Marquese, M. 1994 *Anyone But England: Cricket and the National Malaise*, London, Verso.
Mayer-Schonberger, V. 2009 *Delete: The Virtue of Forgetting in the Digital Age*, Princeton University Press.
Mazower, M. 1998 *Dark Continent: Europe's Twentieth Century*, London, Penguin.
McCourt, D. M. 2011 'Rethinking Britain's "Role in the World" for a New Decade' in *British Journal of Politics and International Relations* 13.
McLaughlin, K., Ferlie, E. and Osborne, S.P. eds. 2002 *New Public Management: Current Trends and Future Prospects*, London, Routledge.
Meades, J. 2012 *Museum Without Walls*, London, unbound.
Metzger, R. 2007 *Berlin in the Twenties: Art and Culture 1918–1933*, London, Thames and Hudson.
Metzger, R. 2012 *London in the Sixties*, London, Thames and Hudson.
Miller, L. 2009 'E-petitions at Westminster: The Way Forward for Democracy', in *Parliamentary Affairs* 62.1.
Milliband, R. 1969 *The State in Capitalist Society*, London, Weidenfeld.
Milward, A. 1992 *The European Rescue of the Nation State*, London, Routledge.
Morozov, E. 2011 *The Net Delusion: How Not to Liberate the World*, London, Allen Lane.
Mount, F. 2012 *Mind the Gap: The New Class Divide in Britain*, London, Short Books.
Muller, J-W. ed. 2002 *Memory and Power in Post-War Europe*, Cambridge University Press.
Mumford, L. 1966 *The City in History*, Harmondsworth, Penguin.
Nairn, T. 1988 *The Enchanted Glass*, London, Hutchison Radius.
Nairn, T. 2011 *The Enchanted Glass: Britain and Its Monarchy*, 2nd ed. London, Verso.
Nash, K. 2008 'Global Citizenship as Show Business: The Cultural Politics of make Poverty Hhistory' in *Media, Culture and Society* 30.2.
National Audit Office. 'Ministry of Defence: Chinook Mk3 Helicopters' 04 June 2008.
Nemirovsky, I. 2007 *Suite Francais*, London, Vintag.
Noyce, P. 2002 *The Quiet American* (film).
Orwell, G. 1936 *Keep the Aspidistra Flying*, London, Gollancz.
Osborne, J. 1956 *Look Back in Anger* (play).
Pace, M. and Cavatorta, F. 2012 'The Arab Uprisings in Theoretical Perspective: An Introduction' in *Mediterranean Politics* 17.2.
Page, T.1984 *Tim Page's Nam*, London, Thames and Hudson.
Parkin, F. 1972 *Class Inequality and Political Order*, London, Paladin.
Passmore, J. 1970 *The Perfectibility of Man*, London, Duckworth.
Paxman, J. 2011 *Empire: What Ruling the World Did to the British*, London, Viking.
Pham, J. 2004 'Ghost Hunting in Colonial Burma: Nostalgia, Paternalism and the Thoughts of J.S. Furnivall' in *South East Asia Research* 12.2.
Polanski, R. 2010 *The Ghost Writer* (film).
Pollard, S. 1971 *The Idea of Progress*, Harmondsworth, Penguin.
Pollock, A. 2005 *NHS PLC: The Privatization of Our Health Care*, London, Verso.

Porter, B. 2004 *The Absent Minded Imperialists*, Oxford University Press.
Porter, R. 2000 *Enlightenment: Britain and the Creation of the Modern World*, London, Allen Lane.
Potter, D. 1981 *Pennies from Heaven* (BBC film).
Potter, D. 1986 *The Singing Detective* (BBC film).
Potter, D. 1993 *Lipstick on your Collar* (BBC film).
Preston, P.W. 1981 *Theories of Development*, London, Routledge and Kegan Paul.
Preston, P.W. 1994 *Europe, Democracy and the Dissolution of Britain*, Aldershot, Avebury.
Preston, P.W. 1997 *Political/Cultural Identity: Citizens and Nations in a Global Era*, London, Sage.
Preston, P.W. 2004 *Relocating England: Englishness in the New Europe*, Manchester University Press.
Preston, P.W. 2009 *Arguments and Actions in Social Theory*, London, Palgrave.
Preston, P.W. 2010 *National Pasts in Europe and East Asia*, London, Routledge.
Preston, P.W. 2012 *England after the Great Recession: Tracking the Political and Cultural Consequences of the Crisis*, London, Palgrave.
Rafael, F. 1976 *The Glittering Prizes* (BBC film).
Reisz, K. 1960 *Saturday Night and Sunday Morning* (film).
Richardson, T. 1959 *Look Back in Anger* (film).
Richey, P. 2001 *Fighter Pilot*, London, Cassel.
Rickman, H.P. 1976 *Wilhelm Dilthey: Selected Writings*, Cambridge University Press.
Roeg, N. 1970 *Performance* (film).
Roger, B.R. 2002 *The Penguin History of Economics*, Harmondsworth, Penguin.
Rorty, R. 1989 *Contingency, Irony and Solidarity*, Cambridge University Press
Rorty, R. 1998 *Achieving our Country: Leftist Thought in Twentieth Century America*, Harvard University Press.
Rose, S.O. 2003 *Which People's War: National Identity and Citizenship in Wartime Britain 1939-1945*, Oxford University Press.
Rudolph, C.R. 1953 *The Quatermass Experiment* (film).
Rushdie, S. 1981 *Midnights Children*, London, Jonathan Cape.
Rushdie, S. 1983 *Shame*, London, Jonathan Cape.
Russell, K. 1962 *Elgar* (BBC film).
Russell, K. 1968 *Song of Summer* (BBC film).
Russell, K. 1969 *Women in Love* (film).
Russell, K. 1970 *The Music Lovers* (film).
Said, E. 1994 *Representations of the Intellectual*, London, Vintage.
Saussure, F. 1990 *Course in General Linguistics*, London, Duckworth.
Schlesinger, J. 1962 *A Kind of Loving* (film).
Schlondorff, V. 1979 *The Tin Drum* (film).
Scott, R. 1982 *Bladerunner* (film).
Scott, R. 2008 *Body of Lies* (film).
Shipway, M. 2007 *Decolonization and Its Impact*, Oxford, Blackwell.
Sillitoe, A. 1958 *Saturday Night and Sunday Morning*, London, W.H. Allen.
Skidelski, R. 2004 *John Maynard Keynes 1883-1946*, London, Macmillan.
Smith, G. 2006 *30 St. Mary Axe: A Tower for London*, London, Merrell.
Smith, J. 'Introduction' (Britain in Europe Special Edition) in *International Affairs* 88.6.

Stone, O. 1987 *Wall Street* (film).
Strange, S. 1988 *States and Markets*, London, Pinter.
Street, J. 2004 'Celebrity Politicians: Culture and Political Representation' in *British Journal of Politics and International Relations* 6.
Street, J. 2010 *Mass Media, Politics and Democracy*, 2nd ed. London, Palgrave.
Szasz, T. 1961 *The Myth of Mental Illness*, New York, Harper.
Tett, G. 2009 *Fool's Gold*, New York, Little Brown.
The Beatles 1963 *Please Please Me* (LP).
The Daily Telegraph.
The Financial Times.
The Guardian.
The Independent.
The New York Review of Books.
The News of the World.
The Times.
Thomas, J. 2007 'Bound by History: The Winter of Discontent in British Politics' in *Media, Culture and Society* 29.2.
Thompson, E. 1968 *The Making of the English Working Class*, Harmondsworth, Penguin.
Tony, R. 1961 *A Taste of Honey* (film).
Toye, R. 2012 'From "Consensus' to "Common Ground": The Rhetoric of the Postwar Settlement and its Collapse' in *Journal of Contemporary History* 48.1.
Urwin, D. 1997 *A Political History of Western Europe Since 1945*, London, Longman.
Usherwood, S. and Startin, N. 2013 ' Euroscepticism as a Persistent Phenomenon' in *Journal of Common Market Studies* 51.1.
von Trier, L.1991 *Europa* (film).
Vonnegut, K. 1969 *Slaughterhouse Five*, New York, Delacorte Press.
Walker, C. and Whyte, D. 2005 'Contracting Out War: Private Military Companies, Law and Regulation in the United Kingdom' in *International and Comparative Law Quarterly* 54.3.
Ward, S. ed. 2001 *British Culture and the End of Empire*, Manchester University Press.
Ward, S., Gibson, R. and Lusoli, W. 2003 'Online Participation and Mobilization in Britain: Hype, Hope and Reality in *Parliamentary Affairs* 56.
Wargnier, R. 1992 *Indochine* (film).
Wasserman, H. 2009 'Book Review: Sofia Johansson, Reading Tabloids' in *Media, Culture and Society* 31.
Webster, W. 2005 *Englishness and Empire 1939–1965*, Oxford University Press.
Weitz, E.D. 2007 *Weimar Germany: Promise and Tragedy*, Princeton University Press.
Whitlock, G. and Carter, D. eds. 1992 *Images of Australia*, University of Queensland Press.
Wilkinson, R. and Pickett, K. 2009 *The Spirit Level*, London, Allen Lane.
Williams, R. 1961 *The Long Revolution*, London, Chatto.
Williams, R. 1963 *Culture and Society 1780–1950*, Harmondsworth, Penguin.
Williams, R. ed. 1974 *George Orwell: A Collection of Critical Essays*, Englewood Cliffs, Prentice Hall.
Williams, R. 1980 *Keywords*, London, Fontana.

Winch, P. 1958/1990 *The Idea of a Social Science and Its Relation to Philosophy*, 2nd ed. London, Routledge and Kegan Paul.
Woodiwiss, A. 1993 *Postmodernity USA*, London, Sage.
Worsley, P. 2008 *An Academic Dancing on Thin Ice*, Oxford, Berghahn Books.
Wright, P. 1985 *On Living in an Old Country*, London, Verso.
Wright, P. 1987 *Spycatcher: The Candid Autobiography of a Senior Intelligence Officer*, New York, Viking.
Wright, P. 1993 *A Journey through the Ruins: A Keyhole Portrait of British Postwar Life and Culture*, London, Flamingo.
Wright, P. 1995 *The Village that Died for England*, London, Jonathan Cape.
Wright, P. 2007 *Iron Curtain: From Stage to Cold War*, Oxford University Press.
Wu, T. 2010 *The Master Switch: The Rise and Fall of Information Empires*, London, Atlantic.
Young, M. and Willmott, P. 1957 *Family and Kinship in East London*, Harmondsworth, Penguin.

Index

Note: Locators with letter 'n' refer to notes.

Abortion Act of 1967, 124
Abortion law reform, 124
Abse, Leo, 124
activism, e-activism/networking, 188–9
Adenauer, Konrad, 126
adventitious, 246–7n40
advertising, images, 135
agents, arguments and, 9
aggression, corporate media and, 174–5
Aherne, Caroline, 88
Al Jazeera, 170
al Qaeda, 173
alcohol industry, 136
alternative music, 128
alternative press, 128
alternatives, neo-liberal, 144–5
alternative society, 117, 127–8
American dream, 32
Amis, Kingsley, 95
anaylsis, of texts, 5–8
Anderson, Lindsay, 128
Anderson-Naim thesis, 128–9
Anglo-sphere, 252–3n2
angry young men, 82–3, 86–7, 92, 99, 103, 235n1
Antonioni, Michelangelo, 128
appeasement plus military upgrade, 222n11
Arab Spring, 159, 179
Arabian Gulf, 29
arc of empire, 220n40
architecture, modern, design and, 50–2
Army Education Corps, 45
art-house films, 7
artist-as-brand, 169–70

art(s)
  fine, satire in, 134
  future of, 86–7
  high, 10–11
  popular organizations, post-war, 1950s–60s, 89
  role in deconstructing Cold War, 78–9
  see also music
Atlantic Charter, 44
attack journalism, 174–5
audience
  corporate media and, 162
  for texts, 12
authenticity, issues of, 131
authoritarian populism
  of Hall, 247n42
  of Thatcher, 152–3

baby boomers, post war, 15–16, 113–14
Bader-Meinhof, 126
Barstow, Stan, 88
Bauhaus, school of modern design, 50–2
BBC television, 101, 107–8, 118
  iPlayer, 161
  licence fees and, 248n13
  monopoly, 160
Beatles, the, 123
Beauvoir, Simone de, 125
Bennett, Alan, 90
Berlin airlift, 67
Berlin Wall, 68
Berlusconi, Silvio, 150
Bernays, Edward, 70
Betjeman John, 123
Bevan, Nye, 55
Beveridge Report, 45, 55
Black, Conrad, 150

Blair, Eric, 74
Blair, Tony, 168–9
bloc system
  creation of, 65–9
  Manichean division, cost of, 71–2
bloc-think, 57, 119
  art, role in deconstructing Cold War, 78–9
  cultural policy serving, 69–71
Bloomsbury group, 93
Blow Up (movie), 132
Blunt, Anthony, 231n16
bonuses, ban on corporate, 245n22
Booker Prize, 95
Bourneville Village, 52
Braine, John, 87
Bretton Woods, 20, 21, 31, 47
British Railways, 47
bubble economy, 148
bureaucratic-rational states, 3
Burgess, Anthony, 78
Butler Education Act, 45

Callaghan, James, 139, 143, 145
Callaghan government, failure of, 221n47
Cambridge division, Cold War and, 67–8
Cambridge Spies, 67–8, 74–6, 81
  see also spies
Cameron, Prime Minster, 216–17
Canadian identity, 224n34
cannabis, legalization of, 244n60
Capello, Fabio, 165–6
capitalism, mass consumer, 136–7
Carré, John Le, 72–6
Cathy Come Home (play), 123–4
CCTV, 182, 184, 187–8, 251n7
celebrity
  corporate media and, 171–2
  popularization of, 168–70
censorship, end of high culture, 129
chavs, 236n29
China Central Television, 170
Churchill, Winston, 66
Churchill option, 220n43

cities
  contemporary human social life and, 48
  industrial-capitalist, 49
Civil Rights Movement, U.S., 112–13, 119, 125
Clarke, Arthur C., 183
class
  activities of, 11
  conflicts, 236n29
  de-alignment, 116–17
  inclusion and, 25
  subaltern, 83, 201
CNN news, 170
Cold War, 15, 29, 62
  arts during, 78–9
  Berlin Wall and, 68
  bloc-system and, 65–9
  bloc-think and, 69–71
  Cambridge division, 67–8
  commentary on, 79–80
  construction of, 64–71
  countries involved in, 77
  culture, 232n34
  domestic paranoia, 206
  elite reach within population, 78
  elite/state-level actions and, 64–5, 78
  in Europe, 62–3
  legacies of/repetitions, 80
  loss of trust during, 73–6
  Manichean division, 68–9, 71–2
  as manufactured, 77
  public sphere and, 71–6
  in retrospect, 76–7
  state-empire, costs of dissolution of, 72–3
Colonial Development Act, 45
colonialism withdrawals from, 119–20
  see also decolonization
colonies, Commonwealth and, 27–31
command economy, 115
commercial arts, 10–11
commercial television (ITV), 101
  nature and role of, 108–9
  reaction to, 107
commercial world, state and, 10
commonwealth, state-empire system and, 27–31

Commonwealth Games, 31
Commonwealth Summits, 31
communication systems, digital technology and, 180–1
Communist Party, 45
community studies, 241n5
compromise, post-war contested, 140–3
compulsory national service, 120
computer-based management systems, 184
computer-generated images (CGI), 181
computers
    analytical programmes, 181
    data storage, 179–80
    data transmission, 180
    high speed processing, 179
    software, 180
    see also internet; privacy
conglomerates, media, 154
Conran, Terrence, 116
conservatism, pre-war, 58
consumer goods, in 1950s, 92
consumerism, welfare-based, 197
consumers, logics producers and, 11–12
consumption, celebration of, 148–9
contemporary culture
    arguments in public sphere, 199–200
    elite factions in, 200–1
    national past, contested, 202–3
    subaltern classes and, 201
contemporary political culture
    collective memory and, 210
    critique of, 207–9
    history, tradition and, 205
    layers of, 206–7
    nationalistic story, 209–11
    political-cultural logic, 210–11
    poodle option, status quo, 212–13
    power, legitimacy and, 211–12
    storytelling, 210
    United States and, 213
    war and, 37–8
Continent, politics of, state-empire collapse and, 32–3
corporate ethos, football and, 167
corporate football, 163–8

corporate media, 176
    advance of, 159–60
    aggression and, 174–5
    audience relationship, 162
    expansion of, 157–9
    politics, power/celebrity and, 171–2
corporate power, rise of, 145–6
corporate world
    control of digital technology, 191–2
    digital technology and, 184–5
    e-corporate surveillance, 188
    football and, 166–7
    images, 135
Council for the Preservation of Rural England, 89
Crosland, Anthony, 90
cross-platform media, 159–60
Crown Corporation, 107
cultural meanings, 8
cultural studies, 130, 237n30
cultural texts, 6
cultural uniformity, 100–1
culture
    angry young men and, 92
    bloc-think and, 69–71
    Cold War, 232n34
    contemporary, see contemporary culture
    contemporary political, see contemporary political culture
    end of censorship of high, 129
    high arts, in Britain, 12–17
    impact of loss of empire and, 24–5
    of public service broadcasting, 172
    welfare state and, 56
cyber-realism, 193, 194
cyberutopianism, 193

data, digital, gathering, 190–1
data storage, computing, 179–80, 182–3
Davies, Terrence, 88
decolonization, 85, 221n2, 224n43, 226n5
Delaney, Shelagh, 88
denial
    elite, of empire dissolving, 26–7
    of state-empire collapse, 203
deregulation, financial, 147–8

270 Index

design, architecture and, 50–2
digital technology
 characteristics of, 179–80
 communication systems, 180–1
 computer-based management systems, 184
 corporate world, use of, 184–5
 development of, 177–8, 194–5
 e-activism/networking, 188–9
 e-corporate surveillance, 188
 e-democracy, 186–7
 e-entertainment, 189
 e-government, 187
 electronic media, 180–1
 enthusiasm/disappointment with, 192–3
 e-state surveillance, 187–8
 information capacity, 181–2
 information overload, 190
 net enthusiasts, against, 193–4
 opacity of, 183
 population-surveillance systems, 184
 privacy issues and, 190–1
 private use of, 185–6
 speed/reach of, 178
 state/corporate control of, 191–2
 state uses of, 183–4
Diski, Jenny, 123, 137
disposable income, 239n10
distribution of wealth/income, 255n33
Dix, Otto, 134
domestic paranoia, Cold War and, 206
dot-com bubble, 159
drugs, 117, 128
Dunn, Nell, 88
duopoly, broadcasting, 99

e-activism/networking, 188–9
economic advance, of 1950s, 92
economic austerity/recovery, 33
economic growth, post-war, 115
economic system, effect of war on, 84–5
economy
 Cold War construction and, 64–5
 deregulation of, 147–8
 mixed, welfare state and, 46–8, 55, 60
e-corporate surveillance, 188
e-data gathering, 190–1
e-democracy, 186–7
e-entertainment, 189
e-government, 187
Egypt
 Canal Zone, 29
 invasion of, 85
electronic media, 180–1
elite
 angry young men attack, 99
 attacks on, 103
 change, structural, 217
 Cold War construction and, 64–5
 control of state-empire system, 20
 critiques of ruling, post-war recovery and, 90
 denial of, state-empire failure, 26–7
 end of high culture censorship, 129
 Europe and, 216–17
 factions of, 200–1
 intellectuals and, 231n24
 metropolitan, accommodating change, 38–9
 patrician, *see* patrician elite
 response to collapse of state-empire, 23–4, 36
 Russian Revolution and, 80
 scandals, 104
 social construction of enemy, sponsors of, 78
 welfare state as project of, 43
embedding (war-time reporters), 243n53
engagement, three forms of, 220n31
Engles, Friedrich, 129–30
Enlightenment project, 220n32
entertainment websites, 185–6
epistemology, 246n25
equipment, poor planning and, 34–6
e-rubbish, 251n14
e-state surveillance, 187–8
Euro summit, 2011, 216–17
Europe
 division of, 65
 in 1960s, 126–9

European Coal and Steel Community (ECSC), 21
European Economic Community (EEC), 21
European Free Trade Association (EFTA), 21, 214
European social theory, 2
European Union, 213–14, 255n31

Fear of Flying (Jong), 124
Female Eunuch, The (Greer), 124
Feminism, rise of, 124–5
Festival of Britain, 85
fields, arguments and, 9
films, alternative, 128
financial crisis, 2008/10, 148, 153, 211, 221n48, 229n54, 245n16
financial deregulation, 148
Flemming, Ian, 225n59, 233n41
folk memory, 164
football, popularization of, 163–8, 249n20
Fortuyn, Pym, 174–5
Foster, Norman, 54
Foucault, Michel, 127
France
  student protests in, 126
  wars of, 120
Frankfurt Schools, 154

gap year, 137
Garden City, 52
Gaulle, Charles de, 113, 126
gay liberation, 124
gender, rise of feminism and, 124–5
geographical territory, 221*n*2
Germany, politics in, 126
Giffords, Gabrielle, 175
Gillray, James, 134
global liberal trading, 142
Golden Notebook, The (Lessing), 124
Google, 251–2n17
GPS systems, 185
Grass, Gunther, 73–6
Great Depression, 19
Great Tradition, 253n4
Greenaway, Peter, 7
Greer, Germaine, 124
Grosz, Georg, 134

Hall, Stuart, 129, 130–1, 247n42
Healy, Denis, 143, 145
hedonism, 136
hegemony, 203, 207
Heller, Joseph, 78
heritage, architecture and, 53
hermeneutics, analysis of texts and, 5–6
high arts, 10–14
  see also art(s)
high culture censorship, end of, 129
high-technology, 182–3
historicism, 227n15
history, tradition and, 205
Hodgson, Roy, 166
Hoggart, Richard, 90, 130
homosexual law reform, 124
Hornsea College, 124
housing bubble, 245n16
Howard, Ebenezer, 52
Hughes, Robert, 170
human language, social production of meaning and, 4–5
human social life, contemporary, 48

ideas
  hegemonic, 207
  of nation, 212
  of political culture, 207
  urban form and, 54
  of welfare state, 56–8, 61
identity, 163–4
  political-cultural, 218n2
images, digital, 181
independent television (ITV), 118
industrial capitalism, science-based, 2–3
industrial era, 132
industrialist-capitalist cities, 49
information
  capacity, 181–2
  overload, digital technology and, 190
  state gathering, 10
infotainment, 170–1
infrastructure, post-war, 97
instrumental, 246n40
intellectuals, 93–4, 153, 231n24
international rebalancing, 215–16

internet
   technology, information and, 180
   see also digital technology
interwar period, 235n66
invention, process of, 92
invisibility-by-virtue-of-familiarity, 203
Iraq, 235n67
Iron Curtain, 57, 80
   see also Cold War
Iron Curtain Speech, 66
Islamo-fascism, 250n35
Israel, 173
Italy, 126–7

Japanese economy, 142–3
Jarrow March, 43, 45
Jewish state, 29–30
jokes, stereotypes and, 225n53
Jong, Erica, 124
journalism, attack, 174–5

Kennan, George, 66–7
Kennedy, J.F., 122, 125
Kennedy, Robert, 125
Kent State University, 120
Keynes, John, 47–8, 115, 140
Keynesian economics, 141
Keynesian informed active state, 59–61, 115
King, Martin Luther, 119, 125
Krier, Leon, 53

Lady Chatterley's Lover (Lawrence), 104, 129
Laing, R.D., 127
language
   English, state-empire collapse and, 31–2
   human, social production of meaning and, 4–5
   public sphere, idea of and, 199
   received pronunciation, 100–1
Larkin, Philip, 95, 123
Lawrence, D.H., 104, 129
Leary, Timothy, 128, 242n28
Leavis, E.R., 130
legacy, of welfare state, 61
Lessing, Doris, 124

liberal *vs.* democratic polity, 154–5
licence system, 161
literature, post war, 87–8
Loach, Ken, 88, 123–4
logics
   arguments and, 9
   producers and consumers, 11–12
London School of Economics, 124
long boom, 97–8, 114–15
lying, instrumental, 233n36, 246n40

Macmillan, Harold, 14, 30, 82, 104–6
management systems, computer-based, 184
Mandela, Nelson, 224n38
Manichean division
   Cold War and, 68–9
   cost of, 71–2
Manichean politics, 206, 208
market-based media, 159–60
market segmentation, plus mass, 162–3
market solutions, 146
Marxism Today, 129
Marxist analysis, opinion and, 128–9
McClaren, Malcom, 11
McClaren, Steve, 165
meaning
   cultural, analysis of, 8
   layers of, 14–17
   social production of, language and, 4–5
media
   alternative press, 128
   arts in deconstructing Cold War, 78
   attacks, on political/elite figures, 103
   Cold War and, 69–70
   commercial sphere of, 11
   conglomerates, 150–1, 154
   corporate, rise/advance of, *see* corporate media
   corporate populism of, 153
   electronic, 180–1
   mass, changing in 1960s, 118
   in 1950s, 101–12
   1950s–60s public sphere, 89
   popularization of football and, 163–8

post-war changes in, 99
public service broadcasting, 107–8
retreat of public service
broadcasting, 160–1
right-wing populist press, 154
scandals and, 104
melancholia, 233n40
memory, collective historical,
state-empire system, 203–5, 210
middle classes, 201
Middle East
British involvement in, 21
state-empire role in, 29
military
Cold War construction and, 64–5
demobilization of, 33
exterminism, institutionalization of,
206, 208
Millett Kate, 124
Milliband, Ralph, 90
minimal impact thesis, 24, 223n20
mixed economy, welfare state and,
46–8, 55, 60
mobile phones, 185
modern world, shift to, 13
monetarism, 146
money, football and, 167–8
Monroe, Marilyn, 169
moral rights, 238n65
Morrisonian socialism, 227n24
Mosely, Max, 174
Murdoch, Rupert, 150, 160
music
alternative, 128
Beatlemania, 123
post-war, 100–1

National Coal Board, 47
National Health Service (NHS), 47
national idea, construction of, 132
national past, contested, 202–3
National Trust, 53, 89
negro, 241n6
neo-classical theory, 140–1
neo-liberal project, 155–6
alternatives, 144–5
consumption, celebration of, 148–9
corporate power, rise of, 145–6
deployment of, 139–40

deregulation of economy, 147–8
financial deregulation, 148
mainstream media, represented, 153
market solutions, preference, 146
media conglomerates, 150–1
post-war contested compromise,
140–3
privatization, of state assets, 146–7
state functions, privatization of, 147
neo-liberals, 236n29
neocolonialism, 224n37
net centrism, 193–4
networking, e-activism/networking,
188–9
New Deal, 47, 66
New Elizabethan Age, 24–5, 34, 56,
92, 103
New Left, 93–4, 128–9
New Left Review (magazine), 128
New Reason (magazine), 128
New Right, 16, 60, 139
news, rolling, 170–1
News International, 154, 160, 172,
240n30, 246n36, 248n11
News of the World, 174
night of the long knives, 104–5
Nineteen Eighty-Four (Orwell), 63, 74,
223n17
1950s, 84–6, 89
arts, popular organizations in, 89
media and, 109–10
post-war reconstruction and, 86–91
in retrospect, 91–4; *see also* public
sphere, in England
social rebellion in 1950s, 84–6
working class, hope for future and,
87–8
1960s
abortion law reform, 124
Beatlemania, 123
Cathy Come Home, political
implications of, 123–4
changing mass media in, 118
colonial withdrawals, 119–20
in Europe, 126–9
feminism, rise of, 124–5
homosexual law reform, 124
legacy of, 136
political culture, changes in, 118–21

274 *Index*

1960s – *continued*
  protests, 124
  social activism of, 121
  social change in, 116–17
  social doubt, 122
  social liberalization, 112–13
  student rebellions, 124
  in United States, 125–6
1970s, end of post-war boom, 138–9
non-governmental organization (NGO), 30
Northern Ireland Civil Rights Movement, 119
NPM, political-cum-management theory, 245n14

Oil price rise, 143
opacity, of high technology, 183
Orwell, George, 45, 63, 73–6, 223n17, 233n43
Osborne, John, 87
Oswald, Lee Harvey, 242n23
Ottoman Empire, 29

Palestine, 29–30, 173
parliamentary politics, 170
Penguin Books, trial of, 104
people's empire, 24–6
people's war, 24–6
personalization, celebrity politics and, 173
photographs, modern world of images, 132–5
photojournalism, 134–5
political culture
  identity, 218n2
  logic, 210–11
  contemporary, war and, 37–8
political discourse, change in nature of, 16
political figures, attacks on, 103
political identity, 164
political unit, 221n2
political violence, 125–6
politics
  celebrity, 173
  Cold War construction and, 64–5
  corporate media and, 171–2

  images and, 132
  Westminster, 170
  see also polity; scandals
polity
  changing structure of British, 196–9
  collective memory of, 210
  contemporary British, 17–18
  denial/confection, 198–9
  institutional mechanisms, change, 197
  legislators and, 220n30
  liberal *vs.* democratic, 154–5
  no united Britain, 209–10
  power relations changes, 197
  poodle option, status quo, 212–13
Popper, Karl, 60, 90
popular arts, 10–11
popularization
  of celebrity, 168–70
  celebrity politics and, 173
  corporate money, nationalism, football and, 163–8
population
  elites reach within a, 78
  mobilized, 99
  state addresses, 9–10
population-surveillance systems, digital technology and, 184
populism, 173
post-war boom, end of, 138
post-war consensus, 97, 226n2
Potter, Dennis, 90
Poundbury, 53
power
  corporate media and, 171–2
  domestic, 211
  rise of corporate, 145–6
  Thatcher route to, 149–50
Prague Spring, 113, 136
Prince Charles, 53
Princess Diana, 169
print media, 102
privacy, digital technology and, 190–1, 251n8
  see also CCTV; surveillance
private finance initiatives (PFI), 147

privatization
  of state assets, 146–7
  of state functions, 147
producers, consumers, logics and, 11–12
production oriented system, of state planning, 100
profit-oriented media, 159–60
Profumo, John, 105–6
propaganda, post-war, 85
protests, 1960s, 124
proto-monetarist, 139, 145
proto-rebellions, 112–13
psychotropic drugs, 128
public record-keeping, digital technology and, 183–4
public service broadcasting, 99
  corporate *vs.*, 172–3
  nature and role of, 107–8
  retreat of, 160–1
public sphere, in England, 3–4
  arguments in, 199–200
  arts, popular organizations, 1950s–60s, 89
  changes in structural patterns, 211–12
  changing technologies, 106–7
  Cold War and, 71–6
  debate and, 13–14
  elites, critiques of, post-war, 90
  future, hope for in arts, theater, literature and, 86–7
  liberalization of, 131
  location, forms of argument deployed and, 8–12
  1950s in retrospect, 91–4
  1950s media and, 109–10
  1950s post-war reconstruction and, 86–91
  optimism, new technology-3, 102
  resources, layers of meanings and, 14–17
  social change, theorizing, artists intellectuals, 89–90
  social doubt, 122
  subaltern classes and, 90–1
  text, text-analogues, readings and, 8
  welfare state and, 55–8

working class, 1950s, hope for future and, 87–8
writers, Cold War politics, risk and, 73–6
punk-monetarism, 145

Queen Elizabeth, 24–5

race, 241n6
Radio Luxembourg, 118, 160
Raphael, Frederic, 90
Rawls, John, 154
reading, text analogues and, 7
received pronunciation, 100–1
recovery, post-war, 82–3
Red Brigades, 126
reform
  domestic, 214–15
  international rebalancing, domestic and, 215–16
  welfare state project and, 41–55
reformism utopian, 49
repetitions, welfare state and, 61
revision, process of, 148
rhetoric, of contemporary political culture, 2076
right-wing populist press, 154
riots, urban violence, 126
Roeg, Nicholas, 128
rolling news, 170–1
Royal Family, 169
Ruby, Jack, 242n23
rural craft life, 52–3
rural life, romantic reading of, 227n27
Russian Revolution, 80
Russia TV, 170

satire
  authenticity ad, 131
  in fine art, 134
scandal(s), 104, 240n18
  News International, 246n36, 248n11
  night of the long knives, 104–5
  Profumo affair, 105–6
  see also polity
Scarfe, Gerald, 134
Schonenberger, Viktor Mayer-, 190–1
Scot, Ridley, 7

Seaton, Arthur, 86, 88, 101, 115, 239n10
Second World War, *see* World War II
security industry, 70–1
Sellers, Peter, 123
Sexual Offences Act, of 1967, 124
Sexual Politics (Millett), 124
Sillitoe, Alan, 88
sit-ins, 1960s, 124
slum clearance, 51
Snowden, Edward, 252n23
social activism, 121
social behavior, experimentation, 127
social change
    artists/intellectuals, 89–90
    of 1960s, 116–17
social complaints, 95–6
social consequences, of state-empire disintegration, 21–2
social development, welfare state and, 54–5
social disturbances, 211
social doubt, 122
social function, of public sphere, 3
social groups, post-war change and, 95
social market, 47
social media websites, 185–6
social production of meaning, language and, 4–5
social rebellion, 83–4
    in 1950s, 84–6
social world, image-drenched, 132–5
soft oligarchy, 187, 197, 200, 211
soft power, 19, 221n1
software, computer, 180
Soviet Union, Cold War and, 63–4
    see also Cold War
spies, 15, 67–8, 73, 75–6, 81, 105, 206, 231n16, 234n50, 234n52, 252n23
    see also Cambridge spies
sport, social role of, 167
spy novels, 234n47
state
    addresses population, 9–10
    assets, privatization of, 146–7
    Cold War construction and, 64–5
    commerce, social world and, locations and agents, 9–10
    commercial world ad, 10
    digital technology, control over, 191–2
    factions in, 200–1
    high technology, uses of, 183–4
    historical trajectory of, phases and, 12–14
    information gathering of, 10
    social/economic arguments for action, 141
state-empire system, 13
    British rule of, 1
    collective historical memory of, 203–5
    commonwealth, 27–31
    continuing Britain, 33–4, 36
    costs of, loss of status and, 72–3
    elite control over, 20
    general crisis for, 76–7
    legacies/repetitions, 36–9
    loss of, denial, addressing loss of, 26–7
    poor equipment/planning setbacks and, 34–6
    in present, 216–17
    reforging nation, 38–9
    standing alone, 34–6
    war/wartime, 34
state-empire system, collapse of
    compensating for, 91–2
    crucial episode for British rule, 15
    continent and, 32–3
    denial of, 203
    dissolution (1945–56), 23–36
    English-speaking peoples and, 31–2
    social consequences of, 21–2
    violent dissolution, 40
    World War II as beginning of, 19–23
state functions, privatization of, 147
state-level rational policy, 142
state planning, production-oriented system of, 100
status quo evolution, 214–15
Steel, David, 124
stereotypes, 225n53, 250n35
structural power, patterns of, 32
student rebellions, 124, 126
sub-Saharan Africa, 30

subaltern classes, 83, 90–1
  celebration of lives, art and, 129–30
  contemporary culture and, 201
  increased visibility of, 101
  voices of, 103
Submission (van Gogh), 175
surveillance systems, 184, 187–8
  see also CCTV; e-corporate surveillance
symbolic episodes, 123
Szasz, Thomas, 127

tabloids, 246n35
Tea Party Movement, 175
technological reductionism, 193–4
technology
  changing, 106–7
  Cold War media and, 69–70
  digital, *see* digital technology
  high, 182–3
  new, media and, 161–2
  social change and, 16
television
  licence fees, 248n13
  post-war growth of, 7, 97, 101–2, 239n6
  see also BBC television
territorial sovereignty, 3
terrorism, 173
texts
  art and, 10–11
  text analogues and, 5–8
Thatcher, Margaret, 145, 146
  authoritarian populism, 152–3
  route to power, 149–50
Thatcherism, 168–9
theater, end of censorship of, 129
Theatres Act of 1968, 129
Thompson, E.P., 129
totalitarian, 230n7
Town Planning Act, 45
trade
  global literal, 142
  patterns of, 142
  surpluses, 227n23
tradition, history and, 205, 254n20
trial, of Penguin Books, 104
triple-dip recession, 60

Truman Doctrine Speech, 66
Turner, Ted, 170

United Nations, 20, 47
United States
  Civil Rights Movement in, 112–13, 119, 125
  nationalism, 229n1
  New Deal, 47
  political violence in, 125–6
  as soft power, 32
  state-empire crisis and, 63–4; *see also* Cold War
  Vietnam War and, 112
  war protests, 120
  weapons research in, 67–8
  youth rebellion in, 117
Universities and Left Review (magazine), 128
urban environment, modern, welfare state and, 48
urban form(s)
  debating, welfare state and, 48–50
  ideas as, 54
urban violence, 126
utopian reformism, 49

van-Gogh, Theo, 175
Vietnam War, 112, 120, 125
violence, political, 125–6
von Hayek, Friedrich, 60, 90

war
  images of, 133–4, 135
  reframing, 34, 37–8
War Game, The (movie), 135
war mobilization, 58
Ward, Stephen, 105–6
Warhol, Andy, 135, 169
Warsaw Pact, 65, 113
Waterhouse, Keith, 88
Waugh, Evelyn, 89
weapons of mass destruction, 206
weapons research, in U.S., 67–8
Wednesday Play, The, 123–4
Weimar Republic, 114
welfare
  ameliorative research on, 253n12
  post-war years, 33

welfare-buttressed consumerism, 197
welfare-ism, 226n3
welfare state, 40–1
  arguments for, 44–6
  cultural impacts of, 56
  heritage, architecture and, 53
  idea of, 56–8
  Keynesian informed active state, 59–61
  legacies/repetitions, 59–61
  mixed economy and, 46–8, 55
  modern architecture, design and, 50–2
  post-war domestic reconstruction and, 42–4
  post-war era, 58
  present, 53–4
  project of, 41–55
  public sphere and, 55–8
  rural craft life and, 52–3
  social development and, 54–5
  urban environment, modern, 48
  urban forms, debating, 48–50
Welwyn Garden City, 52
West Germany, political rebellion in, 113
Westminster politics, 170
Westwood, Vivienne, 11
white dominions, 222n8
Williams, Raymond, 130
Wilson, Harold, 122
working class
  celebration of lives/art of, 129–30
  communities, 236n30
  football as game of, 166–7
  1950s post-war recovery and, 87–8
World War II, 13, 15
  as beginning of end, state-empire system, 19–23
  domestic reconstruction, post, 42–4
  economic austerity/recovery, 33
  holocaust, 30
  as new foundation, myth, 36
  official/popular memory of, 203–5
  people's victory, 25–6
  post-war era, 15–16, 58, 91–4
  reconstruction, 57
  recovery years, 82–3
  social rebellion, recovery and, 84–6
writers, Cold War politics and, 73–6

Yalta, meeting at, 56–7, 65
youth, rebellion of, 1960s, 113, 117
youth culture, growing, 121, 136

Zionists, 29–30

Printed and bound in the United States of America